Michael Novak

The Spirit of Democratic Capitalism

A TOUCHSTONE BOOK
An American Enterprise Institute/Simon and Schuster Publication
NEW YORK

Library of Congress Cataloging in Publication Data
Novak, Michael.
The spirit of democratic capitalism.
Includes bibliographical references and index.
1. Economics—moral and ethical aspects. 2. Capitalism—Moral and
ethical aspects. 3. Democracy—moral and ethical aspects. I. Title.
HB72.N68   330.12′2   81-21365
AACR 2
ISBN 0-671-43154-4
ISBN 0-671-43155-2 Pbk.

The author is grateful for permission to reprint excerpts from the following works:
  The Breakdown, volume 3 of *Main Currents of Marxism,* by Leszek Kolakowski,
translated by P. S. Falla. Copyright © 1978 by Oxford University Press and reprinted
by their permission.
  The Wealth of Nations by Adam Smith. Copyright 1937 by The Modern Library.
Copyright renewed in 1965 by Random House and reprinted by their permission.
  The Protestant Ethic and the Spirit of Capitalism by Max Weber, translated by
Talcott Parsons. Copyright © 1958 by Charles Scribner's Sons and reprinted by their
permission.
  The Church in the Power of the Holy Spirit by Juergen Moltmann, translated by
Margaret Kohl. English translation copyright © 1977 by SCM Press, Ltd. Reprinted
by permission of Harper & Row.
  The Crucified God by Juergen Moltmann, translated by R. A. Wilson and John
Bowden. Copyright © 1974 by SCM Press, Ltd. Reprinted by permission of Harper
& Row.
  "Religion, the Reformation and Social Change" in *The European Witch Craze of
the Sixteenth and Seventeenth Centuries and Other Essays* by H. R. Trevor-Roper.
Copyright © 1969 by Harper & Row and reprinted by their permission.
  Reflections on America by Jacques Maritain. Copyright © 1958 by Jacques Maritain.
Reprinted by permission of Charles Scribner's Sons.

(continued at the back of the book.)

In memory of
William J. Baroody, Sr.
and
In homage to
Pope John Paul II

Many things, having full reference
To one consent, may work contrariously;
As many arrows, loosed several ways,
Fly to one mark; as many ways meet in one town;
As many fresh streams meet in one salt sea;
As many lines close in the dial's center;
So may a thousand actions, once afoot,
End in one purpose, and be all well borne
Without defeat.

—*King Henry V,* act I, sc. 2

Contents

Introduction: Capitalism, Socialism, and Religion—An Inquiry into the Spiritual Wealth of Nations

Of all the systems of political economy which have shaped our history, none has so revolutionized ordinary expectations of human life—lengthened the life span, made the elimination of poverty and famine thinkable, enlarged the range of human choice—as democratic capitalism. Recall the societies of the Roman Empire and Carolingian period. Contemplate the Catholic and Protestant powers of the seventeenth century, colonial and mercantilist. Examine the many forms of socialism in the present day. Each of these systems of political economy has had its theological admirers. Yet no theologian, Christian or Jewish, has yet assessed the theological significance of democratic capitalism. Consider, by contrast, the importance Marx and Engels attached to the capitalist revolution:

> The bourgeoisie, during its rule of scarce one hundred years, has created more massive and more colossal productive forces than have all preceding generations together. Subjection of Nature's forces to man, machinery, application of chemistry to industry and agriculture, steam-navigation, railways, electric telegraphs, clearing of whole continents for cultivation, canalization of rivers, whole populations conjured out of the ground—what earlier century had even a presentiment that such productive forces slumbered in the lap of social labor?[1]

This book, then, is about the life of the spirit which makes democratic capitalism possible. It is about its theological presuppositions, values, and systemic intentions.

What do I mean by "democratic capitalism"? I mean three systems in one: a predominantly market economy; a polity respectful of the rights of the individual to life, liberty, and the pursuit of happiness; and a system of cultural institutions moved by ideals of liberty and justice for all. In short, three dynamic and converging systems functioning as one: a democratic polity, an economy based on markets and incentives, and a moral-cultural system which is pluralistic and, in the largest sense, liberal. Social systems like those of the United States, West Germany, and Japan (with perhaps a score of others among the world's nations) illustrate the type.

The premise of this book may startle some. In the conventional view, the link between a democratic political system and a market economy is merely an accident of history. My argument is that the link is stronger: political democracy is compatible in practice only with a market economy. In turn, both systems nourish and are best nourished by a pluralistic liberal culture. It is important to give attention to all three systems. The full implications of a system which is threefold, rather than unitary, are developed through all the pages of this book.

To begin with, modern democracy and modern capitalism proceed from identical historical impulses. These impulses had moral form before institutions were invented to realize them; they aimed (1) to limit the power of the state, in defense against tyranny and stagnation; and (2) to liberate the energies of individuals and independently organized communities. Such impulses gave birth to modern European cities, whose first citizens took as their battle cry "City air makes men free."[2] Such citizens sought liberation from the crippling taxation, heavy bureaucracy, and dreary regulations of state and church. The moral vision of such citizens demanded forms of self-government in "city republics" and "free cities." It led them to cherish economies based upon free markets, incentives, and contracts. Gradually, such citizens developed polities based upon covenants, suffrage, the separation of powers, and the declaration of individual rights. The two revolutions—political and economic—in practice, but also in theory, nourished each other.[3] Karl Marx recognized this link in his term of contempt: "bourgeois democracy," he called it. Both spring from the same logic, the same moral principles, the same nest of cultural values, institutions, and presuppositions.

While bastard forms of capitalism do seem able for a time to endure without democracy, the natural logic of capitalism leads to democracy.[4] For economic liberties without political liberties are inherently unstable. Citizens economically free soon demand political freedoms. Thus dictatorships or monarchies which permit some freedoms to the market have a tendency to evolve into political democracies, as has happened in recent years in Greece, Portugal, Spain, and other nations. On the other side, the state which does not recognize limits to its power in the economic sphere inevitably destroys liberties in the political sphere. There are, as yet, no instances of dictatorial socialist states becoming democratic (although in 1981 one watched Poland with fascination). Democratic states which are sometimes described as socialist (Sweden, Israel, West Germany) invariably retain large components of private property, markets, and incentives.

Another point must be noted. Democratic polities depend upon the reality of economic growth. No traditional society, no socialist society—indeed, no society in history—has ever produced strict equality among individuals or classes. Real differences in talent, aspiration, and application inexorably individuate humans. Given the diversity and liberty of human life, no fair and free system can possibly guarantee equal outcomes. A democratic system depends for its legitimacy, therefore, not upon equal results but upon a sense of equal opportunity. Such legitimacy flows from the belief of all individuals that they can better their condition. This belief can be realized only under conditions of economic growth. Liberty requires expanse and openness.

In addition, liberty also requires social mobility. While statistical differences between strata necessarily remain, *individuals* must be free to rise from one level to another. Many move from poverty to reasonable economic sufficiency; some move to wealth. Others move up and down in many ways over a lifetime. A graduate student may be classified as "poor" on a graduate student's income, and again after retirement, yet in between may have high status and high income.

The reality of economic growth breaks one vicious circle; social mobility for individuals breaks another. The same democracy which without growth manifests self-destructive tendencies, leads to "balkanization," and inspires factional struggle acquires under conditions of growth a peaceable, generous character and is buoyant and expectant in each of its parts. It yields freedom to dream and realistic fulfillment of dreams. In the trap of a zero-sum economy, the Hobbesian "war of all against all" makes democracy come to seem unworkable. Liberated by economic growth, democracy wins common consent.

Not only do the logic of democracy and the logic of the market economy strengthen one another. Both also require a special moral-cultural base. Without certain moral and cultural presuppositions about the nature of individuals and their communities, about liberty and sin, about the changeability of history, about work and savings, about self-restraint and mutual cooperation, neither democracy nor capitalism can be made to work. Under some moral-cultural conditions, they are simply unachievable.

"Democratic capitalism" is a complex concept, depending in theory and in practice upon a threefold system. In its complexity, democratic capitalism is unlike both the historical societies which preceded it and the collectivized planned society that some wish to build in the future. Many who cherish it sense but cannot state the source of its originality.

1   The Historical Achievements of Democratic Capitalism

Consider the world at the beginning of the democratic capitalist era. The watershed year was 1776. Almost simultaneously, Adam Smith published *An Inquiry into the Nature and Causes of the Wealth of Nations* and the first democratic capitalist republic came into existence in the United States. Until that time, the classical pattern of political economy was mercantilist. Famines ravaged the civilized world on the average once a generation.[5] Plagues seized scores of thousands. In the 1780s, four-fifths of French families devoted 90 percent of their incomes simply to buying bread—only bread—to stay alive. Life expectancy in 1795 in France was 27.3 years for women and 23.4 for men. In the year 1800, in the whole of Germany fewer than a thousand people had incomes as high as $1,000.[6]

"The poor you will always have with you," Christ tells us. At the beginning of the nineteenth century who could doubt it? Travelers from Europe, inured to homegrown poverty, were appalled by the still more unspeakable conditions they found in Africa and Asia. In most places, elementary hygiene seemed unknown. In Africa, the wheel had never been invented. Medical practice in vast stretches of the world was incantatory. Illiteracy was virtually universal. Most of the planet was unmapped. Hardly any of the world's cities had plumbing systems. Potable water was mostly unavailable. Ignorance was so extreme that most humans did not know that unclean water spreads disease. Except in Adam Smith's book, the concept of development did not exist. In 1800, a judgment like that of Ecclesiastes, "There is nothing new under the sun," blanketed a mostly torpid world.

In 1800, popular self-government was uncommon. Democracies (notably Great Britain and the United States) were few. Nearly all states were authoritarian. In most regions, economic enterprises stagnated. In 1800, there were more private business corporations in the infant United States (population: four million) than in all of Europe combined.[7] Liberty of religion and speech was rare. In most cultures, absolute rulers reigned simultaneously over political, economic, and moral-cultural matters. In such a world, in most places, traditional Christianity and Judaism lived under severe constraints.

The invention of the market economy in Great Britain and the United States more profoundly revolutionized the world between 1800 and the present than any other single force. After five millennia of blundering, human beings finally figured out how wealth may be produced in a sustained, systematic way. In Great Britain, real wages doubled between 1800 and 1850, and doubled again between 1850 and 1900. Since the population of Great Britain quadrupled in size, this represented a 1600 percent increase within one century.[8] The gains in liberty of personal choice—in a more varied diet, new beverages, new skills, new vocations—increased accordingly.[9]

The churches did not understand the new economics. Officially and through the theologians, they often regarded "the new spirit of capitalism" as materialistic, secular, and dangerous to religion, as in many respects—being in and of the world—it was. They often protested the rising spirit of individualism. They seldom grasped the new forms of cooperation indispensable to the new economics. They tried to douse the new fire.

Pope Pius XI said that the tragedy of the nineteenth century was the loss of the working classes to the church.[10] An even deeper tragedy lay in the failure of the church to understand the moral-cultural roots of the new economics. Standing outside, it did not infuse. Attached to the past, the church did not leaven the new order with the same combination of critical distance and sympathetic hope with which it had inspired the feudal order, the guilds, and the civic life of medieval Europe.

Yet the possibilities of the new order are manifold. Theology is sustained reflection upon God and his dealings with the human race: *logos* and *theos*, systematic inquiry about God. Judaism and Christianity are distinctive among the world religions because they understand salvation as a vocation in history. It is the religious task of Jews and Christians to change the world as well as to purify their own souls; to build up "the Kingdom of God" in their own hearts and through the work of their hands. At several points, Old and New Testaments alike name Jahweh "Providence," the Provider, and speak in metaphor of "the economy of salvation." Both Jews and Christians are pilgrim peoples. Both in their long history have experienced many different forms of political economy. Both see their religious task as working in and through the institutions of this world. It is the vocation of laypersons, in particular, to fire the iron of politics, economics, and culture to Jahweh's vision.

The Lord of History is purposive. Through his word, human existence aspires upward. Robert Nisbet in his brilliant *History of the Idea of Progress* (1980) shows, against J. B. Bury, that the sense of a future different from the past was crucial to Judaic and Christian theology.[11] Religions like Judaism and Christianity require "historical consciousness," for they are going somewhere, being narrative religions which live by memory and hope. The tentative efforts of the last fifteen years to bring theology to "political consciousness" may yield too much to Marx but do, at least, show concern for shaping history. St. Augustine wrestled to make the City of God discernible in the City of Man. Aquinas attended carefully to the rule of princes, natural law, and civic virtue. Sophistication about history and politics avails little today, however, without sophistication about economics. Yet in no major sphere of life have the traditions of theology fallen further behind. For many centuries, of course, there was no science of economics and no sustained economic growth. So the lack was hardly felt. Today it is a scandal.

2　From Practice to Theory

For two centuries, democratic capitalism has been more a matter of practice than of theory. This practicality has been deliberate. After the divisiveness and bitterness of the religious wars of the seventeenth century, writers like Montesquieu, Smith, and Madison wished to avoid theological disputes. They were eager to describe methods of collaboration which would not entail prior metaphysical agreement. They wished to construct a pluralistic system open to persons of all faiths and visions. Furthermore, their specific genius lay in the practical order. They sought as much as possible to invent methods of compromise and adjustment. They wanted the "new order" they envisaged to grow by experience, by concrete collaboration, and by trial and error. They wrote constantly of their project as "an experiment." Eagerly they referred one another to obscure accounts of practical experiments which one or another came upon in dusty libraries. They were a new breed: philosophers of practice. The system they championed quite naturally rewarded practitioners more than theoreticians. Two centuries later, Jacques Maritain could still write:

> You are advancing in the night, bearing torches toward which mankind would be glad to turn; but you leave them enveloped in the fog of a merely experiential approach and mere practical conceptualization, with no universal ideas to communicate. For lack of an adequate ideology, your lights cannot be seen.[12]

For many generations, the practical superiority of democratic capitalism was as evident as the commercial proverb "Build a better mousetrap and the world will beat a path to your door." The superiority of practical men to theoretical men seemed verified by history. But there is another proverb, equally potent: "Without vision, the people perish." Furthermore, in a world of instantaneous, universal mass communications, the balance of power has now shifted. Ideas, always a part of reality, have today acquired power greater than that of reality. One of the most astonishing characteristics of our age is that ideas, even false and unworkable ideas, even ideas which are no longer believed in by their official guardians, rule the affairs of men and run roughshod over stubborn facts. Ideas of enormous destructiveness, cruelty, and impracticality retain the allegiance of elites that benefit from them. The empirical record seems not to jut through into consciousness to break their spell. The class of persons who earn their livelihood from the making of ideas and symbols seems both unusually bewitched by falsehoods and absurdities and uniquely empowered to impose them upon hapless individuals. (Cf. Chapter IX.)

In previous generations, taking its spiritual inheritance for granted, democratic capitalism felt no acute need for a theory about itself. It did not seem to need a moral theory, a theory about the life of the spirit, since it—erroneously—relied upon its own moral-cultural leaders to maintain one. The age of such innocence has long since passed. The glaring inadequacies of actual socialist societies do not seem to discourage newborn socialists. Entire nations, like Gadarene herds, cast themselves over the precipice. Within democratic capitalist societies as well, humans do not live by bread alone. Inattention to theory weakens the life of the spirit and injures the capacity of the young to dream of noble purposes. Irving Kristol in *Two Cheers for Capitalism* describes a moral vision "desperately needed by the spiritually impoverished civilization that we have constructed on what once seemed to be sturdy bourgeois foundations." He discerns the loss suffered by "a capitalist, republican community, with shared values and a quite unambiguous claim to the title of a just order" when it does not rethink its spiritual foundations and is thoughtlessly "severed from its moral moorings."[13]

The first of all moral obligations is to think clearly. Societies are not like the weather, merely given, since human beings are responsible for their form. Social forms are constructs of the human spirit.

Is there, then, a form for political economy most consonant with Judaic tradition and the Christian gospels? In *Integral Humanism* (1936), Jacques Maritain tried to express such a "proximate ideal," not yet realized by any human society and yet within the reach of human achievement. In other books, he tried to elucidate its presuppositions and its principles. Most astonishingly of all, in *Reflections on America* (1958), written after his firsthand experience of the United States, he admitted, to his own surprise, that the actual form of American society closely resembled the proximate ideal he had sketched in *Integral Humanism,* far more so than he had anticipated.[14] His chapter on the American economic system is especially important. Maritain saw the need for a new theory about the American system, but never gave sustained reflection to it himself. Neither has any other philosopher or theologian. John Courtney Murray, S.J., assayed the political system in *We Hold These Truths* (1960). Walter Lippmann tried to fill the gap with *The Public Philosophy* (1955). Reinhold Niebuhr in *The Irony of American History* (1952) and in other books also blazed a trail across deserts and mountains, but stopped short of the vision.[15]

Such books give me confidence that my own intuitions have not been eccentric. No society in the long history of the Jewish and Christian people owes more than our own to the inspiration of Jewish, Christian, and humanistic traditions. By no means is the political economy of the United States to be identified with the Kingdom of God, which transcends any historical political economy. It is not the "City of God." The transcendent religious commitments of Jews and Christians call us beyond the status quo, are always a source of judgment upon the status quo, and demand ever more profound reforms. Indeed, they transcend any conceivable achievement of reform and place all of history, even the most perfect form of human life, under the judgment of God.

Still, it is surprising that the authoritative documents of the Roman Catholic church, including the encyclicals of recent popes, proceed as if democratic capitalism did not exist. Few references to societies of the American type occur in papal documents; for the most part, these are terse, pejorative, and inaccurate. As Father Joseph Gremillion points out in *The Gospel of Peace and Justice,* a compendium of recent papal teaching on political economy, the horizon of Catholic teaching on the subject seems to have been bounded by a geographical quadrangle enclosed by Paris, Brussels, Munich, and Milan.[16] It is altogether surprising, moreover, that American theological scholars have given so little sustained reflection to the American experience. Father Arthur McGovern, S.J., has lavished more systematic attention on Marxism, in *Marxism: An American Christian Perspective,* than any Jesuit (or any other American Catholic) has yet given to the distinctive theory and practice of the American form of political economy. The record of Protestant theology—notably in official statements on political economy by the World Council of Churches and the National Council of Churches—is not better and in some ways worse.[17]

Not long ago, the United States was a colony of Europe's greatest power. Not long ago, it was trapped in the same immemorial poverty and underdevelopment as other nations. At its founding, it was at least as poor as the colonies of Spain in Latin America. These two Americas, North and South, equally colonies and equally underdeveloped, were founded upon two radically different *ideas* of political economy. The one attempted to recreate the political-economic structure of feudal and mercantilist Spain. The other attempted to establish a *novus ordo seclorum,* a new order, around ideas never before realized in human history. One would expect Christian theologians to have had a special interest in the outcome of these two experiments in the New World, since both were attempting to realize contrasting Christian ideas. It is astonishing to find, instead, theological silence.[18] My aim is to break that silence.

It seems important to state clearly why I have broken with the tradition of Christian socialism in which I was reared. For many of my adult years I thought of myself as a democratic socialist and allied myself with democratic socialist writers. What happened to make me break from this tradition? Nothing spectacular happened, but observation of human affairs and more intense reflection on economic matters gradually persuaded me that I could not, despite the will to do so, remain a socialist, even a "democratic socialist." On the other hand, one of my recent books involved me in a study of the beginnings of the United Mine Workers during the massacre of strikers in Lattimer, Pennsylvania, in 1897.[19] How could I think kindly of capitalism and corporations? A few words of autobiography—typical, I think, for many religious persons—may be in order.

For many years, I studied to become a Catholic priest, and later, as I continued my studies in the history and philosophy of religion as a layman, the specialty I loved most and paid most attention to was "the social teachings of the churches." The general scheme under which I learned to think of the modern era was "secularization." Many of the architects of democracy, capitalism, and moral-cultural pluralism considered organized religion—especially the Roman Catholic Church and the Church of England—as central pillars of the ancient establishment whose yoke they must throw off. On the Continent, both anti-clericalism and hostility to traditional religion were common. In Anglo-Saxon lands, the assault on religion tended, by contrast, to be against its "establishment" but not against religion in itself. Reading this history, no one can fail to note the conflict between traditional Catholicism and modernity. From very early days, it seemed to me that this conflict had been unnecessary and was based on serious misunderstandings. I took delight in the efforts of many to show how democracy and respect for natural human rights belonged to the authentic Catholic tradition. I welcomed the attempts of the Catholic church to "modernize" itself. I wrote one book about the need of the Catholic church to come to terms with the specifically American Catholic experience, and another, *The Open Church,* about the *aggiornamento* then taking place within the Catholic church during the Second Vatican Council (1961–65).[20]

Nonetheless, welcoming democracy and pluralism, I still judged capitalism harshly. For me as for the younger Maritain, capitalism remained something of a dirty word. The ancient and medieval tradition had not known capitalism. Unlike democracy and pluralism, it seemed less than spiritual, less than communal, and—more strongly—disruptive of community and tradition. My family heritage sprang from tiny farms on the hilltops of eastern Slovakia and, in America, in the smaller industrial towns of Pennsylvania and Connecticut. I identified with the sense of community of the European villages and the familial neighborhoods of my youth, and with "labor" rather than with "capital." In those days, capital had an ethnic and religious connotation as well as an economic one. Capitalists seemed almost always to be Protestants, either Calvinist or Episcopalian.

As I read the European Catholic intellectuals of the last two centuries—Lamennais, de Maistre, Chesterton, Belloc, Scheler, Marcel, and many others—I was won over by the contrast they drew between British (Protestant) philosophy and Catholic philosophy. On the one side, they and I lined up individualism, utilitarianism, pragmatism; on the other side, personalism, community, "solidarism." The underlying images in this literature contrasted the machines, slums, alienation, competition, and loneliness of modern secular man with the orderly, communal, holistic life of the Catholic past and (romantic) future. The thinkers of "the Catholic Renascence"[21] were not, however, solely nostalgic; many of them tried to imagine a new "third way" between capitalism and socialism. To "Protestant" conceptions of individualism they contrasted Catholic "personalism." To the pervasive materialism of modern life they contrasted a liturgical life of poverty of spirit and social action. Reinhold Niebuhr once wrote that what he most admired about the Catholic intellectual tradition was its constant emphasis upon the social nature of humans.[22] On the other hand, the popes from Leo XIII through Pius XII had also strenuously condemned the false beliefs of socialism and state tyranny.

In analyzing my own imagination at that time, I see how it was formed by a large component of nostalgia for the medieval village. This was the ground both of its ideal of community and of its revulsion against the democratic capitalist "lack" of community. Further, there was a Platonic or mildly Hegelian layer in my imagination, by which I tried to think of humanity as a "Mystical Body," somehow organically united as the human body is united. Writers who stressed "corporatism," "solidarism," or even non-atheistic forms of "socialism," therefore, struck my imagination as more in tune with the reality of life. When in college I first began to read English writers like Hobbes, Locke, and Mill, and American writers like James, Peirce, and Dewey, I experienced their underlying images as alien and offensive. Their talk of (as it seemed to me) atomic individuals forming "contracts" and "compacts," and their way of thinking in a narrowly empirical, pragmatic way, seemed to me not only foreign but spiritually *wrong*. My own sense of myself was familial, a member of a people whose history was hundreds of years old and stretching out into the unseen future. I did not experience myself as a lonely individual looking for a social contract. I had been born into several overlapping communities.

In these respects, I found the European critique of British individualism and contract theory quite attractive. The writings of the Continental phenomenologists and existentialists—not only Emmanuel Mounier, who had most influence upon Catholics of my generation, but even Scheler, Sartre, Camus, and Merleau-Ponty—seemed far closer to the inner reality of freedom and spiritual risk. Furthermore, I read most deeply of all in the writings of St. Thomas Aquinas and his modern interpreters like Gilson and Maritain. My favorite book was Aristotle's *Nicomachean Ethics* and the *Commentary* of St. Thomas Aquinas on it. They wrote of "distributive justice." They had little to say about the justice of producing wealth and creating economic development (possibilities which simply did not arise during their eras). The center of gravity of my education was Catholic Europe. Democratic capitalism lay largely outside this circle, as did the Anglo-American tradition. It may seem odd to say so, but as an American Catholic I was to discover Anglo-American intellectual life as an outsider.

There are three specific reasons why this is so. In the long Catholic ages, Catholic thought was fashioned to deal with a static world. It was, properly, fascinated by distributive ethics; it ignored questions of production. Secondly, its attitudes toward money were based on premodern realities. It did not understand the creativity and productivity of wisely invested capital. Thirdly, it took justifiable pride in the sense of community it succeeded in inspiring even within the rather inhospitable world of feudalism. Its satisfaction with the organic sensibility of medieval society and with its sense of the order of being and the hierarchical society allowed it to overlook the structures of domination inherent in feudal relations. It has ever since tended to idealize the corporate community of the medieval guilds, villages, estates, and courts, while discounting their grievous human costs. It had been, at times, so identified with the *ancien regime* that it came to resist the social revolutions of modernity, and perhaps particularly the liberal revolution effected in Great Britain, the United States, and a few other places. It has tended, particularly because of the Vatican's location within Italy, and also because of the great strength of still largely feudal societies in the Latin world, the Austro-Hungarian Empire, and Ireland, to rest uncomfortably in the past with only a tenuous connection to liberal societies. In a word, it has stood outside of and has, I think, misread the liberal democratic capitalist revolution.

Maritain once wrote, citing Aristotle, that a man cannot write well about ethics until he is at least fifty. Reading that at twenty-two, I faced a problem: What to do till age fifty? I decided to do what Maritain and Aristotle had done in their youth: to learn about one sphere of human action after another. In my case, this meant exercises in fiction, writing for television, and journalism but, above all, studies of the church, politics, ethnicity, the United States presidency, sports, and labor unions. I saved economics, the most complex, until last. The more I learned, the more I had to change my earlier views. If a neo-conservative is a liberal who has been mugged by reality, I do not quite qualify. The ideals of socialism began to fail me, it is true. More significant, I discovered spiritual resources in democratic capitalism I had long repressed in myself. To praise capitalism violates taboos. Well, intellectuals are supposed to question everything. The more I questioned, the more original the structure of democratic capitalism seemed to me, and the more I came to value it for what it is. Meanwhile, many of my Catholic friends were moving in exactly the opposite direction. Radicalized by the Vietnam War, they were drawn to Marxian analysis and to socialist ideals.

Father Arthur McGovern, S.J., accounts for the recent upsurge in the attraction of Marxism among American Catholic intellectuals in this way:

> . . . many Christians are deeply troubled by conditions in the world, by the vast gap between wealthy, affluent peoples and desperately poor ones, by vast expenditures on military weapons and luxury goods while basic human needs go unmet, by the growing power of giant corporations, and by a culture that undermines Christian values and true human needs.[23]

These sentiments move me as well. Yet if one keeps uppermost in mind the material needs of the poor, the hungry, and the oppressed, rather than one's own state of feelings, one asks: What is the most effective, practical way of raising the wealth of nations? What causes wealth? I have come to think that the dream of democratic socialism is inferior to the dream of democratic capitalism, and that the latter's superiority in actual practice is undeniable.

Democratic socialism now seems to me incoherent. It is consistent with democracy only where large components of democratic capitalism remain. The issue of planning, as such, no longer divides democratic socialists from democratic capitalists. To plan ahead is human, and political agents as well as economic agents must do so. The debate is, first, about the nature of the state (the limits of politics) and, second, about the degree of independence best left to economic agents. Many democratic socialists have joined democratic capitalists in criticism of centralized, bureaucratic state planning. What, then, is the new democratic socialist theory of the state? If an economy is planned—coercively—it cannot be democratic. If it is democratic, fashioned by local communities, it cannot be centrally planned. It will *look* a lot like a democratic capitalist economy.

Democratic socialists are eloquent about visions of virtue. Yet they seem to me nostalgic and wistful about political and economic institutions. As mine once were, their images of the participatory future are drawn from the town meetings of the eighteenth century, and their images of community are based on early village life. They are hostile to capitalism, but vague about future economic growth. Their strength lies in the moral-cultural system, their weakness in political and especially in economic analysis. Moreover, this weakness no longer seems to be merely innocent; it seems to be an unwitting precursor of tyranny. Their measures invariably enlarge state power. To regard the future as a warm, mothering presence up ahead, and to regard a dreamy socialism as beneficial and humane, is to ignore dozens of historical examples. The record of existing socialisms is plain, and so is the prognosis of future socialisms. Whatever the high intentions of its partisans, the structures they build by their actions promise to increase poverty and to legitimate tyranny.

One point remains to be stressed. Democratic capitalism, young as it is, has changed often. In trying to understand our present system, I have not tried to revise the entire tradition of historians of capitalism, nearly all of whom have been at least mildly anti-capitalist. A critical look at this tradition is badly needed.[24] The informing prejudices most of us inherit with our education are transparent. John Locke once wrote that the inventors of new economic processes and products—quinine, for example—were greater benefactors of humankind than earlier givers of charity.[25] There is a crying need for a more just inspection of those the humanists have, with barely concealed venom, attacked as "robber barons." Even the mine owners who played such an unsavory role at Lattimer Mines must, in all justice, be given credit for the inventive genius which opened new worlds to those they "exploited." No elite on earth has been without its victims, but not all have equally liberated and enriched the many. Fair and exact judgment has scarcely been rendered.

My own aim, however, has been to leave such questions aside. I am not trying to reinterpret the past but to understand the present. More precisely, I am trying to understand within the present those institutional ideals and systemic sources by which a better future may be shaped. If it suits the reader to suppose that the conventional picture of the exploitation of the poor by the captains of industry is a fair picture, about which they have no nagging questions, so be it. I keep my skepticism about conventional historical accounts to myself. My own attention is directed to the future.

This book, like its subject, is divided into three parts. In Part One, I try to put into words the structural dynamic beliefs which suffuse democratic capitalism: its *Geist,* its living spirit. In Part Two, I examine briefly what is left of the socialist idea today, so as to glimpse, as if in a mirror, a view of democratic capitalism by contrast. In Part Three, I try to supply at least the beginnings of a religious perspective on democratic capitalism. In large measure, I must here deal with rival theological approaches, again for the sake of contrast. I would like to persuade many religious persons, of my own faith and others, that a fair examination of the American system of political economy provides wisdom of great value to the future of the Jewish, Christian, and perhaps other religious peoples.

Democratic capitalism is neither the Kingdom of God nor without sin. Yet all other known systems of political economy are worse. Such hope as we have for alleviating poverty and for removing oppressive tyranny—perhaps our last, best hope—lies in this much despised system. A never-ending stream of immigrants and refugees seeks out this system. Peoples who imitate this system in faraway places seem to do better than peoples who don't. Why can't we put into words what attracts and what works?

Through the lonely pioneering work of John Courtney Murray, S.J., the experience of religious liberty under democratic capitalism finally, after so much resistance, enriched the patrimony of the Catholic church. So also, I hope, arguments in favor of "the natural system of liberty" will one day enrich the church's conception of political economy.

The world as Adam faced it after the Garden of Eden left humankind in misery and hunger for millennia. Now that the secrets of sustained material progress have been decoded, the responsibility for reducing misery and hunger is no longer God's but ours.

One

The Ideal of Democratic Capitalism

The purpose of Part One is to put into words the underlying moral structures which make the practices of democracy and capitalism work. Nations which lack such moral structures often reject democracy or capitalism, as a human organism sometimes rejects a heart transplant.

Democratic capitalism is not just a system but a way of life. Its *ethos* includes a special evolution of pluralism; respect for contingency and unintended consequences; a sense of sin; and a new and distinctive conception of community, the individual, and the family. The following nine chapters unpack these underlying moral structures one by one.

I

What Is Democratic Capitalism?

Throughout the world, capitalism evokes hatred. The word is associated with selfishness, exploitation, inequality, imperialism, war. Even at home, within the United States, a shrewd observer cannot fail to note a relatively low morale among business executives, workers, and publicists. Democratic capitalism seems to have lost its spirit. To invoke loyalty to it because it brings prosperity seems to some merely materialistic. The Achilles' heel of democratic capitalism is that for two centuries now it has appealed so little to the human spirit.

This failure is not commanded by stars conjoining in the sky. It is a failure not of iron necessity but of intellect. If the system in which we live is better than any theory about it, as Reinhold Niebuhr has suggested, the guardians of its spirit—poets and philosophers and priests—have not penetrated to its secret springs. They have neither deciphered nor taught its spiritual wisdom. They have not loved their own culture.

Clearly, this deficiency shows something wrong at the heart of democratic capitalism. In recent years, Daniel Bell in *The Cultural Contradictions of Capitalism* has tried to name the flaw. A generation ago, Joseph Schumpeter with uncanny accuracy foretold its course.

The ironic flaw which such writers discern in democratic capitalism is this: that its *successes* in the political order and in the economic order *undermine* it in the cultural order. The more it succeeds, the more it fails. Here are a few of the most commonly heard indictments.

(1) *The corruptions of affluence.* Moral discipline yields successes. But success corrupts moral discipline. Thus the system's ironical momentum heads toward hedonism, decadence, and that form of "self-fulfillment" which is like gazing into the pool of Narcissus. Instead of seeking discipline, citizens seek "liberation." Instead of saving, individuals spend and borrow. Instead of committing themselves to hard work, citizens live for "weekends." The health of a democratic republic depends upon a disciplined citizenry, but the political order of democratic capitalism is undermined by laxity. The economic system depends upon a sense of duty, disciplined innovation, and savings, but it also emits siren calls of pleasure. Productivity falls; debts grow; inflation roars; the system stagnates. In this sense, the new phenomenon encountered by economists—"stagflation"—is at bottom a disease of the spirit, which silently spreads decay even when unobserved by economic indicators. Citizens desire something for nothing—and they get it. Inflation and recession follow.

(2) *Advertising and moral weakness.* The leaders of the economic system permit advertising to appeal to the worst in citizens. They encourage credit-card debt, convenience purchasing, the loosening of restraint. Their workers, their customers, and they themselves—following such solicitations—reap the whirlwind.

(3) *Structural irresponsibility.* The leaders of the political order take advantage of a structural weakness in all democratic societies. Unable to depend on strong political parties, political leaders face the people alone and vulnerable, clothing themselves in symbolism and wishes. Their promises of benefits have become a special form of bribery endemic to democracy. Since each politician is on his own, none has an institutional reason to worry about who will eventually pay the costs. The careers of political leaders are shorter than the consequences of their actions. The state acquires ever heavier financial responsibilities, and yet the public incessantly clamors for *"More!"* The political leader spends, spends—an undignified activity Mr. Dooley would have lucidly diagnosed as bribes, bribes—since votes are seldom to be won by *lowering* benefits. All sectors of society desire more, so politicians promise more. They spend money not their own, money the system does not have. The structural flaw in all welfare democra-

cies is the desire of every population to live beyond its means. Weak human nature triumphs over common sense, in public as in private life.

(4) *An ambitious adversarial class.* The number of persons grows who see in expanded government empires to conquer, personal security and wealth to accumulate, and personal power to acquire. Moreover, these growing numbers are increasingly led by an intelligent, able, persistent, and ambitious elite strong enough to rival the business elite in brains and purpose and power. In order to grow wealthy and powerful in a welfare democracy, two roads now lie open where only a short time ago one lay open. This single road used to lie through the private sector. Now a high road has been opened through the public sector. Like Mt. Everest, the limited state once towered in solitary silence, waiting to be taken. The occupying troops have multiplied. The state has become an anthill of activity. Those in control of it are gaining control over the private sector as well. For the private sector is under law while those who make, multiply, and enforce laws have powers of coercion. Lust for power—*superbia*—is deeper, more pervasive, and more widespread than lust for wealth—*cupiditas*.

(5) *The declining status of aristocracy.* The leaders of the moral-cultural sector have long suffered under the market system of democratic capitalism from a profound loss of status (which through domination in the media they have recently been regaining). In traditional societies, an archbishop holds status he cannot possibly command under a fully differentiated system separating church from state. In traditional societies, scholars and artists received patronage and status they cannot readily command in the commercial marketplace. Truly rare works of genius can be appreciated by a very few; the market discerns them poorly. In the old days, artists and scholars hoped to bring their patrons (and themselves) immortality. They belonged to an aristocracy of spirit within an aristocratic culture. Aristocratic elites cherished artistic elites so that the two might forevermore be linked: excellence of intellect and aristocratic taste. In Great Britain, the artist may be "knighted," so inscribed into the aristocratic order.

By contrast, the dominant class within democratic capitalism has been the commercial class. The standards of the market are only rarely the standards of artistic and intellectual excellence. The mass market may indeed recognize great talents like those of

Dickens, but for the most part it seems to favor those talents which flatter the conventional wisdom. In the marketplace, the claims of high excellence are much attenuated.

A socialist state affords its artists and intellectuals higher status. Authoritarian schemes of life enforce respect, affording honor and privilege to compliant intellect. Bourgeois cultures offer liberty but confer little of the status which systems of the traditional or of the socialist sort have it in their power to confer.

(6) *Envy.* In democratic capitalism, the resentments of the intellectuals are bound to fester. Monetary rewards for high intellectual and artistic talents, while in the vagaries of the market sometimes lavish, are more frequently less than rewards for top performers in corporate management, athletics, and entertainment. That fan dancers command moneys many a scholar can scarcely dream of cries to heaven for justice. That a top talent in the field of corporate management commands a salary commensurate with that of a movie star rankles in the breasts of top academic and artistic talents. A less gifted brother of a brilliant social scientist goes to work for a corporation and draws a higher salary. Is that fair? Is this meritocracy? The Lord Jehovah, knowing its potency in the human breast, forbade covetousness twice in ten commandments.

(7) *Taste.* The culture of democratic capitalism is loathed—with perhaps the deepest loathing—for its "bourgeois" and "philistine" tastes. Yet some corporate managers seem to have tastes at least as high as some professors of sociology. Thus the loathing is most exactly directed at the market mechanism, toward which, as Yugoslav socialist Bogdan Denitch puts it, "socialist theorists with rare exceptions" cherish a "dogmatic, almost puritanical attitude," being offended by the passion of Eastern European youths for jeans. The market encourages a "consumer sovereignty that socialist intellectuals all too often think is bad for ordinary mortals." Denitch adds:

> There are two sides to this aversion. One is a predilection of socialist intellectuals toward neat, organized plans run by experts not too unlike themselves; the other is a notion that if customers of the lower orders are turned loose, they will not choose things that are good for them.[1]

Free to choose, a democratic people luxuriously manifests vulgarity. Plastic roses offend the sensitive. Rudeness and vulgarity in "shopping strips" assault the intellectuals. The tastes of ordinary citizens in Hamtramck, Newark, and South Boston scrape against refined tastes like a fingernail across a blackboard.

Trouble arises because both markets and democratic procedures introduce leveling pressures. Majorities of consumers, like political majorities, often choose what some think is not good for them. Socialists who are intellectuals frequently desire the democratization of the economic system, offended both by the existence of economic elites and by the aesthetics and moral mediocrity of free market consumers. Socialism is a neat solution to both grievances. It raises up a new elite to a position empowering it to impose a better way. Thus its attack upon the aesthetics of democratic capitalism is an important step toward "the reintegration of the political and the economic."[2] Such a "reintegration" embodies a moral-cultural vision which is to be obligatory for all.

In sum, democratic capitalism appears to the orderly eye a morass of cultural contradictions. Not many poets, philosophers, artists, or theologians have smiled kindly upon it. It seethes with adversarial spirit.

To these complaints must be added scores of others. It is charged that the skies, water, and lands are polluted. Discarded chemicals "poison" populations. The new civilization is called "cancerous." The wealthy, it is claimed, get wealthier, while the criminal-justice system oppresses the poor. The great corporations are viewed as internally undemocratic and hardly compatible with democracy at all. The "imperialism of money" keeps the Third World in "dependency." The material success of developed nations "causes" the poverty of the less-developed nations. It is hardly any wonder that, for those who believe these things, capitalism is an evil system.

Can any political system or economic system long survive whose moral-cultural guardians loathe it so? Those of us who have acquired our educations in the humanities and social sciences have heard little praise of the system in which we were reared. In 1937, a distinguished panel of Protestant theologians meeting at Oxford, upon mature reflection, described our actual lives so:

> When the necessary work of society is so organized as to make the acquisition of wealth the chief criterion of success, it encourages a feverish scramble for money, and a false

respect for the victors in the struggle, which is as fatal in its moral consequences as any other form of idolatry.[3]

In *Religion and the Rise of Capitalism*, R. H. Tawney discerned as the dominant spiritual theme in democratic capitalism the vulgar itch of acquisitiveness. Max Weber described later capitalism as an "iron cage," whose bureaucratic steel would crush the human spirit.[4] A towering theologian, Paul Tillich, described democratic capitalism as "demonic."[5]

In good faith, who can be, by conviction and by a willingness to commit one's life to its defense, a democratic capitalist? Those who would do so are everywhere embarrassed by the lack of an intellectual tradition that would nourish them; a theory that would satisfy them; a description of the world of their actual experience which is recognizably true. Too many, repelled by the adversaries of democratic capitalism, are nevertheless also dissatisfied with the theories about democratic capitalism inherited from Adam Smith, Jeremy Bentham, Ludwig von Mises, Frederick von Hayek, Milton Friedman, and others. The typical mistake of classic thinkers on this subject is to have laid too small a foundation to support the lived world of a democratic capitalist society as we have experienced it. They have too chastely considered the economic system in abstraction from the real world, in which the political system and the moral-cultural system also shape the texture of daily life.

To a large extent, the few explorers of this terrain find themselves alone. They learn from classical writers, and also from the traditions of democratic socialism. When their teachers fail them, the guides are few. They are obliged to consult afresh their own experience, which goes beyond delivered wisdom.

What then is the spirit of democratic capitalism? Let us begin by meeting Max Weber (1864–1920), the first great sociologist to study world history in order to understand the originality of the modern West. Most literate persons in the West have encountered his theories through such common phrases as "the work ethic." His little classic *The Protestant Ethic and the Spirit of Capitalism* has been read by three generations of college students.[6] He was the first to assay the questions we take up afresh.

Max Weber was an agnostic, yet his studies of world civilizations encouraged in him an unusual interest in the religious dimension of all social systems. He was fascinated by the *Geist,* the spirit, that gave similar activities quite different cosmic and humble operational meanings in different cultures. Buying and selling, for example, are immemorial human activities found in every major culture and era. Great trading civilizations—like that of the ancient Phoenicians (today's Lebanese)—have persisted down through history, or come upon the stage, made their mark, and disappeared. Nonetheless, the *Geist* suffusing such activities shows staggering variation from culture to culture.

Weber was particularly interested in the clash between traditional cultures and modern culture. In our day, even the most casual watcher of the television news has been able to see in the Iran of the Ayatollah Khomeini the sort of conflict between the modern and the traditional that fascinated Weber. What makes modern capitalism new? What makes it seem like such a threat to all forms of traditional culture? It is not so much, Weber thought, that the specific activities of a modern commercial culture differ from those of analogous cultures down through the ages. In the past, there had been commerce, banks, industries, factories for silk and other goods. What, then, is different? Weber observed that in capitalist societies commerce is given a new *meaning*. It becomes part of a new sort of cosmic order, a new vision of human history. It is carried out in a new *spirit*. It is not easy to define the *Geist* of a civilization, but Weber bent every resource of intellect to invent a way of articulating it.

Max Weber knew from his own experience whereof he was writing. A Protestant "evangelical" family, the Webers were among those Protestants driven from Salzburg by the infamous Catholic archbishop Leopold of Firmian in 1731. Settling in Bielefeld, Weber's grandfather ran a comfortable linen business in a pre-capitalist mode. Although he was a buyer and seller, his grandson observed, he lacked "the capitalist spirit." He hardly sought to improve his business; he was content to take a modestly comfortable living from it. To the dismay of the family, Max's Uncle Karl, the eldest son, who inherited the business, from somewhere caught "the capitalist spirit." He was not satisfied with a static world; he chose development. He worked hard to rationalize, modernize, and improve the business. Systematically he collected lists of customers and cottage-industry suppliers, employed designers, and began to organize both demand and supply. By contrast, Max's father, Max senior, abhorred the disciplines of business and enjoyed the more relaxed, freer atmo-

sphere of politics. He freely made those compromises required by
his ambitions. Easygoing in his amiable public life, he was at
home a complete autocrat. Max junior, sensitive and conscientious
to a fault, had a tremendous internal struggle with his father, with
whom for many years of his young adulthood he was forced to
live.

Max's mother brought a sizable dowry to the family, wholly
controlled (without any outward sign of gratitude) by Max senior.
She was as thoroughly devout a Calvinist as her husband was lax.
Often her compassion led her to help the poor and to take part in
religious discussions in ways that became a constant source of
familial conflict. Max junior described himself as lacking an ear
for religion. In this he disappointed his mother and more nearly
resembled his father. The son thought he owed his voracious appetite for work—his need for it, his relentless drive—to his
mother. She was the force of conscience and energy in the family;
his father, except in the home, was far more relaxed.

In 1898, at the age of thirty-four, two years after a furious
outburst in which he ordered his father out of his house and, seven
weeks later, next saw his father dead, Max Weber suffered a
severe nervous breakdown. For four years he was almost totally
incapacitated. He did not resume teaching again, or even meeting
with students, for another fifteen years. During his convalescence,
he was able to resume his studies part-time. The first piece of
writing he felt strong enough to accomplish consisted of the two
long articles he published in 1904 and 1905, which later appeared
jointly as *The Protestant Ethic and the Spirit of Capitalism*. Before
his death in 1920, Weber was able to revise these essays (mostly
in the footnotes rather than in the text), which had already
launched a storm of discussion and achieved status as a classic.
The argument has continued throughout the sixty years since. The
bibliography of the controversy is enormous.[7]

What did Weber mean by "the spirit of capitalism"? I propose
to stress an aspect of the argument not stressed by Weber, but
present in his text, and then to come back rather closely to his
own words.

The most dramatic breakthrough of the capitalist spirit, for
Weber, is its theme of *sustained growth*. Profit is by no means a
new concept in world history; it is as ancient as camel caravans
and sailing ships. But until the capitalist era, the world had been
understood as relatively static. The ancients distinguished cycles

of prosperity, lean years from years of plenty. But the notion that the sustained application of practical intelligence to economic activities could open up new and unprecedented horizons awaited the capitalist spirit. Weber distinguishes the spirit of sustained incremental effort from adventure, piracy, luck, a windfall.

This sense of opening up the world's horizons coincided with the discoveries of the "new world." But there is an important difference between the recognition that entire continents promised new sources of spice, gold, furs, and other goods and the conviction that economic activities at home could be organized in a new way. For many generations after the discovery of America and the opening of sea routes to the Far East, mercantilism—a state-controlled economy—remained the dominant theory and practice of economic activities. There may have been new goods to buy and sell, but methods and techniques remained rather what they had been for centuries. Except in "free cities," the state tended to control economic activities.

It may have been John Locke (1632–1704) who first articulated the new possibility for economic organization. Locke observed that a field of, say, strawberries, highly favored by nature, left to itself, might produce what seemed to be an abundance of strawberries. Subject to cultivation and care by practical intelligence, however, such a field might be made to produce not simply twice but tenfold as many strawberries.[8] In short, Locke concluded, nature is far wealthier in possibility than human beings had ever drawn attention to before.

Permit me to put Locke's point in theological terms. Creation left to itself is incomplete, and humans are called to be co-creators with God, bringing forth the potentialities the Creator has hidden. Creation is full of secrets waiting to be discovered, riddles which human intelligence is expected by the Creator to unlock. The world did not spring from the hand of God as wealthy as humans might make it. After the Fall, ignorance and disorder became commonplace.

There was born in Locke's vision a novel and invigorating sense of the human vocation. History was no longer to be regarded as cyclical. After Locke, reflection on God's ways with the world—theodicy—was altered. The way God works in history was now to be thought of as progressive, open, subject to human liberty and diligence. The vocation of the human being came to seem ennobled. No longer were humans to imagine their lot as passive, long-suffering, submissive. They were called upon to be inventive, prudent, farseeing, hardworking—in order to realize by their obedience to God's call the building up and perfecting of God's Kingdom on earth. Slamming the doors of the monastery shut, as Weber put it, the Reformation had carried the energy of certain human virtues out into worldly callings. Progress and economic growth—not only personal but for the entire world— were seen to be the will of God. Progress imposed its disciplines, a kind of "otherworldly asceticism." This earth was now seen to be full of promise for science, the arts, religion, and even the humble comforts of human life. To be a good Christian and to evince the highest of civic virtues would be, simultaneously, to labor for human progress.

On the Continent, many of the partisans of progress were defiantly secular and often vitriolically anti-religious. Religion, in particular the Catholic religion (but also Protestant Geneva), was regarded as the bastion of resistance to progress. *"Ecrasez l'infame!"* Voltaire could write. In the Anglo-Saxon world, secular thinkers usually treated religion rather more benignly. Even if its doctrines and pieties were not for them, religion on the whole, they thought, played a useful and probably indispensable social role. Montesquieu's dictum that the English were known throughout Europe for three distinctive excellences—piety, commerce, and liberty—pleased Weber.[9]

Max Weber had experienced in his own family history all the elements we have so far described. His grandfather was still part of the traditional society of commerce. His Uncle Karl introduced—much to the disgust of many in the family—the new "capitalist spirit." And Weber came to see in the "work ethic" of his mother and his uncle a powerful synthesis of religion and economic striving. He knew from his own family history that many of those engaged in economic activities in the new spirit, like his uncle, were only marginally religious, while many devout persons like his mother were only marginally interested in economic activities. But what he noticed, or thought he noticed, is that the legitimating, sacralizing force of religion in lives like that of his mother was often being married to economic traditions being born in a family like his uncle's.

When Weber turned then for a classic statement of the new "spirit of capitalism" he was not at all abashed to choose as a chief spokesman for this viewpoint, along with religious preachers like Baxter and Wesley, a man only mildly Deist, hardly at all religious, surely far removed from strict Puritanism: Benjamin Franklin. Weber cites specifically from Franklin's *Advice to a Young Tradesman* (1748) and *Necessary Hints to Those That Would Be Rich* (1736). What startled Weber was the frank rejection by Franklin of traditional Christian warnings against riches. Without question, Franklin explicitly counseled a rigorous asceticism and advised constant watchfulness in even the smallest details of dress and deportment. Equally without question, Franklin's asceticism was astonishingly worldly. Yet, most to the point, Franklin *praised* wealth and riches. He saw in them goals of moral striving. His counsel revealed a shockingly new moral attitude toward the world. The cosmos itself, the imperatives of historical progress, the call of the Creator of all things, were seen by Franklin to be impelling young men toward wealth. Franklin did not think that such a call is in the least corrupt, sinful, or out of accord with the wisdom of the saints or sages of the past. Quite the opposite. While turning on their heads the traditional counsels against worldliness, riches, and concentrated earthly striving, Franklin imagined himself to be speaking with the authority of the religious and humanistic past. Consider one text of many in his *Autobiography:*

> It was about this time that I conceived the bold and arduous Project of arriving at moral Perfection. I wish'd to live without committing any Fault at any time; I would conquer all that either Natural Inclination, Custom, or Company might lead me into.[10]

Here, thought Weber, lay a true revolution in the *Geist* of the West and indeed of all human history. Whereas in previous ages and cultures, both Christian saints and the humanist sages of Stoicism had counseled against excessive worldly striving, against ambition, and against wealth, Franklin turned what was earlier thought to be evil into virtue itself. It is not so much that men and women of commerce in the new age would perform different sorts of activities than the men and women of the past. It is, rather, that they would do so in a wholly new spirit. They did so as humanists. They did so with "religious conviction." As is plain by Weber's choice of the frankly secular Franklin, this new "religion" is susceptible of a quite secular form. But it does function as religions everywhere have always functioned. It gives the cosmos and human history a meaning and also a commanding power. It gives each of its devotees a sense of personal identity and a sense of community with all other "progressive" persons. It sets forth tables of virtues and vices, with a thoroughgoing casuistry for interpreting every detail of concrete behavior in their light. It conveys the energy of purposiveness, and a method for dealing with defeat, discouragement, and setback. It constitutes a novel ethos in world history, a new *Geist*, "the spirit of capitalism."

To be sure, this spirit could not have had historical force without the concomitant growth of many institutional procedures. Taken independently, none of these institutional developments is wholly new. Taken together, they might without the new *Geist* that suffused them have resulted in a very different sort of culture and economy. Weber does not wish to say either that the human *spirit* alone is the cause of institutional developments, or that the development of social *institutions* is the cause of the shape which the human spirit assumes at any one time. He is a determinist neither of mind nor of matter.[11] What he does wish to do is to point out that an adequate historical explanation requires attention to both factors. The factor he finds most neglected by the social thinkers of his own time, influenced chiefly by Marx, is the factor of the spirit.

But it is important also to come down to earth. And so in trying to define the set of institutions suffused by "the capitalist spirit," Weber struggles manfully to distinguish the indispensable institutional preconditions. He offers a preliminary definition of capitalism:

> Capitalism is identical with the pursuit of profit, and forever *renewed* profit, by means of continuous, rational, capitalistic enterprise. . . . A capitalistic economic action . . . rests on the expectation of profit by the utilization of opportunities for exchange, that is on (formally) peaceful chances of profit.[12]

But this must have dissatisfied even him, for he follows it with a discussion of six of its elements which goes far beyond his initial effort.[13] Each of the elements in this definition has significance.

(1) *Free labor* is critical, because the system is not one of

slavery or serfdom or forced labor. The precise quality which Marx sees as so inhuman—that labor is treated as a commodity— Weber sees as the condition of its liberty. If men are to choose their work, they must have multiple possibilities of employment and reward, under conditions of mobility. Few societies can be so simple that each person is self-sufficient. A division of labor is necessary. Thus, free men will necessarily trade their labor so as to obtain in exchange what they desire. One's time, energy, strength, and attention are, in a sense, one's capital. Weber notes that the liberty of exchange makes calculations possible for both the employer and the employee, according to which each can measure profit and loss in each exchange. Each can ask: "Is it worth it?" Where such a discipline is present, under liberty, capitalism can take root. Without such liberty, there is peonage or serfdom. Compared to that of the aristocrat or of the owner of the means of production, the laborer's freedom may be less; but it is more than the freedom of the serf or peon. The age of capitalism, accordingly, is also the age of great migrations.

(2) *Reason* is central to capitalism. Capitalism is very much (as the word suggests) a system of the head. Practical intelligence orders it in every detail. It promotes invention and fresh ideas. It strives constantly for better forms of organization, more efficient production, and greater satisfaction. It plans for the long run as well as the short. It orders materials, machines, producers, salesmen, and consumers. It organizes means and ends. It constantly studies itself for improvement. It is ordered toward continuous enterprise longer than the life of any individual. Oddly, instead of being merely a means to a human end, the rationalized economic system becomes in some ways an end, organizing human beings to its purposes. The economic system need not wholly absorb them or completely dominate them; other demands of life hold it in check. But it cannot be said to be merely an instrument. Recall again Montesquieu's quip that the English excel in three things, piety, commerce, and liberty. Each of these is, in a sense, a means; each is also an end. Piety cannot be the whole of life, if one's calling is to labor in the world. Nor can commerce if piety and liberty are to be served. Nor can liberty, since liberty is *for* as well as *from*. Foreshadowed here is a point that Weber does not make, a point which differentiates our "spirit of democratic capitalism" from Weber's "spirit of capitalism." Democratic capi-

talism is a tripartite system: economic, moral, and political at once. Weber did not go quite so far.

(3) The new capitalism is not a matter of adventure or piracy but of *continuous* enterprise, planned and organized, evaluated for profit and loss. Without the invention of double-entry bookkeeping, without mathematical sophistication, without the techniques of analysis made possible by modern science, continuous calculation would not be possible.

(4) The separation of the workplace from the household—although older than capitalism—raised capitalism to a degree of *impersonality* not possible under agrarian or feudal familism. Under capitalism, a man is not born into his station; questions about his life history became, in a sense, irrelevant. The economic contract does not absorb his entire life. The economic system stands outside the older cultural system. This duality opens up a psychological gap in the life of individuals. The differentiation of systems changes the sense of individual identity. This new duality breaks older organic ties and permits new liberties. Emotionally, it brings costs as well as gains. As exchange on the market becomes impersonal, religion, race, and nationality become less relevant. A purchaser of goods or services often does not know the seller or the maker. (As the American South became more capitalist after World War II, distinctions of race lost rationale.) The move from household to workplace permitted production for the masses as well as for the few. The new differentiation may be seen as alienation or as liberty—opposite sides of the same experience.

(5) Calculation, organization, investment, and exchange could not take place over long periods of time without *stable networks of law*. The gradual invention of corporate law was especially significant. The legal distinction between the corporation and the family permitted new forms of calculation and new forms of activity. Corporate law empowered nonprofit corporations as well as those organized for profit. It encouraged almost infinite varieties of voluntary association and social participation. The corporation in its varieties is the most distinctive agency of democratic capitalism. It transcends the individual person. As a "legal person," it is registered in law. Commerce requires stability and the peaceful resolution of conflict. Although law may choke it, it needs law and favors its development.

(6) The new capitalism grew up most rapidly and broadly in *cities and towns*. The urban spirit instructed human beings in new forms of association. It stimulated intellect and invention. It made possible the break from agrarian rural ways. In the cities law thickened, novel forms of social organization were tried, and modern liberties were experienced. Rural areas remained closer to old traditions; they were agrarian rather than capitalist. Even though marketing and risk, profit and loss, independence and self-reliance, are immemorial characteristics of rural life (in the Soviet Union today, farmers remain a bastion of so-called capitalist habits), these do not constitute the essential originality of capitalism. Capitalism depends upon and generates the culture of cities, a culture of a distinctively modern type. Its texture of habits and laws, perceptions and energies, rhythms and manners, laborers and markets, is distinctively urban. (Even in the twentieth century, rural America long retained an antipathy for Wall Street and the other urban centers of capitalism.)

There are a number of flaws in Weber's definition of capitalism. My own intention in the following chapters is to go beyond it. For our present purposes it suffices to note that Weber was fascinated by the *Geist* or *ethos* that (a) held all these six characteristics together and (b) suffused them with symbolic meaning and spiritual value. Oddly, Weber pays little or no attention to Montesquieu, Adam Smith, James Madison, Thomas Jefferson—persons who thought they were bringing about "a new order of the ages." They thought they divined what God intended to be discovered in his creation and had left for human beings to bring to realization. They saw themselves as agents of the progress which God intended the world to make or, in some cases, as agents of the progress which traditional religion, its towers blocking the sun, had passionately resisted. In either case, for such men and women, science, technology, and practical economic development were godly tasks or, at least, the highest of human imperatives.

Weber's definition of "the spirit of capitalism" falls short of the historical reality in two ways. Weber failed to analyze the necessary connection between economic liberty and political liberty. This necessity is not one of logic but of fact. Although, conceptually, the two notions are different, nonetheless, in the real world, each without the other suffers grievous weaknesses. Thus, Weber ought to have written, but did not, about the spirit of *democratic* capitalism. He saw that capitalism is an *economic* system dependent upon a moral *spirit,* but those are only two of the three essential components of the existing system. The *political* system is also a powerful force, setting up rival institutions, meanings, and powers of its own. Weber should have seen more clearly—as Schumpeter was later to see—the gargantuan struggle even in his day taking shape between the state system and the economic system. When capitalism reverts to state control (as it did under fascism and does under forms of socialist collectivism), it ceases to be capitalism and becomes once again the patrimonial state. Differentiation between the economic system and the political system is then swallowed up again in primeval unity.[14] The state rules all.

This is why Robert Heilbroner, in some ways the most honest of contemporary socialists, has become (perhaps despite himself) a harbinger of the authoritarianism he sees descending upon us all. "Bourgeois rights," he continues to remind those who nourish softer illusions, cannot survive under a state system of effective planning and effective control.[15]

In addition, Max Weber misdiagnosed the nature of practical intelligence within democratic capitalism by describing it as "rational-legal." It is, in fact, far more than "rational" in his sense, and far more than merely "legal." When Weber argues that democratic capitalism produces "an iron cage," he may have been observing in the temper of the Prussian burgher a zest for precision, rule, law, and lock-step discipline. He was not describing the hedonism, decadence, breakdown of values, amorality, and wildness which Berthold Brecht was soon to observe in the Berlin of the era of the Weimar Republic. He did not capture the ebullience and the bombast of the beer halls of Munich. Much more was to happen than Weber anticipated in the Germany of the period after the disastrous Treaty of Versailles. Still more was happening, under quite different conditions, in other centers of democratic capitalism, whose vitalities are far more than "rational-legal."

Weber seemed to understand by "rational" the rationality of engineers, who put time clocks to the analysis of industrial production. But the application of scientific rationality to industrialization is not confined to democratic capitalism; it is just as endemic to scientific socialism. Rationality of that sort does not properly define democratic capitalism. In his eagerness to distinguish capitalism by contrast with traditional and charismatic societies, Weber missed some essential vitalities.

Weber overlooked, for example, the role of insight and practical wisdom in entrepreneurship and skillful management. Successful management in a large firm depends upon an ability to understand people, to inspire, and to draw the best out of them. Such forms of insight are difficult to teach, and some individuals are more highly endowed with them than others. Managerial talent is rare. In entrepreneurship, as well, invention plays an indispensable role. Modern commerce to an extraordinary extent depends upon a continual stream of innovations in every step of the economic process, from concept to production, from distribution to marketing. A firm bound by the rational-legal habits of yesterday is almost certain to fossilize. Weber, in brief, overlooked the multiple types of rationality implicit in democratic capitalism. He defined rationality too narrowly, overlooking its capacities for revolutionary dynamism.

Far from coming to resemble the "iron cage" of the rolling last paragraphs of *The Protestant Ethic,* the real world of democratic capitalism is demonstrably open. It has been "revolutionized" again and again. In the United States, the political system empowered labor unions in the Wagner Act of 1935; defined the forty-hour week; banned child labor; and established social security. The dynamism of the political system has tremendously affected the economic order. Furthermore, wholly new inventions—from the typewriter to the automobile to the miniaturized computer—have again and again altered the bases of industry, the workplace, and the common life. Rational-legal? The new economic system delights in the marvelous. It often seems more like magic than like bureaucratic reason. It stirs primitive wonder.

Moreover, the new system speeded up the rate of change in the world. The industrial revolution has already given way to the "post-industrial age." From generation to generation, styles of management have changed. Thus, if the economic system is dynamic in ways that shatter its earlier paradigms, the moral-cultural system also changes. Over the decades, "life-styles" have changed rapidly and "new moralities" have several times appeared. These days, few dread too much stability, too much iron sameness. Some indeed warn us of the opposite: "future shock." The charismatic vitality of the forms of practical intelligence embodied in democratic capitalism makes Weber's description of the "rational-legal" iron cage untenable.

The spirit of democratic capitalism is the spirit of development, risk, experiment, adventure. It surrenders present security for future betterment. In differentiating the economic system from the state, it introduced a novel pluralism into the very center of the social system. Henceforth, all societies of its type would be internally divided—and explosively revolutionary.

II
Pluralism

$\mathbf{M}$ax Weber was right to look to the *spirit* of democratic capitalism. Apart from some new spirit, it is almost impossible to define capitalism.[1] Its economic features do not define it. Neither industry nor factories, neither commerce nor profits, neither private property nor incentives, neither the division of labor nor international trade, appeared first in modern times. Yet something new is universally held to have appeared—even if Weber failed, finally, to define it exactly—and that something new is pluralism.

A pluralistic spirit decisively distinguishes democratic capitalism from either traditionalist or socialist societies. Every other form of society the world has ever known imposes a collective sense of what is good and true. In all other systems, every decisive economic, political, and moral-cultural power is exercised by one set of authorities. Democratic capitalism is unique among all forms of political economy by reason of its pluralism.

How is pluralism to be understood? Can such pluralism in politics, economics, and moral-cultural matters yield order? If no one philosophy spreads a "sacred canopy" over our teeming liberties, how is anarchy to be avoided? No issue we face is more complicated, and so we must proceed through four brief inquiries. First, a pluralist order must be distinguished from a traditional (or socialist) order. Next, we explore pluralism as it bears on economics, on politics, and on religion.

1
Unitary Order

The human race commonly manifests a kind of mysticism about order. In the religious consciousness of the West, for example, there is a deeply buried habit of thinking of history as a unified field. There is a deep desire to find meaning in it. Traditional societies in the West have exhibited this desire, as more recently have socialist societies. In this sense, monotheism has had profound effects upon political consciousness.[2] If there is one God who shapes nature and history, then there "must" be meaning, purpose, direction in history.

In theistic versions of the meaning of history, the legitimacy of a social order resides in its cleaving to the order in the mind of the Lord of nature and history. Thus, citizens "participate," although darkly, in the purpose of God. Spokesmen of the churches play a large role in discerning the order desired by God, although the individual consciences of the laity may also be charged with discernment. Murder, mayhem, injustice, and other characteristics are seen to be offenses to legitimate order and must be set right.

There are also atheistic versions of the monotheistic impulse. In some secular visions, history is conceived to be purposive. Individuals acquire moral weight from lending their shoulders to the wheels of progress. "The future"—imagined as better than the present—is seen to make moral claims upon persons of goodwill. It is imagined that there are tides, trends, and causes being realized in events which it is obligatory for sensitive persons to support. One is ethical not only by the way in which one lives one's private life but by the quality of the progressive causes one supports. Those who resist such causes are thought to be insensitive, obdurate, or bad. Marxism is an atheism of this sort, monotheistic in its underlying theory of history. It is not difficult for certain theists to identify the sense of progress willed by God with the dialectic of "liberation" discerned by scientific socialism. Through identifying themselves with it, they may feel a part of a story far larger than their own brief and otherwise perhaps pointless lives. Such a vision of order in history has ethical bite. It issues commands for action now.

Democratic capitalism is not such a moral order. One of the key accusations against it is that it is in some ways amoral; that it leads to widespread anomie, purposelessness, and loss of vision. Thus Aleksandr Solzhenitsyn in his Harvard address of 1978 discerns at the heart of democratic capitalism a "moral poverty, which no one could have imagined even as late as in the nineteenth century." This new order of the world did not make spiritual purposes central to its inner order. It left the circle of freedom bare. The great Solzhenitsyn thus finds democratic capitalism wanting:

> Everything beyond physical well-being and accumulation of material goods, all human requirements and characteristics of a subtler and higher nature, were left outside the range of attention of the state and the social system, as if human life did not have any higher meaning.[3]

Solzhenitsyn's good society is based upon a traditional vision of social order. This vision is explicitly religious, perhaps even theocratic. The Orthodox society he envisages would discipline liberty and would shape human beings by this vision.

Roman Catholic popes from Leo XIII (1891) to Pius XI (1931) have also looked with disapproval upon liberal, pluralistic societies of the British and American type.[4] They interpret these societies from afar as examples of radical disorder. In their eyes such societies cannot be suffused with justice or love, for they depend solely on the choices of individuals unrestrained by commanding social imperatives. They must end in moral disorder. The pontiffs fear an individualism so radical that it will end in tyranny.

Thus, democratic capitalism is an affront both to traditional and to socialist conceptions of unitary order. If the system genuinely permits pluralism, does it not, in effect, lack unitary vision? Does it not set humans at cross-purposes? Does it not permit some to engage in what to others seems to be evil behavior? Is not its moral *laissez-faire,* howsoever dignified by the name of tolerance, an impermissible concession to errant consciences? For a time, critics think, hidden values may sustain such a society. But as the logic of individual conscience works its way, the moral texture of such a society would appear to become incoherent. Solzhenitsyn comments:

> Two hundred or even fifty years ago, it would have seemed quite impossible, in America, that an individual could be granted boundless freedom with no purpose, simply for the satisfaction of his whims. Subsequently, however, all such limitations were eroded everywhere in the West; a total emancipation occurred from the moral heritage of Christian centuries with their great reserves of mercy and sacrifice.[5]

Even social scientists, whose standpoint is supposed to be free of perspectival taint, often judge democratic capitalism from a nostalgic sense of order. Many regard the emptiness at the heart of pluralism as a flaw. Its consequences among individuals are looked upon as illnesses: anomie, alienation, loneliness, despair, loss of meaning, etc.

But all this is to attempt to judge pluralism by a standard appropriate to a traditional sense of order. The "new order of the ages" was intended to be quite different. The founders of the new order feared absolutism more than they feared pluralism. They were willing to launch a new experiment, even though its ultimate shape might be hidden from them.

Moreover, the experience which some describe as alienation, anomie, purposelessness, and the like may be regarded from a quite different point of view. It may be regarded as the necessary other side to any genuine experience of liberty. For if in relationship to the values and symbols of my family, my church, and my culture I am free to ask such radical questions as "alienate" me from them, it does not follow that I am ill, misused, or deranged. The human capacity to raise questions is testimony to our capacities for the more than finite. "Our hearts are restless, Lord," St. Augustine prayed, "until they rest in Thee." Those who find all finite things tasteless and barren have not placed themselves outside the Western tradition. To see through those solidities of daily life which once seemed rocklike, and to see them suddenly as shadows dancing on the walls, like Plato, is an ancient experience. The human spirit is not imprisoned by the realities of its culture. Occasionally, it slips outside to see as if from outside in.

In any free society, within which citizens are taught to question all things, such experiences may be expected to multiply. One must expect frequent testimony to "the view from underground," reports on the absurd, nausea, restlessness, alienation. Indeed, such experiences become so frequent in a truly free society that their expression may come to seem sophomoric. Bright youngsters learn to feign them. Some who do not feel an "identity crisis" may come to think that something must be wrong with them. Of course free persons will feel alienation! The opposite would be to feel so connected as not to be free. To appropriate one's own liberty is to learn—sometimes against one's will, forcibly—to be detached from all things.[6]

Some writers speak of the patterns of plausibility which all cultures erect—a sense for what shall be taken to be real, true, good, beautiful—as a "sacred canopy."[7] Cultures differ in such patterns. To go from one to another is commonly, therefore, to experience a kind of "culture shock." All one's expectations are out of focus; one's grip on reality seems weak. To live in an energetic, dynamic, free society is to experience culture shock frequently. Perhaps within certain cognitive enclaves one may live under a "sacred canopy," in which all share in the same meanings, make similar moral and aesthetic judgments, laugh at the same jokes. In such enclaves, one may relax among friends. Outside this temporary shelter, however, there are within pluralism, by design, many such sacred canopies, and some things one group takes to be sacred are mocked in another. Life in a pluralistic society, accordingly, teaches one to avoid social land mines. As often as we go out among our fellows, we are made to feel our limits.

In a genuinely pluralistic society, there is no one sacred canopy. *By intention* there is not. At its spiritual core, there is an empty shrine. That shrine is left empty in the knowledge that no one word, image, or symbol is worthy of what all seek there. Its emptiness, therefore, represents the transcendence which is approached by free consciences from a virtually infinite number of directions. (Aquinas once wrote that humans are made in the image of God but that since God is infinite He may be mirrored only through a virtually infinite number of humans. No concept of Him is adequate.) Believer and unbeliever, selfless and selfish, frightened and bold, naive and jaded, all participate in an order whose *center* is not socially imposed.

But is the center of pluralism in the United States really so empty? Human beings, according to the Declaration of Independence, are endowed with inalienable rights by the Creator. Abraham Lincoln and other presidents have freely reverenced the Almighty. On coins and notes of deposit one reads: "In God we trust." Is not God at the center? For those who so experience reality, yes. For atheists, no. Official religious expressions are not intended to embarrass or to compromise those who do not believe in God. They have a pluralistic content. No institution, group, or person in the United States is entitled to define for others the content signified by words like "God," "the Almighty," and "Creator." These words are like pointers, which each person must define for himself. Their function is to protect the liberty of conscience of all, by using a symbol which transcends the power of the state and any other earthly power. Such symbols are not quite blank; one may not fill them in with any content at all. They point beyond worldly power. Doing so, they guard the human openness to transcendence.

There are other symbols of pluralism whose content is not empty. Free speech, a free press, and free intellectual inquiry, for example, permit enormous diversity to flourish. But each of these values imposes its own disciplines on all. Each demands of every participant much restraint, tolerance, and willingness to be patient with arduous democratic procedures. Individuals are instructed thereby that the common good transcends their own vision of the good, however passionately held.

It is in the light of such transcendence that progress is inspired and reforms are called for. At no moment in history is it appropriate to say "We have enough justice now" or "Liberty has been secured once for all." The moral progress to which democratic capitalism calls is not utopian; but it is never at an end in history. The fact that the center is kept empty does not mean that it lacks vitality, but rather that its vitality exceeds the limits of any one instrument by which its nature might be adequately defined. The values and habits required to maintain this transcendent center, however, entail a spirit of cooperation, mutuality, and common striving. A "sacred canopy" of this sort—practical rather than creedal—allows for unity in practice, diversity in belief.

By contrast, traditional and socialist societies offer unitary vision. They suffuse every activity with symbolic solidarity. The human breast hungers for such nourishment. Atavistic memories haunt each free person. The "wasteland" at the heart of democratic capitalism is like a field of battle, on which individuals wander alone, in some confusion, amid many casualties. Nonetheless, like the dark night of the soul in the inner journey of the mystics, this desert has an indispensable purpose. It is maintained out of respect for the diversity of human consciences, perceptions, and intentions. It is swept clean out of reverence for the sphere of the transcendent, to which the individual has access through the self, beyond the mediations of social institutions. The domain of the transcendent, of course, is mediated by literature, religion, family, and fellows. But it is finally centered in the silence in each person.

Democratic capitalism not only permits individuals to experience alienation, anomie, loneliness, and nothingness. Democratic capitalism is also constantly renewed by such radical experiences of human liberty. While it is true that humans are social animals, and that there are many vital mediating institutions in which humans live, move, and have their being, still, humans are not, in the end, fully plumbed by the institutions in which they dwell. Each experiences a solitariness and personal responsibility which renders him (or her) oddly alone in the midst of solidarity. Conscience is the taproot of democratic capitalism. It is because individuals are capable of the experience of nothingness—that is, able to raise questions about all schemes of community, order, purpose, and meaning, and able to choose in darkness—that individuals have inalienable rights. Democratic capitalism respects this transcendence by limiting its own reach.

A pluralist conception of order is radically different from the unitary order of traditionalist (and socialist) societies. Pluralism *by design* violates older conceptions.

2
Not by Free Enterprise Alone

What the founders of democratic capitalism most feared is the gathering of all power into one.* No human being, they believed,

*The degree to which the founders were also theorists is often underestimated. Their books exhibit intense theoretical passions. Yet they were

is wise or good enough to be trusted with undivided, unitary power. For this reason, they separated moral-cultural institutions like the press, the universities, the church, and voluntary associations of free speech from the state. But they also separated economic institutions from the state.

In earlier eras, clergymen and aristocrats alike had much to say about economic life. Bureaucrats of church and state controlled economic activities, bestowed licenses, imposed taxes and tariffs. Similarly, clergymen meddled in politics and political leaders in religion. Both censored intellect and the arts. It is a distinctive invention of democratic capitalism to have conceived a way of differentiating three major spheres of life, and to have assigned to each relatively autonomous networks of institutions.

This differentiation of systems sets individuals possessed of the will-to-power on three separate tracks. Political activists may compete for eminence in the political system, economic activists in the economic system, religious activists and intellectuals in various parts of the moral-cultural system. But the powers of each of the three systems over the others, while in each case substantial, are firmly limited. It is not likely that one person or party can gain complete dominance over all three systems, and should such misfortune come to pass, there remain plural roads by which offended forces may attack each pretender at his weakest points.

Oddly, many scholars have missed the fact that capitalism—the economic system—is embedded in a pluralistic structure in which it is designed to be checked by a political system and a moral-cultural system. Max Weber, for example, failed to note the political ethos of which so much is made in *The Federalist* and in Adam Smith's *The Wealth of Nations*. Democratic capitalism is not a "free enterprise system" alone. It cannot thrive apart from the moral culture that nourishes the virtues and values on which its existence depends. It cannot thrive apart from a democratic polity committed, on the one hand, to limited government and, on the other hand, to many legitimate activities without which a prosperous economy is impossible. The inarticulate practical wisdom embedded in the political system and in the moral-cultural system has profoundly affected the workings of the economic

---

preeminently practical thinkers, determined to bow to experimental evidence. The system they designed was also intended to be experimental. It seems proper to think of them as "founders" rather than as "theorists."

system. Both political decisions and the moral climate encouraged this development. At various times in American history, both the political system and the moral-cultural system have seriously intervened, positively and negatively, in the economic system. Each of the three systems has modified the others.

The fact that humanists and political scientists have scarcely studied the history and workings of the economic system, as Irving Kristol has remarked, has probably created a larger gap in our culture than the celebrated gap between "the two cultures" of literature and science of which C. P. Snow spoke.[8] Ignorance of economics has probably caused, as well, more harm to more people in more places than any other ignorance. A further result is that most writing about the business system is done by economists, who are not so professionally concerned about the political system and the moral-cultural system as about the economic system in abstraction. The abstract knowledge they have thus produced compounds the general ignorance through distortion.

Thus, for example, an authoritarian nation like Brazil, which claims to favor "free enterprise," is improperly linked to the democratic capitalist tradition. On inspection, one notes that the social structure of Brazil is heir to an aristocratic mode in which a relatively few families, by governmental license in the past or in the present, own most of the land and most of the instruments of production. Moreover, the bureaucratic state under military leadership functions like the state of the Sun King, Louis XIV, and its economic fiats are like those of eighteenth-century mercantilism. Brazil and other nations have systems like those against which democratic capitalism first rebelled. They are more like the *ancien regime* than like "the new order of the ages."

Should such nations, over time, manage to diffuse property rights—the ownership of homesteads and homes, the public ownership of industry through stock ownership—and extend literacy, mobility, and opportunity, they may evolve into something they now are not. They are not now examples of democratic capitalism.

Democratic capitalism is not a free enterprise system merely. Its political system has many legitimate roles to play in economic life, from protecting the soundness of the currency to regulating international trade and internal competition. Its moral-cultural system also has many legitimate and indispensable roles to play in economic life, from encouraging self-restraint, hard work, discipline, and sacrifice for the future to insisting upon generosity, compassion, integrity, and concern for the common good. The economic activist is simultaneously a citizen of the polity and a seeker after truth, beauty, virtue, and meaning. The differentiation of systems is intended to protect all against unitary power. It is not intended to protect anyone from a fully integrated personal life. The burden of living in a free society, however, is proportionately heavy upon each one of us. It is especially heavy in politics, the arena in which competing claims are negotiated. Our aim in the next section is to place the discussion of "interest group" politics on a new intellectual base.

3
Pluralism in Politics

One of the forms of tyranny of which the authors of *The Federalist* were most afraid was the tyranny of a majority.[9] They sought, therefore, to construct a system which would empower many factions and interests. Building a coalition of such interests into a majority, they thought, would require political acumen and a spirit of compromise. Concrete issues would have to be addressed one by one. Coalitions would shift, as factions and interests lined up in kaleidoscopic variations, each group making judgments according to its own firm sense of reality. In order for political accord to be achieved, a majority of widely dispersed constituencies would have to concur that the agreed-upon policy was good for them. Any policy which won the realistic concurrence of a majority of such widely dispersed groups, the founders believed, would most often not be too far wide of reality and the common good. And even if majorities erred, experience would furnish new arguments to dissenters until the error could be corrected—as later happened, for example, in the case of Prohibition.

No *one* group may be trusted to see the common good whole and entire, as if by immediate inspection. But the assemblage of many partial realistic judgments must, at least, strike not too far wide of the mark. For the founders took aim, not at some abstract good, but at fairly tangible realities which significant factions and interests judged to be good, each by its own partial lights. In a famous painting, Raphael depicts Plato pointing upward, Aristotle at the earth. The authors of *The Federalist* sought less the Platonic Good than earthly Aristotelian goods judged to be such by practical wisdom.

The Aristotelian tradition is useful here in getting at an important point.[10] Some people wish to argue that democracy depends upon virtue. They think its vitality rests with the idealists, who in every issue follow the direct path of visionary conscience. Others think its vitality rests with the pragmatists, who on every issue seek the incremental gain which is presently realizable. Unfortunately, this discussion is usually foreshortened because of a deficiency in our current philosophical language. Shortly after the rise of democratic capitalism, British and American political philosophy was largely preempted by the utilitarians. Much that is good, practical, and even idealistic may be—and often has been—argued for in the language of that tradition. Yet several problems arise within that language. For example, the famous principle of "the greatest good of the greatest number" may be very damaging to minorities. Utilitarianism does not well express some important ideas of fairness and other forms of idealism. In my own experience, it has been more useful to articulate the American experience in a language which goes beyond utilitarianism. I learned this language through reflection on the American experience and my own Thomist tradition. It does three things better. It better states the dangers inherent in idealism, the uniqueness of the person, and the special advantages of the practical (as distinct from the theoretical) order.

Let me begin with a recent accusation. Certain writers attack democratic capitalism as though its intellectual base were utilitarian. They sneer at its "interest-group liberalism." Professor Theodore Lowi writes: "Interest-group liberalism seeks pluralistic government, in which there is no formal specification of means and ends. In pluralistic government there is therefore no substance. Neither is there procedure. There is only process."[11] Such complaints are frequent among political idealists. Interest-group politics, they say, is always narrow, selfish, and expedient. They are rather more certain that they know what is good.

Such persons are seldom content with a "formal specification of means and ends" which is not *their* specification. They assume that there is a Good in the light of which means and ends may be specified, and that at least the enlightened may discern it. This assumption leads sooner or later to a unitary political power, able to enforce its vision of the Good on all. The pluralism of democratic capitalism has a quite different understanding of political goods. In order to uncover it, one must distinguish it from the conceptions of utilitarians.

The tradition of Jeremy Bentham, John Stuart Mill, and others associated with British utilitarianism has many noble features. It is of all intellectual traditions one of the least morally pretentious, aiming as it does at genial tolerance. As though in reaction against stuffy clergymen and aristocrats convinced of their own superior honor, taste, and insight, the utilitarians understated their own righteousness. They tried to choose general, plain, and homely words to stand in the center of their system, words like "utility," "pleasure," and "desire," which might, from person to person, case to case, be affixed to an exceedingly broad set of objects. While susceptible of refined and noble use, each of these words is on the face of it and in plain intention a word of rather low and undercharged moral status. By choosing such words, utilitarians may have purposely been mocking the "beautiful thoughts" of the religious idealists, the "righteous wrath" of the avid sectarians, and the "proud thoughts" of aristocrats of the old order. They perhaps intended their way of thinking to seem uninspiring. A favorite word of theirs, "calculus," is icy with arithmetic. Moreover, when wed to "the dismal science" of economics, utilitarianism may seem positively deflating.

"Utility," for example, may suggest using persons as means. "Pleasure" may suggest hedonism, even if at times of a refined sort; it is clearly rather far from the stern stuff of heroism, duty, and self-sacrifice. "Desire" may suggest the subservience of critical judgment to less than noble impulses. Altogether, such terms are of the sort sometimes aimed at the lowest common denominator.

Moreover, the utilitarians employed an image of society as though it first consisted of atomlike individuals—individuals first, then society. This highly individualized and fragmented image was badly distorted by being drawn into the images later evoked by Darwin and Spencer: the rugged individual competing against nature, society, and the elements in a fierce self-centered struggle to survive.

If one matches these utilitarian images of society to actual experience, however, they don't quite fit. Thus, in recent years, John Rawls has tried to disengage liberal feelings about life from raw utilitarianism and to wed them to a sterner morality based upon Kant.[12] My own purposes are quite different. Rawls is correct that the utilitarian images do not quite satisfy our longings. But he, too, begins with the primal image of an "original position" in which individuals come first, social arrangements second.

In actual fact, each of us first begins to experience and to reflect *within* lived social worlds. We are born into families. The moral and aesthetic traditions in which our sensibilities and our minds are nourished are first given us by traditions, institutions, a people, which we did not choose for ourselves. Only later do we come to discern, reflect upon, criticize—and either appropriate or reject—our social inheritance. In this, the conservative critics of the utilitarians, like Edmund Burke and Alexis de Tocqueville, were surely correct. Human beings experience themselves first as social animals, shaped by traditions and nourished by symbols, languages, and ideas acquired socially. Our individuality emerges only later. For much of our lives we are more shaped than shaping. We owe more to our ancestors than at first we recognize. (A conservative, a British saying has it, is one who thinks his grandfather was at least as smart and good as he.)

The utilitarian image which long nourished liberalism often trades upon the symbols of enlightenment and liberation. We are taught that we were born and nurtured in a kind of darkness, from which we ought to become enlightened. We are taught that we should be liberated successively from each social cocoon in which we have been nourished. Such radical individualism has always seemed artificial. In the sharply more communal cultures of Germany, Eastern Europe, and the Latin lands, both conservative and socialist forces strongly opposed it. In freeing individuals from too much dependency, individualism plays an important role. Taken too far, it is plainly wrong about human life.

On the good side, liberal utilitarianism pays tribute to the role of realism in history. It holds that beneath the seemingly anarchic face of a society composed of multiple individuals there is a transcendental order of reality beckoning to each person's reason and sentiment. When enough individuals pay heed, it suggests, there will be moral progress.

The problem for such individuals is how to distinguish subjective desire from what real circumstances objectively demand. Unwilling to turn for guidance to tradition, church, or family, liberalism trusts only the individual conscience. A progressive social order, therefore, depends upon the individual's willingness to reason objectively. The course of progress, the substance of the liberal order, is hidden in concrete situations. It is to be discovered by individual conscience. There is something heroic, even romantic, in this conception.

Yet this way of looking at the world goes beyond utility, desire, and pleasure—all the way to conscience.[13] Its hidden assumption is that history conveys moral imperatives which conscience follows. The most rosy liberal view is that the world is ultimately harmonious, so that all persons of goodwill must end up on the same side of all important issues. The more tragic view is that human beings do not, in fact, agree about substantive goods, but that conflict, while inevitable, can also be creative. Practical solutions can be worked out; muddling through will in the end be better than moral pretense. What must *not* be done is to blunt individual conscience.

Interest-group pluralism, in this scheme of things, serves the search for realism by assembling the many different angles from which the reality of things is perceived. When a majority of groups agree upon a policy or program, there must be *some* reality to it; it can scarcely be completely wrong. More than that, a program worked out through the clash of different perspectives is more likely to strike closer to the good, the true, the real than any program simply imagined by one party alone, however noble or disinterested it may think itself. In American life, in particular, there are not wanting many groups who believe their own vision of morality to be not simply superior but correct. They believe they speak for the Good. They believe they speak for a common cause, as opposed to selfish individual private causes. They have faith that their sectarian views, whether religious or purely rationalist, conform to reality. Partisans of interest-group pluralism are skeptical about such claims. For one thing, they have learned through experience that reality seldom conforms to any clear rational vision. For another, groups that claim to be disinterested, unselfish, and nonprivate are usually quite mistaken about their own rationality. Self-deception makes them more like others than they imagine. More crimes may be committed through claims to greater virtue than through commitment to vice.

Those who favor interest-group pluralism simply do not trust claims to special idealism, rationality, and moral insight. They think that concrete realism is better discovered through more humble conflicts. But it is a mistake to imagine that they do so through ignoring substantive goods in the name of procedural goods. It is true that procedures of conflict resolution are dear to them. But this is so precisely because they value substantive goods—and because they value the most trustworthy modes of human access to them—not because they ignore them. How this happens is best articulated in three steps. The articulation of these steps places the theory of interest-group pluralism on firmer philosophical grounds than those provided by utilitarianism.

The first step is to purge liberalism of a too-simple view of the way rationality and morality work in history. In unexamined corners of their minds, many liberals hold the conviction that all the positive values in which men have believed must, in the end, be compatible, and must perhaps even entail one another. This belief, more than any other, Isaiah Berlin writes in *Four Essays on Liberty,* "is responsible for the slaughter of individuals on the altars of great historical ideals."[14] It springs from too much faith in direct access to truth and morality. Persons who believe that the truth is so easily discovered often react with moral revulsion against conservatives or reactionaries who disagree with them. Since truth is so intellectually clear, those who do not see it must be persons of bad will. Daily experience teaches that this is not so.

It simply is not true that all right-thinking persons, in all conscience and with all goodwill, hold the same vision of the good and judge moral acts similarly. Pluralism in moral vision is real. To recognize this is not to surrender to moral relativism. It does not follow from the fact that persons (and groups) stand in radical moral disagreement that "anything goes," "to each his own," etc. It may well be that when persons or groups stand in radical moral disagreement, only one is correct. The problem for a free society is to discern which.

The second step consists in grasping certain peculiar characteristics of the human spirit, which may best be brought out in the distinction between an *individual* and a *person.* The tree in my yard and the kitten much loved by my children are individuals, one distinctive maple among millions, one kitten unlike any other. Human beings are also individuals in this way. Beyond that, however, they are also originating agencies of insight and choice. They are persons. The concept of person has a fascinating intellectual history which helps to make the point clear.[15] Personhood entails the right—the *vocation*—to be different. Individuality alone entails no such right, not for trees or cats, and not for humans insofar as they are merely expressions of a common social order. As expressions of a common social order, individuals may readily be organized in collectives, socialist or traditional, in which persons would feel restless and confined. Individuals do not require "bourgeois rights" or need "bourgeois liberties" as birds need air. Persons do. A democratic capitalist society mirrors the infinity of God through the conflicting, discordant, irreconcilable differences of huge numbers of persons, each of whom is an originating agency of distinctive insight and distinctive choice. Thus John Wesley said:

We ought, without this endless jangling about opinions, to provoke one another to love and to good works. Let the points wherein we differ stand aside: here are enough wherein we agree, enough to be the ground of every Christian temper and of every Christian action. . . . Then if we cannot as yet think alike in all things, at least we may love alike.[16]

Once one understands the limitations and the variation ineradicable from human life, and once one grasps the fact that it is the vocation of personhood to be singular in insight and in choice, it does not follow that the world of practice must collapse in anarchy. Recognizing both their limitations and their need of each other, human beings may well decide to respect the personal search of each for his or her singular vocation while also inventing structures, institutions, and activities in which they can cooperate. Perhaps they may never reach agreement in theory about the nature of the substantive goods each seeks. Nonetheless, they may take up the practical challenge of inventing institutions which respect personal liberties while providing large areas of mutual collaboration. As persons, each may jealously guard a terrain of singular choice and vision. As individuals, each may share common burdens of survival, prosperity, community, suffering, and death. Well might they agree to take up such burdens fraternally.

The invention of democratic capitalism was aimed at the discovery of *practical principles* that would make such common life possible, while holding sacred the singular sphere of each human person. Democratic capitalism is not a system aimed at defining the whole of life. Its aim is to establish the practical substructure of cooperative social life. Traditional societies aimed to provide considerably more than this. They provided a (usually) religious vision. Socialist societies, too, attempt to suffuse political and economic structures with moral values like justice and equality. Solidarity—not only in practical cooperation but in moral values and meaning—is the common aim of all social systems except democratic capitalism.

Alone among the systems known to humankind, democratic capitalism has tried to preserve the sphere of the person inviolable. It glories in divergence, dissent, and singularity. It has done so by inventing a set of practical principles, embodied in institutions, and jealously guarded by rival interests each of considerable power, by which social cooperation may be achieved, without prior agreement on metaphysical, philosophical, or religious presuppositions. In order to agree to observe such practical principles, persons do not have to hold the same reasons for supporting them, nor do they need to have the same ends in view. Furthermore, when such practical principles prove their worth by their fruits, these practical principles themselves become worthy of honor. They themselves become substantive goods of a sort. They are not *mere* procedures. They become a proven body of practical principles, respect for which makes the pursuit of substantive goods possible. They are loved in and through the respect of persons for substantive goods. They are loved because they preserve the integrity of substantive goods and the pursuit by free persons of such goods. It is as proper to love the means which make ends attainable as to love the labor of writing for the work achieved.

The philosopher Jacques Maritain described adherence to such principles of practice as a *secular* faith, a *civic* faith, rooted in the practical nature of human beings.[17] It is not a religious faith or a world view. It springs, in different languages and in different intellectual horizons, from the nature of practical life. Its secrets have not been universally discovered. In some cultures, practical cooperation is discouraged between persons of differing faiths.

Prior agreement in faith and vision is considered necessary, no matter the practical costs. In the name of a single vision of humanity, inhumanities are often justified. So this civic faith, this practical faith, while accessible to all human beings, is not universally embraced and never perfectly fulfilled. Maritain describes it so:

> Thus it is that, men possessing quite different, even opposite metaphysical or religious outlooks, can converge, not by virtue of any identity of doctrine, but by virtue of an analogical similitude in practical principles, toward the same practical conclusions, and can share in the same practical secular faith, provided that they similarly revere, perhaps for quite diverse reasons, truth and intelligence, human dignity, freedom, brotherly love, and the absolute value of moral good.
>
> We must therefore maintain a sharp and clear distinction between the human and temporal creed which lies at the root of common life and which is but a set of practical conclusions or of practical points of convergence—on the one hand; and on the other, the theoretical justifications, the conceptions of the world and of life, the philosophical or religious creeds which found, or claim to found, these practical conclusions in reason.[18]

Consider "practical faith" in the United States. Although other societies may be equally or more pluralistic in composition, few have been settled so thoroughly by persons of so many diverse cultures, from every region of the entire planet. To enter such a society, one need not surrender one's native culture, religion, conception of life, scheme of values, way of philosophizing, or personal vision. No statement of unitary belonging is required, no denunciation of world views previously held. One must pledge only to respect the practical principles set forth in the Constitution. The Constitution itself exemplifies a practical, rather than a creedal, vision of the good society.

A sound theory of pluralism, therefore, is based on rather more than "interest-group jockeying." But it is also based on rather less than a "specification of ends and means," a unitary vision of the meaning of social life. It is something less than "substantive" in the way socialists would desire, commanding the socialist virtues and repressing "anti-socialist" and "nonprogressive" behavior. Yet it is considerably more substantive than the inherited rubrics of interest-group liberalism have allowed. It seems to be exactly tailored to the difference between the human being's highest aspirations for human unity and his limits of insight and purity of heart. Too low a system for angels, it seems not to be too high for humans as they are. It stretches them a little.

So much for pluralism in economics and politics. Now to religion.

4
The Attempt to Christianize the System

A rather harsh thesis is forced on those who would like to "Christianize" a pluralist society, "bring Christ to the marketplace," and "suffuse the system with Christian values." Such expressions derive from a traditional conception of social order. They project a unity of moral vision which, under pluralism, is inappropriate. In a *command* society—socialist or any other—one can imagine the "suffusion" of Christian values. Those who wish the social order to be based upon commanded "substantive" morality cannot be in favor of pluralism.

A democratic capitalist society is, in principle, uncommitted to any one vision of a social order. For such a commitment is a violation of transcendence. Any society which commanded it would trespass upon the precincts of conscience and personhood. If such a society were to be formally committed in its central institutions to a Christian vision of justice and love, it might still retain some elements of democracy and some elements of markets and incentives. For there is an inner consonance between the inherent (although, alas, not always observed) respect for free acts of faith and conscience common to Judaism and Christianity and the rights protected by democracy.[19] Indeed, without certain conceptions of history, nature, person, community, and the limited state, the very notion of "human rights" makes little sense. Respect for the transcendence of God and for full freedom of conscience—respect for the common human wandering in darkness—is better served, however, even in Christian and Jewish terms, by the reverential emptiness at the heart of pluralism than by a socially imposed vision of the good.

For grave dangers to the human spirit lurk in the subordination of the political system and the economic system to a single moral-cultural vision. Daily life is (as Christians believe) a contest with the world, the flesh, and the devil. An attempt to impose the Kingdom of God upon this contest is dangerous not only to human liberty but to Christianity itself (and to any other religion similarly tempted). For darkness and recalcitrance always demand their due and corrupt those who would replace them.

In the world as it is, humans as they are are often and unavoidably enmeshed in lies, betrayals, injustices, and sinful energies of every sort. Prematurely, before the endtime, to attempt to treat any society of this world as "a Christian society" is to confound precious hope with a sad reality. Human beings, even the most devout and serious Christians, cannot be expected to act always and in all ways as Christians ought to act, under the sway and impulse of God's grace. A political system based upon such expectations must necessarily end in disaster. An economic system based upon such expectations must necessarily confound illusions with realities. In the world as it is, as Reinhold Niebuhr warned throughout his exemplary intellectual life, "the children of light" are in many respects a greater danger to biblical faith than "the children of darkness."[20]

The moral-cultural system is embodied in *institutions*. Its reality is not confined to the inner psyche or the privacy of conscience. There are churches, synagogues, universities, newspapers, publishers, television networks, associations of philosophers and poets, etc. These institutions are plural and in mutual conflict. Their influence over the symbols and values which promote and inhibit action is immense. Political leaders often cannot do what they would do because such institutions will not permit them. Business leaders necessarily become involved in issues not at all justified by merely economic imperatives. In other words, the institutions which shape the system's ethos are powerful. Lacking such an ethos, in certain cultures neither democracy nor capitalism makes sense. Where moral and cultural visions of certain sorts prevail, a democratic polity and a capitalist economy are not feasible. The important distinction is this: Christianity has helped to shape the *ethos* of democratic capitalism, but this ethos forbids Christians (or any others) from attempting to *command* the system.

It is particularly difficult for religious bodies to adjust to a role which removes them from command and places them outside the center. Their natural inclination is to suffuse every part of life with their own holistic vision of human nature and destiny. Since human beings are social animals, creatures of flesh and blood, religious bodies properly resist being shunted aside into the private spaces of the individual heart. They desire a public social role. Under democratic capitalism, they have such a role. But it is neither in command nor at the center.

Religious leaders *believe* that their vision is a vision of reality itself. Some Christian leaders can hardly help wishing to make theirs a Christian civilization; some Jewish religious leaders to make Israel a religiously Jewish state; some Islamic leaders to make their civilizations Islamic. Moreover, they are sorely tempted to do so directly, at the center, from the top, thoroughly. To think that they must attempt their important work only indirectly, by inspiring millions of individuals and through the competition of ideas and symbols in a pluralistic marketplace, must inevitably seem to some too demanding. Yet all this democratic capitalism asks of them. Like them, business leaders coping with political regulations and political leaders coping with pluralistic pressures feel equivalent frustrations. The system is designed to frustrate the totalistic impulse.

Still, a plural society has its own kind of order. It is marvelous to live in a society in which simple instruments work, and persons seem to have an interest in keeping their part of the system working. It is marvelous to find cooperation in nearly all details of daily life (and to scream when it is absent). Yet the order of democratic capitalism is not the order of a unitary society. It is not a commanded, overseen order. It springs from a multiplicity of motives, incentives, presuppositions, and purposes. Such an order calls forth not only a new theology but a new type of religion. The institutional force of religion is dramatically altered under it: strengthened in some respects, weakened in others. Ways of life, beliefs, and styles compete. Each shares an equal lack of social enforcement.

Yet if Jewish and Christian conceptions of human life are sound, and if they fit the new social order of pluralism, the widespread nostalgia for a traditional form of social order may be resisted. This is so even if such nostalgia takes the form of projection into the future rather than into long-gone Eden. For the full exercise of their humanity, being both finite and sinful, free persons require pluralist institutions. Such structures will not produce utopia. They will not eliminate sinfulness from human life. The expectation of sinfulness in every social order makes pluralism necessary. The renunciation of utopia makes it sufficient.

Christian symbols ought not to be placed in the center of a pluralist society. They must not be, out of reverence for the transcendent which others approach in other ways. Yet as the following chapters will demonstrate, the underlying philosophy of pluralism is consonant with Jewish and Christian understandings of human life. These include a vision of history, sin, and community.

III

Emergent Probability

It would be against the perfection of the universe if no
corruptible thing existed, and no power could fail . . . it
would be contrary to the meaning of Providence, and to the
perfection of things, if there were no chance events.
—St. Thomas Aquinas, *Summa Contra Gentiles*[1]

A plural social order is designed to fit within a world process
open to liberty, evil, and surprise. Is that the way the world
works?

Even while we pursue this inquiry, practical persons elsewhere
are hard at work on startling inventions the rest of us will not learn
of until tomorrow, their sense of adventure stimulated by the
"energy crisis." Someone somewhere is struggling to invent better batteries for electric cars. Someone is pushing toward a breakthrough in hydrogen-powered engines (more energy in a gallon of
seawater than in a gallon of crude oil). Someone is trying to
unlock energy from some material no one else has thought of.
Thousands of bright young men and women are now competing—
to serve humankind; to acquire fame like Edison's; to launch
whole new industries, even a new era of world history; and,
perhaps, to make a personal fortune, too. Inventors are competing
to end the oil age, primitive and polluting as now in its passing it
appears to have been. The "limits" of the earth are not yet
known. Limits are a frame of reference bounded by one time. In
the light of another time, today's limit marks a frontier.

Pessimism runs in cycles. At the birth of democratic capitalism, the gloom of Thomas Malthus clouded knowing souls. Lean years and scarcity were in the offing.

Pessimism in itself is healthy; the fault lies in giving moral weight to temporality. Neither the past nor the present nor the future conveys moral obligation. This point is not as obvious as it seems. Those who discern an "age of limits" see duty in the present frame of reference; claim to *know* the limits, and to impose them as a moral obligation. There are others, in the days of kings, who received obligation from the past as past. Maintaining the harmonies as they had been handed down seemed to them of gravest moral weight. Still others imagine that the future has higher moral status than the present, that God is the God of the future, that the future will usher in a morally better age, which places today under moral command. The main tide of history, they say, is "the liberation of the oppressed." All humans of good-will, all true Christians, should stand "on the side of history," should not resist the "tides of change."

Most interesting arguments about the world have hidden in them a theory of time, a kind of metaphysic, a vision of what being, reality, and history are like. I do not want in these pages to become ensnared too deeply in metaphysics, for the necessary point is a humble one. Every human action is part of a narrative. Socialists, for example, argue from a sense of the way history is flowing and feel called upon to serve history's purposes. Some may be atheists, but they certainly have faith. But so does everyone who believes in "change." Democratic capitalism has also been a revolutionary force in history. It stimulates invention, enterprise, feverish activity; it delights irreverently in change; its two favorite words are "new" and "improved." What, then, is its implicit view of history?

The scholar who, to my mind, has set forth the underlying scheme most clearly, although he was concerned with a far larger canvas than democratic capitalism, is Bernard Lonergan in *Insight: A Study of Human Understanding*.[2] His conception of "emergent probability" has extraordinary power, though of a very general sort, and I mean to adapt it here to the purposes of this inquiry. Lonergan states quite clearly the sort of assumptions most of us in democratic capitalist societies take for granted, assumptions that have not seemed obvious in our earlier history or in other cultures. Like all such attempts to comprehend the world process in which we find ourselves, they may be quite wrong. They are distinctive assumptions nonetheless.

In the background of their minds, some persons carry images of biblical faith, of Creation, Providence, and sin, of history conceived not only as a kind of pilgrimage but as a kind of "economy" ordered to God's meaning. History is not regarded simply as absurd. Nor is it dumb. Darkly, it tells a story. To understand it is not easy. But inquiry and action are worth their costs. There are meanings to be discerned, breakthroughs to be achieved, possibilities to be grasped and realized, riches to be wrested from silent nature. Nature is not regarded as achieved, complete, finished. Creation is unfinished. There are things human beings have yet to do. Surprises lie in store. If there are horrors yet to face (there always have been), God is with us. The future may not have an upward slant, except as Golgotha had: So be it.

To enter Lonergan's frame of reference, however, it is important for the moment to forget this religious backdrop of our culture and to think, rather, of its scientific, practical side. There are on this planet entire continents in which inventions known elsewhere—the wheel, for example—never were invented but were imported. Scientific discoveries and practical inventions have their own logic. One cannot split atoms until one has discovered their existence, learned much about them, and developed instruments for isolating and experimenting with them. Absent earlier developments, later ones are most improbable or strictly inconceivable. But process occurs in the real world as well as in the world of discovery and invention. There would not now be coal and oil if in the earlier history of the planet decaying plants had not undergone millennia of stress and transformation underground. Thus, the world of our experience—the world of nature and the world of human inquiry both—undergoes development. One cannot speak of it as "world stable" or "world complete." One says, fairly enough, "world process." But what sort of "process" is it?

For Lonergan, it is important to draw attention to the occurrence of insight among human beings. This occurrence is so common in our lives that we seldom notice how interesting it is. The bright experience insight often, in virtually every transaction of the day. The dull experience it less frequently, learning much by rote and imitation. The advance of science is constituted by the occurrence of insights but also by the further act of a more complex form of insight, the *verification* of insights—sorting out which of the bright ideas may be confirmed in fact. It is useful to "brainstorm," but not all ideas pan out. Reality imposes tests. To fashion insights to the contours of such tests requires time, development, and—often enough—entire breakthroughs in underlying paradigms and expectations. The attempt to understand everything that may be understood about the world follows a history and logic of its own. And the world, too, is changing. So, in a sense, history has two tracks: changes in the world to be understood, and changes in our understanding. The world changes, and we change. The two tracks, moreover, interact. Human beings change the world, and the world seems ever to insist upon changes in human understanding.

These remarks are utterly general, yet consider their bearing upon such slogans as the following. "Progress is our most important product." "Building a better world through chemistry." "Ford has a better idea." Consider, too, the role of ideas, arguments, and experiment on the part of that small body of humans who first conceived of the institutions of democratic societies. "We are testing," Abraham Lincoln said at Gettysburg, "whether this nation, or any nation so conceived and so dedicated, can long endure." Or consider the long generations of ideological inquiry, dispute, manifesto, and utopian conceptions that preceded the establishment of the first socialist state in 1917. The role of insight is not negligible in the human attempt to construct a social order fitted to human nature and to the possibilities of this planet. It is hard to believe that this struggle for insight is at its end.

Employing a language of extreme generality, Bernard Lonergan has made the following observations about world process, including development both in nature and in human history. So as not to be involved in the technicalities of his argument, I report them in the language of common sense. It may help to imagine oneself as the chief executive officer of a major corporation—General Electric, let us say—who with his top management team is trying to decide whether to invest 200 million dollars in new operations in a distant country. What image of the world operates in the recesses of their minds as they must make such a decision?

(1) Such rationality as world process manifests does not proceed by cold logical necessity. All sorts of things may happen.

(2) "Things" that may happen, events, may not proceed by cold logical necessity, but neither are they perfectly random.

Events are of kinds; like kinds recur; and so probabilities may be assigned to them. Even wildly improbable things, which are of so low a probability in a short frame of time as to appear to be merely random, have some probability. Murphy's Law playfully exaggerates this point: "Anything that can go wrong will go wrong."

(3) Thus, events, being neither necessary nor merely random, occur in accord with schemes of probabilities.

(4) Probabilities of the emergence of events are affected by their position (and relative concentration) in space and time. In some places and times, they are highly likely, in others unlikely. Such probabilities are especially affected by the lengths of time assigned them. Given enough time, every probable event will occur.

(5) Probabilities must be assigned not only to the emergence of schemes of recurrence but also to their survival. Schemes of recurrence whose probabilities depend upon the occurrence of earlier events may or may not emerge. If they do emerge, they may or may not survive. Their emergence and their survival depend upon the fate of their preconditions.

(6) World process is open to events and to schemes of recurrence which have never before emerged, subject to the fulfillment of their preconditions.

(7) World process is open to breakdowns and to reversals, as when events or schemes of recurrence which finally succeed in emerging do not succeed in surviving.

(8) Human intelligence is not entirely helpless in coming to understand events, their probabilities, and their preconditions. Nor is it entirely helpless in intervening so as to make their emergence and survival more or less likely.

From past experience, in other words, the CEO of General Electric knows that the world is open to human intelligence and intervention; that the application of intelligence affects the probabilities of success or failure; but that the complexity of events, the schemes of probabilities, and their uncertainties make none of his decisions a sure thing. He and his team know that success depends upon setting many preconditions in place. They know as well that some preconditions of success escape their own full control; they need some "breaks." When they finally reach their decision, they will have tried to think of every "relevant" scheme of recurrence they might later have to deal with. But they cannot be certain, particularly if the operation is in an area new to them, that their own criteria of relevance have been broad enough. From experience, they know that many a promising operation has come to naught for want of planning for a contingency no one ever thought of (but perhaps, being wiser, might have thought of). They may decide that some other operation, in some other place, bears fewer risks. They may decide that the human benefits to be derived from their investment justify the acceptance of higher risks than usual, especially since the work they contemplate will, eventually, have to be done by somebody, and they are confident that they can do it best.

The habit of mind designated by a term like "enterprise" depends for its very existence upon belief in a world of emergent probability—a world not logical, geometric, perfectly predictable, on the one hand, nor on the other hand totally mad, irrational, and impervious to intelligence. The most intelligent of efforts can end in failure. Sheer luck can sometimes bring success. But over the long run, humans face a world of risk to which intelligence is sufficiently matched to wrest significant successes. A single individual, grasping probabilities no one else has ever perceived and setting in place the preconditions to move them to actuality, can change the world and bring forth in it things never seen before. Success is by no means guaranteed. But the battle of wits, exhilarating in itself, often enough breaks in favor of the bold.

One can imagine worlds, unlike our own, in which a metaphysic of emergent probability would be out of tune with reality. A world of blind necessity would rule out successful human intervention aimed at changing history. A perfectly absurd world, in which events systematically diverged from schemes of recurrence (so that no events were like any others or related to any others) would defeat intelligence at every turn. The world of "scientific socialism," whose ultimate secrets Marx, Engels, and Lenin believed they had penetrated, moves upon iron tracks of necessity; no man can stay its course, and those who wish to stand "on the side of history" can only submit with glad or reluctant cooperation.

Yet the sharpest contrast to a world view based upon a sense of emergent probability lies in the world from which democratic capitalism itself emerged. Democratic capitalism did not emerge by cold logical necessity; neither was its emergence by random accident. A few individuals saw new possibilities in human history, articulated them, made a case for them against heavy opposition, and were sufficiently practical to make their case prevail. They saw the importance of *system*. They saw that the design of the system matters.

Here we may borrow another distinction from Bernard Lonergan.[3] A *good of desire* is a good that fulfills a particular need, as bacon, eggs, and coffee satisfy the morning craving of a hungry camper. But a *good of order* occupies a more intellectual plane, constituting a scheme of recurrence, as when an ordinary man can count upon having breakfast every day without too much thought about it. Goods of order—systems for providing goods on a recurrent basis—are easy to take for granted. They are goods of order precisely because they can be taken for granted. One notices their reality most sharply when they are taken away, as when during the Depression, despite such an abundance of goods that farmers were spilling milk in ditches and slaughtering cattle, many were going hungry. Missing were neither the necessary goods of desire nor the desire to have them, but the system which heretofore had joined the two in familiar routine. The Depression was a breakdown in the system. A good of order was lost.

To a greater extent than is usually brought to consciousness, the systems through which the ordinary goods of daily life are brought to us are themselves goods of order. Systems count. The insight that human beings can gain some control over the economic system on which they depend as a good of order appeared very late in human history. Adam Smith may be regarded as the genius chiefly responsible (although by no means solely) for the expression of this insight. His *An Inquiry into the Nature and Causes of the Wealth of Nations* (1776) is the classic pioneering text on the bold and original idea, new for that time, of sustained economic development produced as a matter of intelligence. Once Smith's ideas began to be carried out, wherever their writ ran famine was eliminated and the idea that material improvement is possible began to grip the imagination of the world.[4]

Smith attempted to provide a good of order, a system, an intellectual understanding of the way the world might be organized so as to raise the wealth of all nations. His emphasis lay not upon the possession of great natural resources, nor upon political status (whether as an independent nation or as a colony), nor upon underpopulation or overpopulation, nor upon ownership of the means of production by the state, nor upon better and more detailed planning, nor upon decentralized democratic decision-making, nor upon religious rules of justice and charity, nor upon the organization of states by the military, nor upon any of the other conceptions of a good of order then current or exemplified in previous history. Arguments about how best to overcome poverty or to cope with scarcity are arguments about alternative goods of order. Which good of order best matches a world of emergent probability? Which is more in tune with reality?

This insight into the role of *system* as a good of order had special bearing in the late eighteenth century. It had acute relevance in Europe, still in the pre-capitalist order of the *ancien regime*. It had profound relevance in the New World, in which two contrasting experiments in order, in South America and North America, were being tried. Smith saw the significance of these two contrasting *ideas* of political economy and predicted, accurately enough, their probable futures. (See Chapters XVI, XVII, and XVIII.)

In inquiring into the causes of the wealth of nations, Smith discovered that societies equally rich in resources might through different *systems* achieve remarkably different outcomes. A system designed as closely as possible to fit human character, Smith argued, is best designed to unleash human creativity. The key to the wealth of nations lies in human creativity more than in any other source. The key to that lies in "the natural system of liberty."

Near the end of the eighteenth century, Smith's idea was not yet widely shared. It seemed to many counterintuitive. The prevailing instinct was that governmental control, planning from the top, would be both more orderly and more efficient. Smith and others recognized the good intentions behind paternalism, but poked effective fun at its historical record of unintended consequences. (More on this in Chapter IV.)

To persuade others of these paradoxical ideas, so that they might try the social order he hoped to put in the place of the existing order, he had to argue his case. His probabilities of success were high, for many of the presuppositions he needed to draw upon were already falling into place. Among them were some of the moral-cultural values Max Weber later attempted to codify under the name "the Protestant ethic."[5] Whether in the strict sense Protestant or not, a new ethos stirred the air. With such a breeze in its sails, the new order took to sea.

Adam Smith believed that he had glimpsed an important secret in the way the world works. The best way to try to understand it is not from the top down, but from the bottom up, along the fullest extent of its base in individual citizens. The best way to make the economic system rational is not to impose upon it the rationality glimpsed in the minds of one person or a few, but to empower the individual rationality of every individual. Cumulatively, individual rationality, close to the emergent texture of daily events, in the end adds up to a far more rational form of economic order than a rationality imposed upon the collective from some distance above daily events. Smith adduced sound reasons, based on many cases illustrating the way things actually work, for believing that trust in individual rationality would not lead to anarchy but to a new sort of order.

In some areas, no doubt, the political system will wish to have its say in economic affairs. Smith gave many examples in which he judged such political intervention useful and commendable. There can be no doubt, however, about the main thrust of Smith's argument: that markets as free as possible from governmental and religious command best serve the common good. Such a system frees the intelligence, imagination, and enterprise of individuals to explore the possibilities inherent in world process, which he conceived of—to employ the language of this chapter—as a universe of emergent probabilities.

Adam Smith believed that the new order would benefit all without exception, not only in Britain but in the entire world. It would lead humankind to new heights of moral achievement, but by a paradoxical route. Moralists of the past had stressed vision, goals, purposes, and motives. Smith drew attention, instead, to outcomes. He conceived of the abolition of famine, the raising up of the poor, and the banishment of material suffering from all humankind as an outcome morally to be approved of. Very well, then, if that is the desirable outcome, what is the best system for attaining it? The paradox consisted in attaining a highly moral outcome by placing *less* stress on moral purposes. Toward the desired moral outcome, the exercise of rational self-interest on the part of every citizen is, in the real world of historical examples, a far more successful means than the exercise of other motivations.

This does not mean that other motivations are less important, less admirable, or less socially useful. It means only that they do not as regularly, as thoroughly, or even as morally bring about the desired outcome. In the real world, moral motives do not suffice. The bafflements of emergent probability do not yield their meaning to good intentions.

On the other hand, rational self-interest even in the large sense described by Smith is not sufficient for social life. It is not sufficient even within the economic system. Narrowly construed, self-interest alone counsels caution and self-protection. In order to be creative—to venture into new areas, to experiment, to pioneer—one must be willing to lose what one has, to replace security with insecurity. Again, economic contracts and corporate decision-making always involve some measure of trust between person and person. Thus rational self-interest alone does not exhaust the range of moral attitudes necessary for a dynamic economy. Precisely because rational self-interest does not always result in moral outcomes, religious (and other) values are indispensable to democratic capitalism. Some argue for a public spending limitation, for example, as a restraint upon political self-interests. Self-interest is a creative but not a sufficient vitality in human affairs.

Apart from an implicit vision of world process as emergent probability, neither democracy nor capitalism makes much sense. Through it, the quiet stability of the medieval vision of order was broken through. In an important sense, this was a moral breakthrough. It was even, if you please, a theological breakthrough. It suited Judaism and Christianity, narrative religions, just fine.

Since emergent probability does not mean automatic progress, this world suffers decline as well as progress and often there are trade-offs. Humans err through ignorance, but also at times through apathy, envy, or greed. Sin is, alas, a factor in human history. So also are unintended consequences and self-interest of several kinds, some virtuous, some neutral, and some immoral. The plot thickens.

IV
Sin

Why wouldst thou be a breeder
of sinners? I am myself indiffer-
ent honest; but yet I could accuse
me of such things that it were
better my mother had not borne
me. I am very proud, revenge-
ful, ambitious; with more of-
fences at my beck than I have
thoughts to put them in, imagination to give them shape, or time
to act them in. What should such
fellows as I do crawling between
heaven and earth? We are arrant
knaves all; believe none of us.

—*Hamlet,* act 3, sc. 1

A free political economy wears sin like a scarlet letter. Soft neon
lights beckon, alas, to massage parlors and "adult" (that is, ado-
lescent) magazines. Democratic capitalist societies exhibit the
lives of human beings not perhaps as they should be but as they
are, for they have been conceived in due recognition of the errant
human heart, whose liberty they respect. In this, they follow the
example of the Creator who knows what is in humans—who hates

sin but permits it for the sake of liberty, who suffers from it but remains faithful to his sinful children.

Three points must be made about the special sense of sin which informs democratic capitalism. First, it regards sin as rooted in the free personality, beyond the reach of any system, an ineradicable given from which all realistic thinking about political economy must begin. Secondly, a way to defeat sin—a way to transform its energy into creative use (and thus to take on Satan the best revenge)—is offered by the workings of unintended consequences. A system trying to put ineradicable sin to creative purposes need neither rely on perfect virtue nor aim directly at pure intentions. Thirdly, moral virtue is a significant part of self-interest. Thus, a free society, without aiming so high as perfect virtue, must insist upon a core of common indispensable morality and can under suitable checks and balances wrest a reasonable degree of goodness, decency, and compassion from less than perfect materials. One must be satisfied in systems, Aristotle once wrote, with "a tincture of virtue," even though rather more than that may sometimes be obtained.

1
Freedom and Sin

Political economy must deal with humans as they are. Yet remarkably different hypotheses are entertained about human beings. Who are we? What may we hope? What ought we to do? These, Immanuel Kant suggested, are the perennial questions behind political economy. Every system of political economy represents at least an implicit answer to them. Each system allows only so much scope to individuals. Each favors some instincts in the human breast and penalizes others. Each embodies a conviction about the most dangerous evils, which need to be watched with care or carefully repressed.

Consider for a moment three different forms of political economy. Traditional societies are aimed against disorder. Socialist societies are aimed against inequality. Democratic capitalist societies are aimed against tyranny.

Traditional societies are preoccupied by problems of order and stability. Their enemy is "the war of all against all."[1] They have vivid memories of plunder, murder, rape, riot, and civil war. Cities have been sacked, the countryside terrorized by marauding bands, economies disrupted, daily life rendered desperate. Leaders who have brought order out of chaos, united peoples, and created conditions of stability are highly praised. Their work may seem like God's work, as if they had brought about on earth the harmony and regularity which humans observe at night in the quiet patterns of the stars. God, then, is often imagined to be a God of order, of lawlike rationality, of harmony and peace. Sins against order are regarded as sins against God. Punishments for acts of disorder—as in medieval European societies—have been direct and brutal. Hands are cut off. Tongues are cut out. Adulterers are stoned.

In socialist societies, the enemy of human development is thought to lie in inequalities of economic wealth and power. These being removed, it is imagined that society will be cooperative and the human breast at peace with itself. In extreme forms of socialism, all forms of private ownership are to be abolished, as the source of inequalities and restlessness. The gap between rich and poor is regarded as the mainspring of injustice. In moderate forms, which respect the connection between liberty and private property, income differentials still seem to be a scandal. The assumption seems to be that envy is the central passion in the human breast. Socialists seem to think that humans *should* feel envy, even if they don't. For socialism, the fundamental evil is the conflict between classes. "Socialism," writes R. H. Tawney, "would end the conflict by ending the economic and legal conditions by which it is produced. Its fundamental dogma is the dignity of man; its fundamental criticism of capitalism is, not merely that it impoverishes the mass of mankind—poverty is an ancient evil—but that it makes riches a god, and treats common men less than man."[2]

Democratic capitalism has a rather different understanding of itself from the one imputed by Tawney. Far from impoverishing the mass of humankind, it has intended to generate a greater improvement in the material conditions of every portion of humankind. Far from making riches a god, democratic capitalism promotes a pluralism of interests and purposes. The ideal in whose light it judges the bigness of corporations is pragmatic: does bigness promote or injure the common goal? Democratic capitalism is not identical with corporatism—a system of large corporations.

What democratic capitalism fears is tyranny, most notably by the state, but also by excessive private power. It fears the mean pettiness of regimented equality. It propounds an openness about economic wealth and power. It regulates the trusts. It foments rapid mobility, recognizing that old fortunes decline and new ones arise. In some forms of disparity in wealth and power, it sees utilities from which all benefit. For other forms of disparity, it establishes several correctives: a plural scheme of checks and balances; legitimate power in the political system and in the moral-cultural system to restrain, temper, and check the economic system; and stimulation of the due circulation of elites and the economic mobility of individuals.

Under democratic capitalism, inequalities of wealth and power are not considered evil in themselves. They are in tune with natural inequalities which everyone experiences every day. Nature itself has made human beings equal in dignity before God and one another. But it has not made them equal to one another in talent, personal energy, luck, motivation, and practical abilities. On the other hand, inequalities of every sort are potential sources of evil and abuse. Human beings are insecure. Often, even as little children, they engage in petty rivalries and tear one another down. Long before the rise of democratic capitalism, even in biblical times, envy was potent. Nature itself generates inequalities of looks, stature, intellect, and heart. Should a good society repress inequalities, or should it respect them, while teaching cooperation and respect? Democratic capitalism is loathe to repress natural human energies which manifest obvious inequalities. Such energies are perennial, universal, and irrepressible; the attempt to repress them breeds yet more dangerous evils. Yet even persons in many ways unequal to one another may respect one another in other ways as equals, may cooperate, and seek mutual benefit.

Any society which does not promote and support its best natural leaders punishes itself and weakens its probabilities of survival and progress. In all fields, genius is rare and high talent is in relatively short supply. Any political economy which wishes to be as creative as possible must try to invent a system which permits persons of talent in all fields to discover their talents, to develop them, and to find the social positions in which their exercise bears maximal social fruit. Necessarily, such a system must encourage massive programs of self-discovery and self-improvement. Such a system must promote considerable fluidity and mobility. It must reward performance and learn to seek out talent wherever it may be found. Such a system requires vital local communities which identify and promote talents appearing in their midst. Under the pressures of high technology and its demands, democratic capitalist societies (like others) face keen difficulties, stemming from government, business, and even the mass media, in keeping subsidiary communities vital, in not overwhelming them, and in promoting their self-reliance and creativity. Too little thought flows in this direction, and then the ideals of democratic capitalism are themselves undercut.

Democratic capitalism does not promise to eliminate sin. It certainly does not promise equality of results (an outcome which, in any case, would run counter both to nature and to justice). It does not even promise that all those who have wealth or who acquire wealth will do so according to moral merit. Its sense of meritocracy is not a judgment upon individuals but is based upon the system *qua* system. It holds that a system which permits individual families over time to rise and to fall in wealth in accord with their own actions and circumstances will, *on the whole,* better reward familial performance than any other form of society.[3] The judgment of individual cases may be left to God.

It is, so to speak, the chief virtue of democratic capitalism that, in giving rein to liberty, it allows tares to grow among the wheat. Its political economy is not designed for saints. Whereas socialists frequently promise, under their coercive system, "a new socialist man" of a virtuous sort the world has never seen before, democratic capitalism (although it, too, depends upon and nourishes virtuous behavior) promises no such thing. Its political economy, while depending upon a high degree of civic virtue in its citizens (and upon an especially potent moral-cultural system separated from the state), is designed for sinners. That is, for humans as they are.

Most social revolutions promise a reign of the saints. Most promise a new type of moral man. And most intend to produce this higher type of morality through the coercive power of the state. This is precisely the impulse in the human breast which democratic capitalism finds to be the most productive of evil. Against it, tolerating other evils, it most resolutely sets its face.

There are, in this respect, two main traditions of revolutionary thought, the utopian and the realist. Utopian revolutionaries imagine that the source of human evil lies in social structures and systems and that in removing these they will remove evil and virtue will flourish. By contrast, realists hold that the source of human evil lies in the self and in the necessary limitations of every form of social organization. Realists hold that no real or imagined social structures and no system, however ingeniously designed, will banish sin from the field of human liberty. "The revolution," Charles Péguy once wrote, "is moral or not at all."⁴ But what makes a revolution moral? For the utopians, morality flows from structures and systems. (At one extreme, Stalinists hold that any act by individuals to bring about socialism is objectively a moral act.) For the realists, morality flows from individual will and act.

In the realist tradition, a moral revolution in political economy depends upon creating a system within which, to the maximum extent history makes possible, liberty for individuals will flourish. Such a system necessarily means that sin will flourish too. Yet the system *qua* system will be moral if two conditions are met. First, the design must include pluralistic institutions which permit both liberty and virtue to prosper. Second, the system of moral and religious culture must instruct individuals in the ways of liberty and virtue. Such a design rests upon an exact diagnosis of human frailty on the one hand, and of the effects, intended and unintended, of institutional arrangements on the other.

The realist revolutionary does not believe that the overthrow of an evil system will guarantee a better to replace it. He does not glorify the revolutionary struggle or the revolutionary moment, for he does not conceive that the source of evil lies in the system to be overthrown. The realists do not imagine that there has been, is now, or ever will be a political economy from which evil will be banished. Wherever there are human beings, there will be evil. Because they do not believe in a paradise on earth, or in an innocent system, the realists are often dismissed as mere "reformers." In fact, their vision is revolutionary precisely because they reject the moral pretenses both of ancient traditional orders and of contemporary utopian orders. The utopias of the modern age strike them as too like the theocracies and moral tyrannies of the past.

Theological traditions ground both the utopian and the realist strains of revolutionary theory. Many scholars trace both to Calvinism. One strain arises from the humility involved in recognizing, as John Wesley did, inevitable differences in individual conscience. The other arises from the millennialism of Joachim of Flora and the Muenster Rebellion. Both strains begin with a profound awareness of the sinfulness of this world. From one strain comes a realism which concentrates moral attention upon checking the evil always present in the human heart. The other is fired by a passion for purification from evil, through the destruction of evil institutions and the dawn of a new era. Karl Marx traces the origins of scientific socialism to the latter. Democratic capitalism has its origins in the former. Both speak of a "new order of the ages." Each is the ground of a new sort of liberation theology.[5]

In Latin America today, the utopian strain has been gaining ground among Catholics and Protestants alike. Thus, when liberation theologian Juan Luis Segundo describes the choice between capitalism and socialism as the "theological crux" for Latin America, he explicitly prefers the utopianism of socialism to the realism of democratic capitalism.[6] The economic successes of the realist tradition have changed the material horizon of the peoples of the Third World. But the *ideas* of the realist tradition have had surprisingly little impact upon its intellectual elites. For theologians reflexively hostile to democratic capitalism, the socialist vision seems all the more commendable for being utopian. They see in it the perfectionism of Christianity. They dream about a new society of equality, justice, autonomy, and brotherhood. One reads them in vain for descriptions of the exact institutional structures by which these dreams will be realized.

Democratic capitalism places its strongest emphasis upon practice. The British empiricists and American pragmatists alike highly praised "the experimental method." In a sense quite different from that of Karl Marx, they held that the point of philosophy is not merely to reflect the world but to change it. Since what they feared most was the abuse of public power through state tyranny, they developed a theory of the limited state. Since they were mindful that men are not angels, they tried to design a system that would diffuse power broadly through a system of differentiation. Since they did not believe that parchment alone governs men, they tried to establish a dynamic system of competing interests of many sorts, political, economic, and moral-cultural. Since history showed that not even the church of Christ can be purified of sin, they did not expect the earthly city to be pure. Instead of trying to cleanse the earth of sin, they set out to construct a framework of laws, institutions, and plural purposes, within which no one sector, and no one interest, might impose unitary dominance.

The seminal thinkers who set democratic capitalism upon its historic course were exceedingly practical men, thoroughly sobered by the human capacity for sin and illusion. While some scholars interpret their work as though they were sunny rationalists,[7] the opposite is nearer the truth. Thinkers like Montesquieu, Adam Smith, and James Madison were counter-rationalists. They were not optimistic about the human capacity for reasonableness or virtue. Ironically, the modest virtue they claimed for democratic capitalism laid the system open to charges that it encourages the worst in the human breast. Some have accused it of licensing greed and making riches god. Still others accuse it of radical individualism, moral anarchy, and destructive competitiveness. Some sunny rationalism.

2
The Doctrine of Unintended Consequences

In political economy, there are two self-frustrating ways to defeat sin. One is to convert individual hearts. The other is to construct a system which imposes virtue by force. Democratic capitalism chose a third way. Through close study, its founders observed that in political economy personal intentions characteristically lead to unintended consequences. There is a gap between "moral man" and "not-so-moral society."[8] Thus, political economists must pay less attention to individual intentions and more attention to systemic even if unintended consequences. In free societies, at least, there are so many agents, intentions, and actions that the line between intentions and results is too complex for the human mind to discern in advance.[9] If there is a social order, its rationality may become apparent after the fact. Its order cannot be planned or commanded in advance.

This doctrine of unintended consequences is central in the theory of democratic capitalism. It represents the conservative strain within the Enlightenment. It is counter-rationalist. By contrast, socialism is clearly rationalist, depending as it does on the ability of the human mind to ram its own intentions through social reality. Equally by contrast, anti-capitalist conservatives resist the dynamism, change, and progress which democratic capitalists favor. Friedrich Hayek is probably correct in his essay "Why I Am Not a Conservative" in identifying democratic capitalism as an inheritance of the Whig tradition—of Montesquieu, Smith, Burke, de Tocqueville—rather than of the conservative tradition.[10]

The doctrine of unintended consequences turns the eyes of the political economist away from the moral intentions of individuals and toward the final social consequences of their actions. More than that, it turns his attention to systems *qua* systems. This led to the insight that, among competing alternatives, the hopes for a good, free, and just society are best reposed in a system which gives high status to commerce and industry.

Consider the alternatives. The clergy had a demonstrated record of fanaticism, intolerance, and misuse of power. The military had a record of despoliation. Lords and nobles had a record of hauteur, luxury, and indolence on the one hand, and of martial adventure on the other. The state and its bureaucracies, through the system of royal privileges and grants, had long been parasitic upon the prosperity of nations. Bureaucracies of state and church, producing nothing, drove away producers by their arrogance. To which central activity, to which class, then, ought those who favor liberty to turn? Men of manufacturing and commerce might be an unsavory and disagreeable lot. Yet certain features in the formal structure of their own activities allied their own interests to those of liberty.

Men of manufacturing and commerce often have their origins outside existing establishments. Once successful, they may be scorned as *nouveaux riches,* but nonetheless social mobility is important to them. Their activities, moreover, depend upon stability and law, for they must make investments long before the fruits of manufacturing and trading bring them return; their instruments are trust and contract. For another thing, men of manufacturing and commerce have an interest in small increments and marginal savings; their habits of mind incline them to productivity and to moderation. Finally, they have an interest in expanding prosperity for many others, in reaching out to other nations and peoples, and in maintaining ties of peace and order abroad (lest their overseas investments be confiscated by powers suddenly turned hostile).

For all these reasons (and others), the founders of democratic capitalism looked to the formal structures of manufacturing and commerce for real interests that might undergird a political economy of liberty. Perhaps it is worth singling out yet another attractive feature of the world of trade. Its medium is money—cold, impersonal, insensitive to station, class, creed, race, or person. The very qualities which some find so unattractive in money led the partisans of liberty to see in it a respecter not of persons but of laws. The ancient proverb *Radix malorum cupiditas* was often translated in the vernacular as "Money is the root of all evils." The evil uses to which money can be put need no stress. But money has within it moral as well as immoral potency, and its use opens the political economy to men of every class, race, and creed. Its impersonality has good as well as ill effects in societies historically battered by class and religious strife.

The founders of democratic capitalism had a further structural reason for giving greater scope to men of manufacturing and commerce than had obtained under any previous form of political economy. They wished to build a center of power to rival the power of the state. They separated the economy from the state not only to unleash the power of individual imagination and initiative but also to limit the state from within and to check it from without. They did not fear unrestrained economic power as much as they feared political tyranny. For they believed that restraints upon economic power are many, partly from competitors but even more from the hazards of economic mortality. Business ventures frequently fail, nature is unpredictable, markets fluctuate, and new technologies make old centers of power obsolete. One may imagine "economic power" in the abstract as formidable, but enterprise by enterprise, industry by industry, it is always subject to swift and sudden failure. Like states, centers of economic power are tempted to abuse their power. That is precisely why the state retains ultimate legal and coercive power, and why the moral-cultural system is kept free of direct dependence either upon the state or upon the economic system.

Neither Montesquieu nor Smith nor Madison was a merchant or an industrialist. None had a high opinion of merchants or industrialists, or pictured the latter as moral idealists. Smith in particular cited evidence that such men, as a class, were often vulgar and crass. Still, it was not to the motivation or virtue of merchants and industrialists that democratic capitalism looked for the social basis of a law-abiding, dynamic, free society. It is the *structure* of business activities, not the intentions of businessmen, that are favorable to rule by law, to liberty, to habits of regularity and moderation, to a healthy realism, and to demonstrated social progress—demonstrably more favorable than the structures of churchly, aristocratic, or military activities. It is in the interests of businessmen to defend and to enlarge the virtues on which liberty and progress depend.

This view stands on its head the usual accusation against democratic capitalism. Those who prefer ecclesiastical, aristocratic, or martial values commonly deplore the values of a society undergirded by the moral imperatives of business. Yet democratic capitalism looks to the record, rather than to the intentions, of rival elites. None had produced an equivalent system of liberties. None had so loosed the bonds of station, rank, peonage, and immobility. None had so raised human expectations. None so valued the individual.

Under democratic capitalism, individual persons began receiving and using proper names.[11] They began to enjoy rights of privacy. They began thinking of themselves as agents responsible for altering their own future and that of the world. De Tocqueville observed how all through the United States a kind of spiritual energy coursed through mechanics and artisans, farmers and carpenters, men and women of every station, who felt charged to make their own world.[12] Under all other systems of political economy, traditional or socialist, priority is given to collectives: orders human and divine, station and rank, classes and systems. Uniquely, democratic capitalism makes the insight and choice of the human person the determining power of history.

Yet democratic capitalism is not a system of radical individualism (as is often alleged). Parties and factions loom large in it. Family is central to it. Structures, institutions, laws, and prescribed procedures are indispensable to its conception. In economic matters, its chief social inventions are the business corporation and the free labor union. Its theory of sin makes such complexity necessary. Its theory of sin makes creative use even of self-interest.

3
Virtuous Self-Interest

R. H. Tawney described the age of capitalism as the age of acquisitiveness. Marx described it as the reduction of every human relation to the cash nexus. Pamphleteers for generations have denounced its licensing of greed. Yet simple reflection upon one's own life and the life of others, including the lives of those critics who denounce the system from within, suggests that there are enormous reservoirs of high motivation and moral purpose among citizens in democratic capitalist societies. The history of democratic capitalism is alive with potent movements of reform and idealistic purpose. As the world goes, its people do not in fact seem to be more greedy, grasping, selfish, acquisitive, or anarchic than citizens in traditional or in socialist societies. If democratic capitalism is to be blamed for sins it permits to flourish, the virtues it nourishes also deserve some credit.

In practice, the bone of contention seems most often to be the central concept of self-interest. A system committed to the principle that individuals are best placed to judge their real interests for themselves may be accused of institutionalizing selfishness and greed—but only on the premise that individuals are so depraved that they never make any other choice.

The founders of democratic capitalism did not believe that such depravity is universal. Furthermore, they held that the laws of free economic markets are such that the real interests of individuals are best served in the long run by a systematic refusal to take short-term advantage. Apart from internal restraints, the system itself places restraints upon greed and narrowly construed self-interest. Greed and selfishness, when they occur, are made to have their costs. A firm aware of its long-term fiduciary responsibilities to its shareholders must protect its investments for future generations. It must change with the times. It must maintain a reputation for reliability, integrity, and fairness. In one large family trucking firm, for example, the last generation of owners kept too much in profits and invested too little in new technologies and new procedures, with the result that their heirs received a battered company unable to compete or to solve its cash-flow problems. Thus a firm committed to greed unleashes social forces that will sooner or later destroy it. Spasms of greed will disturb its own inner disciplines, corrupt its executives, anger its patrons, injure the morale of its workers, antagonize its suppliers and purchasers, embolden its competitors, and attract public retribution. In a free society, such spasms must be expected; they must also be opposed.

The real interests of individuals, furthermore, are seldom merely self-regarding. To most persons, their families mean more than their own interests; they frequently subordinate the latter to the former. Their communities are also important to them. In the human breast, commitments to benevolence, fellow-feeling, and sympathy are strong. Moreover, humans have the capacity to see themselves as others see them, and to hold themselves to standards which transcend their own selfish inclinations. Thus the "self" in self-interest is complex, at once familial and communitarian as well as individual, other-regarding as well as self-regarding, cooperative as well as independent, and self-judging as well as self-loving. Understood too narrowly, self-interest destroys firms as surely as it destroys personal lives. Understood broadly enough, as a set of realistic limits, it is a key to all the virtues, as prudence is.

Like prudence in Aristotelian thought, self-interest in democratic capitalist thought has an inferior reputation among moralists. Thus it is necessary to stress again that a *society* may not work well if all its members act always from benevolent intentions. On the other hand, democratic capitalism as a system deliberately enables many persons to do well by doing good (or even purporting to do good). It offers incentives of power, fame, and money to reformers and moralists.[13]

The economic system of democratic capitalism depends to an extraordinary extent upon the social capacities of the human person. Its system of inheritance respects the familial character of motivation. Its corporate pattern reflects the necessity of shared risks and shared rewards. Its divisions both of labor and of specialization reflect the demands of teamwork and association. Its separated churches and autonomous universities reflect the importance of independent moral communities. The ideology of individualism, too much stressed by some proponents and some opponents alike, disguises the essential communitarian character of its system.

Regrettably, the theory of democratic capitalism was left too long to economists. While economists are entitled to specialize, theologians also have such rights. A theology of democratic capitalism requires a larger view, of which economists freely concede the legitimacy. Thus, Milton and Rose Friedman in their best-selling *Free to Choose* consciously stress

> . . . the broad meaning that must be attached to the concept of "self-interest." Narrow preoccupation with the economic market has led to a narrow interpretation of self-interest as myopic selfishness, as exclusive concern with immediate material rewards. Economics has been berated for allegedly drawing far-reaching conclusions from a wholly unrealistic "economic man" who is little more than a calculating machine, responding only to monetary stimuli. That is a great mistake. Self-interest is not myopic selfishness. It is whatever it is that interests the participants, whatever they value, whatever goals they pursue. The scientist seeking to advance the frontiers of his discipline, the missionary seeking to convert infidels to the true faith, the philanthropist seeking to bring comfort to the needy—all are pursuing their interests, as they see them, as they judge them by their own values.[14]

Under self-interest, then, fall religious and moral interests, artistic and scientific interests, and interests in justice and peace. The interests of the self define the self. In a free society, persons are free to choose their own interests. It is part of the function of a free economy to provide the abundance which breaks the chains of the mere struggle for subsistence, and to permit individual persons to "find themselves," indeed to define themselves through the interests they choose to make central to their lives.

In brief, the term "self-interest" encodes a view of human liberty that far exceeds self-regard, selfishness, acquisitiveness, and greed. Adam Smith attempted to suggest this by speaking of *rational* self-interest, by which he meant a specification of human consciousness not only intelligent and judgmental, beyond the sphere of mere desire or self-regard, but also guided by the ideal of objectivity. In *The Theory of Moral Sentiments* (1759), he argued that what is truly rational must be seen to be so not merely from the point of view of the self-interested party but from that of a disinterested rational observer as well. He called the achievement of such realistic judgment "the perfection of human nature." The whole system, as he imagined it, is aimed toward the acquisition of such realism: "We endeavour to examine our own conduct as we imagine any other fair and impartial spectator would examine it." Again: "To feel much for others, and little for ourselves . . . to restrain our selfish, and to indulge our benevolent, affections, constitutes the perfection of human nature."[15]

Democratic capitalism, then rests on a complex theory of sin. While recognizing ineradicable sinful tendencies in every human, it does not count humans depraved. While recognizing that no system of political economy can escape the ravages of human sinfulness, it has attempted to set in place a system which renders sinful tendencies as productive of good as possible. While basing itself on something less than perfect virtue, reasoned self-interest, it has attempted to draw from self-interest its most creative potential. It is a system designed for sinners, in the hope of achieving as much moral good as individuals and communities can generate under conditions of ample liberty.

Can human society imitate Providence?

V

Providence and Practical Wisdom

Human affairs are darkened by those who blow conscience out and willfully choose night. As if to make things worse, human affairs abound in unintended consequences.

The ancients imagined God as the lucid *Nous,* the all-knowing and all-seeing God of harmony, who moved the stars and planets in mathematical orbits. By contrast, they saw the cosmos in tense balance ever at risk of breakdown. Yet as human insight into the tangles of history has become more plural and uncertain, the image of God has also changed. In the thirteenth century, Thomas Aquinas began to abandon the image of God as *Nous* and to choose as a more useful metaphor *Providence.* This represented a shift from the God of geometry to the God of historical singulars, a shift in metaphor from theoretical reason to practical wisdom. In the Jewish-Christian view, Providence knows every lily of every field, every hair on every head. Providence is Lord of the absurd, the idiosyncratic, the slip of the tongue. This shift was especially marked in Aquinas's tract against the Islamic scholars Averroës and Avicenna, in which Aquinas stressed the respect of God for a world of concrete contingencies, secondary causes, liberties, and sin.[1]

Parallel to this shift in theology, a problem arose for the polity. By what human instrument can humankind best cope with the impenetrability of history and sin? How can political economy be Provident? To imitate Providence, it is not enough to have an all-knowing plan. A practical system must often be counterintuitive, since reality does not lie limpid before us. Useful presuppositions can be learned only through study and experience, and the resulting knowledge is better called wisdom than science.

In practice, many things go wrong which are not caused by faulty theory—as when, in football, a perfectly executed diagram fails because the open receiver stumbles. Thus practitioners confront hazards more complicated than those of theoreticians. Since this chapter is about practice, it is, accordingly, the most complex in the book. I urge the reader to keep in mind that each of its five parts—its discussions of time, the market, the so-called invisible hand, profit, and the zero-sum society—develops a lesson learned from experience about the way the world works in practice. This terrain is untidy because life is. I have tried to concentrate on theological assumptions. Economists discuss these matters somewhat differently.

1
Time and Intelligence

INDUSTRY: *Lose no time: Be always employ'd in something useful: cut off all unnecessary Action.*
—Benjamin Franklin, *Autobiography.*[2]

The word "capitalism" first came into usage, it appears, at the end of the eighteenth century,[3] but it did not acquire broad currency until Marx and Engels made it famous a half century later. In this new system, time gained new significance. In earlier periods, when economic development had not yet been glimpsed as a moral imperative, the consciousness of human beings was naturally oriented more toward the past than toward the future. Thus, even the artistic breakthroughs of the Renaissance were described in a backward-glancing term. Peoples of "the Book" gave tradition great weight. Ancient classics guided cultural life. Paradise lay in the past.

Quite suddenly, in the new age, consciousness was thrown

forward into the future. Belief in the coming Kingdom of God had, of course, prepared the way. The narrative sense of history which is part of a biblical inheritance had opened minds to the future.

Still, belief that the future could actually be changed depended upon conditions which were only slowly met: the emergence of science and technology, the growth of northern European cities, the stimulation of markets and manufacturing, and the weakening of the feudal order. The Dominican scholar Cajetan (1469–1534) appears to have been the first theologian to break from conceptions of a static economic world to those of a changing world. For him, the "just wage" could not solely be measured by what was "appropriate to one's station" (imagined to be unchanging) but by what was appropriate to one's contribution (shifting with changes in the world).[4]

In early literature, a common symbol for economic evil was the miser, who through avarice hoarded his money. The miser was evil because, in a static world, with valuables in short supply, what one person hoarded was subtracted from the common store. Yet the miser who sat in his countinghouse counting up his money was soon made to appear foolish. His figure disappeared from literature. For now the capitalist ethos valued the *time* through which money might be used. This ethos profoundly changed the role of practical intelligence. It saw in idle money a resource for transforming the future. Money alone is not "capital." But money taken from idleness and made active through practical intelligence became something new and needed a new name. Centuries of biblical faith had nourished trust in human intelligence, and in due time economic activists began to draw upon this trust to change the world. "God saw that it was good," the Book of Genesis said of the earth; but human beings only gradually awakened to how much good was yet to be discovered in it. The Belgian anthropologist Léo Moulin shows how much trust in Creation was needed before men would venture into the bowels of the earth to fuel industry.[5]

In this respect, although he goes too far in speaking of altruism and love, George Gilder's reflections on the basic trust implicit in the democratic capitalist view of the world seem sound.[6] Anthropologically, the European adventure in modernity was made possible because miners trusted the dark innards of the earth, alchemists were not fundamentally afraid of the elements of nature, inventors did not hesitate to bring forth novelties, investors parted with tangibles in the intangible hope of future returns. They did so despite the romantic, even reactionary, tradition which taught humans to fear nature and to see modernity as Frankenstein. Humankind could give rein to a generous instinct, trusting that God's nature would offer reward in kind. Up and outward went the thrust of democratic capitalism. First came investment and effort, later the return. The spirit was not that of the zero-sum nor that of the miser nor that of primitive fear, but that of the experimenting follower of dreams.

Time itself came to be seen as a record of human experiments from which instruction might be drawn. "When in the course of human events," the American Declaration of Independence begins, drawing such a lesson. It closes, then, with "a firm reliance on the protection of divine Providence." Trust in practical intelligence is linked to trust in Providence. Experiments are legitimate. "Making history" is an appropriate human vocation. De Tocqueville commented on the spirit of the future that seemed to sweep through every family in the New World.[7] Individuals broke out of the ancient sense of imprisonment within eternal cycles and began to work toward, save for, and invest in the future. Migrants poured from the countryside, immigrants crossed frontiers and set sail upon forbidding oceans.

Practical intelligence grasped new schemes of probabilities. Married to practical intelligence, inert money acquired two new values: a time value and a productive value. The use of money in investments made it subject to loss; one needed trust in order to invest it. Yet investment gave money a dimension beyond that of mere exchange. The rationale for regarding interest payments as a sin—as usury—was thereby weakened. The time through which idle money was put to use yielded new value, for which it began to seem proper to exact a price. Money, no longer static, invested wisely, could grow. Invested at 10 percent over seven years, it could double. It could do so because productive investment increased the world's store of valuables. Wealth could, therefore, generate new wealth without taking from anybody else, through creative and intelligent use. These new discoveries about practical intelligence and investment led Walter Lippmann to observe quite shrewdly:

For the first time in human history men had come upon a

way of producing wealth in which the good fortune of others multiplied their own. . . . They actually felt it to be true that an enlightened self-interest promoted the common good. For the first time men could conceive a social order in which the ancient moral aspiration for liberty, equality, and fraternity was consistent with the abolition of poverty and the increase of wealth. Until the division of labor had begun to make men dependent upon the free collaboration of other men, the worldly policy was to be predatory. The claims of the spirit were other-worldly. So it was not until the industrial revolution had altered the traditional mode of life that the vista was opened at the end of which men could see the possibility of the Good Society on this earth. At long last the ancient schism between the world and the spirit, between self-interest and disinterestedness, was potentially closed, and a wholly new orientation of the human race became theoretically conceivable and, in fact, necessary.[8]

Theologians have not sufficiently reflected on the psychological nature of money. New inventions in accounting and contract law, and later still in the monetizing of public debts, turned attention away from the physicality of money. Less and less did individuals handle physical money; more and more money became a bookkeeping record. Money in this sense became intellectualized. Gold, silver, and materials of barter were largely supplanted by symbolic paper. Moreover, this paper came to depend to an unprecedented degree upon public trust. Thus, in our day, economists measure "consumer confidence," "inflationary psychology," "business confidence," "investment climate." The stability of societies has become an important factor in the value of their public currencies and their economic assets.

Money, in short, has become less materialistic. It is in part a symbol of social health and confidence in the future, and it is linked to potential productivity. The investment of money is regarded in a quite secular sense as an act of faith, trust, confidence, and even fraternity. It has come to be seen as the key to development and peace and justice. It is awarded as a grace (more fancifully, even as an indulgence) as credits are extended or refinanced so that practical productive activities may be launched. In this sense, financial institutions and banks are commonly described, particularly in respect to less-developed nations and regions, in the language of justice, fiduciary responsibility, creativity, and even forgiveness. This is an ironic switch, for the theological language of redemption (buying back) was originally derived from commercial metaphors.

Thus, the ethos of capitalism transformed the nature of money by linking it to practical intelligence and future productivity. This ethos legitimated the completing of creation as it sprang from the care of Providence. The value of money springs from foresight into the future: from *pro* + *videre*. This new conception of money, therefore, also altered the conception and value of time.

For it now became apparent that "time is money." Time lost its neutrality and came to be regarded as an ideal dimension, imposing upon individuals a duty not to "waste" it. Under the goal of a better future, time came to exert a discipline over the natural rhythms of the body and the psyche. The pace of human life seemed to quicken. Economic activities were no longer oriented merely toward survival or sufficiency but toward a kind of spiritual goal. They acquired purposiveness. The new sense of time demanded abnegations of the body and the emotions not unlike the mortifications of the monks at their monastic "hours." It launched vast new movements of self-education and self-improvement. Within one's lifetime one was now expected to invest each moment in activities which would help one to realize one's potential in the future. Time thus imposes disciplines and obligations. Capitalism is not so much a material as a self-making ethos. The modern age, supposed to be so materialistic, imposed its own spirituality. Consider the daily regimen adopted by Benjamin Franklin (see page 102).[9]

Among the modern religious orders, new congregations committed themselves to "the active life" and adopted disciplines of historical originality. (Among these are the Jesuits, the teaching orders, congregations of nurses, and missionary communities.) Such disciplines have crowded out, more than they ought, the poetic, contemplative, meditative side of life, and in religion the peoples of the West have become too activist. This is a serious failing, which many recent movements toward meditation and contemplation are trying (often badly) to redress. What cannot be denied is that a new conception of time and practical intelligence became a cultural life form of extraordinary power.[10] By comparison, traditional cultures, however vital in their own terms, seem to have been "asleep." When today one speaks of the "awaken-

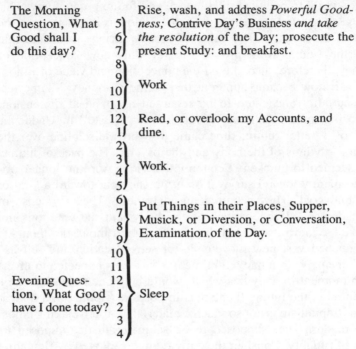

The Precept of *Order* requiring that *every Part of my Business should have its allotted Time,* one Page in my little Book contain'd the following Scheme of Employment for the Twenty-four Hours of a natural Day,

The Morning Question, What Good shall I do this day?	5 6 7	Rise, wash, and address *Powerful Goodness;* Contrive Day's Business *and take the resolution* of the Day; prosecute the present Study: and breakfast.
	8 9 10 11	Work
	12 1	Read, or overlook my Accounts, and dine.
	2 3 4 5	Work.
	6 7 8 9	Put Things in their Places, Supper, Musick, or Diversion, or Conversation, Examination of the Day.
Evening Question, What Good have I done today?	10 11 12 1 2 3 4	Sleep

ing" of the Third World, it is into this novel life form that they are in fact entering.

Economic activism is central to this awakening. For the economic system produces the wherewithal through which the realm of choice is enlarged. Poverty may not be evil in itself, but it does restrict choices. The key to increasing the wealth of nations lies, then, in stimulating economic activism. The chief good to be gained through such activism is increased personal liberty. Thus, increased personal liberty is both a goal in itself and a means toward other goals, a method of stimulating economic activism.

Still, when classical writers discuss the components of economic wealth—land, rents, capital, and labor—they nearly always overlook the most important ingredient: practical intelligence and the organization of personal life. It is intelligence that grasps new methods of cultivation and makes the land yield greater harvests. It is intelligence that devises new systems of transport, new methods of distribution, and new marketing strategies. On the other hand, without a suitable discipline in personal life, practical intelligence cannot be a guiding force. For this reason, the moral-cultural system of democratic capitalism must resist hedonism and decadence with all its power, and not merely accommodate itself to fashion. For this reason, too, entire cultures, insofar as they wish to enjoy the benefits of wider liberties, must grasp the decisive importance of breaking the grip of animism, magic, and the other nonrational forms of traditional cultures.[11] Individuals must be encouraged to permit practical wisdom to guide their economic behavior. Some cultures refuse this permission. They pay a price for this refusal.[12]

In *The Responsible Society,* Eugen Loebl and Stephen Roman observe that Marxists—and even many Westerners—have made too little of the primacy of intelligence in democratic capitalism.[13] Roman is president of one of Canada's most important corporations; Loebl was minister of foreign trade in the Marxist government of Czechoslovakia, before his imprisonment and subsequent exile. They object to discussions which proceed as if democratic capitalism were interested only in the material world. What is most striking, they argue, is its emphasis upon intelligence and thus upon the life of the spirit. "Human capital" is its dynamic force.

Practical insights are the primary source of wealth. Consider two laborers, one working unintelligently and by rote, the other inventing more practical and efficient techniques. It is intelligence that results in the increased value of the second's output. Intelligence is also the primary form of capital. Oil lay beneath the sands of Arabia for thousands of years, relatively without value to the human race, until the application of human intelligence found a use for it. Countless parts of God's creation lay fallow for millennia until human intelligence saw value in them. Many of the things we today describe as resources were not known to be resources a hundred years ago. Many of those which tomorrow may come to be of value still lie fallow today. The bridge to wealth is constructed chiefly of intelligence. The cause of wealth lies more in the human spirit than in matter.

Time and intelligence made "capital" of useless miser's gold.

The alchemists who sought to turn base metals to gold overlooked the real source of wealth.

2
The Market

When millions of human individuals become economic activists it seems intuitively as if their activities must be anarchic. Only a lucid commanding intelligence, intuition tells us, can apply resources efficiently to places of need according to rational criteria, eliminate duplication, and avoid waste. Traditionalists and socialists take the direct road to economic rationality. They occupy the commanding heights and try to impose order.

In practice, however, even the most lucid experts do not seem to be able to see into the future with sufficient clarity to estimate correctly the actual flows of demand or the actual availabilities of supply. In most economic markets, particularly those with millions of participants, no single human intelligence seems adequate to grasping the needs of individuals. Central planners have a record of building up wasteful surpluses in some areas, precipitating unplanned-for shortages in others. Queues and illicit black markets result. Between direct rationality and reality there yawns a great gap. Perhaps worse, incentives to individual intelligence are few and the common fund of invention shrinks.

The founders of democratic capitalism sought intelligibility by a different route, indirect rather than direct, counterintuitive but effective. They understood that predictions about scores of millions of economic transactions by millions of free economic agents exceed the capacity of human intelligence. They sought a humbler way. They saw great worth in liberty, and this bias no doubt carried them in a new direction. Their study of historical experiments convinced them of its practicality.

For economic activity is less anarchic in practice, even when free, than intuition expects. Wherever economic activism flourishes, people are drawn together. Urban centers grow. Markets are established. Lines of transport and communication multiply. Individualization is furthered by higher levels of activity and choice, while tribal and familial forms of closeness are sharply altered. The social life of economically active individuals is in many ways richer and more intense than life in "sleepier" eras, and interactions between persons multiply. Some of these interactions are impersonal, but others are not. Economic activism generates excitement and intellectual stimulation out of increased human interaction. Markets "bustle." Cosmopolitanism flourishes. Economic activity generates vortices of human energy, expressed in the history of cities. Urban life lacks agrarian charm, but it is certainly not poorer in human interaction. The interdependence it forges is unlike the relative self-reliance and isolation typical of rural life; but it generates solitude and self-reliance of its own.[14]

Economic activity is impossible in isolation, since it consists in intelligent, voluntary transactions. The word "commerce" means not only buying and selling, but the coming together of peoples. Its transactions are reasoned, lawlike, contractual. Moreover, they occur under tangible constraints of scarcity and plenty. If there were total abundance, immediately accessible to all, economic activity would be pointless. But under conditions of scarcity, human beings need each other. It is scarcity that calls economic activism into being. Where exchange is free, consensual, and reasoned, laws of supply and demand direct the flow of economic activity. This fact alone diminishes anarchy. Quite general laws discipline all, and bind all together under significant constraints.

How many goods of a certain kind ought to be produced? The answer is best left to the contingency plans of actual buyers and sellers. The reason is not simply that individuals are the best judges of their own real needs. It is also that the pattern of their choices plays an important informational role. When the number of economic agents willing to expend resources upon certain goods is great, inadequate supply is likely to force prices up until some buyers, at least, change their minds. The prices that result from negotiations between buyers and sellers summarize large quantities of information with computerlike speed. Those who specialize in certain goods or certain markets follow such information closely. Mistakes are costly. They have reason to develop contingency plans.

Market prices provide more than information. They also generate new activities and stimulate inventions. As the price of oil rises, solar energy and other possibilities attract the enterprising. The cycle of new technologies, furthermore, promotes social mobility. Practical intelligence does not seem to be distributed only to the wealthy, the privileged, or the highly educated. Many, perhaps most, leaders of major industrial and marketing concerns spring from poorer families. Their advantages may include not only a fresh sense of novelty but also a sharper realism. For in a market system, some who begin poor hunger to "get ahead," and some who were formerly wealthy squander their inheritance. Markets yield patterns of rationality; they are open; and they make things happen.

Most of human living does not take place in markets, and no one is bound to enter into them more than subsistence requires. Yet it is in the interest of markets to include all. In a market system things move; wealth grows; opportunities open; breakthroughs are made; new groups rise to wealth. Practical intelligence assesses existing arrangements in order to invent others, to offer new services, to meet unmet needs, to discover better ways. The inventiveness encouraged by market systems may be their most important characteristic.

Socialists make four fairly common objections to a market system: (1) Markets resolve problems according to the purchasing power of those who have money. One dollar may be analogous to one vote, and those who have more dollars have more votes than those who have fewer. (2) Modern advertising distorts the judgments of those who have money, so that market decisions are far less rational than they ought to be. (3) Large corporations are able to place administered prices on their goods, either in collusion with other suppliers or through their power over particular markets. (4) Markets work in such a way that the rich get richer, the poor poorer.

Since proponents of the market system do not argue that the system is utopian and flawless, only that it is economically the most productive, intellectually the most inventive and dynamic, and politically the only system compatible with liberty, these objections might simply be taken as the price which must be paid for the benefits gained. Taken one by one, however, these four objections have less weight than at first appears.

While it is true that money talks and that those with more money enjoy a wider range of choices that those with less, it is also true that a market system has an inherent interest in the many which is far more substantial than its interest in the few. Corporations which seek mass markets have a far larger economic base than those which specialize in items exclusively for the rich. Not long ago, for example, the ownership of a coach-and-four was limited to few; but market systems over the years have led quite naturally to the mass production of automobiles affordable by millions of families. There were 57 million families in the United States in 1978, for example, and 103 million automobiles in use.[15]

The second objection concerns distortions attributed to advertising. Yet if this objection is valid, then the idea of democracy is in great jeopardy. Under the heading "Individual Incompetence," Charles E. Lindblom makes an astounding statement in his much-acclaimed *Politics and Markets:*

Obviously an optimum is impossible when persons are ignorant of their own preferences or of the qualities of the goods and services they buy. In actual fact, no consumer is competent across the range of his purchases: insurance, medical care, mechanical and electronic equipment of many kinds, and foods treated with additives. This is of course a problem in all forms of organization: decision makers are never wholly competent in any form of politico-economic organization.[16]

One cites here, against Lindblom late, Lindblom early, who in *The Intelligence of Democracy* and *A Strategy of Decision* showed how decentralized systems of acquiring and using knowledge are better than centralized ones.[17] In an advanced society, important inequalities of knowledge and technical understanding multiply. Every citizen is incompetent in many areas. No one of us understands the scientific theory or engineering principles behind most of the ocean of knowledge which supports us. It does not follow that rule by experts is an intelligent response to the new inequalities.[18] It is still wise to trust the ordinary wisdom of plain human beings on juries, in the voting booth, in the development of public dialogue, and in the ordinary decencies of daily living. So also, it would seem, a wise society trusts individuals to spend their hard-earned dollars as they judge best. Choices made by some in the marketplace will often seem to others less than rational. This is true, as well, of the religious practices and moral principles to which individuals commit themselves. The marketplace suffers from ignorance, whimsy, passion, and relative irrationality. So do all other forms of free behavior. Moreover, the case against advertising requires a certain care. The history of advertising is full of quirks and failures. Many a highly advertised book falls flat. Not even the lavish advertising of American auto companies in the winter of 1979–80 seemed to bring consumer choice to prior levels. Advertisements compete with one another, so that while individual advertisers might *wish* they had the power often ascribed to them, they seldom do. Moreover, purchasers have their own experience as a check upon the millions of advertisements they are exposed to; they are not merely passive. Nor does there seem to be much evidence that highly sophisticated citizens (professors, for example) are superior to ordinary people in their ability to determine their own real interests, whether in politics or in economics. Furthermore, the conventional taboos and pieties which press upon intellectual elites—and their occupational remove from many of the rough places of common experience—may in fact distort perception far more than advertising does.[19] "Discriminating" consumers, like discriminating voters, seem equally blended of the rational and the irrational. Finally, the problems posed by advertising in economics seem quite different in structure from the problems posed by state propaganda in command economies.

The third objection, concerning administered prices, was made prominent in public discussion by John Kenneth Galbraith,[20] but it has by no means persuaded all economists. It certainly does not persuade executives even of the largest corporations who have often seen the market turn away from them. Galbraith's point is partly a truism. Products on the market today often result from research and development, complex processes of production and distribution, and sophisticated national marketing strategies and advertising budgets. Such factors make the task of putting price tags on a blender, coffeemaker, or camera a more complex calculation than in simpler times. Yet there are also today many more products competing simultaneously for the consumer's dollar.

In part, a supplier must make an educated guess, in advance, about the size of the particular market in which he intends to offer the blender, coffeemaker, or camera. In part, he must also recognize that the public, for one reason or another, may concentrate its purchase upon some *other* item at similar cost. A blender priced at $29.95 competes not simply with other blenders but with many other possible consumer purchases in other departments entirely. Some customers will seek discount stores, wait for sales, or look for "rebates." Many firms, imagining a far larger market for citizen-band radios than, in fact, turned out to exist, found themselves overstocked with merchandise they could not move. Many products in which manufacturers place high hopes—the Edsel, Corfam shoes, etc.—may fail to win public acceptance. The graveyard of ballyhooed products is enormous.[21] Even if some prices were administered in the sense that Professor Galbraith intends (economists will have to settle the argument), it does not follow that citizens can be clubbed into purchasing the particular products involved. Finally, it seems odd for a socialist to object to administered prices.

The notion that *markets* make the rich richer and the poor poorer—a dictum of Barbara Ward's[22]—seems not to match the historical record. Under market economies, the historical record shows unprecedented gains in real incomes for the poor. Many Marxists properly complain about the *embourgeoisement* of the proletariat. Regrettably, from their point of view, many workers nourish hopes that a market system will reward them economically with greater generosity than a command economy. In the Third World, too, as P. T. Bauer has pointed out, the nations least touched by market economies are poorest, and within nations those regions least open to markets are in worst economic and human shape.[23]

Yet markets do not work equally and simultaneously for all parts of the population. Getting people *into* markets is the hardest task. In an extremely backward country, where the economic starting point of most of the population is below a desirable subsistence level, where economic skills (even literacy and stamina) are low, the most difficult hurdle appears to be that between ground zero and something like $1,000 of annual income per family. In such cases, a floor of subsistence must somehow be put in place by methods beyond that of the unaided market. Once that level is reached, however, the market appears to be a dynamic economic force without equal. Cuba, for example, has apparently had success in raising the lowest fifth of its population to a modest level, but has failed to find a method for further dynamism and progress for all.[24]

Markets reward unequal skills and unequal efforts, and offer opportunities for enterprise, invention, adaptation, and social mobility. Market societies characteristically produce many *nouveaux riches,* diminish the role and power of landed aristocracies, create a broad middle class, and raise standards of health, literacy, and mobility among the poor. Moreover, in the transition between traditional economies and market economies, expectations and standards rise. In rural areas, the absence of running water, indoor plumbing, and paved streets is altogether common; in cities the same absences seem unjust and primitive. In rural areas, child labor is common, the forty-hour week is not observed, wages and annual income are only a fraction of urban income, and progress of every sort is delayed. Markets create cities; cities create visibility and impose higher modern standards.

Without markets, local industries lack incentives. The skills nourished in a market economy—in industrial crafts, transport, management, clerical staffs, bookkeeping, marketing, research, and the like—call forth talents in the population which traditional societies neglect. Max Weber suggests that one reason capitalism was born in England was that its insular position made the need for a standing army minimal. Thus, peasants unable to support themselves on the land were not tempted by such minimal pay as the military and police forces of traditional societies elsewhere provided to the unemployed, but were available as a massive work force for industry.[25] Industry generates white-collar jobs, broad professional classes, and new types of social workers as well as industrial jobs. It has an inherent interest in the education of the poor.

Finally, a word must be said about the occupational hostility of intellectuals, not only socialist intellectuals, to the very conception of the marketplace. An exception must be made for a free market in ideas; to this market, of course, intellectuals are much attached. As we have seen, intellectual and artistic work of a high order cannot always be appreciated by those who lack developed tastes and skills. Like other aristocracies, intellectuals may be of two minds regarding ordinary people. In moments of romance, they may glorify the folk, fancy themselves to be populists, and pose as the vanguard of the working class. In actual contacts with ordinary workers, however, the spiritual aristocracy may find its refined sensibilities offended. In a passage which nicely blends the aristocratic sensibilities of the past with those of modern intellectuals, Henry Fairlie commented in the *Washington Post* upon the massed delegates at the Republican Convention of 1980:

Here was the common man and, yes, the common woman, too, come to take possession of their century at last. . . . Narrow minded, book banning, truth censoring, mean spirited; ungenerous, envious, intolerant, afraid; chicken, bullying; trivially moral, falsely patriotic; family cheapening, flag cheapening, God cheapening; the common man, shallow, small, sanctimonious . . . exactly those who in Germany gave the Nazis their main strength and who in France collaborated with them and sustained Vichy.[26]

This passage scarcely exemplifies the civility and reason it means to commend to others. Yet its sentiments seem conventional enough among many intellectuals.

Conventions of ridicule extend to polyester suits, McDonald's, American-made automobiles, televised football games, shopping malls, and other forms of what is called, with audible disdain, "mass culture" and "consumerism."[27] An underlying assumption seems to be that if intellectuals were in command of markets and behaviors, people would soon purchase what is good for them and learn their place.

Nevertheless, there is a difference between a defense of the free market and a defense of democratic capitalism. Even socialists may concede the superiority of the free market as a system of *exchange*. They may even agree that the free market properly results in some limits upon government and in some of the good features of a liberal polity. But they still do not accept capitalism.[28] Accepting the market principle—and calling the result social market democracy—they may still wish to build certain moral preferences into economic activities over and beyond the freedom of the market. They may wish to build public housing, give income supplements to the poor, provide health care from public funds, and the like. Since these things may also be done under democratic capitalism—which is not an economic system merely— socialists at this point are not so easy to distinguish from those who approve of social welfare programs on nonsocialist grounds. Many "neo-conservatives" like Irving Kristol and "neo-liberals" like Senator Daniel Patrick Moynihan—the differences between the two deserve to be remarked—remain committed to social-welfare democratic capitalism. They may be as critical of governmental abuse and corruption as socialists are of abuses and corruption in the large corporations. But they ground their own vision of social welfare, not in socialism, but in the imperatives of the moral-cultural system of democratic capitalism. Thus, beyond social welfare, socialists need to stake out new ground of their own. Some call the new socialist ideal "economic democracy," by which they mean the submission of the economic system (or at least the large corporations and financial institutions) to political controls. They may accept some limits upon government action over markets, especially for farmers, cooperatives, and small businesses, and some institutions of the liberal polity. But they do not accept the separation of the political system from the economic system. In the name of the moral-cultural values of socialism, they desire to subordinate the economic system to the political system, thus collapsing the triune order of democratic capitalism into the unitary order of socialism. They say that this unitary socialist order will be "decentralized" and "democratic." If so, it will encounter the same diffusion of choices as does the free market. In order to effect socialist values, they will eventually have to use the coercive powers of the state.

Theologically speaking, the free market and the liberal polity follow from liberty of conscience. Yet those religious persons who prefer the public enforcement of virtue find obvious attractions in socialism. What censorship is to free speech, the command economy is to the free market. What an established religion is to a traditional society, a collective moral vision publicly imposed is to a socialist society. There will not be wanting Christian, Jewish, and secular socialists to whom a socialist society promises methods of suffusing their views throughout every activity which no free society affords them.

In this sense, a defense of the free market is, first, a defense of efficiency, productivity, inventiveness, and prosperity. It is also a defense of the free conscience—free not only in the realm of the spirit, and not only in politics, but also in the economic decisions of everyday life. It is, thirdly, a defense of the pluralist order of democratic capitalism against the unitary and commanded order of socialism.

The image of God underlying socialist thought is *Nous:* the all-seeing, commanding intelligence. The image of God underlying both the free market and the triune system of democratic capitalism is *Phronimos,* the practical provident intelligence embodied in singular agents in singular concrete situations.

3
An Invisible Hand?

Critics of the market seldom fail to mock the fabled "invisible hand" mentioned by Adam Smith. The unaware are led to imagine that the invisible hand looms large in Adam Smith's writings. Actually, Smith uses this metaphor but twice, each time briefly and glancingly, once in *The Theory of Moral Sentiments* and once in *An Inquiry into the Nature and the Cause of the Wealth of Nations*.[29] The latter book numbers 903 pages, and if one looks hard for it, one will find the offending expression on page 423 in a chapter on "Restraints on Particular Imports." It enters the discussion casually.

> As every individual, therefore, endeavours as much as he can both to employ his capital in the support of domestic industry, and so to direct that industry that its produce may be of the greatest value; every individual necessarily labours to render the annual revenue of the society as great as he can. He generally, indeed, neither intends to promote the public interest, nor knows how much he is promoting it. By preferring the support of domestic to that of foreign industry, he intends only his own security; and by directing that industry in such a manner as its produce may be of the greatest value, he intends only his own gain, and he is in this, as in many other cases, led by an invisible hand to promote an end which was no part of his intention. Nor is it always the worse for the society that it was no part of it. By pursuing his own interest he frequently promotes that of the society more effectually than when he really intends to promote it. I have never known much good done by those who affect to trade for the public good. It is an affectation, indeed, not very common among merchants, and very few words need be employed in dissuading them from it.[30]

Why should an *in*visible hand be so objectionable? Undoubtedly, the critics mean to suggest that no such hand exists and that the phrase is a piece of mystification. Is it?

What sort of thing would we be looking for in searching for an invisible hand? The metaphor occurs in an argument in favor of free international markets. The "hand" we are looking for, then, is not coercive. The metaphor, simply put, draws attention to unintended consequences. The *motives* of individuals, it suggests, are not the same as the *social consequences* of their actions. The logic of economic behavior lies on a plane different from that of the logic of motives. Actually, the socialist conception of "structural sin" makes a similar point. Regardless of the moral rectitude of individual agents, socialists say, *the system* of which they are a part leads to injustice. One must inspect the "invisible hand" of the system, not simply the visibly expressed motives of its participants. Whether one regards it as sinful or as beneficial, there is in any case a system, a logic, an order, beneath the seeming individuality of individual choices. This is Smith's central point.

Market systems are not, then, as anarchic as intuition may lead one to suppose. Buyers may have motives of limitless variety and may intend quite personal consequences. Sellers may have an equally broad array of motives and intentions. Yet this vast array of purposes somehow results in orderly kinds of behavior which reduce many economic activities to rather dull routines. Indeed, while much imagination and risk may go into inventing new products, or into finding new ways to bring products into new markets, the inherent tendency of economic systems is to establish orderly, dependable routines. One critic may accuse market systems of anarchy, and another may accuse them of lock-step regimentation. It is worth noting, though, that markets do tend to allow greater freedom than traditional or command economies, while at the same time producing dependable routines. Food arrives in the stores, taxis move on the streets, offices open like clockwork. Those who fear anarchy must find nine-to-five boredom the marvel. Those who fear overorganization—"Do not bend, fold, mutilate, or staple"—must marvel at the novelties, varieties of motivations, and liberties of choice that abound.

The order provided by markets differs from the order provided by command. In dealing with government agencies, citizens come to expect to wait in line. In dealing with markets, they expect efficiency as a right and resent waiting in line as an affront. The reason this is so is that market exchanges are voluntary. Besides, markets are expected to process information with great rapidity and encapsulate it as price. One expects to step up, pay the price (or turn away from it), and go.

Interestingly enough, then, a system which on the face of it leaves historically unprecedented liberty to economic agents—both in supply and in demand—and which involves an array of motives as complex as the mixed motives of millions of individuals, remains orderly. The order is far from perfect. Yet, compared to other systems, an amazing array of complex functions seems to work. A market system embodies order, on a level different from the level of the motives and intentions of those who make it happen. This is one meaning for the metaphor "led by an invisible hand."

But there is a second meaning as well. The order which emerges from an aggregate of decisions made by individuals may turn out, surprisingly, to be more rational than any order imposed by rational planners. The reason the hand is "invisible" is that the rationality of a market is not commanded. If naked intelligence were omniscient, planners could plan in advance the appropriate levels of supply and demand. No such intelligence is in sight. The order which results from individuals' acting upon their own judgments is quite remarkable—so remarkable that it *seems* "led by an invisible hand." But, of course, there is no such hand. An intelligible order there plainly is, but not commanded by anyone's hand, nor consciously intended by anyone's intellect.

To think that for order to exist there must be commands may seem obvious. Persons of socialist temperament frequently publish books with titles like *Who Runs America?* and *Who Rules America?* They search eagerly for "interlocking directorates," "corporate elites," and "commanding heights of the economy." In a sense, the parable of the invisible hand is a parable told for persons of such a temperament. It is a bit of red meat tossed out to those who cannot grasp that order may emerge on its own from the exercise of liberty. Were such order impossible, democracy itself would be impossible. Human liberty would be a euphemism for anarchy. Religious liberty would empty the churches and make unity of belief depend upon coercion.

4
Profit and Commercial Values

While markets encourage the exercise of choice, they stand accused of corrupting morals. Money, markets, and profits are thisworldly, not otherworldly, terms. They seem to symbolize Mammon, and to run against the perfectionist strain in Christianity. As Irving Kristol has pointed out, certain Christian traditions reflect hostility to commerce unknown in Jewish traditions.[31] Just as some forms of Christianity have harbored excessively negative attitudes toward sex, so some also harbor negative attitudes toward monetary commerce. In particular, the long tradition of hostility toward lending money for profit ("usury")[32] seems to have spilled over into moral antipathy toward profit. "Is the profit motive compatible with humane purposes?" is for some a slow-pitch question whose answer is in the resounding negative.

Yet commerce is not without its own moral structure. The inventors of democratic capitalism—Montesquieu, John Adams, Adam Smith, Benjamin Franklin, Benjamin Rush, James Madison, Thomas Jefferson, and others were not themselves primarily men of commerce or manufacturing. They saw clearly both the perennial abuses typical of commercial life and the deficiencies even of its virtues. Such matters, known to Homer and Vergil, are reflected in ancient proverbs like *Caveat emptor* (Let the buyer beware). In trying to imagine a "new order," the founders of democratic capitalism considered the historical record. They found serious structural difficulties in the civic orders of ancient Greece and Rome, in those of the Holy Roman Empire, and in the various *anciens regimes* of their experience. In the old regimes, "the king had his glory, the nobles their honor, the Christians their salvation, the citizens of pagan antiquity their ambition."[33] In all such orders, privileges were preserved for too few. Contemplating the historical parade of aristocratic pretension, religious persecution, cults of heroism and glory, and the public presumption of deference to the powerful, the founders of democratic capitalism thought these bred "extravagant rashness and folly," and were at bottom "absurd."[34] Although each of the old orders of political economy appealed to high ideals of disinterestedness, nobility, and honor, these masked much "avidity and injustice" in high places. Based upon human ideals too high for the ordinary mundane business of life, their perfectionism was out of touch with reality. Under their influence, over many centuries, the lot of the ordinary mass of humanity had scarcely advanced at all.

The old orders endowed each man of high birth and inherited status with false notions of "self-sufficiency and absurd conceit of his own superiority."[35] They sold too short the capacities of commoners to direct their own activities, to form their own practical judgments, and to make their own choices. Moreover, they overlooked the tremendous economic potential of practicality, inventiveness, and enterprise on the part of free individuals.

Aristocratic pride produces no wealth, Adam Smith argued.[36] Even from situations of great original wealth, it produces laziness, extravagance, poverty, and ruin. Spain and Portugal did not become rich from the enormous wealth they expropriated from the mines of South America; they were propelled, instead, upon historical decline. Aristocratic taste with its preference for elegance may generate high art, works of beauty, palaces and churches ornately decorated in silver and gold. But, corrupting practical wisdom, it in the end impoverishes.

Thus, the founding fathers rejected aristocratic morals in favor of the common, the useful, the mundane. Favorite words in their new vocabulary were common sense and utility, which they thought to be in tune with the plain teaching of the gospels. In the essay of which I have been making extensive use in this section, Ralph Lerner speaks not of democratic capitalism but of "the commercial republic," a republic which places the moral qualities required for successful commerce at the center of its social life. In such a republic, commerce is by no means the whole of life. Yet in it commerce is given greater freedom, and its prospering is made to be more central to the purposes of the state than in any previous form of civic order.

The ethic of commerce furnishes a school of virtue favorable to democratic governance. This ethic is not pretentious in its conception of reason and human nature. It enhances the cooperative spirit, since economic tasks cannot be accomplished by one person alone. It increases attention to law. It singles out the self-determination of the individual as the main source of social energy. It places limits on the state and other authorities. It incites imagination and industry. It disciplines all to common sense. It teaches respect for "an exact attention to small savings and small gains"[37] which, in turn, are the single most significant engine of sustained economic growth, since progress takes place at the margins and depends upon increments of new investment and new invention. It breaks the grip of those high utopian ideals of earlier civic orders which, while pretending to represent Reason in one or another of its lofty forms, proved in fact to be so impoverishing for real people. It is a system in tune with emergent probability, the limitations of human intelligence, and the unreliability of the human heart. The ethic of commerce is proportioned to man as he is, not as dreams would have him, and plainly appeared to the founders to support "the natural system of liberty and justice."

Early travelers to America observed this "new order" in practice. De Tocqueville noted that everywhere in America citizens were "calculating and weighing and computing."[38] Since practical intelligence yields tangible progress, men and women had an incentive to acquire it, to become savvy, to develop each of their crafts to new heights of inventiveness and effect. In Europe, the code of the gentleman required that one not appear to be too industrious, intent, or sweaty in one's work; everything, it was thought, ought to appear effortless, spontaneous, natural. In America, the market taught men and women to roll up their sleeves, to dirty their hands, and to shrug off "that inconsiderate contempt for practice" typical of aristocrats.[39] European attitudes may have required contempt for crass practicalities and respect for loftiness of station. In America, even the landed gentry took pride in physical labor and attention to practical detail.

Religion, too, was brought down to earth by the new American order. De Tocqueville commented. "In the very midst of their zeal one generally sees something so quiet, so methodical, so calculated that it would seem that the head rather than the heart leads them to the foot of the altar."[40] Montesquieu blamed churchmen for their centuries-long condemnations of commerce and the misfortunes they thus visited upon common people. He blamed them even more for fanning the flames of intolerance, including the persecution of the Jews, and for glorifying ideals too perfectionist for ordinary life. John Adams was equally hard on the emphasis of the ancient Greeks upon virtue, particularly of an aristocratic sort; Sparta, in particular, distorted humans beyond recognizable shape, "destitute of all business, pleasure, and amusement, but war and politics, pride and ambition."[41] "Commerce cures destructive prejudices," Montesquieu wrote; it "polishes and softens barbaric morals." It makes men less provincial and more humane. "The spirit of commerce unites nations." Commercial nations seek gain, not conquest, and gain in the long term rests on mutual satisfaction through voluntary exchange. Commerce obliges nations to be "pacific from principle."[42] Commerce "diminishes the spirit both of patriotism and military defense," Thomas Paine wrote.[43] Benjamin Rush viewed it as "the means of uniting the different nations of the world together by the ties of mutual writs and obligations."[44] David Hume wrote that in a commercial civilization, as opposed to a martial, aristocratic, or religious civilization, "Factions are then less inveterate, revolutions less tragical, authority less severe, and seditions less frequent."[45] Free to pursue their own happiness, he hoped, individuals would become less ferocious and brutish than their ancestors. He believed that commerce gives "authority and consideration to that middling rank of men, who are the best and firmest in public liberty."[46] For Adam Smith, whereas men had before "lived almost in a continual state of war with their neighbors, and of servile dependency upon their supervisors," under a system committed to commerce they might enjoy "order and good government and, with them, the liberty and security of individuals."[47]

A commercial civilization breaks the monopoly of public service enjoyed by the great. Even the humblest person has opportunity both to improve his station and to enrich the republic. Ambition courses through millions who, under other regimes, would seem sullen and inert. Individuals set goals for themselves—to be a master carpenter, or foreman, or linesman, whatever each might rationally aspire to—and enjoy the satisfaction of self-improvement, whereas the aristocrat "shudders with horror at the thought of . . . continued and long exertion of patience, industry, fortitude and application of thought."[48] More romantic social orders stimulate great passions, de Tocqueville observed, but citizens in a commercial republic exhibit love of order, regard for conventional morality, distrust of genius, and preference for the practical over the theoretical. "Violent political passions have little hold on men whose whole thoughts are bent on the pursuit of well being. Their excitement about small matters makes them calm about great ones."[49] But this is not exactly right. For trade and navigation are seen to be surrogates for war. Great deeds and heroic exertions are borne, not solely for the self, but usually for family and often for the pure achievement of the thing. The man of commerce treats all of life "like a game of chance, a time of revolution, or the day of a battle."[50] Building industries where none stood before yields creative satisfactions.

In the new order, ordinary people feel a lift in self-esteem. Their aspirations realistically reach higher than their fathers'. Their efforts, not in every case but in a sufficiently large number of cases, have continued to be rewarded. Their personal goals, if proportional to their abilities, have a good chance of being realized. Self-realization becomes a common aim. Commerce also teaches that no one can be right all the time, since nearly all sometimes experience failure. The market puts a ceiling on ambition, proportional to each. Not all succeed equally. Luck and timing play important roles. The market raises up many who under other regimes were last, and tumbles many who in earlier regimes were first. New cycles of progress and technological development continue this process. The resulting social system is highly mobile and fluid, compared to others.

A market system entails great human losses. For realists, this was a foregone conclusion. Montesquieu counted the cost of old communal ties, which would be replaced by the less effective ties of mutual interests in liberty and order.[51] Adam Smith was even more aware of the human losses to be expected. The new order would narrow and demean the human spirit, such that the "heroic spirit" would be "almost entirely extinguished."[52] The rapacity of some merchants would lead them to try to close open markets through monopolistic practices. Competitive markets are not sustained by magic; they must be maintained through vigilance on the part of the public and the state.[53] The division of labor would force some into tasks that would mutilate their minds, encourage gross ignorance and stupidity, and corrupt "the nobler parts of human character."[54] Society would have to find compensatory means to redress these injustices; the market alone would not do that. Moreover, since every virtue may be corrupted, the commercial virtues may degenerate into avarice, social meanness, cowardice, and hedonism. Since the greater dangers lay in the indolence and extravagance of aristocracy, in the intolerance of the clergy, and in the despotism of the state, these costs can be borne; but they must be seen to be costs.

Finally, the success of democratic capitalism in producing prosperity and liberty is its own greatest danger. The virtues required to "increase the wealth of nations" are less easily observed once wealth is attained. Parents brought up under poverty do not know how to bring up children under affluence. Moreover, as more and more citizens are taken from productive work and their own non-profit work is supported by the productivity of others, new vested interests are established. A new sort of social aristocracy is born, not through inherited status, but through professional interests and ambitions. As "the new class" of commerce took center stage in 1776, so later a "new class" of intellectuals—so Schumpeter saw[55]—would try to dominate the commercial class by seizing the power of the state. De Tocqueville had foreseen that the passion for equality inherent in the new order might lead, in time, "to servitude or freedom, knowledge or barbarism, prosperity or wretchedness."[56]

The commercial virtues are not, then, sufficient to their own defense. A commercial system needs taming and correction by a moral-cultural system independent of commerce. At critical points, it also requires taming and correction by the political system and the state. The founding fathers did not imagine that the institutions of religion, humanism, and the arts would ever lose their indispensable role. They did not imagine that the state would wither away. Each of the three systems needs the other.

Yet they did understand that an economic system without profit is merely spinning its wheels, providing neither for the unmet needs of the poor nor for progress. Even "small gains and small savings" have extraordinary impact. A growth rate averaging just 2 percent a year was sustained in Great Britain from 1780 until 1914,[57] and made that tiny nation the world's leading power. To have invented a system capable of such sustained development was a gain for humanity. For in the wake of economic development came political and moral-cultural developments of great importance, including a great flowering of individual possibility, the arts, and good works (including many not for profit).

Thus, neither commercial virtues nor profits are merely economic in their character or in their effects. On the other hand, they are not sufficient for a full human life. They play an indispensable role in the achievement of the common good, and societies which lack them struggle in swamps of hopelessness unknown to those that possess them. One may believe the commercial virtues to be less than the highest of virtues, but it is not contrary to biblical faith to honor them for their instrumental role.

5
The Zero-Sum Society

The zero-sum game is really the most ancient way of thinking, found in all primitive societies and highly exaggerated in peasant mentality.

—Jack D. Douglas, "The Welfare State
as a Zero-Sum Game"[58]

"Economic activity," writes Thomas Wilson in a volume commemorating the bicentennial of Adam Smith's *Wealth of Nations,* "is not a zero-sum game, although there may be a deeply rooted inclination, especially in Britain, to suppose that it is so."[59] Belief in zero-sum society, Milton Friedman writes in *Free to Choose,* is the source of most economic fallacies. To fall into it, one must overlook Adam Smith's key insight, which is "misleadingly simple: if an exchange between two parties is voluntary, it will not take place unless both believe they will benefit from it. Most economic fallacies derive from the neglect of this simple insight, from the tendency to assume that there is a fixed pie, that one party can gain only at the expense of another."[60] A few months after Milton Friedman's book appeared, Lester Thurow published *The Zero-Sum Society,* an elegant description of how a society which increasingly adopts socialist goals and socialist purposes falls back into the zero-sum game. The drive for economic security, he suggests, represents the spirit of socialism:

As we deliver economic security, we undercut the implicit

assumptions of capitalism, democracy, and individual initiative. Economic failure won't hurt, because failures will be protected by government. This both reduces the rate of economic progress and removes the rationale for having capitalism in the first place. If government protects and controls, it might just as well own.[61]

Reflection on the socialist ethos helps to illuminate, by contrast, the ethos Adam Smith hoped to generate.

Suppose that there are two deeply rooted psychological tendencies in the human breast, one self-protective and inward-turning, the other rooted in what Erik Erickson calls "basic trust," outward-going and ready to take risks.[62] The capitalist ethos, based on self-improvement and growth, is founded on the latter. The socialist ethos, based on the quest for security and equality, springs from the former. The contrast between West Berlin and East Berlin is startling. West Berlin is bright, dazzling, busy, flamboyant, lacking in the restraint proper to the moral virtues. East Berlin is no more conspicuous for virtue, but its activity is far more sluggish, its light more wan, its people far more inward-turning. This contrast is repeated between other sectors of the democratic capitalist and socialist worlds; between South Korea and North Korea; between Hong Kong (or Taiwan) and mainland China; between Vienna and Bratislava; between the Havana of old and Castro's Havana. Moreover, advances in the desire for equality and security within Western nations, as in Great Britain, appear to bring with them the "zero-sum game" Professor Thurow sees descending upon the United States. Socialism *is* a zero-sum game. Democratic capitalism is not.

The impulse toward security is aversive to risk and creativity. At an extreme, it is an impulse aversive even to liberty. As John Dewey wrote in *The Quest for Certainty,*[63] certainty can be won only at the price of stifling empirical science and experimental method. In a world of emergent probability, risks cannot be avoided by an attempt to make the world predictable and safe. Such an attempt runs against the grain of things. It has a paralyzing effect on investment, research, experimental probes, advances in productivity, and progress itself. A people committed to security constricts the circle of its future.

A society in which all have identical incomes is not necessarily a just society. The attempt to achieve it is certain to have many evil consequences, some intended and some unintended. Among *intended* consequences are a restriction of liberty and the expansion of the coercive powers of the state. Further, the attempt to impose equality of incomes changes the focus of economic activity from production to distribution. This is a reversion to premodern economic conceptions. Such a step backward is certain to reduce savings, investment, and productivity. It necessarily results in a society more static than a free society. Concern for equal opportunity is consistent with incentives and inequalities. Concern for equal results is not. The latter must produce a zero-sum game. If rewards are by allocation, all will be living in dependency.

Among the *unintended* consequences of the pursuit of equality of results is a heightening of sullenness and resentment. A society judged less upon its dynamism, opportunities, liberties, and mobilities and more upon the equal allocation of its benefits feeds the fires of envy it is presumably intended to quiet. Its procedures of allocation are necessarily bureaucratic, legal, and general. They therefore focus attention upon group characteristics rather than upon individual performance. In practice, allocative systems give superior benefits to those groups with superior organizational power. In Great Britain, certain labor unions exert such power. In U.S. cities, now that local "machines" have lost their clout, municipal unions fill the vacuum on election day, for a price. It does not seem that the promise of security and equality has rendered the populations of Great Britain, or other jurisdictions where socialist principles have been put into effect, happier or more content.

It is a mistake to base one's hopes for happiness upon the enforcement of security and equality. *In principle*, both desires are insatiable. Both run counter to the human condition. No individual or society is secure in a world of emergent probability and sin; and the talents with which human beings are endowed are unequal. The desires for security and equality run counter, further, to the requirements of liberty. To exercise liberty is to take risks, to embrace uncertainties, and to arrive at variable outcomes. Finally, one speaks of the "pursuit" of happiness precisely because happiness transcends each present moment. Successful persons, then, are not likely to be "happy" with their relative success. The poor in America are not likely to observe that they are rich by comparison with a majority of persons elsewhere. Even the wealthiest and most powerful persons are likely to feel envious, in some respects, of some others. One must expect human beings, whatever their achievements or their status, to compare their lot, not to that of those with less than they have, but to infinite possibility. Happiness with material achievements is unobtainable, except through renunciation and detachment, as the Stoics long ago saw.

Societies designed to bring security and equality are, on those terms, foredoomed to failure. They cannot effect the security and equality they are pledged to effect. Worse, even if they could, that achievement would not suffuse their populations with happiness, contentment, or a sense of justice achieved.

By contrast, democratic capitalism aims at the widest possible diffusion of liberty. It recognizes that individuals exhibit incredible variety from person to person, and that some cultures, better than others, prepare their participants to embrace liberty of opportunity with intelligence, verve, and demonstrable effect.

By pursuing a course of liberty, democratic capitalism in the United States escaped the age-old tyranny of the zero-sum game. Instead of focusing attention upon sources of envy and resentment, democratic capitalism focuses upon future possibilities. Ideally, it permits no single person to feel trapped, except by his own misjudgments or actions. It does not promise equal futures for every group. But it does promise opportunity for every group and for every individual. It does not presume that all individuals and all groups have equal capacities for seizing such opportunities. It does not expect all to succeed equally. Those who lack *opportunity* for self-advancement have a legitimate grievance against its promises. Those who can demonstrate *unequal results* have no such legitimate grievance. A free society is necessarily committed to unequal results. For under conditions of liberty, individuals as well as groups make different choices and follow divergent paths.

In a stagnant, no-growth society, the same pie must be divided generation by generation. In a dynamic, growing society, three different characteristics appear. First, even if the relative position of each family stays the same (in fact, it does not), all enjoy better futures. Secondly, the dynamism of growth erodes the technological base on which the wealth of some families is based and throws up new technologies and new sources of wealth. Thirdly, the dynamic churning of technologies and elites creates many open spaces for multitudes who are neither the owners of industry nor the inventors of new processes or products. Opportunities appear by serendipity and by foresight, by fortune and by intelligent preparation. In a society committed to growth, even when the relative proportions of income shared by various percentiles of the population remain constant, the *individuals* and *families* represented within these percentiles change. Some individuals rise from one percentile to another, others decline. But an even stronger point may be made: Democratic capitalist societies improve the relative equality of percentiles, and show a more equitable distribution than traditional societies.[64]

To be sure, growth by itself does not guarantee equality of opportunity. What it does guarantee is larger future sums, so that all at every level may have reasonable hopes of material improvement in their condition, if they do what is in them to do. More important, the reality of growth permits attention to be focused on the future, while in the zero-sum game it is withdrawn to the present. Ironically, socialists, who once dreamed of the cooperative society, are counseling against resentment and bitter group conflict over the cutting of a fixed pie. Socialists have come to be partisans of restricted horizons, while those who cherish the ideals of democratic capitalism are intent upon changing the future.

It is sometimes argued against the existence of Providence that, being omnipotent and omniscient, a good God would have created a world more just than this. The fact that a democratic capitalist society does not produce a perfectly just world may also be held against it. It is obviously not the City of God or the New Jerusalem. Yet the foregoing reflections on practical matters like time, the market, the so-called invisible hand, profit, and the zero-sum society do indicate that, while democratic capitalism is not utopian, its institutions embody a practical wisdom worthy of admiration, whose relative virtues attract migrants from all parts of the world. Often, with the faith of converts, these see its ethos with fresh eyes and pay it honor, even though they see its faults quite clearly. By not claiming as much as its rivals, and by doggedly working to fulfill what it does claim, democratic capitalism represents a plain sort of wisdom suited to this world. It shows practical concern for economic development, whose urgent relevance aristocrats and clergymen tend to underestimate. It also generates new forms of community. Here, too, it turns up new problems and addresses them in new ways. It is a creation as unfinished as God's.

VI
Community

The liberal ideology . . . asserts itself in the name of economic efficiency for the defense of the individual against the increasingly overwhelming hold of organizations, and as a reaction against the totalitarian tendencies of political powers. Certainly, personal initiative must be maintained and developed. But do not Christians who take this path tend to idealize liberalism in their turn . . . while easily forgetting that at the very root of philosophical liberalism is an erroneous affirmation of the autonomy of the individual in his activity, his motivation and the exercise of his liberty?
— Pope Paul VI, *Octogesima Adveniens*[1]

The meaning of community in traditional societies is clear, even if tinted rose with nostalgia. It is the community of the small village, in which all share the same values. Such images are like memories of childhood. We long—impossibly—to experience them again.

In religious circles, democratic capitalist societies—sometimes called "liberal" societies—are accused of disrupting the traditional sense of community, which they do, and of denying the social nature of human beings, which they do not. The popes have approached democratic capitalist societies as if they were "Protestant"—individualistic, anarchic.

Some proponents of democratic capitalism do carry radical individualism to ridiculous extremes. No doubt, too, a pluralistic society differs dramatically from a traditional society, and religious understandings often seem nostalgic for the latter. Yet pluralistic societies develop their own powerful forms of community, overlooked by those who share traditionalist or socialist assumptions. We must look afresh at democratic capitalist practice—but first at elements of its forgotten theory.

1
The Forgotten Theory

The very structure of democratic capitalism—even its impersonal economic system—is aimed at community, not of course in the nostalgic sense of *Gemeinschaft,* but at a new order of community, the community of free persons in voluntary association.

There are four fundamental elements in the structure of democratic capitalism which lead to new forms of community. These elements belong to the system *qua* system, independently of the motives and attitudes of those who participate in it.

(1) *World development.* The dynamics of the economic system are aimed—in the phrase of Adam Smith—not at the wealth of individuals and not at the wealth of Scotland or Great Britain, but at the wealth of all nations. The intention of the system *qua* system is to raise the material base of the life of every human being on earth. It is a system designed to unleash the powers found within every human individual. It instructs nations as well as individuals to seek development of their own wealth. It awakens individuals and nations to their own capacities for imagination, self-improvement, and growth.

These are not the only ideals now cherished by the human race. But they are accessible to all human beings without exception. Even in the teaching of great socialist leaders—notably Mao Tsetung—self-reliance has found an honored place. Archbishop Roger Heckel entitles one of his seminal commentaries on the teachings of Pope Paul VI and Pope John Paul II *Self-Reliance.*[2] This pamphlet is as close as the Vatican has come to articulating one of the major ideals of democratic capitalism in an international context.

Thus, with the birth of democratic capitalism, an international dream of justice entered the world. Every nation without exception has been called to develop its own wealth. No longer are the peoples of the world expected to respond with passive resignation to poverty, famine, and an average human mortality of under thirty years, or with the despair dramatized in Brueghel's paintings of the plagues and rapine of early-medieval Europe. No longer are the world's peoples to conceive of justice as resignation to implacable fate.

Democratic capitalism discovered the secret to sustained economic development for all nations. It uncovered heretofore unsuspected capacities for production. Most of the ideals now regnant throughout the world are ideals which first emerged under democratic capitalism in the West: development, modernization, social justice, national liberation, independence, self-reliance, etc.[3] These ideals were thought from the beginning to be universal. It was also thought that the advance of every part of humankind advanced the benefit of all.

Thus when after World War II the economies of Japan and Europe lay in shambles, it was not only in the interest of the United States to assist in their rapid recovery, it was also a fundamental imperative of the system. The fact that today the economies of Japan and Western Europe rival that of the United States is a happy outcome. It is expected that by the 1990s, the economy of a consortium of nations in Southeast Asia—Japan, Taiwan, Hong Kong, South Korea, Singapore, and others—may approximate the highest living standards in the world. Meanwhile, the invention of the piston engine and the techniques of oil recovery have conferred enormous wealth on oil-producing nations in the Middle East, Nigeria, Mexico, Venezuela, and elsewhere. These and other developments are neither unfavorable to the United States nor contrary to the ideals of a system committed to increasing the wealth of all nations. Only when every nation is able to take its place in a system of law and progress will those ideals be realized. Their intention is social and universal.

(2) *The corporation.* The system of democratic capitalism brought into prominence a novel social instrument: the voluntary association committed to business enterprise, the corporation.

The assumption behind this invention is social, not individualistic. It holds that economic activity is fundamentally corporate, exceeding the capacity of any one individual alone. It requires a social life form which goes beyond the power and the lifetime of one individual. This cooperative principle is essential to a capitalist economic system.

To begin with, investors pool their resources. They must then develop social organizations to make concrete business decisions. Social forms for owners and for managers come to be differentiated. There are some social losses to this procedure. Thus business corporations, at least when they expand, frequently lose the familial, paternalistic direction of a single family. If they further attempt to raise capital by offering shares to the general public, they become by that degree more "impersonal." By treating them as legal persons, emergent corporate law disengages the state from their workings. If a company fails (and most do), the losses are borne by the investors. Thus, at least in earlier generations, when all corporations were relatively small, the public purse was not implicated in their failure. From this arrangement, the state gained much useful experimentation, private energy, and productive capacity. The wealth of the nation was improved without any commitment of public funds.

This is not the place for a long disquisition on the growth of corporations and the complex relations of states and private corporations.[4] The important point to underline is the *corporate* character of economic enterprise. Its corporate nature is not what the ideology of "the rugged individual" leads one to anticipate.

Consider the life of the chief executive officer of a large corporation. A high proportion of his time is spent in making decisions about personnel and in conveying a spirit of unity, coordination, and morale throughout a farflung organization. Many of the decisions to be reached involve kinds of expertise beyond his own. These become, necessarily, team decisions. Such a manager can scarcely be an autocrat. He must have the trust of many and must inspire many. The more his actions are inspired by all the moral virtues, not excluding all that is intended by the Christian concept of *caritas*,* the better his relations with others will

*In English, charity—in the sense of a genuine, mature, realistic love for one's fellows. See Chapter XX.

be. He depends heavily on such relations, for he is relatively easily replaced. The average tenure in his office is about six years.

The immense literature on the problems of management today gives fascinating attention to human problems, employee relationships, and styles of personal communication. The industrial and commercial process is long and complex; a failure at any one point is a weak link in a chain. Unity of purpose is a necessary ideal. Ninety percent of a manager's problems, the textbooks say, are human problems.

The human problems within a large corporation are also faced by the heads of many other large organizations. In its special ethos, one order of religious men or women differs from another. So does one corporation differ from another. Industries differ in the types of persons and skills they attract. Some (chemicals, drugs, electronics) depend on large numbers of highly educated managers, many with doctoral degrees. Some depend on invention and research, and favor creative atmospheres like those of universities. The *culture* of specific industries and individual corporations requires much closer inspection than it is usually given. Problems of cooperation and morale differ in each.

From level to level within a corporation, forms of association are critical. Throughout the enterprise, the ability of workers and managers to improvise, to improve productivity, and to solve practical problems (which arise at every point along the way on an almost hourly basis) is highly significant. When managers are not close enough to the concrete actions of their employees, quality controls suffer. Some critics of U.S. auto manufacturers believe that precisely this sort of gap has arisen in recent years, with disastrous competitive results by comparison to foreign performance. The fault is fairly assigned to management.

A successful corporation is frequently based upon the principle of subsidiarity. According to this principle, concrete decisions must be made on the level closest to the concrete reality.[5] Managers and workers need to trust the skills of their colleagues. A corporate strategy which overlooks this principle—and many do—falls prey to all the vices of a command economy, in which all orders come from above. Corporate life places many constraints upon "rugged individualism," whether in executive offices or in the field. Many critics complain of excessive communal pressure and conformity. Corporate managers appear to meet together more often to discuss common strategies than do parish priests and bishops. By comparison with the degree of cooperation shown by corporate managers, professors of theology, philosophy, and literature seem to be rugged individualists indeed.

Because a corporation is not an instrument of the state, it does not follow that it lacks social form and social function. Only a few corporations have as many employees as the Jesuits have members or as large universities have faculties and staffs; none is as large an organization as the Methodist church. All such forms of community face problems of organization and morale specific to their large size. But all are, each in its way, communities. Within each are to be found horror stories of lapses in basic human virtue. Within each are also to be found much admirable social cohesion.

(3) *Interdependence*. From the beginning, the founders of corporations argued that a commercial civilization would outperform clerical, aristocratic, and military civilizations in making the world "interdependent." Nearly every breakthrough of technology and trade which has since made the world more like a "global village" was pioneered by the achievements of business corporations, from the airplane to the radio, television, and telecommunications.

Beginning with Lenin's book on imperialism, many critics, particularly in the Third World, have recognized the international community which democratic capitalism has brought into existence but have accused it of being malign. Today, especially in Latin America, critics hold that democratic capitalism proceeds by making smaller and more distant nations "dependent," just as the cities within which a market system first takes root tend to make the rural areas on the "periphery" dependent.[6] In deploring the international dynamism of democratic capitalism, such accusations nonetheless underline the social nature of the system.

Pius XI warned in 1931 that while exchange between equals may be fair because based upon mutual consent, exchange between peoples and institutions of unequal power is likely to be less so. Yet the pontiff hastened to add that all the various nations ought to promote "a healthy economic cooperation by prudent pacts and institutions, since in economic matters they are largely dependent one upon another, and need one another's help."[7]

The first theoreticians of democratic capitalism early grasped this interdependence. Their arguments for free trade did not depend upon the abolition of political respect and moral-cultural restraints. They argued that commerce and trade, of their very nature, must create an interdependent world, in which the logic of law and peaceable relations would suit the real interests of all. Since the short-term interests of nations would lead to protectionism, they did not think to banish sin and injustice. They hoped these would be mitigated, even more through the long-range mutual benefits of the system *qua* system than through short-term motives and intentions.

(4) *The ethos of cooperation.* The system *qua* system depends upon a community of values. Not just any values will do; particular values are required. When a Soviet flier defected with his jet to Japan, he was transported to the United States, in which he sought asylum, on an American aircraft carrier. He expressed his amazement at the way crewmen on the carrier cooperated in their duties, as if teamwork were second nature to them, without waiting for explicit orders. No such experience had been available to him in the Soviet armed forces.[8] Similarly, in many areas of life, the behavior of Americans makes sense only if one grasps the unifying ethos which they share. (The social cohesion of other democratic nations like Japan and Germany is still more remarkable.) In order to value social cooperation, it is not necessary for a people to be socialist. John Dewey argued that such cooperation is the essence both of democratic and of scientific life.[9] Indeed, only those cultures which nurture in their peoples inner social disciplines are capable of democratic politics and capitalist economies. Cultures in which individuals are not taught how to cooperate, compromise, and discipline themselves to practical communal tasks can make neither democratic politics nor market economies work.

These four elements are the backbone of the forms of community democratic capitalism has invented. They have made possible a new type of human being, neither an individualist nor a collectivist.

2
Community in Practice

Between individualism and collectivism, there is a third way: a rich pattern of association. Just because individuals are not collectivized it does not follow that they are not communal.

Thus, the Catholic philosopher Jacques Maritain reported his own shock on coming to know the United States. For him, capitalism had always been an evil word. In *Reflections on America,* he wrote: "The American economy is growing beyond capitalism, in the proper classical sense of this word." The United States has discovered a new direction "beyond capitalism and beyond socialism . . . personalist and community-minded at the same time." Under democratic capitalism—one from among the names he suggested to describe the new reality—"free enterprise and private ownership function now in a social context."[10]

Maritain's witness is important.[11] America as he experienced it was not as he had read about it. Like Maritain, each of us in our families has through experience a fund of knowledge about the system which is independent of books. Beyond ideology, there is experience. In a pluralistic system, such experience is amazingly various. The experience of the Irish in the United States is not exactly like that of the Poles, Italians, or Hispanics. The experience of individuals is more various still. Yet all such experience points to community.

For example, my wife and I found a memoir written some ninety years ago by an ancestor of hers. He was Charles E. Brown, the first Baptist missionary in the Iowa Territory, who journeyed westward with his family from upstate New York in 1842. One of the most stunning features of his memoir is that nearly all the daily activities he reports were cooperative and fraternal.[12] Families helped each other putting up homes and barns. Together, they built churches, schools, and common civic buildings. They collaborated to build roads and bridges. They took pride in being free persons, independent, and self-reliant; but the texture of their lives was cooperative and fraternal.

These pioneer experiences of fraternity were not unlike those of later waves of immigrants, who began coming to America about 1870, notably to the minefields and smaller industrial cities of the northeast. They too lived richly communal lives. They built fraternals, lodges, and associations of many sorts. They too built many of their own homes and common buildings. While it is true that many of them left Europe as individuals, breaking from their own families, their lives in America continued to be intensely familial and associative. Many were active in the labor unions. Virtually all were active in churches, clubs, and many other associations. The experience of my wife's family and mine were not, then, those of "rugged individuals" alone.

It is true that life in America was rather less tribal, less limited to kin, and less homogeneous than in Europe. Neighborhoods and villages tended to be "melting pots" or, as some were later to say, "little leagues of nations." Both the public and the parochial schools tended to unite persons of many diverse backgrounds and linguistic traditions. The idea of fraternity was sharply real. It was not without friction.

The great mobility and patterns of opportunity in America began, however, to change the nature and meaning of community. For many, there still remained many forms of *Gemeinschaft,* that closeness of belonging, kinship, and common memory and faith which their ancestors had known in Europe. Yet every American family has also known the experience of uprooting, often more than once, and virtually all have been aware that their neighbors and friends in the New World belong to kinship networks, cultures, religions, and races different from their own. Pluralism is part of everyday experience. The huge dislocations of World War II, moreover, dramatically introduced even previously distant groups of Americans to one another in military service, in travel, at work. Lads from mining towns and city ghettoes took basic training in the South, visited California, served abroad.

In the years following World War II, mobility and interchange increased. Through these changes, the American people in all their variety continued to manifest loyalties to family, to civic life, and to countless forms of association. Yet in their freedom they have also experienced much rupture of close ties, many separations, and significant loneliness.

One reason problems of community are so acute among Americans is that most of us live between two experiences. More than is commonly thought, a great many of us have known a strong familial, neighborhood, and village life. We are fairly close to the experience of traditional societies known to our grandparents. On the other hand, we know new liberties. This is especially true of those more highly educated professionals whose jobs may carry them anywhere in the nation or the world. Such freedom disciplines the human spirit to the kind of "detachment" which religious superiors used to preach to young priests and religious. The latter's frequent changes of assignment, they were instructed, would oblige them to be uprooted often and to disrupt close human associations many times. They would accept these disciplines for the common good and for their own inner development.

This example shows that "community" is a reality of many kinds. My wife often teases me that I could be happy anywhere, as long as I could have my books and some writing paper. This made me recognize that many of my best friends and kindred spirits—whose books I lug with me from place to place—have been dead for hundreds of years. There are real communities of the spirit, which we carry with us even in solitude. At the Catholic Mass, as in the Jewish sabbath services, one recalls consciously that one is part of a community stretching across thousands of years. Intimate proximity is not essential to community.

In our sentimental age, however, there is a tendency to desire a different sort of community, less a community of the spirit and the inner life than a community of sentiment, emotional support, and often expressed intimacy. Such communities are no doubt precious, but they are also often dubious, cloying, and imprisoning. Community is not a simple reality. The much celebrated "loss of community" is not, correspondingly, all loss.

There is one form of community worth stressing here. It is a community of colleagueship, task-oriented, goal-directed, freely entered into and freely left. Its members have much respect for each other, learn much from each other, come to expect truth from each other, and treat one another fairly. Still, they may not have much emotional attachment to each other, spend much time looking into each other's eyes for moral support, or be particularly intimate with one another. They may enjoy comradeship in fighting the same battles, in enduring together the slings of hostile fortune, and in taking up each other's necessities.

Such community is not like the closeness of medieval villagers, nor does it require having the same faith, world view, or vision of reality. There are "bands of brothers" who do not occupy the same metaphysical ground. Add to this form of community many years of comradeship, growing mutual esteem, and the competitive urging of each other to new heights of development, and one experiences within it a form of friendship not unknown to the ancients, yet quite distinctively modern. For much modern work requires intense collaboration over long periods of time with skilled and dedicated colleagues. Democratic capitalism is not, I think, inferior in nurturing many such communities. Sports offer an approximation through extended experiences of teamwork. Later life goes far beyond sports.

Thus, in discussing community, I have found it useful to ask: Acording to which ideal? The sorts of community known to villages and neighborhoods are quite admirable, but they have their own limitations and liabilities. Affective communities which seek to vibrate together on compatible wavelengths also have their attractions and their limits. Collective solidarity seems strong and ennobling; yet it renders dissent and individual difference suspect. Communities of "joy, love and hope"—to cite the words of one contemporary Catholic hymn—inspire gladness but seem superficial. (Psalms of grief, enmity, and despair strike me as truer, deeper, more reliable.)

In order to experience the community of colleagueship, one needs an ethos deeper than individualism and collectivism, an ethos of association, teamwork, and collaboration, oriented by tasks and goals, voluntarily entered into. The ethos of democratic capitalism is rich in such encouragement. This is not the only form of community, but it is a noble one. It is not, however, given. It must be created.

Thus the social life of Americans remains so associative that it is often difficult to get parents and children to sit down together for one meal each day. Eight-year-olds belong to more groups than two parents can supply drivers for. During political campaigns, strangers from all parts of the country converge on states like Iowa and New Hampshire and, without delay, establish patterns of teamwork and swift cooperation.

Some critics accuse Americans of too little individualism. They sometimes describe Americans as too highly organized, too quick to be "joiners," too socially activist, too conformist. David Riesman's famous book *The Lonely Crowd* suggested that too few

Americans show that firm inner backbone, that inner-directedness, which used to be the hallmark of one type of individualism.[13] Many are too "other-directed," too quick to take their signals from their associates. The group instinct is too strong.

I have had occasion to visit my mother's family high in the mountains of eastern Slovakia. From the hilltops, on a clear day, one can see into Poland toward Krakow, at one time the greatest trading center in Europe. By sheer chance, I discovered in a sheepherder's hut at some distance from the village some colored pages from an old Sears catalog nailed to the rude walls. The shepherd offered me a cut of goat's cheese on his knife. As he talked, he revealed that he had been born in America in the same hospital in the same city in the same year as I had. His father had brought him home to Slovakia as a child, and the war had prevented their return.

It was impossible not to know that there had been significant transformations between the life forms of those rural villages and those of the cities of the United States (or of Kosice or Bratislava, for that matter). Yet I could not bring myself to feel that the advantages of living in the United States were solely material. I know and value the quality of the lives of those I met in the villages of Brutovce and Dubrava. Yet I felt profoundly grateful to my migrant grandparents for *spiritual* privileges, precisely for a thicker and richer social existence than was possible in the mountain villages of my ancestors.

I do not mean to pen a rhapsody to the social life of America. There is much wrong with it. Yet it would be wrong to be entirely silent about the distinctive forms of community it does build. The experiences America has given to my family, and to many millions of other families, have been so rich in opportunity, in possibility, in dream, that they cannot easily be fathomed. The enormous wealth produced by a free system sometimes masks these social benefits from our sight.

In *Socialism,* Michael Harrington observes that many of the spiritual realities intended by the name "socialism" have been realized under another name, the name "America."[14] Among these are not only political democracy and opportunity, but also marvelously strong traditions of family and association, cooperation and fraternity. A pluralistic society, in particular, draws out in each of us skills in tolerance, collaboration, and mutual respect that are all the more remarkable when compared to the still-bitter antagonisms between groups, religions, and cultures in the lands from which we are derived.

Still, the transition from the village life we remember through our parents and grandparents to the looser associations of our own lives is hard on all of us. Many teenagers seem overwhelmed by the confusing freedoms of their futures and by loss of regular contact with adults. The inroads of crime and drugs are alarming. The horrid *busyness* of nearly everybody's life kills the more relaxed forms of community even our universities used to know. The mobility and travel which, on the one hand, stimulate our minds and enlarge our perceptions leave us, on the other, frayed and seldom fully "present," our whole restful attention available to those among whom we find ourselves. Our moral and cultural traditions have not kept pace with our economic possibilities. We try to match new demands with a spiritual life not designed for them. Democratic capitalism suffers from the underdevelopment of guidance for a spiritual life appropriate to its highly developed political and economic life. To some extent, the leaders of our moral-cultural institutions must accept the blame. They have too often been followers, arriving breathless on battlefields only in time to erect monuments.

In any era, in any culture, it is difficult to become all that one can become. In our time it is exceedingly difficult, because the guiding voices are contradictory, and because one loses so much time groping up so many wrong alleys into so many deadends. Societies as hugely free as ours create enormous problems for individuals seeking to "find themselves" and result in much aimless wandering. One feels, sometimes, like those dry leaves Dante saw swirling outside the gates, more blown than choosing. We desperately need teachers, models, guides—not those who steal our freedom from us but those who teach us to grasp it surehandedly. The life of the spirit is far from stifled by democratic capitalism, but in the absence of strong moral guidance, it is often squandered. Our moral-cultural institutions do their job less well than our economic institutions do theirs. The twain are not yet matched. We need a spirituality appropriate for democratic capitalism as it is, and we do not have it.

Some common misperceptions seem to block us from even starting to acquire it. When I think of the many families in America known to me, most of the descriptions of Americans common to sociological and literary conventions do not seem to fit. In particular, descriptions like "the consumer society," "greed," and "materialism" seem very wide of the mark. These are not saintly families, only ordinary human beings. Yet the more one knows about them, the deeper and more worthy of respect they seem to be. If we would help them to become better than they are, we must at least come to know them as they are. Their generosity may be historically unparalleled. It is a generosity not of financial giving only but of an enormous network of volunteer activities. Faced with a problem, Americans almost by instinct form a committee. Their contributions to humanitarian purposes around the world and to their neighbors are not inferior to those of traditional or socialist societies. [15]

It is tempting to believe that the instinct for community so vital and alive among Americans—"caring," "compassion," "sensitivity," and even "love" are words used so often in American public life as to have become cloying—is due mainly to the political culture of democracy and to the moral-cultural values of Jewish, Christian, and humanistic inheritance. No doubt this is largely true. On the other hand, the specific forms of capitalist *economic* life are actually experienced by most Americans in ways far from "the cash nexus." With respect to their own private lives, money is an almost taboo subject among Americans. Most often, one does not know the salaries of one's associates and, beyond that, whatever financial resources they may have inherited. It would be gross to inquire. At universities, the children of the wealthy seem to be among the most diffident about wealth, the most eager to hide advantages. John Barron reports in his book on the KGB that the Soviets find it almost impossible to recruit American agents through ideology or political conviction; their recruiters are advised that, in approaching Americans, money is the only safe avenue. [16] The Soviets attribute this to capitalist greed. It seems far more attributable to the American sense that a transaction reduced to money seems mundane and innocent.

It is sometimes said that capitalism introduces a "competitive" system, a "rat race," "dog-eat-dog." One does not notice that athletes from socialist nations are any less competitive than those from democratic capitalist lands. Nor is the competition for political power in socialist states any less fearsome than the competition for the more various forms of power open to the citizens of democratic capitalist societies. Still, most persons in America do *not* seem to want to rise to the top. Many compete mostly with themselves. They set goals for themselves and try to realize them in their own way and at their own pace. Taking it easy, playing it as it comes, easy does it—these attributes seem to be at least as widely celebrated and realized as the competitive drive. Individuals choose their own roads—even children from one family go in multiple directions.

The ideal of a democratic capitalist society is to guarantee the right of each person to pursue happiness. (Happiness itself is not guaranteed.) Thus the system as a whole must be open to enormous variety. It must afford satisfactions at work as well as in free time. Since it is in the nature of humans to be social, the ideal is also to build decent and even affectionate relations among those who work together. For many Americans, there is almost as much friendship and mutuality with colleagues or buddies on the job as in the family. Indeed, for some, there may be a larger store of shared values with workmates than with the whole extended family at Thanksgiving dinner, at which they must sit down with persons whose politics they abhor, whose religious views they cannot abide, and whose occupational biases, ideas, values, and even social class may be far removed from their own. We may within limits choose our communities.

In short, even the economic system within democratic capitalism has its own internal impulses toward community, though of a different sort than any known before. Concerning these, we need far more careful thought than anywhere is yet in evidence. They have produced a new type of human being, the communitarian individual. Perhaps we have not seen what is around us because we are too close to it—and have learned too many clichés about the bourgeois man and woman, the middle class, ourselves.

VII
The Communitarian Individual

The mathematicability of reality, the cult of reason, free
trade, liberalism, the abolition of slavery, of censorship, the
contractual idea of the state, constitutionalism, individualism, socialism, nationalism, internationalism—these were
not aristocratic ideas. For bourgeois means something more
than a social class: it means certain rights and privileges,
certain aspirations, a certain way of thinking even more than
of living. . . . The bourgeois standards and habits of thought
were constantly changing; and what was characteristic of
them was not their fixity *but the way in which they have
been changing*. (Had the aristocracies had their way there
would have been little change.)
                          —John Lukacs, *The Passing of the Modern Age*[1]

Nothing is more common in anti-capitalist literature than rhetorical assaults against "bourgeois individualism." Although most
Americans might have to consult a dictionary to learn all the
nuances of contempt which Europeans often pack into the term
"bourgeois," nearly everybody knows that to be called "bourgeois" is not a compliment. Or is it?

It is useful to consult the alternatives. To be called "noble" is
to receive a compliment. Yet would one really wish to support a
feudal order? To be called "comrade" is a sign of solidarity. Yet
would one really wish to support a socialist order in which all real
goods are owned by the state and all possibilities of dissent are
controlled by the state? Democratic socialists face a quandary.

The builders of Soviet socialism have been able to cite chapter and verse from Marx to justify their worst oppressions. Perhaps they neglect the good, humanistic Marx, but there is enough in the other Marx to legitimate totalitarianism. Moreover, where there is no personal control over one's own economic life—no private property—liberty is empty. The unlimited state controls all. There are no examples of socialist states which permit the liberties desired by democratic socialists.

Thus, democratic socialists commonly argue that they intend to preserve the political liberties won by bourgeois political democracy, but to extend these through the further revolution of economic democracy. Here the most sophisticated among them, like Michael Walzer,[2] are careful to portray the welfare state, the centralized administrative state, as an enemy against whom the revolution must be launched. They favor "decentralization," "participatory democracy," "communities at the base." They thus recognize a role for private property. Large landholdings, for example, will be broken up so that peasants may own their own land. Cooperatives will permit socially owned private property. Factories will be owned (and managed) by their workers. To an important extent, therefore, democratic socialism sounds uncannily like bourgeois democratic capitalism. When Michael Walzer lists the values for which democratic socialism stands, they are astonishingly bourgeois values:

> And yet, the deep principles of the Left also have their origins in the pre-liberated world. Where else could they have their origins? . . . The list is well-known: Individual freedom, dignity, responsibility, equality, mutual respect, hard work, craftsmanship, honesty, and loyalty. And two more, less commonly acknowledged, authority and property.[3]

This description falls far short of the communal virtues highly prized by Adam Smith and others who tried to formulate the ideals of democratic capitalism. The tradition of British individualism has played a mischievous role, however, in masking these ideals. Under the mask, the hidden ideal of democratic capitalism is that of the communitarian individual.

1
"Das Anglo-Saxon Problem"

Anglo-Saxon culture appears in this respect to be peculiarly mis-understood among the other cultures of the world. Its leading figures speak openly of the importance of the individual, but in practice Anglo-Saxon customs and traditions nourish remarkable social orderliness and a splendid cooperative spirit. One sees it in British common law and in that peculiarly British love of liberty combined with respect for law. (As Britain becomes more social-ist, daily life seems to grow less civil and more embittered.) Individualism in Great Britain is not what it appears; it has limits and complexities. It is not at all "Every man for himself." The British may not be as socially disciplined as the Germans; they value their eccentricities too much. But it is a grievous mistake to underestimate their capacities for organization and sociality.

This clue to the underlying practice of British society, as dis-tinct from its public emphasis on the individual, leads one to reexamine the classic texts of democratic capitalism. A rereading of Adam Smith brings out quite clearly the important role he claimed for sympathy, benevolence, the good opinion of others, and other social determinants of virtue.[4] Smith is far from repre-senting the sort of "autonomy" and errant individualism the popes and theologians impute to such as him.

German critics, in particular, have been perplexed by the con-tradiction they seem to find between Smith's *The Theory of Moral Sentiments* (1759) and *Wealth of Nations* (1776). They read the first as emphasizing fellow feeling, common sympathy, and be-nevolence, and the second as emphasizing self-love and self-in-terest. They refer to this conflict as *Das Adam Smith Problem*.[5] Since many years after publishing the second book, Smith edited a new version of the first, it cannot be imagined that between the two volumes he renounced his earlier views. Actually, his second book takes the first for granted, as many textual evidences show—and as the ordinary practice of British life shows clearly enough.

In *The Theory of Moral Sentiments,* Smith points out that every self is both individual and social, and has both selfish and benevolent interests. As to which represents the higher virtue, it is absolutely clear to him "that to feel much for others, and little for ourselves, that to restrain our selfish, and to indulge our benevolent affections, constitutes the perfection of human nature."[6] The virtues of benevolence and sympathy, however, often need to be broken free by an exercise of reason. Egotism deceives; an impartial observer is more discerning:

> We can never survey our own sentiments and motives, we can never form any judgement concerning them, unless we remove ourselves, as it were, from our natural station, and endeavour to view them as at a certain distance from us. But we can do this in no other way than by endeavouring to view them with the eyes of other people, or as other people are likely to view them. Whatever judgement we can form concerning them, accordingly, must always bear some secret reference, either to what are, or to what, upon a certain condition, would be, or to what, we ought to imagine, ought to be the judgement of others. We endeavour to examine our own conduct as we imagine any other fair and impartial spectator would examine it.[7]

Smith finds such virtues common among Englishmen, and he cites the example of "every thoroughly good soldier" who would willingly "throw away his life when the good of the service required it." He believes such virtues to be only common sense. "When the happiness or misery of others depends in any respect upon our conduct, we dare not, as self-love might suggest to us, prefer the interest of one to that of many. The man within immediately calls to us, that we value ourselves too much and other people too little, and that, by doing so, we render ourselves the proper object of the contempt and indignation of our brethren."[8]

On the other hand, Smith is a realist. Since at least the days of Duns Scotus (1265–1308), the British have had a reputation for stressing the individual. Duns Scotus did so in the principle of *Haeccitas,* highlighting the "thisness" or individuality of all things, a view much cherished by the Jesuit poet Gerard Manley Hopkins.[9] Smith, too, stands in this tradition. "Every man is no doubt, by nature, first and principally recommended to his own care; and as he is fitter to take care of himself, than is any other person, it is fit and right that it should be so."[10] But Smith did not stop at self-reliance:

> If he would act so as that the impartial spectator may enter into the principles of his conduct, which is what of all things he has the greatest desire to do, he must upon this, as upon all other occasions, humble the arrogance of his self-love, and bring it down to something which other men can go along with.[11]

Finally, Smith insists upon fair play. Individualism must be held in check by moral-cultural ideals. "In the race for wealth, and honours, and preferments, he may run as hard as he can, and strain every nerve and every muscle, in order to outstrip all his competitors. But if he should jostle or throw down any of them, the indulgence of the spectators is entirely at an end. It is a violation of fair play, which they cannot admit of."[12]

In *An Inquiry into the Nature and Causes of the Wealth of Nations,* similar statements appear. But Smith now emphasizes the *unintended consequences* of moral sentiments. In the move from "moral man" to "immoral society"—to use key words from the title of Reinhold Niebuhr's famous book[13]—Smith observes a paradox. Sometimes less than moral sentiments result in superior moral outcomes. There is no direct link between personal intentions and social outcomes. He concludes that a sound economic order should not be based on good intentions alone but on respect for social outcomes.

Here Smith avoids a mistake many contemporaries make. He regards "the economy" *not* as a system of aggregates and averages studied by economists, but as a system of individual acts by individual purchasers and suppliers. Businessmen, not economists, lie at the center of his imagination. He does not think to stimulate "the economy," but to stimulate individuals.[14] He grasps thoroughly the importance of incentives, personal goals, and personal realism. He was more interested in real-world psychology than in statistical aggregates. If individual agents become economically active, the statistics will take of themselves. "It is not from the benevolence of the butcher, the brewer, or the baker that we expect our dinner," Smith dryly observes, "but from their regard to their own interest. We address ourselves, not to their humanity but to their self-love, and never talk to them of our own necessities but of their advantages.''[15]

Anyone who has bartered for goods in a Mediterranean bazaar knows that what Smith here observes is not true. Professions of great love and concern are voiced, profusions of generosity and goodwill, exclamations of personal need and long tales of personal misfortune. Of course, both parties know that such words mask the desire of buyer and seller to reach an agreeable accommodation that leaves both feeling gratified. Whatever their many expressions of mutual benevolence and sympathy, buyer and seller are at bottom weighing their own present interest. Each knows that the other must gain something. The aim of even the most animated exchange is realistic compromise.

But the subject bears further examination. The butcher, the brewer, and the baker are not usually motivated solely by selfishness. They have families to feed, loved ones to provide for. Their ''self-love'' is social in nature and includes those to whom they are bound by natural sympathy and benevolence. Were their behavior that of Scrooge, British society would condemn them. The perfection of human nature is ''to feel much for others, little for ourselves.''

Just the same, in economic activities a certain realism is only reasonable. Sympathy may temper, but should not remove, hardheaded considerations. The butcher, the brewer and the baker have a right to a fair return on their labor. For work in and of itself is not costless. The butcher's bench is bloody, the brewery is dark and smelly, the bakery is hot. Human beings do not bear hard work without hope of fair return. Given a chance, human beings would prefer ease:

> It is the interest of every man to live as much at his ease as he can; and if his emoluments are to be precisely the same, whether he does or does not perform some very laborious duty, it is certainly his interest, at least as interest is vulgarly understood, either to neglect it altogether, or, if he is subject to some authority which will not suffer him to do this, to perform it in as careless and slovenly a manner as that authority will permit.[16]

Socialist societies learn this elementary lesson the hard way. Smith's idea was to erect a system of incentives in which each participant might judge his return just and see in it prospects of betterment for himself and those dear to him. This sort of self-love is not vicious.

Utopians are bound to wish that human beings would work solely out of a spirit of love and communal dedication. If men were angels, they would. To a large extent, in small communities they must and do. In a small town, each worker and each merchant knows that his reputation follows him. Good business requires neighborliness. In larger urban settings and in more complex and impersonal relationships, there is more opportunity for self-love and greed to grow unchecked. But this is true not only in matters of commerce and money. It is true as well in matters of political favors, party belonging, and exchanges of power and privilege.

Hector St. John Crèvecoeur, writing in the year 1780, and observing the new American nation in light of the European experience, commented:

> The American ought therefore to love this country much better than that wherein either he or his forefathers were born. Here the rewards of his industry follow with equal steps the progress of his labour; his labour is founded on the basis of nature, *self-interest;* can it want a stronger allurement? Wives and children, who before in vain demanded of him a morsel of bread, now, fat and frolicsome, gladly help their father to clear those fields whence exuberant crops are to arise to feed and to clothe them all; without any part being claimed, either by a despotic prince, a rich abbot, or a mighty lord.[17]

"A man is never so innocently occupied," Samuel Johnson once observed, "as when he is getting money."[18] A commercial society is less to be feared than the old order.

Adam Smith's hope was that the self-love of human beings might be transformed into a social system which benefited all as no other system had ever done. Thus his purpose in granting human self-interest its due was to transform it into a system of order, imagination, initiative, and progress for all. Such a system would, he thought, evolve interests larger than those of self-love, sentiments of love and gratitude for the system itself as a good of order. Each individual would then participate in a good society, in such a way that his self-love would come to include the whole.

And the work of democratic capitalism will not be done until a
sound material base has been laid beneath every human life on
this planet. The bourgeois ideal, though measured, is spacious. It
is not utopian, but it rewards big dreams.

2
The Assault on the Bourgeoisie

Catholic writers, nonetheless, have been particularly hostile to the
"bourgeois" ideal. Democratic capitalism is pluralistic; there is
ample room within it for Catholic ideals. Yet its pluralism and
this-worldly focus make it, admittedly, less than a full expression
of Christianity. In a recent volume of essays by major Catholic
theologians, *Christianity and the Bourgeoisie,* the authors describe the bourgeoisie as though it were Protestant, Calvinist, sick
with that sort of inwardness the theologians Sören Kierkegaard
and Karl Barth castigated.[19] They attribute to it a false individualism and utilitarianism. They think it puts a cheap sexual love in
the place of genuine sexual community.[20] (All the vices of modern
civilization are bourgeois. All its virtues are socialist.)

Is the bourgeoisie inward-turning? The builders of industry,
inventors of new technologies, constructors of skyscrapers, builders of roads and architects of all the immense transformations of
modern life during the past two hundred years may more plausibly
be accused, one would think, of too much activism and too much
extroversion. As we have seen, the motive of the system *qua*
system is communal. But the kind of *personality type* which it
nourishes is also communitarian. The anti-bourgeois ideology deserves an empirical critique.

Who, for example, belongs to the bourgeoisie? The term seems
first to have entered usage to describe those owners of their own
homes in the infant cities of northern Europe, persons who were
neither of the aristocracy nor peasants, but usually craftsmen,
artisans, or merchants. Marx gave the term ideological use by
tying it to the "owners of the means of production." This usage

has fallen upon many difficulties. When the state owns the means of production, not much improvement in the human condition appears to become visible. Workers seem no happier, wages are not higher, and neither sullenness nor alcoholism nor "alienation" seems to be diminished. Under democratic capitalism, the owners of small businesses may be "bourgeois" in an earlier sense, but the ownership of publicly owned corporations is diffused among all who purchase their public shares. Among the large purchasers thereof are pension funds, insurance companies, and banks. If the bourgeoisie includes all those who derive income and dividends through ownership of the means of production, all those workers covered by pension plans, insurance, and holdings of stocks or bonds are also among the bourgeoisie. Most of the academic critics of the bourgeoisie would appear to stand among those they loathe. Many own their own homes. Many are covered by pension funds. Most have status as highly trained professionals. The Catholic theologians in the study under consideration seem to feel some discomfort about their own *embourgeoisement*.

Thus, new attempts are constantly being made to redefine the bourgeoisie to make the concept fit the Marxian scheme in which one class oppresses another. Sophisticated socialists recognize that corporate executives are also hired professionals and thus, in a sense, highly paid proletarians like football players and rock stars. The search for the bourgeoisie then turns into a search for "the power elite." Generally, this elite is imagined to be composed of "the upper ten thousand" decisionmakers, as one author puts it.[21] These may include not only the chief owners of private wealth but also the top managers and top leaders in each of the three systems of democratic capitalism. In every form of society, there is an elite. Most of its members may be presumed to love the system of which they are a part. The elite in a democratic capitalist society, in this tautology, is the elite in a democratic capitalist society.

"Fewer and fewer citizens class themselves as proletarians," a West German author writes.[22] The same author scathingly attacks the bourgeoisie, while wishing to preserve "individual freedom and the use of reason as a criterion." He admires "freedom in the sense of the right of all individuals to full development of their unique individuality, and reason in the sense of a way of life and mode of production based on rational goals which are open to inspection by all in a free discussion." Lest this sound like an endorsement of democratic capitalism, he expresses a final hope that the human race will "shake off the influence of 'bourgeois' capitalist industrial civilization, but without thereby abandoning its valuable achievements."[23]

Why this antipathy combined with grudging admiration? Detached observation suggests that bourgeois institutions nourish high moral qualities. In the first place, a bourgeois has *economic independence,* perhaps as a shopkeeper in his or her own enterprise. A bourgeois *owns property.* A bourgeois (normally) shares the *cultural life of the city* rather than that of the rural countryside.[24] These are not trivial matters for the life of the spirit. Not until Europe began to break free from the fixed status of the feudal order did the bourgeoisie attain sufficient critical mass to define a significant new social class. A new politics, a new economics, a new culture, and a new morality were generated by their coming center stage in history. Much that we hold dear was won by the bourgeoisie.[25]

To some extent, the bourgeoisie violated significant taboos of feudalism. Their growing competence, ambition, wealth, and power constituted a threat to the authority of the aristocratic class. They upset feudal conceptions of status and place. Their "new morality" gave higher value to the economic order—to industry, savings, the acquisition of wealth, upward mobility, and economic rationality—than the "old morality" of aristocrats, churchmen, monks, and humanists. As the bourgeoisie gained in influence and power, aristocrats began a long descent and, with them, many humanist scholars and artists. By contrast, peasants and yeomen who could never aspire to noble birth or the privileges of aristocracy could aspire to "better their condition" by entering the bourgeois class. The bourgeois class was, in a sense, the most open, dynamic, and expansive class. Aristocrats who chose to play by the new economic rules could join it, and so could former serfs, peasants, and the urban or rural poor. Karl Marx imagined that the "class war" of the nineteenth century would pit the bourgeoisie—the new owners of the new instruments of production—against the growing urban proletariat. The reality appears to have been that most proletarians aspired to, and succeeded in embodying, *embourgeoisement.* The new middle class turned out to have political, economic, and moral attractions which many intellectuals have overlooked.

What are these attractions? A measure of economic independence and well-being is certainly one. Compared to the mud floors, glassless windows, inadequate sanitation, crowding, lack of warmth, and other inadequacies of the medieval farm hut, common all through Europe during the eighteenth and nineteenth centuries (and still seen in rural areas of Eastern Europe even today), the increasingly sturdy and independent dwellings of the bourgeois class exerted admirable attraction. Moreover, the philosophical and legal basis of the "freehold" or "private property" saw to it that not even the king had the right of entry and search.[26] This fact made the independently owned home of the bourgeois as well defended as a castle, for which the law provided a kind of spiritual moat. "Independence" and "liberty" have attractions above and beyond the material order. The bourgeoisie may have lacked the high status of noble birth; yet as historical carriers of the dream of personal independence and liberty, they struggled for rights formerly reserved to royalty and the aristocracy.

Finally, the bourgeoisie by their industry and competitive habits nourished a new cultural excellence. The privately owned, family-centered enterprises of France still set worldwide standards for the arts of daily living. A good wine, delicious bread, inimitable cheese, lace of the finest workmanship, elegant hats, imaginative sartorial arts, sophisticated cuisine—such excellence France has long supplied through the small enterprises of the bourgeoisie. Scholars and artists who recall with nostalgia the high status of aristocratic patronage may continue to have contempt for the bourgeoisie. But palaces, monuments, and salons were virtually never executed by aristocrats. They were produced by craftsmen in competitive bourgeois enterprises. In one of the choice ironies of intellectual history, many great scholars and artists of the first rank, themselves children of the middle class, celebrated the virtues of aristocracy in preference to those of their own class.

It does not appear that the bourgeois is, as charged, uniquely self-satisfied, secure, or smug. Characteristically, the bourgeois likes to be made fun of, accused, made to feel guilty. The arts produced by and for the middle class uniquely delight in shocking the middle class. Berthold Brecht and Henrik Ibsen, Eugene Ionesco and Jean-Paul Sartre have been clasped to the heart. The children of the middle class thrive on the adversarial culture of the universities; it is a culture perfectly suited to late adolescence. The cinema, television, the major literary publications, the great newspapers, and the slick magazines delight in mocking bourgeois manners and mores, sins and fantasies, ideals and values. What is relatively rare is a work celebrating the middle class as heroes, saints, adventurers, the salt of the human race. Socialist literature in socialist nations, epics honoring kings and warriors and aristocrats, and folk songs honoring the poorer classes—all other forms of literature celebrate the class that sponsors them. The middle class seems to be the first class in human history to delight in self-ridicule and self-criticism. Many of its intellectuals seem to pride themselves on being adversarial to their own class.

It is further said that the middle class is blind to the "invisible" poor.[27] Since the early 1960s, however, it can hardly be said that the poor are "invisible." Indeed, few American citizens, as George Gilder points out in his stunning portrait *Visible Man,* are more highly visible in the U.S. media today than the militant young black male on welfare and perhaps on the edge of desperation and revolt.[28] His picture has appeared around the world. Rather more rarely does one see the young black or other poor person who has become successful in chemistry or engineering or English literature and is looking ahead to an intelligent, cultivated life. The taboo is not against poverty. It is against success. Many middle-class persons, typically sentimental, seem to cherish appeals to compassion and sympathy.

Moreover, Latin America liberation theologians and others may accuse, voice outrage, and threaten retribution upon the bourgeois class, but if one listens closely, they also appeal to the *ideals* of the middle class, and specifically to its religious and moral ideals. The ideas and ideals brought into historical actuality by a bourgeois civilization, inspired by the yeast of Christian, Jewish, and humanistic wisdom, are required even in the act of pointing to injustices and inequalities. Such appeals, lost on those who are merely egotistic, ruthless, and coldly calculating, testify to a moral inheritance which is quite precious.

The individual of the democratic capitalist ideal recognizes allegiance to values which transcend historical eras or cultural boundaries, ideals like personal dignity, liberty, justice for all, and human rights. Bourgeois life is thick with activism, voluntarism, and mutual association. It is often, to a fault, willing to entertain accusations about its own guilt. Hearing such appeals too often, of course, it may react with practiced boredom and apathy—but expect its cheerleaders and gadflies to continue to nag. Appeals to it for help from every quarter of the world bump into each other in their frequency. The ideal of the middle-class man or woman is not to be a rugged individual, isolated and alone. To be independent, yes, and also self-reliant. Yet also to be an active member of many communities, to be open to appeals from the needy, to be informed about the world at large, and to care about its problems. The middle-class ideal is communitarian. Its manifold activities, charities, and voluntary endeavors can be explained in no other way.

Yet if the democratic capitalist ideal is communitarian, the family is its school of realism and self-governance *par excellence*.

VIII
The Family

It is no accident, as the Socialists say, that Socialism and Sex (or "free love") came in together as "advanced" ideas. They supplement each other. Russian dissident Igor Shafarevich, in his profound book *The Socialist Phenomenon,* explains that the Socialist project of homogenizing society demands that the family be vitiated or destroyed. This can be accomplished in good measure by profaning conjugal love and breaking monogamy's link between Sex and loyalty. Hence, in their missionary phases Socialist movements often stress sexual "liberation," and members of radical organizations may impose mandatory promiscuity within the group, everyone sharing a bed with each of the others, each equally related to each. It is the ultimate in leveling. . . .

Few Americans will buy a bottle labeled Socialism. The cunning of the Socialist hive has consisted largely in its skill in piggybacking on more attractive things. Like Sex.

—Joseph Sobran[1]

To this point, I have argued that democratic capitalism presupposes and nourishes certain values, perceptions, and virtues. In this chapter, I stress some virtues necessary for its effective functioning. From one point of view, the institutions of democratic capitalism are designed to function with minimal dependence upon virtuous motives. From another, they cannot function at all without certain moral strengths, rooted in institutions like the family. The moral-cultural institutions of the system, including churches and neighborhoods, are vital to the threefold system. The system is far from heartless; the family is far more than a haven. The family is a dynamic, progressive force. If it is ignored or penalized, its weakening weakens the whole.

Population specialists speculate that 4 percent of all the human beings who have ever lived upon this earth are living now. We may conclude, alas, that barely 1 percent of all human beings in history have enjoyed the fruits of liberal self-government.[2] The enemies of that form of political economy are virtually unanimous in their hostility toward the "bourgeois family." Such enmity provokes a question. Perhaps the family is indispensable to republican government, democratic institutions, and the liberal tradition. Perhaps the actual texture of life under democratic capitalism is not quite centered on the individual but on the family. This is the thesis we now explore.

Conveniently, in 1980, the White House Conference on Families focused national attention on the subject. Its history is instructive. In 1975, Jimmy Carter, virtually unknown outside Georgia, listened to an idea for a White House Conference to honor the traditional family. Some months later, the nominee of his party, he designated Joseph Califano to begin planning a program on the family for the new administration, and still later, in September 1976, he opened his campaign with a Labor Day speech on the family. Almost at once the infighting started. Professionals in the social science establishment insisted that the name of the conference be changed to the White House Conference on Families— plural, not singular, any hint of a normative ideal carefully excised.

Sensing the political passion aroused by this normative ideal— 85 percent of all Americans, according to Gallup, count the family "the most" or "one of the most" important elements in their lives[3]—President Carter pushed the White House Conference away from the White House out into the states. Local constituencies began to elect delegates who believe in the family. Alarmed, the planning staff began to "balance" the delegations with hand-picked appointees so that at least 40 percent were professionals "in family-related fields"—and of approved politics.

Members of the planning staff of the White House Conference spoke openly of the "nostalgic family," by which they meant the heterosexual couple united in matrimony and bringing up children. They included as "families" any household somehow in-

volved in "nurture" or "fulfilling one another's basic needs"—
homosexual liaisons, childless and unmarried couples living together, communes, and similar affinity groups. They did not seem
anxious to exclude any arrangement. This bias was startling to
those who considered the demographics.

Firgures from the U.S. Department of Commerce for 1978
indicate that there were then 101,000,000 husbands and wives in
the United States. (By contrast, there were 2,274,000 men and
women living as unmarried couples.) There were 49,700,000 single, widowed, or divorced adults; 49,132,000 children were living
with two parents, and 11,710,000 were living with one parent.[4]
What the staff members of the White House Conference on Families were pleased to call the "nostalgic family" actually included, then, a solid two-thirds of the nation's population. In
addition, single parents with children constitute families in the
quite traditional sense according to which, in the past, disease or
accident often brought early death to one or both spouses. Of
those adults in childless households, most were over forty-five.
Though their children had left home, few may be assumed to have
regarded the traditional family with contempt. Finally, millions of
widows and widowers living alone invest emotion in the families
of their children. The "nostalgic family" seems to include as a
living reality all but a vocal minority of Americans.

No doubt high divorce rates and other statistics of family
"breakup" indicate that not all is well with the family in America. It never was.[5] A free society encourages such great mobility
that grandparents today poignantly boast to all who will listen that
their children are scattered across the world, not a one "close to
home." Such mobility (not only geographic but in the regions of
the heart) is partly a source of pride. But it also places strains
upon families comparable to those of the great migrations, wars,
and dispersals of the past.

So the ideal lives. No wonder, since nature must of necessity
constantly reinvent it. Human offspring require some twenty years
of nurture. Three thousand years of civilization must be passed on
to children during those years; without that, progress would halt.
An elementary stability is essential for this process; more than
nature, culture demands it. The original intention of the White
House Conference was to give some small honor and moral support to those who accomplish this noble work. Why were the

professionals so hostile to this simple idea? What were the anti-family professionals up to?

Although there is much vocal contempt for the "nostalgic family," few such critics seem really to propose that having one parent is superior to having two; that prodigal separation, divorce, and infidelity have only good effects; that coupling without marriage and marriage without children best serve the common good; or that the best of all societies would encourage an impermanent, childless, sexual free-for-all. The hostile critics of the family are shockingly vague about what they plan to put in its place, beyond "liberation" and "openness."

Attacks on the family take three forms: derogating its economic, its political, and its moral-cultural accomplishments. The family is called "bourgeois," "repressive," and "narrow." In it are discerned the roots of this nation's political economy, such that radicals who would destroy the latter believe that they must extirpate the former. In a way they don't intend, they appear to be correct. It seems impossible to imagine the democratic governance, a free economy, and a liberal culture apart from the much disdained bourgeois family.

To be sure, classic theoreticians of "the new order of the world" did not write at length, profoundly, or with unmitigated admiration of the family. Some later scholars think they took it for granted as a given of nature and good sense. But the truth is that the great intellectual breakthroughs of the modern era occurred, rather, around the polar concepts of the *individual* and the *state*. Rousseau wrote eloquently, if with a certain detached romanticism, about the family and about childhood, and nearly all the scholars of the Anglo-Scottish Enlightenment, from John Locke through Adam Smith to John Stuart Mill, wrote at least briefly of the family. Yet one must recall the order they wrote *against*.

The feudal world was fixated on inherited status. No newborn child chose the family he was born into, yet birth fixed class, station, religion, and occupation forevermore. In the feudal order, concepts of family were half submerged in less than rational materials like blood, habit, custom, tradition, ethnicity, and religion. Original minds concerned with a central role for intellect, for liberty, and for the flowering of talent wherever it is found were obliged to look beyond the family for the dynamism of a new order. Thus the discoverers of "the natural system of liberty" stressed the distinctive, aspiring *individual* and the self-limiting *state* that would liberate his energies. For generations, political theory, economic theory, and moral theory—preoccupied with the individual and the state—have systematically neglected the social vitality of the family.

In our day, when such genuine freedoms are available that anything may be tried, we are driven to face directly what our forebears neglected or took for granted. It is useful to reflect on our own common experiences in the three areas in which the traditional family is under relentless attack—in the economic order, the political order, and the moral-cultural order.

1

The Economic Order

Even today libertarian scholars, like David Friedman in *The Machinery of Freedom,*[6] place at the center of their analysis the rational will of the free individual, and so do most textbooks in economics. But is the analytic assumption fair to our actual experience? David Friedman dedicates his book to his father, Milton Friedman, and pays prefatory homage to his wife and children; one suspects that whole regions of ordinary experience lie, unanalyzed, behind these brief hints of familial reality.

According to libertarian theory, the economic motivation of individuals arises from rational self-interest. Yet according to the same theory, individual self-interest includes far more than a merely self-absorbed, self-regarding solipsism. As we have seen, it is entirely consistent with the tenor of Adam Smith's thought to recognize that most butchers and bakers endure the blood and the heat of their labors not for themselves alone but for the benefit of their families. The "self-love" Smith writes of is to be taken in a large rather than in a narrow sense, so as to include forms of natural benevolence, duty, and other-centered ambition. Above all, economic self-interest includes the family. But this is an important qualification. Too much economic analysis seems to ignore it.

For in ordinary experience, our own economic starting place in life is given us by our families. Nearly all have multiple reasons to be grateful to the families that gave us birth, nourished us, instructed us, prepared us, and made an endless series of self-denying sacrifices in our behalf, long before we were capable of economic or educational choices of our own. We did not suddenly invent ourselves out of wholecloth. When at last we began to attain to self-consciousness and self-direction, we had already been *thrown,* we were already in motion. Impulses which did not originate with us moved us forward with a kind of imparted gravity. Thus, it is analytically improper to take the individual alone as the sufficient unit of economic analysis. Individual human beings are social animals. More exactly than that, each of us is a familial animal. Our families enter into our very constitution, not only genetically but also psychologically, educationally, and morally.

In many of our family traditions, high priority was attached to education. As Thomas Sowell demonstrates in *Race and Economics* and in *Essays and Data on American Ethnic Groups,*[7] family culture is a critical variable in economic performance. It is through no choice of their own, or at least only in a diminished sense, that some 70 percent of all Jewish youngsters in America find themselves between the ages of eighteen and twenty-two in colleges or universities, and in so many diverse ways directed toward a high use of intelligence. The family is the major carrier of culture, transmitting ancient values and lessons in ways that escape completely rational articulation, carrying forward motivations and standards of judgment and shaping the distribution of energy and emotion, preferences and inclinations.

In many families in America these last many generations, the economic welfare of each individual depended in very large part not only upon the immediate family (father, mother, and siblings) but also upon an extended network of others (grandparents, uncles, aunts, cousins, and in-laws). To some extent, various family members supplied economic role models. On occasion, especially during hard times, one family took another in. Older generations sometimes provided at least some little capital, so that one generation might begin at a higher financial level than the preceding.

But the family network also provided countless exchanges of goods and services, which otherwise individual families could not have afforded. One brother in one business helped out another in another; and each received benefits outside normal markets. A successful family member was a source of jobs, information, or assistance to others; perhaps even the discreet use of his or her name might open doors. Finally, family networks have been sources of invaluable economic lore about techniques for advancement, mistakes to avoid, opportunities to seize. Economic skills rarely develop in a vacuum. Every family, particularly through its brightest and most intelligent members, transmits economic advantages to its entire network, without which individuals would begin life far more ignorant and helpless than they do.

It follows, then, that families defy simple and abstract schemes of equality. Families with an intelligent and effective economic tradition are not equal to families of less developed traditions. Their individual members, unless they choose to neglect the acquired family wisdom, do not begin at the same "starting line" as other individuals of less highly developed family traditions. It is in the interests of a healthy and dynamic society, of course, to upgrade the economic traditions of every family for the sake of every individual. But every single family network that becomes a center of intelligent economic activity and a repository of hard-won economic habits is an immeasurable resource for the nation of which it is a part.

Furthermore, it seems obvious that, each individual life being short, the most profound of economic motives is almost always— and must necessarily be—family-oriented. Economic laborers seldom work only for themselves. It is no doubt true that those who do not have families of their own do work rather more for themselves; but even in such cases one often observes the help generously given by such persons to the elderly, sick, or very young members of their extended families of birth. For those men and women who have chosen to establish families of their own, there can be no doubt whatever that much of their economic conduct makes no sense apart from the benefits they are trying to accrue for their children. The fundamental motive of all economic activity seems clearly to be, far more than economists commonly suggest, family-regarding.

It is for the family's welfare that so much gratification is deferred; that so many excruciating medical, educational, and emotional struggles are engaged in; that so much saving is attempted; and that investments which regard the future so much more than the present are undertaken. One does, indeed, meet parents who say, "You only live once and I intend to enjoy it, leaving my children to fend, as I did, for themselves." This is not, other things being equal, an immoral or even a necessarily harmful choice so far as the children are concerned. But it does not appear to be the common sentiment—or perhaps ever intended to the hilt.

Insofar as democratic capitalism depends for its economic vitality upon deferred gratification, savings, and long-term investment, no motive for such behavior is the equivalent of regard for the future welfare of one's own progeny. Self-interest is not a felicitous name for this regard for the welfare of one's children and one's children's children. Yet it is just this extended motivation which cuts to the quick. This is the motivation that adequately explains herculean economic activities. This is the only rational motivation for long-range economic decisions. For, in the long run, the individual economic agent is dead. Only his progeny survive to enjoy the fruits of his labors, intelligence, and concern.

Through this regard for family, the isolated individual escapes mere self-interest or self-regard. Through it, "charity begins at home." Through it, human sociality achieves its normal full development, in the very territory closest to the knowledge and wise concern of the individual agent. Indeed, until the collectivist state began to take over more and more of its economic functions, it was through familial socialism that most highly developed cultures cared for the poor, the sick, the retarded, the needy, and the very young and very old in their midst. Their religious traditions, meanwhile, taught them as well to care for those most unfortunate of all, the widows and orphans and those who were "homeless."

But if the family is a form of socialism which corrects the exaggerated individualism of capitalist economists, it is also a form of liberty which corrects the exaggerated collectivism of statists. These reflections lead us to politics.

2
The Political Order

As in the economic order, so in the political order of republican governance and democratic institutions it appears that the family is rather less dispensable than political scientists commonly emphasize. First and foremost the right to relative economic independence on the part of the family, the right of the freehold, sets an effective barrier upon the state. A state which controls all the means of production, all the terms of employment, and every aspect of exchange controls the daily reality of its citizens in every sphere. Political revolt under such circumstances is virtually impossible. So many citizens are in the direct employ of the state that spying upon every small beginning of dissent serves the self-interest of the forces of control. State ownership of the printing presses and other media might be thought to be sufficient for total political control. Yet total public control over every economic activity extends political control still further—into every material activity from food to housing, from production to consumption, and from savings and credit to every act of exchange. One can observe such control in China. It is apparent in Cuba. A very large proportion of the earth's population presently lives under such controls. The subject lies open to empirical observation, beyond purely theoretical argument.

The right of a family to own and to transmit property to its progeny is not the sole contribution of the bourgeois family to political liberty. If republican government is preeminently self-government, it is in the family that the habits of mind and will indispensable to the conception and practice of self-government are best taught—only there can be taught. If individuals have no space protecting them from the state, they have no ''self'' for self-government. The family provides such space. The family is the seat of the primary right in education. The state may require certain areas and levels of competency in the education of its citizens; but it may not usurp the right of parents to direct the education of their own children. As the limited state may not infringe upon personal conscience, so it may not infringe upon the intellectual and moral traditions of the family. Human children differ from the young of all other animals in requiring a very long period of physical, emotional, intellectual, and moral nurture before they attain adulthood. The primary agency of such nurture is the family. The family, in that sphere, has inalienable rights. Between the omnipotent state and the naked individual looms the first line of resistance against totalitarianism: the economically and politically independent family, protecting the space within which free and independent individuals may receive the necessary years of nurture.

No self-government can stand where individuals choose to live as slaves and wards. Just as tyrannies may on occasion be benevolent, the powerful modern state may also be paternalistic, providing for the material welfare of its citizens in exchange for the surrender of self-government. Thus nearly every utopian vision of a paternalistic paradise on earth begins by undermining the sanctity of the family. The more the state invades the family, the less likely the prospect of self-government.

It was not by accident that the apparently mad Jim Jones of Jonestown, in launching his explicitly socialist utopian experiment, concentrated first on breaking down the family rights of every family in his community.[8] When each person of each sex was reduced to dependence upon the community alone (it is relatively insignificant that Jones sought their total dependence upon himself), the effective resistance of individuals was also broken. For it is an obscure but important truth of political economy that the self is primarily familial, and only secondarily independent as an individual. When the primary familial self is effectively destroyed, the independence of the individual also disintegrates and nothing is left of self but the will of the community. The practice of totalitarian societies supplies universal verification of this principle. For those who seek totalitarian state control, it is always evident that the independent bourgeois family must be destroyed.

This is so because the individual bound by responsibilities and loyalties to spouse and children is bound, as well, to traditions welling up from the past and extending into the future. In real human life, the family is the ordinary institution of self-transcendence. Through it, the sociality of the self is realized in flesh and blood, gains perspective on past and future, and is made to belong not to the self alone, not to the present alone, and not to the regime of the moment alone, but to a culture thousands of years old. In this light, the pretensions of the totalitarian state wither.

The totalitarian spirit, nourished by abstractions, is inevitably utopian. It impresses the majority through effective, although perhaps disguised, terror. Its appeal to idealists (at least to idealists outside its effective grip) consists in an abstract vision of a society that never yet has been, is not now, and never will be. Family ties lead individuals to count concrete costs. Watching their children, taking thought about their daily family circumstances, husband and wife have concrete evidence of the reality of their brief lifetime. The family is the human race's natural defense against utopianism.

3
The Moral-Cultural Order

Our reflections about morality are still disproportionately colored by the values of the ancient, aristocratic order. When, in a famous essay intended to put everyone in his place, Matthew Arnold distinguished the "barbarians" (the nobility) from the "philistines" (the commercial class), he celebrated the moral imperative of high culture to draw all citizens, from every walk of life, into a higher order of sensibility.[9] Yet there are overtones in that essay of far greater sympathy for "barbarians" than for "philistines" (not to mention "populace"). Many of our terms of approbation, moral and aesthetic—like grace, princely, regal, and the like—are colored by lenses of class and romantic memory. We somehow assume that the aristocracy sets the highest standard of excellence. But is that true? Aristocrats may have paid for excellence and been its patrons; less frequently, it appears, did they achieve it in their persons.

As in the economic order and the political order, so also in the moral order the primary institution of realism is the bourgeois family. The schemes of utopians customarily exclude the family, as they must, for the family is a most un-utopian institution. What it teaches spouses with each other and parents with their children is humble acceptance of human frailty. Those who seek moral perfection, full self-fulfillment, high happiness, and other manifestations of the utopian imagination can scarcely abide the constraints of matrimony and childrearing. For no man is god, no woman a goddess. Each has feet of clay. Moreover, the prolonged exposure of each to each, day after day, year after year, is bound to instruct them in ways they did not expect, both in the manifold faults of the other and—still more dispiriting—in their own faults.

Honesty and sincerity are said to be the most highly praised ideals of sophisticated, sensitive Americans. Yet matrimony induces realism precisely where the immaturity of each of us least desires it: in the destruction of our illusions about our own goodness, virtue, and attractiveness. The other cannot afford to be deceived by our self-illusions. If, in a word, you do not admire unrelenting honesty, avoid matrimony.

From the Declaration of Independence through *The Federalist* and in every wise document of our realist revolutionary tradition, it is confidently asserted that the possibility of self-government rests upon the virtue of its citizens. Nature's own school for virtue—and, hence, that of any political economy based upon self-government—is primarily the family. In the family, one encounters the limitations of one's own sex, vocation, and station in life.

The project of living daily with a person of the opposite sex teaches one a great deal about the unknown mysteries of one's own sex, as well as about those of the other. These mysteries are not easily brought into consciousness, let alone into words, but they are marvelously instructive. They are also laden with requirements of self-discipline. Anyone who would wish to live with another, for better or worse, until death does them part, had better begin acquiring ancient and constantly required virtues. Marriage teaches a realist rather than a utopian discipline.

Childrearing is also instructive in a kind of ordinary heroism. A typical mother or father, without thinking twice about it, would willingly die—in fire or accident, say—in order to save one of his or her children. While in most circumstances this human act would be regarded as heroic, for parents it is only ordinary. Thus nature, and perhaps the Creator, has shaped family life to teach as a matter of course the role of virtue. This admittedly extreme example suggests that family life is not so mundane and empty of transcendence as some of its cultural despisers would suggest. There are many acts of self-denial short of death which parents, hardly thinking about it, willingly perform for their children. Finally, childrearing teaches one lessons about self-governance. The lessons one learns as a child about independence, the rule of law, liberty, and obedience, supply only half the requirements which a self-governing republic imposes upon its citizens. On the other side of the generational divide, for parents, problems of liberty and authority wear a different aspect. A parent cannot avoid the exercise of authority, although our civilization is particularly fertile in suggesting innumerable systems for such avoidance. If one cares at all, one simply must learn to say no. One must also learn to accept the consequences of saying yes and no at precisely the wrong times. The application of discipline to a young child—let alone a teenager—is an enormously demanding act. It cannot be faked by permissiveness. I have seen men and women unafraid of the hosts of hell tremble in the face of their surly children.

Self-government is not possible without self-discipline. It is not possible, either, men and women being what they are, without the whip of the law. The childrearing practices of the citizenry of our republic either strengthen or undermine in its some sixty million families the habits of mind and soul, the moral skills, so to speak, of the republic itself.

Above everything else, the bourgeois family is built on critical judgment. Critical judgment is more than calculation, or logic, or analytic reason, or positivism. For the bourgeois family is quite well known for its practicality, for being religious, and even at times for being sentimental and romantic. Under the sway of "middle-class Christianity," for example, great international religious communities went out to the far corners of the earth, to the slums of the cities, to islands where lepers needed care, to the sick and the insane and the homeless. These religious communities, like the bourgeoisie generally, are known for their practicality more than for their mysticism. Practical wisdom characterizes their charity. Thus in attributing to the bourgeois family a special regard for critical judgment, I intend to attribute no narrow rationalism, but rather the capacity to reflect clearly upon the world of experience, to make practical judgments about it, and to act. The bourgeois family is to be distinguished from the sorts of family that have preceded it and have recently begun to follow after it. It is different from the aristocratic family because its sense of self-worth comes not from noble birth but from self-directed accomplishment; not from attributed status but from status earned through excellence. The children of the successful middle class begin life with inherited advantages, but it does not follow that, like the aristocracy, they can maintain title to these till death; from riches to rags is the story of many of the downwardly mobile. The bourgeois family is different, as well, from the peasant family, chiefly by reason of its affinity for the values of an urban rather than a rural civilization, with its consequent emphasis upon those habits of mind and soul suited to a pluralistic, rapidly changing environment. Again, the bourgeois family is different from the traditional ethnic family (of many different cultures) not only through the experience of transcultural migration but also, and especially, through its emphasis upon the nuclear family and the individual rather than upon the entire family network, the clan, and the ethnic group. Many of us who have experienced in our own lives the tension between the traditional ethnic family and the bourgeois family recognize full well the contrasting values of each, even as we make our own choice.

Finally, in the startling and historically untypical explosion of affluence which followed upon World War II, an entire generation of families in the United States experienced a wave of what at first appeared as liberation, but lately has come to seem like moral confusion and even decadence. Children born in the meanness of the Depression were not prepared, as parents, to bring up children under heretofore never experienced conditions of affluence. Wanting to spare their children their own remembered deprivations, they indulged them rather more than they had ever been indulged. Learning a new cosmopolitanism and experiencing, perhaps, a form of culture shock, they abandoned the forms of authority under which they had been reared. Much influenced by new psychological theories linking discipline to repression and repression to fascism, the parents who fought a war against Hitler—and even more their children—tried desperately not to appear to be authoritarian. One aspect of this immense cultural repression of the natural instinct of parental authority was the sustained effort not to be "judgmental."

Thus a best-selling writer of books of loose sex for children tells a radio talk-show host, who pretends to be admiring, that she "tries very hard not to be judgmental, not to make my readers feel bad about things they might do, like the characters in my book.'' This flight from critical judgment runs precisely against the grain of the bourgeois family. The bourgeois family does make judgments. It does so not only in codes of ethical conduct and in schemes of self-improvement, but also in terms of practical achievement. The code of the bourgeois family is *to measure*—to measure in order to compete against oneself, to inspire self-improvement, to "better oneself.'' By contrast, the family of the new class (the post-bourgeois elite family) fears measurement, disdains competition with the self, and prefers to "find" rather than to "better" the self. The heart of the difference lies in the respect of the bourgeois family for critical judgment, and of the family of the new class for being nonjudgmental.

There are two quite different approaches to the ancient contest between reasoned judgment and the passions. There can scarcely be any doubt that the family of the new class gives greater play to the passions and esteems reasoned judgment less than does the bourgeois family. Indeed, the family of the new class is praised by its champions for its moral superiority—for being "liberated"— in precisely these respects.

In personal life, rule by one's passions and liberation from the disciplines of reasoned judgment are the opposite of what is meant by self-government. While the self may freely choose to follow its passions where they list—to let it all hang out—it would be claiming too much to describe that process as government. Rebellion, dissidence, dissonance, and "letting go" are closer to the mark. Government itself is a bourgeois word, self-government even more so.

Where self-government is not possible in personal life, it remains to be seen whether it is possible in the republic. Every prognosis based upon history would suggest that lack of self-government in the individual citizenry will lead to lack of restraint in the government of the republic. (It does not follow that habits of self-government nourished in families necessarily produces self-restraint in government, as the case of Britain shows.) Personal prodigality will be parallelled by public prodigality. As individuals live beyond their means, so will the state. As individuals liberate themselves from costs, responsibilities, and a prudent concern for the future, so will their political leaders. When self-government is no longer an ideal for individuals, it cannot be credible for the republic.

IX
Continuous Revolution

Against the holistic view of society, I find it more useful to think of contemporary society . . . as three distinct realms, each of which is obedient to a different axial principle. I divide society, analytically, into the *techno-economic structure,* the *polity,* and the *culture.* These are not congruent with one another and have different rhythms of change: they follow different norms which legitimate different, and even contrasting, types of behavior. It is the discordances between these realms which are responsible for the various contradictions within society.
—Daniel Bell, *The Cultural Contradictions of Capitalism*[1]

Pluralism, once institutionalized, spreads out into every department of life. Free to choose, individuals do not necessarily follow in the footsteps of their parents, either in occupation or in avocation, either in political conviction or in religion. These multiple pluralisms of daily life have their origin in a sturdy triune framework—in the division of the political system from the moral-cultural system, and of the economic system from both.

Each of these systems has its own special institutions and methods, disciplines and standards, purposes and limits, attractions and repulsions. Each has its own ethos. Each also creates problems for the other two. These tensions are desirable; a pluralist system is *designed* to foment them. From the stream of sparks flowing from their contact it derives its energy for progress and its capacities for internal correction. It is a system intended to constitute a continuous revolution.

1
The Political System

By virtue of its independence from the moral-cultural system, the political system is free from control by any one church, sect, school of thought, or philosophy. The separation of church and state protects the church but also the state. Nonetheless, clergymen and journalists, preachers and professors often place enormous pressures upon the state—on behalf of temperance or civil rights, to end the war in Vietnam, to develop legislation or to bring controverted cases to trial, etc. Such power is substantial. The form of political power which flows from the barrel of a gun is one form only. Armies and police powers are important. But ideas in people's heads and values in their hearts have demoralized great armies, as was the case when the armies of Iran were disarmed during the Khomeini revolution. Ideas have power. Nations may reform themselves through such power. They may also, following illusory ideas, weaken, impoverish, or destroy themselves. Political leaders may recognize realities invisible to the public, but find their freedom of action gravely hampered by public ignorance. On the other hand, the public may recognize realities which political elites do not, and find its intentions frustrated by its leadership.

As the political system is structurally separated from the moral-cultural system, while yet profoundly affected by it through the power of ideas and values, so also it is structurally separated from the economic system, while yet profoundly affected by it at many levels. Failures in the economic system may lead to grave political crises, as in the Depression or in times of massive unemployment and diminished productivity. Failures in the political system may cripple the economic system. Still, the structural separation of the political system from the economic system protects the integrity of each, even though each system also exercises considerable power over the other. The state has executive, legislative, judicial, and (increasing) bureaucratic power over economic enterprises. It can impede and it can finally destroy an entire private industry, as in the case of the private nuclear-energy industry. It can restrain automakers from building small cars overseas, through setting fleet average mileage standards while not allowing autos built outside the United States to be counted in fulfillment of such standards. It can close any plant anywhere for infractions of laws and regulations (of which there are entire shelves of volumes). It can impose costs, confiscate profits (as in the windfall-profits tax on oil companies), tax, set depreciation schedules, and in many other ways expand or constrict the liberties of business. It may harass executives through wiretaps, FBI visits in the night, investigations, and subpoenas. At the extremity, it can nationalize entire industries.[2]

During the past fifty years, the federal government (in particular) has expanded its activities in and control over the economic system. The various governments within the political system now employ some 15.6 million civilian workers (1978).[3] By contrast, the top five hundred industrial corporations listed by *Fortune* magazine employ 15.8 million workers.[4] Thus the government has created new interests for a sizable new class of citizens, who have a stake in its own expanded wealth and power. The greater the share of wealth and power accumulated by government, the greater the opportunities for ambitious members of this class. This class, moreover, finds many natural allies among those who depend upon government grants, payments, and favors, as do teachers, universities, hospitals, and various clients of social services from social security to aid to mothers with dependent children. In addition, an estimated 4 million workers are consultants to government bodies or work on government contract.[5]

Through legislation affecting social mores, governmental agencies have further acquired powers over hiring and personnel practices. A vast apparatus of mandatory information and secret investigation has been erected. This apparatus extends beyond the economic system into the institutions of the moral-cultural system.

The politicization of moral and cultural issues now extends to the role of women, homosexuality, marriage, family, abortion, renting and selling real estate, busing, educational experiments, and the like. The "new politics" has expanded the reach of the political system. Daniel Bell comments:

> Above all, the basic allocative power is now *political* rather than *economic*. And this raises a fundamental question of restraints. The economic constraint on private wants is the amount of money that a man has, or the credit he is able to establish. But what are the constraints on political demands? . . . today the public household is more than a third sector; increasingly in the modern polity it absorbs the other two. And the major aspect of the public household is the centrality of the budget, the level of government revenues and expenditures, as the mechanism for reallocation and redress. How much the government shall spend, and for whom, obviously is the major political question of the next decades.[6]

The political system, in a word, encroaches significantly upon the economic system and the moral-cultural system.

2
The Economic System

Most literature about democracy takes the economic system as the main adversary of the political system. Most leaders of the moral-cultural system seem also to regard the economic system as their main adversary. For this reason, the problems which the economic system creates for the political and moral-cultural systems are not only well-known but much exaggerated. On the other hand, capitalism has been given far too little credit for what it *has* done for democracy and what it might, *in line with its own ideals,* yet do. Similarly with respect to the freedom and vitality of the moral-cultural system. The plaints and wails of poets and preachers about the sins and errors of the market system screech through intellectual history, while friendly voices are few. Yet no other form of economy has resulted in so many books being published, schools founded, churches built, philanthropies undertaken, and intellectual and religious liberties maintained.

To begin with, "democratic capitalism" is said by some to be a contradiction in terms, since economic institutions are not usually run by democratic methods. The assumption is that democratic methods are universally desirable. But most sectors of the moral-cultural system do not find democratic methods appropriate in every inquiry or action. A majority of persons once believed that the earth is flat. Majority belief did not make this view true. The Ten Commandments are not repealed when a majority no longer offers them obedience. Excellence in philosophical argument is governed by intrinsic criteria, not by conventional wisdom. So democratic methods have an honored place in a democratic society, but their use is by no means intended to be universal. Even within the political system, neither the executive nor the judicial powers are intended to be exercised by democratic majorities. Furthermore, the institutions of representative government are designed to limit majoritarian decision-making, both for reasons of practicality and because majorities are easily swayed by passion, inclined to intolerance, and subject to impulses of tyranny.

Secondly, it may be true that business executives too little honor the genius of professors, writers, and artists, but it seems altogether certain that the reverse is true. In the production of wealth, high excellence is required. The chief executive officers of major corporations have as much claim to high talent as do the top five hundred intellectuals and professors, the top five hundred scientists, or the top five hundred musicians, painters, and sculptors of the land. Their inventions and organizational innovations, their capacities for leadership and practical judgment, are assets which benefit their fellow citizens. Until their activities appeared in history, the human race was far poorer than it is. Yet few minorities in the United States are as subject to ridicule and disparagement in the public media. As Ben Stein reports in *The View from Sunset Boulevard*,[7] the villain in virtually every television plot is a businessman. What is oddest is that the businessman, through advertising, pays for his own vilification.

The theologian John C. Bennett has written that capitalism needs to "be tamed and corrected by democracy," and that "the impulses of democracy and the impulses of capitalism are often in conflict with one another." He elaborates: "Until the rise of effective labor unions, many powerful corporations were, in relation to their workers, industrial tyrannies."[8] While the political system may at times "tame and correct" the economic system, the reverse is also true. Democratic leaders have a tendency to bestow benefits on the voters, in order to curry electoral favor, without accepting responsibility for paying for them. The resources and practical wisdom of the economic system often tame and correct the illusions of the political system.

Not long ago, I undertook a study of one of the most bitter labor-industrial conflicts in American history, the strike by the United Mine Workers in northeastern Pennsylvania in 1897.[9] In the most awful labor massacre in American history until that time, some nineteen miners were shot to death and at least fifty-three others wounded by gunfire from an excited sheriff's posse. So it is true that the economic system has had bloody episodes. But so has the political system (in the Civil War) and so have churches (as in the burning of Catholic convents, the murder of the Mormons, etc.). It is true, further, that the miners at Lattimer Mines in 1897 suffered abuse not only from the mine owners but also from the state government and local citizenry, as well as from major cultural guardians. The *New York Times* and many other papers praised the sheriff's posse and blamed the strikers. Indeed, the record of some churches in the history of labor struggles is not much better than that of "the capitalists" Bennett singles out for blame. The record of the political system is also flawed. Nonetheless, the pluralism of the three systems enabled the miners at Lattimer, at the cost of their own blood, to make their case and ultimately to bring about important transformations in all three systems. Some persons (including some mine owners) in each of the three systems were aroused by injustice. Gradually, all three sectors advanced toward a new correlation of forces. By 1904, President Theodore Roosevelt was in a position, at a dramatic moment, to side with the workers and to bring a favorable conclusion to the Great Strike of that year. The men at Lattimer did not die in vain.

In his important but flawed book *Politics and Markets,* Charles E. Lindblom holds it to be a curious feature of democratic thought that it has not faced up to the private corporation as a "peculiar organization" in an "ostensible" democracy. "Enormously large, rich in resources, the big corporations, we have seen, command more resources than do most government units. They can also, over a broad range, insist that government meet their demands, even if these demands run counter to those of citizens expressed through their polyarchal controls." He points out that as legal persons, large corporations enter into partisan politics, although often on both sides. They exercise "unusual veto powers" and are "disproportionately powerful." He concludes that "the large private corporation fits oddly into democratic theory and vision. Indeed, it does not fit."[10]

As it happens, no single corporation employs as many persons as the U.S. Department of Defense or the combined agencies of Health, Human Services and Welfare. Indeed, the Big Three auto companies—which, in 1980, looked like anything but fearsome giants—had the two largest and the fourteenth-ranked work forces (853,000 for GM, 495,000 for Ford, 134,000 for Chrysler), and only ten corporations (GM, Ford, General Electric, ITT, IBM, Mobil, United Technologies, U.S. Steel, Exxon, and Western Electric) had more than 160,000 employees.[11] Usually, however, only small portions of the employees of a large corporation work at any one location. Few work sites have as many employees at one place as do representative universities like the University of California at Los Angeles (56,000), the University of Michigan (46,000), the University of Texas (36,000), the University of Wisconsin (33,000), Brigham Young University (25,000), and Yale University (13,000).[12]

Most corporations are not "enormously large." One may argue that the few which are have important reasons for being so.[13] The auto companies, for example, compete not only with each other but with large competitors in other lands. The Boeing Corporation has to be large to build large aircraft. Without large national merchandising outlets like Sears and Penney's, many economies of scale could not be passed on to consumers. Moreover, government has far more coercive controls over even the biggest corporations than the latter over the government. The Congress of the United States in 1980 was easily able to confiscate $100 billion in the so-called windfall-profits tax from the oil companies. This confiscation may have been appropriate. But although the funds confiscated rightfully belonged to the shareholders of all the oil companies affected, the political system had no serious difficulty in seizing them. In his campaign for the Republican presidential candidacy for 1980, former governor John Connally of Texas probably had more support from the executives of major corporations than any candidate in history. He raised great sums of money, which availed him to elect one single delegate from all the primaries he entered.

Many writers, like Professor Lindblom, do not attack all corporations equally; they most fear the "big" corporations. Professor Lindblom says the big corporations are "disproportionately" powerful. Compared to what? Corporations have powerful lobbies, but so have others: public employee unions, the National Education Association, the recipients of social security, and many others. Besides, corporations in different industries and regions have conflicting interests. Pressured by many lobbyists from many sides, it is still government that establishes the depreciation schedules, capital-gains taxes, environmental legislation, safety and health rules, personnel guidelines, and many other limits and restraints under which such firms operate. Yet such firms must constantly rebuild their infrastructures for the new technologies of the future, a task in which they have fallen significantly behind their competitors in Japan and Germany. The case that U.S. corporations are not powerful enough to secure even their own liberty to function competitively seems to be a strong one. Professor Lindblom ignores it. The entire public is already suffering and will yet suffer more for political errors with respect to markets.

Does the large private corporation fit oddly into democratic theory? Without the large private corporation, there would be one fewer among the large private forces strong enough to check the growing ambitions of the administrative state. Were the state to acquire control over the large corporations, the political system would thoroughly dominate the economic system. The likely result would be a productive capacity run at about the efficiency of the U.S. Postal Service. The most destructive result would be the diminishment of liberty.

The employees of the *Fortune* 500 are among the best-paid and most-favored in working conditions and benefits in the nation. Corporate life is not organized democratically, like a town meeting, although its forms of internal organization are many and varied. To organize industry democratically would be a grave and costly error, since democratic procedures are not designed for productivity and efficiency. Poor management may not recognize that workmen on the line are fertile in figuring out new and better ways of doing things; but good management does. The more a corporation embodies the principle of subsidiarity in its organization, the closer to its work force it becomes.[14] According to this principle, human life proceeds most intelligently and creatively when decisions are made at the level closest to concrete reality, and when next-higher levels of decision-making are invoked only as a last resort. Experiments to find better forms of organization are part of the history of the economic system, which has real interests in discovering them. But it is naive to demand of a system, whose goal is to increase the wealth not only of the United States but of the world, a form of internal organization inappropriate to the task.

Every encroachment of the political system upon the economic system has its costs. The unintended consequences of such controls are certain to be far more sweeping and destructive than costs calculated in advance. But liberty, too, has costs. In my hometown in Cambria County, Pennsylvania, the red dust thrown into the air by Bethlehem Steel Company used to be a source of pride, a sign of the modernity, verve, and muscle which conquered an idle wilderness. Only in my adulthood was this same dust suddenly perceived as "pollution." For more than a century, peoples from all over the world had streamed to Johnstown and cities like it, glad to find jobs and a better life, and willing to pay the cost of the red dust and the brackish waters of the Stony Creek River. Then values changed. Citizens wanted the dust controlled and the rivers clean. That purpose, in turn, imposed new costs upon Bethlehem Steel, and eventually upon everyone who pays for items in which steel is included. One may think that the corporations can pay such costs. But whatever money the corporations have they receive from purchasers of their products. The citizenry pays for what it chooses.

As the decline of the U.S. steel companies in world markets continues, Bethlehem Steel keeps cutting back its work force in Johnstown. One day, Bethlehem will probably abandon its antiquated facilities there entirely. This corporate decision will impose public costs. Yet the political system of the United States has for years been imposing costs on corporations like Bethlehem Steel. The moral-cultural system has not valued the liberty and social needs of producers. The political and moral-cultural elites with whom corporate leaders must work have taken for granted the wealth generated in the past, but have not thought about its declining infrastructure. These public failures have hurt U.S. steel companies and other corporate "giants." Giants die too. The corporation which, as Lindblom says, "is legally a person" is, like a person, mortal.

Nonetheless, the economic system creates serious problems for the other two systems. In a brief summary of his book, Professor Lindblom argues that "capitalism is now a barrier to a more fully developed democracy because it is a system of inequality in the distribution of power." Businessmen hold a privileged position. "At peril to their own positions, political officials know that they must do everything in their power to meet whatever level of business demands will produce economic stability and growth." In the preamble of the Constitution, this appears to be one of the main purposes of good government. Yet Lindblom would appear to desire the political system to take over the economic system: "A distinguishing characteristic of capitalism is that many of the most important functions to be performed in the society—feeding and housing the population and supplying it with power for its machines, among others—are assigned not to government officials but to a category of major functionaries called businessmen."[15] Free citizens who by right have economic liberty are hardly "functionaries." Moreover, the contest between the leaders of the political system and the leaders of the economic system does not seem to be as one-sided as he claims. Each side makes life more difficult for the other. The division between economic power and political power is deliberate, and so are the headaches involved. This separation can never be perfect, is always fluid, and is properly hotly contested.

With respect to the moral-cultural system, some thinkers argue that the economic system is governed by functional rationality, along an axis altogether different from the axes of political concern or moral rationality. To some extent, this is obviously true. In deciding to close an unprofitable plant, managers may recognize political pressures and moral pressures of many sorts, while still determining that economic rationality alone "leaves them no alternative." Some might further argue that reliance on such rationality also represents, in the larger view, sound political and moral judgment. Their reason is that a polity which subsidizes unprofitable operations penalizes other citizens elsewhere, weakens its own economic future, and, even if in the name of compassion or other noble sentiments, sets in motion pressures for less than moral purposes throughout the society. Some might say, in other words, that economic rationality also ranks among the moral virtues, a form of prudence.

But there is a deeper point. A capitalist economic system may be described in terms that seem to be, as it were, arithmetic and morally neutral, like punctuality, exact accounting, efficiency, honest labor, a fair price, and the like. Just the same, there is a strong consonance between the virtues required for successful commercial and industrial practice and the natural moral virtues. Without Aristotelian temperance and prudence, fortitude and justice, economic rationality lacks root in human character. Economic rationality is not easy to acquire; it must be learned. The act of acquiring it enforces its own disciplines. Managers and workers must show up on time, with regularity and attentiveness. Not for nothing do many voices plead for special programs like the Job Corps to "educate" workers presently unemployable, less perhaps to teach them skills than to instruct them in good "work habits." The training of managers is also, to a high degree, moral training.

Some experts point out that capitalism is "ideologically neutral," and that in developing countries like China, Nigeria, and Nicaragua they can teach the skills of production, management, efficiency, and marketing as pedagogical rules and practical techniques, apart from any reference to "capitalism." Of course. What must be noted, though, is that to learn and to practice such rules is to discipline one's habits and one's acts in specific ways; that is, to learn and to practice classical virtues.

Economic rationality, therefore, is not as merely instrumental or morally empty as some may think. The virtues it requires, and the virtues it nourishes, are indispensable to a self-governing polity and to a sound morality. Obviously, a system vivified by the cardinal virtues is not by that fact alone directed to moral purposes, or within reach of a good moral life for all its citizens. One may imagine a virtuous regime like that of ancient Sparta geared for martial exercise. For such reasons, democratic capitalism does not look to economic rationality alone for the full flowering of its intrinsic moral ideals. Yet the virtues inherent in economic rationality are not without significance to the virtues of its political and moral-cultural life.

3
The Moral-Cultural System

Two contrary propositions seem required by contemplation of the moral-cultural system of the United States—that is, of its institutions of journalism, the universities, the cinema, the churches, and the rest: (1) that this system is the least developed, most neglected, most delinquent system; (2) that it has become the most powerful, most ambitious, most dominating system. If Joseph Schumpeter is the scholar who was earliest and most gravely concerned about the potential danger posed by "the intellectuals" to the survival of democratic capitalism, there are not lacking many scholars who hold that democratic capitalism has for too long neglected its spiritual resources and is using up the spiritual capital it has inherited from the past. Both of the above propositions, then, appear to be true, and each illuminates the other. Those who hold that democratic capitalism will end, perhaps sooner than we imagine, by eviscerating itself do not usually locate its fatal flaw in its political system or in its economic system, both of which are superior to any known to history, but in its moral-cultural system.

The strengths of the moral-cultural system of the United States are many.[16] Its churches are among the most active and best-attended in the world. Its scientific establishments have, in all but a few departments, either no rivals or a bare handful of peers. Its universities include a larger percentage of its population than those of any nation on earth. The arts flourish, including arts (dance, ballet) to which America in an organized way has come relatively late. If there are no American novelists to rival the great Russian, British, and even American authors of the nineteenth century, and no painters as dominant as Picasso, nonetheless, artists from throughout the world in every medium must now exhibit their talents in America, measure themselves by the best to be found here, and absorb world-significant energies from the American experience. Above all, the sheer quantity of moral, religious, and artistic passion generated in America is evidence of enormous spiritual vitality. The great movements of the postwar years, the years of supposed affluence and decadence, have been moral in energy, character and expression: the civil rights movement, the war on poverty, the anti-war movement, environmentalism, feminism, the "pro-life" and "pro-choice" movements among them. Americans seem to judge themselves by high moral standards, to enjoy feeling guilty, to argue about what ought to be done about their errors, and to do it—to do something, anything, ill-advisedly perhaps, but with unmistakable energy. Completely obscure and ordinary people—Martin Luther King, Jr., Michael Harrington, Daniel Berrigan, S.J., Ralph Nader, Betty Friedan, Phyllis Schlafly, Ellen McCormack, Howard Jarvis—seem continually to be thrown up by the nation's churning energies to positions symbolizing constant social change.

During the middle years of the twentieth century, new technologies have given the leaders of the moral-cultural system unprecedented power, for a large and complex society, drawn (quite suddenly) into an international circle of self-consciousness, is extraordinarily dependent on mass communications. The radio, the cinema, the phonograph and the cassette player, television, high-speed presses able to produce international news and photo magazines, and telex and communications satellites for the transmission of newspaper text and photos have lifted the world of ideas and symbols beyond the range of the individual's voice and physical presence. They have created a new nervous system, almost as it were a new collective brain, for the instantaneous transmission of ways of looking at the world. In a sense, ideas and symbols have become more powerful than reality. They are a *new* reality, often (although not always) able to trample upon stubborn fact, to make illusions seem to be realities while long ignoring, as if they did not exist, important realities hidden from public contemplation. The media of communication interpose themselves between individuals in the public and the world around them. It would be naive to expect such *media* to be pellucid windows on reality, subject to no distortion.

The media of communication are, from one perspective, institutions of the economic system or (as in the case of public television) of the political system. Yet journalists quite properly regard themselves as members of a separate estate. Their behavior is governed less by laws appropriate only to commerce than by liberties and responsibilities proper to the world of ideas, values,

and symbols. The domain of the word—the right to free speech—
is specifically protected. Its relative autonomy grants to the moral-
cultural system status as a system, on a plane equal to that of the
economic system and the political system. Special bodies of tradition and law protect its spheres of operation. Its special ideals
and disciplines are shepherded with jealous vigilance.

The culture of the national media, particularly of television,
tends to be the culture of artists and entertainers (directors, producers, camera crews, make-up artists, script writers, lighting
engineers, etc.). This culture has traditionally been sympathetic
to "the left." It nurtures few conservatives and few with compre-
hension of or respect for the economic system. Its special social
location makes it less than a clear window on reality. Its sympathies are often obvious. This fact of life is also a check upon the
system.

The national media are not coextensive with the moral-cultural
system, for many persons and groups justifiably feel left out of
media coverage. In order to have public weight at all, in order for
their very *existence* to be recognized in the new sphere of reality
created by the national media, many persons and groups have had
to learn the strategies and tactics of access. There are many
sources of ideas, values, and ideals powerful and active in the
population which are represented in the national media barely or
not at all. The bishops of the Roman Catholic church, for example, represent important spiritual interests of at least one-fourth of
the population, but it would be silly to imagine that one-fourth of
the weight, so to speak, of media presentations serves such interests. For this purpose, Catholic churches, schools, meetings, in-
stitutes, magazines, newspapers, associations, and families play
a systemic moral-cultural role, as do those of other churches.
They must often do so against the media tide.

Finally, ideas have consequences, nowhere more so than as the
architectonic ideas which inspire systems of political economy. In
our time, scores of new nations are choosing paths of economic
development. In this context, P. T. Bauer of the London School
of Economics has often pointed out that economic development
cannot be said to depend on the possession of great natural resources, since many highly developed nations (Great Britain, Japan, Taiwan, Singapore) are not conspicuously endowed, and
many nations rich in resources remain sadly underdeveloped (as
in Africa). Nor can economic development be said to depend on

small and manageable populations, since many "overpopulated" nations (the Netherlands, Japan, Hong Kong) are economically successful. Nor on noncolonial status, since many of the most highly developed nations have recently been—or still are—colonies. Economic development, he stresses, depends "on people and their arrangements," on "human resources and the will to use them," on "personal qualities," on "social institutions and mores," on "political arrangements."[17] That is to say, *the moral-cultural system is the chief dynamic force behind the rise both of a democratic political system and of a liberal economic system.* The moral-cultural system is the *sine qua non* of the political system and the economic system. Neglect of it bodes ill.

One result of this curious neglect of the moral-cultural resources of our own system is the abandonment of the exposition of these systems to social scientists and technicians. Yet such experts are barred by their disciplines from the very sorts of moral inquiry most required.

The second result is that this system makes no moral presentation of itself to the world. It discusses itself, and allows itself to be discussed, in sheerly material and procedural terms. The intellectuals of those incredibly varied nations ideologically tied together as "the Third World" heap on it a burden of guilt they do not consider attributing to themselves. There has grown up, as P. T. Bauer observes, a dishonorable international politics.[18] It is morally wrong, not only intellectually dishonest, to cooperate with such a tide of ideas and values, and to deny before the world those moral-cultural qualities without which neither economic development nor democratic governance can be achieved.

A third result is that morale is lowered in the West. Human beings do not live by bread alone. They must believe their political and economic activities have moral significance. Their stamina, their perseverance in difficulties, their sense of well-being and purpose—all these depend on the strength of the moral-cultural system in which they participate.

Yet it is, ironically, from the guardians of the moral-cultural system that democratic capitalism, according to Schumpeter, faces its most mortal danger. The most ambitious among them are liable to resent the leaders of the economic system and the political system, whose methods and styles differ so much from their own. Growing rapidly in numbers as the ranks of professionals and technicians expand, emboldened by the new powers over reality which the instruments of communication concentrate in their hands, the "new class" is tempted like any other class to follow the will-to-power wherever it leads.[19] The new class from its base in the moral-cultural system may attempt to dominate both the state and the economy.

The new class is a formidable danger to democratic capitalism. (There is a new class even within the clergy: large numbers of clerics who are neither bishops nor chaplains nor pastors but ecclesiastical bureaucrats.) For the new class has at its disposal both instruments of unrivaled power and a strategic location at the heart of a complex society. Democratic capitalism is more likely to perish through its loss of its indispensable ideas and morals than through weaknesses in its political system or its economic system. In its moral-cultural system lies its weakest link.

The literature on the new class is immense.[20] Some critics rightly point out that persons of high income, high education, and high status (the external determinants of the new class) are to be found on all sides of the ideological spectrum. But two further determinants must be mentioned. A large proportion of this new elite benefits in power, wealth, and celebrity by the growing power and wealth of the state. Secondly, many participate in the "adversarial culture" which plays so large a role in debunking institutions and values which stand in the way of their own new morality, new culture, and new politics. Moreover, the line between being an opponent of the new class and a partisan of it often falls *within* the hearts and minds of individuals, who struggle internally to define their own choice. For this reason, it seems wrong to argue from economic or political determinism.

A war of ideas is being fought in many minds and hearts. Many, battling in this war, change their minds. Within us, there is a battle between the competing ideals of democratic capitalism and democratic socialism. On its outcome, the future shape of our society depends.

Two

The Twilight of Socialism

The most unreported fact of our era is the death of socialism.
—Daniel Bell

X

The Transformation of Socialism

Marxism has been the greatest fantasy of our century. . . .
The influence that Marxism has achieved, far from being the
result or proof of its scientific character, is almost entirely
due to its prophetic, fantastic, and irrational elements. . . .
At present, Marxism neither interprets the world nor changes
it. it is merely a repertoire of slogans serving to organize
various interests.

—Leszek Kolakowski, *Main Currents of Marxism*[1]

Socialist movements continue to grow around the world, particularly in Africa and Latin America. Yet it is not easy today to
state what socialists stand for. This difficulty arises less from the
fact that socialists are divided in their views, although they are,
than from the fact that socialists are embarrassed by the totalitarianism of existing socialist states. So far as intellectual content
goes, the word "socialism" appears to designate—in the West, at
least—two vague and shifting sets of attitudes: first, idealism
about equality; secondly, hostility toward democratic capitalism.

In its central historical vision, whether Marxist or non-Marxist,
socialism was once presented, negatively, as a way of analyzing
the deficiencies of democratic capitalism. Positively, socialism
once meant the abolition of private property; state ownership of
the means of production through the nationalization of industries;
state control over all aspects of the economy; the abolition of
"bourgeois democracy" through the creation of a classless society; and an international order based upon a class analysis tran-

scending national, cultural, and linguistic frontiers. Socialism meant the banishing of the profit motive, which was judged to be the root cause of the exploitation of labor. It also meant the abolition of imperialism, since capital and the profit motive were judged to be the root of empire. Socialism promised a social structure which would end competition between person and person and give to each according to need while taking from each according to ability, a social structure which would thus effect a change in what earlier generations had erroneously regarded as "human nature." Socialism, it was confidently predicted, would bring about a new type of human being, "socialist man." Such a human being would act from motives of human solidarity, community, cooperation, and comradeliness.

Socialism has many intellectual roots, including pre-Marxist traditions of religious socialism.[2] Socialism, some said, is the practice of which Christianity is the religion. Others, like Marx and Engels, rejected "soft" socialism. Such Marxists emphasized that socialism could only come about through violence, since the owners of the instruments of production could not be expected to give up their power and privileges without a struggle. But not all socialists have been Marxists.

In the 133 years since *The Communist Manifesto* and in the 64 years since the Bolshevik revolution, several important lessons have been learned by virtually all socialists. First, the socialist dream has sometimes resulted in a nightmare of oppression, totalitarian control, and ruthless imperialism. Second, national and ethnic loyalties have proved to be stronger than class loyalties. Thus as early as World War I, workers, even socialist workers, manufactured the munitions used by soldiers, even socialist soldiers, in each of the national armies. Since that time, socialist nations have declared war on one another, invaded one another, and publicly and emotionally denounced and threatened one another.

Furthermore, specific elements in socialist doctrine have been shown to be deficient in practice. Nationalized industries do not prevent low wages to workers, do not conspicuously improve working conditions, do not diminish environmental damage, and do not raise levels of efficiency, material progress, and humane attitudes in the work force. On the other side, those small portions of agriculture allowed by socialist regimes to remain in private hands have outperformed collectivized state agriculture by factors as high as 30 to 1, despite far higher concentrations of resources (machinery, fertilizers, roads, etc.) devoted to state collectives. Again, administered prices and wages have been shown to be far less intelligent, efficient, and rational than the market mechanism. In the economic sphere, therefore, nearly every central socialist doctrine has been shown to be in need of critical transformation.

In the political sphere, the central administrative state has proved to be a more thorough instrument of oppression and exploitation than the democratic capitalist state.

In the moral-cultural sphere, no fully socialist state has yet shown that it can tolerate the broad range of dissent, human liberties, and human rights achieved by democratic capitalist states.

Dogmatism and sectarianism bedevil socialist cultures, perhaps precisely because of their claim to represent science rather than opinion. In sum, the socialist frame of mind and socialist practice have been shown to be far less humane than Marx and non-Marxist socialists had expected.

Solzhenitsyn and others have testified that no one behind the Iron Curtain can bear to discuss socialism without at least a sardonic smile. For individuals, the creed is empty, even though it still functions as a powerful instrument of legitimation for Soviet domestic repression and international empire.

Outside the self-declared socialist nations of the Soviet bloc and China, socialists have also been transformed. Few today point to the Soviet Union or to China as models they would wish to emulate. Although some try to place the best face they can upon existing socialist experiments elsewhere, and continue to greet new ones with fresh hope, most insist upon distinguishing what *they* mean by socialism from what occurs within existing socialist states. In this sense, socialism has lost its grip on concrete reality. Most Western and Third World socialists try to rescue the dream from the manifest horrors of actual experimentation. Even as a doctrine, socialism has been revised in almost every part. Thus, for example, the leading socialist social scientist in the United States, C. Wright Mills, took pains in one essay to list the key propositions of socialism, and to show how each of them has been proved by history to be false or misleading.[3]

In the real world, socialism has acquired two decisive centers of gravity. On the one hand, its doctrines legitimate the extension of the empire of the Soviet Union. On the other, among the Western bourgeoisie, it is a catch-all for many types of utopianism and radical individualism, a substitute religion. On both counts, it has precipitated strong intellectual and popular revulsion. This loss of faith is most widespread within the Soviet orbit and, outside it, among formerly socialist intellectuals. Thus, just where the sun should be shining brightest, there is gloom. In *Main Currents of Marxism,* Leszek Kolakowski, until 1968 the Professor of History and Philosophy at the University of Warsaw and Eastern Europe's most distinguished Marxist theoretician, tried to describe why. Kolakowski has not yet despaired of socialism—not, at least, democratic socialism—and he remains in the Polish anti-capitalist tradition. Still, he values liberty and the liberal polity which institutionalizes it. He has taken to describing himself as a "conservative liberal democratic socialist."[4] While it would be hard for an outsider to be as detached and cool and yet as devastating to Marxism as he is in his three-volume study, Kolakowski is not alone among Eastern intellectuals in rejecting Marxism. He summarizes lessons of experience painfully learned by many others of vastly different intellectual commitments, like Aleksandr Solzhenitsyn of the Soviet Union, Mihajlo Mihajlov of Yugoslavia,[5] and Zdenek Mlynar of Czechoslovakia.[6] Kolakowski writes, for example:

> Marxism has been frozen and immobilized for decades as the ideological superstructure of a totalitarian political movement, and in consequence has lost touch with intellectual developments and social realities. The hope that it could be revived and made fruitful once again soon proved to be an illusion. As an explanatory "system" it is dead, nor does it offer any "method" that can be effectively used to interpret modern life, to foresee the future, or cultivate utopian projections. Contemporary Marxist literature, although plentiful in quantity, has a depressing air of sterility and helplessness. . . .[7]

Kolakowski properly gives credit to Marx for drawing attention to the important effects which the social conflicts of an era may have upon the history of politics and the arts. Even those who do not believe that the whole of human history is the history of class conflict, or that the polity and the moral-cultural system have no history of their own because "true" history is the history of instruments of production, have learned from Marx. But Kolakowski faults Marx for imagining that socialism is a science and offers a scientific method for predicting the future. Marxism is not an explanatory theory. Its purported predictive capacities are sheer fantasy.[8]

Some hold that Marx is not responsible for Stalinism, since "the young Marx" was humanistic and democratic. But Kolakowski observes that, after all,

> . . . it was Marx who declared that the whole idea of Communism could be summed up in a single formula—the abolition of private property; that the state of the future must take over the centralized management of the means of production, and that the abolition of capital meant the abolition of wage-labour. There was nothing flagrantly illogical in deducing from this that the expropriation of the bourgeoisie and the nationalization of industry and agriculture would bring about the general emancipation of mankind. In the event it turned out that, having nationalized the means of production, it was possible to erect on this foundation a monstrous edifice of lies, exploitation, and oppression.[9]

According to Kolakowski, Marx inherited a romantic ideal of social unity from the idealized image of the small Greek city-state popular in German philosophy for over a century. This romance fed a common appetite for illusion. There was an element of magic in Marx's view. Abolish capitalists and presto! human beings will become cooperative. Forbid private ownership and presto! human beings will cease to be selfish.[10]

Human needs as far exceed the limits of reality as do romantic dreams. Since to fulfill these is patently silly, Marxists pledged to ensure the satisfaction of "true" or "genuine" needs, not whims and fancies, scorning the "waste" and "vulgarity" of the desires fulfilled through the free market. "This, however, gave rise to a problem which no one answered clearly: who is to decide what needs are 'genuine,' and by what criteria?"[11] When the state undertakes to make such decisions for individuals, "the greatest emancipation in history consists in a system of universal rationing."[12]

It is the same with pledges of perfect equality. Not all goods may be equally divided. Not all goods are sufficiently abundant to yield a share for everyone. Not all workers show equal care, intelligence, and effort. Is it *just* to give each the same reward? "Perfect equality can only be imagined under a system of extreme despotism . . . in real life more equality means more government, and absolute equality means absolute government."[13] As soon as some begin to administer equality, furthermore, some participate unequally in access, information, and power. The ideal of perfect equality is, in practice, self-defeating.

Further, Kolakowski notes, all-embracing economic planning is impossible to achieve.[14] It is incompatible with the autonomy of small producers, regional units, and local groups. A rigorous policy of cradle-to-grave security diminishes innovation and technological progress. The romantic idealism of Marx led him to overlook fundamental antinomies—freedom versus equality, planning versus the autonomy of small groups, social welfare versus inventiveness, government bureaucracy versus efficient management. Marx designed no system of compromise, partial solutions, interest groups, and checks and balances. He concentrated all powers.

Above all, Marx sold liberty short. Kolakowski, still a socialist, strives manfully to rescue his faith in democratic socialism from his loss of faith in Marxism. In his eyes, democratic socialism has nothing to do with an apocalyptic belief in the consummation of history, the inevitability of socialism, the dictatorship of the proletariat, the exaltation of violence, faith in the automatic efficiency of nationalizing industry, or "fantasies concerning a society without conflict and an economy without money." No, by contrast, the purpose of democratic socialism is

> to create institutions which can gradually reduce the subordination of production to profit, do away with poverty, diminish inequality, remove social barriers to educational opportunity, and minimize the threat to democratic liberties from state bureaucracy and the seductions of totalitarianism.[15]

These efforts, for Kolakowski, are firmly rooted in what "Marxists stigmatize as 'negative' freedom, i.e., the area of decision which society allows to the individual." Kolakowski remains anticapitalist, but he is liberal enough to cherish liberty, and specifically a limited state, both as an "intrinsic value requiring no justification beyond itself" and also as "the self-regulating mechanism through which societies reform themselves." Without liberty, "societies are unable to reform themselves."[16] In

Kolakowski's view, Marxism has not suffered death by murder. It has suffocated for want of liberty. Kolakowski prefers for it words like "frozen," "immobile," "sterile," "useless," "dead."[17]

Yet even after it has died as an intellectual theory, Marxism still has enormous power as an instrument of international mobilization. For Marxism has become embodied. It works like a stencil applied to every grievance in human affairs. Wherever there is resentment, wherever there is injustice, wherever there is inequality, wherever there are expectations met too slowly, the Marxist stencil channels frustration and aggression. It announces that all dissatisfactions are against the natural order of things, and that history itself intends immediate and full relief. It directs frustration and aggressiveness against malevolent enemies (whose identity may change upon a moment's notice). It asserts that only such enemies stand between the aggrieved victims and the historical satisfaction of their dreams. The fault lies never in the victims, only in their oppressors. Too late does the victim realize that those who think of themselves as victims decline responsibility for their own condition and surrender their liberty to the absolute state.

As businessmen are the supreme activists of economics, Kolakowski observes, Marxists are the supreme activists of politics. Their trade is grievances. This trade has its own graveyard. "Wherever Communism is in power, the ruling class transforms it into an ideology whose real sources are in nationalism, racism or imperialism," the three hot energies infusing Marxism today. In this way, Communism "has produced its own gravediggers."[18] For such energies are nationalistic and narrow, and spring from hate, envy, and a thirst for power. The coherence of the communist world is, therefore, based on force. It must "be dominated by a single imperialism, or there would be an unending series of wars between 'Marxist' rulers of different countries."[19] As a unifying spiritual force, Marxism is dead. As a mobilizing stencil for grievances—as a center for international training, funding, and logistical support—it continues to live as a "totalitarian political movement."[20]

XI
Socialism as Highmindedness

We were happy a hundred years ago. We knew that there were exploiters and exploited, wealthy and poor, and we had a perfect idea of how to get rid of injustice: we would expropriate the owners and turn the wealth over to the common good. We expropriated the owners and we created one of the most monstrous and oppressive social systems in world history. And we keep repeating that "in principle: everything was all right, only some unfortunate accidents slipped in and slightly spoiled the good idea. Now let us start afresh. . . ."

—Leszek Kolakowski, *The Socialist Idea*[1]

1
What Went Wrong?

Several years ago, a number of lifelong socialists gathered in England to redefine the socialist idea. The actual record of socialism in history had not matched the expectations of their youth. Is something wrong, they asked, in the praxis of socialism, which may be corrected? Or is something wrong with the fundamental *idea*? The outcome of the conference may be summarized as follows: Socialism is not a set of political or economic programs; it is a set of political and economic ideals. In the past, we have misidentified it with programs which do not work, with interpretations of good and evil which were too simple, and with ideals carelessly stated and insufficiently realistic. We must begin afresh.[2] One of the two editors of the conference proceedings, Leszek Kolakowski, is cited above; the other, British philosopher Stuart Hampshire, may be cited here:

> For me socialism is not so much a theory as a set of moral injunctions, which seem to me clearly right and rationally justifiable: first, that the elimination of poverty ought to be the first priority of government after defense; secondly, that as great inequalities in wealth between different social groups lead to inequalities in power and in freedom of action, they are generally unjust and need to be redressed by governmental action; thirdly, that democratically elected governments ought to ensure that primary and basic human needs are given priority within the economic system, even if this involves some loss in the aggregate of goods and services which would otherwise be available.[3]

Two features in recent socialist thought, then, are quite fascinating. First, socialists seem to be in retreat both from theory and from program. A favorite new word is "nondoctrinaire." This may be regarded as disillusionment with doctrine. Secondly, socialists seem to have retreated to the safer ground of moral ideals: about poverty, inequality, and the priority of meeting human needs democratically. One might be tempted to think of socialists as admirable persons who are only voicing ideals quite compatible with democratic capitalism. Why not give them credit for being representatives of the idealism any humane society needs?

The truth is more complex. When I was in college, I was moved by the socialism of Charles Péguy, the French Catholic poet who saw in socialism not so much a doctrine as a way of life.[4] My views of that time may be summarized in passages one frequently encounters, like this one:

> Did the Socialist Party have no higher political ideal than the victory of one class over another it would not be worthy

of a moment's support from any right-thinking individual. It would, indeed, be impossible for the party to gain any considerable strength or prestige. It is the great moral worth of its ideals that attracts adherents to the Socialist movement even from the ranks of the capitalist class, and holds them to their allegiance with an enthusiasm that suggests a close parallel with the early days of Christianity.[5]

In thinking of socialism as a kind of political religion, or perhaps more exactly as a political-economic expression of Jewish-Christian ideals, I tended to give socialists credit for pure idealism. Capitalism might be justified because it works better, but—I tended to agree—it represents an inferior ideal.

The notion that an unworkable ideal is a morally acceptable ideal, however, troubled me. If an ideal doesn't work, isn't that evidence that it is out of touch with human reality? Isn't that a sign that it is a *false* ideal?

In this respect, socialism is unlike Judaism and Christianity. Jews and Christians quite expect this world to be a world of sin. When they entertain images of "the Kingdom of God," they quite properly recognize the transcendence of the Kingdom. They recognize it as a vision and do not expect any earthly institution to embody it fully. Socialism cannot easily accept such realism. The moment socialism allows itself to be judged by realistic criteria, it loses its cachet as a special form of idealism. It becomes simply a competing political economy, to be judged empirically, on its record. If socialism is only a competing political and economic theory, it has no special standing as a kind of secular religion.

Yet it is as a kind of religion that socialists most often justify their beliefs. Seldom do they claim that the superiority of socialism lies in its works, its practicality, its proven fruits. Nearly always they justify it in terms of its vision. "We are *for* equality," Kolakowski writes; "we are for economic democracy." "For me," writes Hampshire, "socialism is not so much a theory as a set of moral injunctions." And again: "It is the great moral worth of its ideals that attracts adherents."[6] Quite commonly, socialists are prepared to admit that democratic capitalism is more productive, more efficient, and far less vicious in practice than socialist theory would lead one to expect; in short, it works better. They rest the case for socialism on its supposed moral superiority over democratic capitalism.

Since nearly everybody interprets the logic of democratic capitalism as inherently less moral than that of socialism, honest persons are often troubled by a "paradox." Democratic capitalism, they think, ought not to bear moral fruit; yet it does. This "paradox" arrested Jacques Maritain:

> This industrial civilization, which I had learned to know in Europe, appeared to me, here, both as gigantically developed (like many things transplanted from Europe over here) and as a kind of ritual dedicated to some foreign goddess. Its inner logic, as I knew it—originally grounded as it was on the principle of the fecundity of money and the absolute primacy of the individual profit—was, everywhere in the world, inhuman and materialist.
>
> But, by a strange paradox, the people who lived and toiled under this structure or ritual of civilization were keeping their own souls apart from it. At least as regards the essentials, their souls and vital energy, their dreams, their everyday effort, their idealism and generosity, were running against the grain of the inner logic of the superimposed structure. They were freedom-loving and mankind-loving people, people clinging to the importance of ethical standards, anxious to save the world, the most humane and the least materialist among modern peoples which had reached the industrial stage.[7]

Jean-François Revel makes an analogous observation.[8]

Yet the nub of this so-called paradox lies in the socialist interpretation of reality. On the premises of democratic capitalism, the happy outcome reported by Maritain and Revel was to be expected. It was, after all, the outcome predicted by the designers of the experiment. Only on the premises of socialism does it come as a surprise.

Furthermore, in the days when I thought socialism represented a moral ideal, socialism required of me no special moral heroism. I did not intend to become an economic activist. I had great ambitions, but not as an entrepreneur, business executive, inventor, or other economic agent. While I attributed high moral idealism to socialism, those who would bear the chief costs of my views were, above all, the wealthy and the economically active. Socialism took no skin off my nose. Moreover, if socialism did not actually work as predicted, the poor and the workers would pay a higher price for economic stagnation that I would. It was a moral position which levied no costs. In the fields of literature, religion, and journalism, moreover, a socialist ideology offers higher status and acclaim. To stand as an adversary seems heroic, visionary, pure, whereas appreciation of the American system is regarded as "selling out," indulging in "compromise," and "making peace with the enemy." This is especially true because of the difference between the literary culture and the broader culture. In the United States, the broader public does not have high regard either for socialists or for their theories. Among the more highly educated, however, and in the dominant literary circles, socialists are afforded moral prestige even by those too realistic to share their views in full.

According to socialist morality, the enemy was clear: the large corporations, the military-industrial complex (not of Japan, Germany, the USSR, Cuba, Nicaragua—only of the United States). One needed only to examine those facts on such matters as confirmed what one already knew. In order to keep one's moral credentials straight, one had only to keep well informed about the latest line of advanced socialist thinking—on busing, crime, affirmative action, sex, and every other issue of the day. In order to help shape the radical consensus, one needed only the wit to draw out the implications for current affairs of socialist premises. Leadership in socialism comes easily enough to the logically rigorous.

Stylistically, at least a hint of socialism enhances the work of a writer or social critic. Since the future is said to belong to socialism, and since advantage accrues to the avant-garde, it is not costly to employ socialism for "critical distance." Since realists tend to become mired in the messiness of facts, they do not seem to be as ideologically reliable and as morally pure as idealists. The socialist world is predominantly literary. It is far easier to organize words on paper than to organize workable programs in reality. In my world, therefore, socialism conferred many advantages.

When I finally decided, on reflection, that I preferred the ideals of democratic capitalism and could not be a democratic socialist, it was at first by considering what works. I was repelled, secondly, by the sense of moral superiority socialism afforded. Finally, I began to reflect upon flaws not only in its practice but also in its theory. I became anti-socialist before I began to turn seriously, for the first time, to an inquiry into the ideals of democratic capitalism.

Perhaps this movement of thought may be explained as follows. Nothing prevents a democratic capitalist from obeying the "moral injunctions" Hampshire lists above. Under democratic capitalism, individuals, parties, and institutions may work effectively to relieve the sufferings of the poor; to try to diminish inequalities of wealth and power through various checks and balances, schemes of redistribution, and legal reforms; and to make the meeting of basic human needs a higher priority than economic growth and the production of goods. A democratic capitalist may, within the system, work for and even achieve all these things. Indeed, others with other priorities are also free to choose what they will work for.

By contrast, democratic socialism has an inherent tendency to impose one set of moral injunctions upon all, even at the expense of other moral injunctions. To be sure, socialist thought assumes that its goals are in harmony with what humans universally desire, and thus does not think of itself as coercive. Yet it does tend to define its opponents as greedy, selfish, oppressive, and hostile to the poor.[9] Such moralism fuels its historical tendency toward coercive behavior and sectarian schism.

Furthermore, since the socialist ideal is presented as an international ideal, with claims that go beyond those of historical institutions, it tends to teach individuals to loathe their own societies. It feeds on the adversarial spirit and has made common cause with "the adversary culture" of literary modernism.[10] It is often hostile to Western institutions and sympathetic to movements of socialist revolution wherever they occur. Most Western socialists, certainly social democrats and democratic socialists, are unremittingly opposed to Stalinism and Soviet-style socialism; some are among its most penetrating and able opponents. Yet socialists typically judge democratic capitalism by the strictest standards of performance, while extending extraordinary sympathy to even the flimsiest claims of socialist revolution elsewhere. When Bernard-Henri Lévy accused the French left of "fifty years of lies" about the Gulag Archipelago, he pointed to this systemic double standard.[11]

2
Definition by Contrast

Stuart Hampshire, we have seen, reduces socialism to three "moral" injunctions: (1) that the elimination of poverty ought to be the first priority of government, after defense; (2) that great inequalities in wealth lead to inequalities in freedom of action and need to be redressed by government action; and (3) that basic needs ought to be given priority by governments, even if this involves some loss in the aggregate of goods and services which would otherwise be available. On the face of it, these injunctions seem to be "moral." Actually, they encapsulate a theory of government and economics. They entail raising up the poor and pulling down the rich. Their aim appears to be to bring about a kind of universal middle income. They look to government as the instrument by which to enforce the desired equality.

Obvious dangers lurk in these three injunctions. First, there is the danger of applying them one-sidedly, so as to create a monstrous government, especially when the injunction to respect the limits of government does not appear to be given equal moral force. Second, there is the danger that "some" loss of aggregate goods and services may be so great as to bring about economic stagnation and decline. Since an impoverished nation has little flexibility in alleviating the lot of its unemployed, its handicapped, and its poor, such loss might place in jeopardy the basic legitimacy of democratic governance, by intensifying the resentments of citizens whose futures show little promise of betterment. Third, there is the danger that attempts to alleviate poverty by a direct and supposedly rational plan may seriously misconstrue the causes of the wealth of nations.

At the very least, Hampshire's three moral injunctions have a statist bias. They appear, as well, to ignore the sources of economic dynamism. These are quite dangerous intellectual errors.

Democratic capitalism has a rather different way of understanding and fulfilling the goals Hampshire has in view. Through its political system, democratic capitalism allows for governmental action in alleviating poverty, enhancing the liberty of all, and fulfilling basic needs. Yet it is deeply concerned lest government overstep its limits and become itself a threat worse than the injuries it sets out to redress. In practice, the limits to be imposed on government may be difficult to discern in advance. Yet the danger of tyranny is great, all the more so when the enlargement of government is made to seem legitimate through appeal to moral principle.

The threat to liberty of action, as Professor Hampshire sees it, arises primarily from "great inequalities of wealth between different social groups." But at least an equal threat arises from the creation of a corrupt, arrogant, and indecipherable government. Furthermore, the principle that all social groups ought to be equal in power and freedom of action cannot be served through the enlargement of government, unless that government is staffed by angels. For the accrual of all powers necessary to enforce equality gives to government officials unequal power. Who will govern government? To assert that a democratically elected people will control bureaucracies is to ignore fundamental problems of governability, and not least the nature of bureaucracies. To rest the hopes of liberty on the ability of bureaucracies to adjudicate the economic power of discrete groups of citizens is to trust bureaucrats more than common sense allows.

Furthermore, Hampshire's implicit principle of equal freedom of action for all runs against the grain of nature. Persons without an ear for music will never have equal freedom of action in matters musical, and those who cannot master elementary logic will never gain equal power in departments of philosophy. Mastery of the English language gives those who possess it a power to express themselves lacking in those less fortunate. It stands to reason that in economic activities persons are likewise of unequal talent. Those of lesser talent (whether of mind, instinct, or energy) are not likely to gain equal economic power and equal freedom of economic action. It would seem to be a truism that those who labor to develop their talents, whether in music, philosophy, or economic activities, do so precisely in order to increase the range of power and freedom of action accessible to them. Professor Hampshire's principle of equality cannot be applied in fields outside economics. Why should it be applied within that field?

By contrast, democratic capitalists hold that *every* person of

talent—musical, intellectual, economic—should have every opportunity to discover and to develop his talents. They hold, further, that natural and developed inequalities enhance the common
good of all. Societies without artistic and intellectual genius are
poorer in every part for such a lack, and so are societies without
economic genius. In traditional societies, in which neither equal
opportunity nor social mobility is operative, existing inequalities
of wealth, status, and hierarchical allocation seem to block the
rise of new and superior talent. In both traditional and socialist
societies, democratic capitalists perceive real offenses against the
common good.

Democratic socialists and democratic capitalists, therefore,
look upon inequalities of wealth in quite different ways. The
democratic socialist wishes speedily to remove such inequalities
as an offense against nature and morality. The democratic capitalist sees them as typical of nature, but judges their morality by the
benefits they bring (including lack of coercion) to the common
good. A confidence in the workings of talent over time leads the
democratic capitalist to expect that, under conditions of equal
opportunity and open social mobility (conditions often not met in
Latin America, for example), families which acquire wealth will
invest it wisely or lose it, and that elites will circulate as new
families producing wealth in new ways replace older elites. "Concentrations of economic power" are, on the one hand, limited.
On the other, they have a way of dissolving over time under the
dynamics of economic change.

Wealth, moreover, is safest in a free, growing society and most
at risk in a decaying society. Thus the wealthy have a real and
abiding interest in the economic, political, and social health of
their societies. Under democratic capitalism, the wealthy have
incentives to be public-spirited, civic-minded, and philanthropic.
This is true not only of the Carnegies, Mellons, Rockefellers, and
Fords, with their libraries, art galleries, and foundations, but of
lesser-known families of wealth in every locality, with their gifts
to hospital wings, college dormitories, city orchestras, and the
like. It is in their interest not to use their own wealth narrowly.
When they do not recognize this interest, a free society brings
many institutional resources to their correction. Not only wealthy
families but great corporations and entire industries rise and fall—
the whaling industry, the railroads, even nuclear energy—under
quite natural rhythms, rhythms related to their own perspicacity

and social vision. Unenlightened management of wealth invites its own punishment. The democratic capitalist, then, need not play God.

Western civilization is possible because it has triumphed over envy. It did so largely through the invention of the market. Exchange in markets requires trust—trust in society's future, trust in the stability of the currency, trust in credit extended, and trust in goods received. It also requires information about the needs of others, for each exchange is other-regarding as well as self-regarding. Where markets exist, information about the needs of others is direct and simple. Where markets do not exist, distant authorities must speculate about needs and assign them rankings. Exchange relations are more fully human than relations of dependency. For this reason, markets take for granted (and promote) elementary equalities and, where such equalities do not exist, slowly generate them. Democratic socialists conclude from this slowness that markets should be abridged in favor of governmental action. In principle, democratic capitalists do not oppose governmental action, but judge it according to whether it generates equalities which bring newcomers into markets or whether it generates dependency. They believe the first course promotes voluntariness, while the second is dangerous and less than moral.

Some of the hidden underpinnings of socialist "idealism" may now be briefly noted. There is a class of persons—usually the most influential in the shaping of public opinion—whose life situation is better served by assumptions that favor socialist ideals. (The success of democratic capitalism, in strengthening this class, strengthens these general assumptions.) Several centuries ago, educated persons learned that human beings could acquire great power and attain great benefits by organizing the forces of nature. It was an easy inference to assume that similar power and similar benefits might be attained by organizing society. Since a single coherent plan, carried out with practical skill, succeeds so well in taming nature, a single coherent plan should be equally successful in taming society. Here lies a powerful bias in favor, if not of "scientific socialism," at least of some form of social planning. An order which is intelligible to planners and carried out with authority seems deserving of higher intellectual status than whatever order emerges from a multiplicity of free choices.

The career most attractive to socialists has characteristically been a career of ideas. "Socialism," Hayek writes, "has never been at first a working class movement. It is by no means an obvious remedy for the obvious evil which the interests of that class will necessarily demand. It is a construction of theorists, deriving from certain tendencies of abstract thought with which for a long time only the intellectuals were familiar. . . ."[12]

Simply as an idea, furthermore, at least in already free societies, socialism has a great rhetorical advantage over liberalism. While liberal thinkers struggle to be practical and realistic, socialist thinkers enjoy the superior power of general ideas. In nation after nation, socialism has first taken root chiefly among that class of general thinkers who comment on everything, who are themselves in need of large general ideas and a vision of an ideal future. In already free societies, socialism has been in competition, not with a contrasting democratic capitalistic ideal, but with an existing state of affairs. Thus a very large body of persons whose expertise lies in retailing new ideas to their constituencies—chaplains, ministers, college presidents, heads of foundations, news reporters, magazine writers, consultants, advisers of every sort—finds in socialism a general framework by which to claim originality and critical distance. In one sense, the dependence of socialism upon ideas is a striking refutation of its materialistic interpretation of history. In another, it makes ideas a source of social power, and thus an equivalent to material interest.

The high mindedness of socialist intellectuals, therefore, has economic significance, just as intellectuals and social activists have their own class interests. Those who are socialist in their thinking acquire the prestige that accrues to those in possession of coherent general theories about the future, by comparison with which liberal ideas seem tepid. Socialism thus brings with it intellectual prestige not available to democratic capitalist ideas. It offers the framework for nearly all general thinking outside narrow specialities, so that persons who try to stay abreast of current ideas must, of necessity, think in mainly socialist categories. Those who use democratic capitalist ideas carry the burden of existing evils, conflicts, and perplexities, and are easily made to seem, by comparison, on the defensive.

3
From Economics to Politics

> We are *for* equality, but we realize that economic organization cannot be based on equality of wages, that cultural backwardness has a self-perpetuating mechanism that no institutional changes are likely to destroy rapidly, that some inequalities are accounted for by genetic factors and too little is known of their impact on social processes, etc. We are for economic democracy, but we do not know how to harmonize it with the competent running of production.
> —Leszek Kolakowski, *The Socialist Idea*[13]

As an idea, socialism has been forced by its own failures to retreat from the field of economics to the high ground of morality. This transformation is especially marked among democratic socialists in the United States, whose chief national organ is *Dissent* magazine.[14] The editor of *Dissent*, Irving Howe, is a literary critic in whose thoughts are deeply embedded many of the principles of the American tradition. In many ways, his work might be interpreted as that of a democratic capitalist, whose personal moral code happens to be socialist. Yet his political vision does entail changing American society so as to meet more closely the socialist ideal.

Howe makes clear the centrality of democracy to socialism:

> Socialism must be committed, without qualification, to democracy—yes, the flawed and inadequate democracy we have today—in order to be able to bring a heightened democratic content to every department of life: political, economic, social, cultural. There can be no socialism without democracy, not any compromise with apologists for dictatorship or authoritarianism in any shape or form.[15]

Furthermore, he identifies socialism neither with the abolition of poverty nor with the nationalization of industry. These are serious acts of revisionism, which he attempts to disguise with ideologically freighted words:

> Socialism must then be redefined as a society in which the means of production, to an extent that need not be determined rigidly in advance, are collectively owned and in which they are democratically controlled; a society requiring as its absolute prerequisite the preservation and extension of democracy.[16]

One notes the gesture toward empiricism: "need not be determined rigidly in advance." Yet the iron gate slams shut in the next phrase: "collectively owned." The lesson Howe has derived from Stalinism comes down, then, to this. The problem lies not in "collective ownership" but in being "democratically controlled." Thus, the newly revised socialism hangs everything upon one "absolute prerequisite"—the preservation and extension of "democracy."

Howe does not show how democracy will be preserved when property is collectively owned. Since a key element in the American constitutional vision is defense against democratic majorities, this lapse is quite damaging. How will the pluralism of minorities, dissenters, and divergent interests be protected under democratic socialism, if all collectivized property is controlled by a majority vote? Howe does seem to admire "the flawed and inadequate democracy we have today." Yet he does not seem to discern how it is rooted in real interests, including property interests, and real incentives for individual purposes. He is much less wise on these matters than Madison in *The Federalist*.

If the root of democracy lies in the rights it confers on the individual, in the incentives it establishes for economic activism (and hence economic growth), and in the strict limits it places upon the reach of the political system, then it is hard to see how democratic socialism like Howe's either preserves democracy or extends it. A skeptic may doubt how much pleasure human beings will take in a community politically bogged down in committee work and economically unrewarding of personal effort. It is not easy to imagine striving, competing, energetic economic activists, political achievers, and moral-cultural dissidents enjoying happiness under the sunny providence of collectivization.

My reasons for finding it difficult to follow Howe and other democratic socialists into thinking of participatory democracy as a universal remedy for worldly ills may be succinctly stated. First, participatory democracy is not an appropriate method for reaching most decisions in the moral-cultural realm, whether in religion, morals, the arts, or literature. In such matters there are intrinsic standards. Second, it is not an appropriate method for reaching most decisions in the economic realm. Neither invention nor economic management, neither personal responsibility on the job nor personal choices in consumption are best adjudicated by a vote in committee.[17]

Third, participatory democracy requires too many meetings, and it suits neither the needs of most citizens nor the purposes of a free society. Some persons *do* like to "participate in all the decisions that affect their lives." But most persons have as little to do with politics as they can. The right to pursue happiness means, for them, the right to fix elected decision-makers with a disapproving eye from time to time, while getting on with the attractions of living. Enforced participatory democracy would be, for most, less attractive than obligatory attendance at church. This may be a disappointment to believers in "civism," as we may call the religion of politics.

It is unlikely that any society in history has ever given rise to so many associations, committees, and action groups as that of democratic capitalism in the United States, and it is not evident that democratic socialism means more than improving upon what already exists. Insofar as it does so, it advances democratic capitalism. But insofar as it strengthens the administrative state, it is a version of statism. Insofar as it abolishes private property and business corporations, it renders citizens the more defenseless against the economic power of the bureaucratic state. Concerned about the disproportionate powers of big business, democratic socialism leaves citizens vulnerable to the disproportionate power of the state.

Finally, democratic socialism trades upon imagery according to which all things private—like businesses and markets—are selfish, greedy, and corrupt, while it neglects even to study the historical record of the selfishness, greed, and corruption of bureaucracies (whether of church or of state) which in the past and the present have claimed to speak for the public. Liberalism arose as a defense of individuals against church and state. Claiming to go beyond liberalism, democratic socialists have created the greatest administrative state power in human history. They have been invincibly innocent concerning the limits of politics. They have been willfully ignorant about the corruption of entire populations through total dependence upon the state.

Democracy depends for its legitimacy not so much upon equality of results as upon a belief among even the least well off that things will get better for them. The legitimacy of democracy rests upon economic growth and the pervasive optimism it generates. In giving economic growth too low a priority, democratic socialism has contributed mightily to making democracies increasingly ungovernable and to destroying their real legitimacy. Thus democratic socialism is not only a romantic illusion. It destroys the very thing it means to save. Since World War II, democratic socialism has swept all other ideas before it, especially in Europe, but at the end of the twentieth century the high costs of its programs are beginning to roll ominously in.

Democracy is not legitimated through socialist solidarity, but through individual economic opportunity. A Rumanian dissident has written:

> What the people of Rumania want is a liberalization of the economy in which they have personal, material incentives . . . Socialism has proved that it has not given a valuable solution to mankind and always comes into conflict with freedom, democracy, and justice. Socialism has failed in Eastern Europe, and in Cuba, and in China.[18]

As we have seen, the reasons for these failures are not circumstantial. They lie in the moral and political ideal of socialism, even of democratic socialism. The ideal is wrong.

4

The Utility of the Rich

On no point are democratic capitalism and democratic socialism more at odds than in their judgment upon the rich. Most democratic socialists recognize that strict equality of incomes is unworkable and also unjust. Some persons work harder than others, some have special talents, some have especially demanding or dangerous work, and some perform in superior ways. Still, to sensitive consciences extreme disparities of income may seem "immoral." Michael Walzer writes that small entrepreneurs and others who invent new ways of serving the public deserve to keep their incomes, but he finds salaries paid to corporate executives "obscene."[19] Is it possible to resolve this difference between democratic capitalists and democratic socialists?

As a first step, we may note that the number of disputed cases is relatively few. In 1978, 354,200 U.S. tax returns, barely more than 0.5 percent, showed pre-tax income of $100,000 or more.[20] Only 69,039 persons had an adjusted gross income over $200,000. The total income of the latter came to $25.5 billion, on which they paid $11.1 billion in taxes.[21] Suppose these 69,039 could keep only $100,000 each ($6.9 billion in total), the rest going to the IRS. With $11.1 billion already collected, that would add $7.5 billion to the Treasury. Would a society be morally better whose government spent this $7.5 billion? A society whose government limits itself, allowing those who earn this extra $7.5 billion to invest or spend it as they see fit, would seem to be a freer, more productive, more inventive, and less dull civilization.

In particular, the salaries of corporate executives disturb some critics, even among those who are not disturbed by the high income of athletes, entertainers, authors, inventors, and self-made entrepreneurs. On average, the chief executive officers of *Fortune* 500 receive salaries of $330,000. In 1980, at least fifteen executives received over $1 million, counting bonuses and stock options. Some object that one could pay the salaries of sixty or more employees at $30,000 each for such amounts. Can any executive be worth that much? One single good executive decision can make a difference to a firm of far more than that.

So the issue is not an easy one. Good managers are rare, and corporations frequently raid one another for talent. To the recruiting corporation, an outstanding executive can make a difference worth millions of dollars, so a high bid for his or her services may seem easily worth the cost. To the company trying to hold on to its talent, generous compensation schemes count as basic self-protection. The market exerts its pressures.

Still, public opinion is not to be scorned. At the very least, great care must be exercised to make it clear that salaries are linked to performance. Boards of directors owe it to the good name of the system to make this link plain. The use of stock options may, for example, be discouraged. Such options are of value because of stock market factors beyond the control of the executives and are, in this sense, harder to link to performance. Sobriety and restraint are admirable moral qualities, and must be placed in the moral balance with incentives. I do not know the answer, but I do see the need for executives and boards to give evidence of moral restraint. This may seem unfair, since a journalist like Dan Rather may make $8 million for five years, and Johnny Carson earns more for a longer period than any CEOs. (Babe Ruth, told that he made more than the president of the United States, rejoined that he had had a better year.) A nation with a Puritan heritage, in any case, ought not to weaken its dislike for extravagance. It particularly ought not to do so on the part of those who in a special way symbolize a crucial part of the system, and whose moral responsibilities are as high as their economic ones.

One of the problems encountered by socialist societies is the drabness of socialist realism. To counter this threat, the British socialist Anthony Crosland imagined a new socialism of

> more open-air cafes, brighter and gayer streets at night, later closing hours for public houses, more local repertory theatres, better and more hospitable hoteliers and restaurateurs, brighter and cleaner eating houses, more riverside cafes, more pleasure-gardens on the Battersea model, more murals and pictures in public places, better designs for furniture and pottery and women's clothes, statues in the centre of new housing estates, better-designed street-lamps and telephone kiosks, and so on *ad infinitum*. . . .[22]

In a brilliant review of Crosland's work, Colin Welch notes that this "enlivening prospect: Paris rather than Moscow, more Toulouse-Lautrec than socialist realism," depends in practice upon private means and private tastes to ensure "the survival, *ambience* and prosperity of many of these charming amenities. That riverside restaurant which we can afford to go to once in a while, on special occasions, is in fact kept going by those who can afford to eat out there often and well: no rich, alas, no restaurant." Crosland's neglect of such facts of life "may in part explain the fearful contrast between the enlivening prospects he offers and the shabby, decaying slum, the haunted house, in which we have been condemned . . . by his egalitarian fervor to live."[23]

The rich are useful because their odd tastes prevent our architecture from being monotonously bureaucratic. Their taste in hotels makes it possible for millions to stay, at least once or twice, in something other than middle-period Holiday Inn. Their mushy ideological sentiments lead them, often enough, to endow foundations which sponsor scholars who write in favor of overturning the system. Not a few museums, galleries, symphony halls, and libraries owe their nonbureaucratic liberties and real human beauties to the grand ambitions of the rich for public immortality.[24] The "robber barons" were not always robbers and seldom barons; most were poor boys, badly educated, barely (if at all) gentlemen, and aesthetically quite insecure.

Often the wealthy invest grandly (if unwisely, thus setting in motion their own decline) in mansions and gardens, public monuments and centers of research, churches and universities. Where there are few or no wealthy, many amenities disappear from the social landscape, life becomes grayer, and the verve of the whole society declines. Politico-bureaucratic decisions about aesthetics lack the freedom and variety of a system of private donors.

In addition, disproportionate amounts of economic investment come from the rich. This, in its way, is a social contribution. To encourage the rich not to be idle, to give them reason not to waste their abundance on yachts and palaces, and to infuse them with a desire to invest and to create is no small advantage for a nation. Not a few of the basic industries of modernity (telephones, radios, autos, television, minicomputers, electronic watches, etc.) owe their origins to the curiosity and perseverance of a rich man in his fascination with a problem or a gadget. Most new technologies are supported in their infancy by marketing strategies aimed first at the rich and then at the masses. Of yore patrons of the arts, many of the wealthy today are patrons of new technologies.

Perhaps one reason I cannot be a democratic socialist is that I find it difficult to be envious. Why covet the wealth of Sandy Koufax, Arthur Schlesinger, Jr., Dan Rather, Joe Namath, Robert Redford, Jay Rockefeller, David Packard, Paul Samuelson, Ray Kroc, John Kenneth Galbraith, John Lennon, Edward M. Kennedy, and others who count as "people" in the magazines? Let them have their wealth. Their lives, on the whole, seem not worse than the lives of the rest of us, and their investments, if wise, create new possibilities.

Any system which can turn the rich to social utility works an alchemy that benefits all. Under democratic capitalism, standards of what counts as poverty have risen dramatically. Many, born poor, have become rich. Many families, once rich, have fallen on hard times. Democratic capitalism has as its ideal the upward push of the poor, the bright, the talented. It keeps alive the knowledge that, with skill or luck (or both), one may yet have a future different from one's present. In most societies, especially in administrative societies and in societies bearing the name of socialism, one knows from the start just how high one can go. The only path upward is political favor. Democratic capitalism has its faults. The alternatives are worse.

Making a political economy work requires more than ideals; one must also deal with recalcitrant facts and with ironic twists in the way the world actually works. Some of these matters of fact and ironic reversals must be addressed in the following two chapters.

XII

Income Distribution and Race

Although this book is mainly about ideals, some questions about those ideals are best met through empirical study. Only in that way can contrasts be sharpened. In this and the next chapter, then, we must deal in summary fashion with three empirical issues: the distribution of income; the rise of blacks in the United States; and transnational corporations. These chapters are a little different from the others in form but experience shows that they are necessary to the overall argument.

1

Income Distribution

As a moral injunction, democratic socialists usually give higher priority to the distribution of wealth than to its production. Most, however, do not believe that all incomes ought to be identical. Most recognize that socialist regimes (like all others) mete out differential rewards. In communist regimes, rewards are assigned by the political allocation of privileges and perquisites: apartments, autos, special stores, vacation spots, travel permits, and other methods above and beyond monetary income. One writer uses Cuba as a model. He points out that top scientists and other highly skilled workers receive eight times the salary of the lowest-paid workers.[1] Shall we take this, or something like it, as the democratic socialist ideal?

Would a society be fair if the categories of income were ranked in an order, for instance, of one to seven, so that the most highly prized talents would receive seven times what the poorest received? Thus surgeons and top engineers, top managers and political leaders, top movie stars and others, would receive approximately seven times the income of the poorest.

Consider now the situation in the United States. The "official poverty level" of the United States (for a non-farm family of four) was set at $7,412 in 1979.[2] According to our abstract scheme, then, let x = $7,000. The top category would then be receiving about $49,000 per year ($7x$). Categories 2, 3, 4, 5, and 6 would be receiving $14,000, $21,000, $28,000, $35,000, and $42,000, respectively. Would this seem to be just?

In a purely formal and abstract way, democratic capitalism meets this pattern, with one major revision. This revision recognizes the social utility of permitting the top 2 percent or so to swing free of restraint to whatever extent the market permits. This revision sets no ceiling at the top. Persons of the highest talents in any field may earn as much as the market will pay.

How, then, does the actual distribution in the United States match the abstract scheme? Since in the next section we shall deal directly with the income of black families, consider here the figures for whites as of 1978. The Census Bureau divides the 51 million white families by income categories into quintiles of equal size (10.2 million families each). Of these the bottom quintile reported income in 1978 of less than $9,500. The second quintile reported less than $15,443. The middle fifth reported less than $21,284. The fourth quintile reported less than $29,332. The top quintile is composed of all those receiving more than this amount. Most of these families receive less than $42,000. The income of those in the top 5 percent is given as an average, and it comes to $46,272. This *average* is a little less than $7x$.

The revision mentioned above occurs in this way. In 1978, 354,200 taxpayers received $100,000 or more in pre-tax earnings. The vast majority of these—285,161—received less than $200,000;

60,075 received between $200,000 and $500,000; 8,964 received more than $500,000.[3]

In other words, 99.5 percent of the population received less than $100,000. For democratic socialists, the existence of this top 0.5 percent is something of a scandal. For democratic capitalists, it is not. For the latter, scandal arises only if it can be shown that the fact of higher income for a minority injures others. Democratic capitalists, on the whole, think that an unlimited ceiling is of benefit to the entire society. They think societies in which it obtains may be morally better—more dynamic, freer, more generous, more colorful—than those in which it does not.

Consider solely the consequences for taxation. The total pretax income of the 354,200 families that earned more than $100,000 came to $63 billion. Of this amount, they paid $19 billion in taxes.

Those families that earned more than $50,000—about 2 percent of all families—paid 24 percent of all U.S. income taxes. The next lower 8 percent of families paid 25.7 percent of all U.S. income taxes. Thus, the top 10 percent paid 49.7 percent of all U.S. income taxes in 1978. Those who earned between about $20,000 and $40,000 in 1978—about 40 percent of the families— paid approximately 50 percent of U.S. income taxes for 1978.

By contrast, the bottom *half* of all families (some 25.5 million) paid only 6.5 percent of all income taxes. Of these, the bottom quintile paid virtually none.[4]

In effect, the wealthiest 10 percent paid most of the taxes for the poorest 50 percent. Some may hold that they should pay still more. Yet some credit should also be given for what they do pay. From the perspective of the moral-cultural and the political system of democratic capitalism, it does seem right that the most fortunate should pay disproportionately more. The question of where to strike the balance between incentives and taxation, between liberty and its proper social burdens, is subject to economic utility, political wisdom, and moral reflection.

It is worth noting that the top 0.5 percent—the 354,200— includes a wide variety of income earners: movie stars, authors, journalists, surgeons, lawyers, inventors, corporate executives, owners of businesses, editors, clippers of coupons, athletes, and many others. The threshold of $100,000 is, after all, not so high. Some years ago in a debate on Italian television, an Italian

Communist pointed out to me that one of the best arguments in favor of capitalism is its effect on distribution. Wherever capitalism takes hold, it brings the workers into the middle class. There is a structural reason, he pointed out, for this development. It is in the interest of democratic capitalism for markets to expand. Mass markets depend upon the purchasing power of the masses. The largest and most successful industries are those which aim to supply everybody, in every family. The loyalty of citizens is based in part on the fact that a system delivers real economic benefits. For other reasons, this observer does not approve of capitalism; but he gives it credit for what it does.

This courteous debater is correct that poverty is a threat both to the economy and to the polity of democratic capitalism. It also supplies a moral stimulus. For this reason, democratic capitalism, however grudgingly, adopts social welfare programs, often initially sponsored by socialists. Social welfare programs fit the logic of democratic capitalism and have a legitimate claim on it. On the other hand, since such values as liberty, markets, incentives, and the creation of new wealth are also important values in democratic capitalism, there is healthy resistance to social welfare measures alone. Where the latter are absolutized, dominate all other values, result in economic stagnation, and corrupt the citizenry through dependence, they are properly subjected to criticism.

Social welfare societies like those of Western Europe and the United States face grave crises in the last part of the twentieth century. A dependent citizenry is a danger. Welfare benefits even at their present levels can only be maintained in economies which continue to grow; present levels of growth seem to be insufficient to meet future demands.[5]

2

The Economic Situation of Blacks

The cumulative annual income of the 25 million American blacks— some $114 billion, according to Andrew Brimmer—is larger than that of all but fourteen of the world's nations, including the People's Republic of China.[6] Black Americans are richer and better educated than any other blacks in the world and most other peoples, besides. On the other hand, compared to white Americans, while doing better on some indices, black Americans do not register as well on other indices.

The democratic socialist approach to the problems of blacks emphasizes distribution and dependency. Predominantly, the left wing of the Democratic Party insists upon government programs as the solution to disproportionate problems of poverty among the black "underclass." When the focus is on jobs and education, such leaders seldom observe that such things cannot be merely given but must be seized through personal initiative. By contrast, as Thomas Sowell—as well as daily observation—makes plain, most blacks are in fact disciplined, ambitious, hardworking, and conscientious in seizing opportunity.[7]

Protestant cultures in history have been distinctive for their emphasis upon the discipline of the organizing mind over the senses and the emotions. This has had consequences for the rise and success of democratic capitalism. Remarkably, some versions of Protestantism among American blacks are quite different from classic forms of Protestantism. Among some black American Protestants, a much higher degree of emphasis seems to be placed upon free forms of expression and the emotions. The rhetorical pitch is far higher. The sense of dream and resurrection is acute. The message seems aimed more at surcease from the day's woes than at an organized plan for tomorrow. All this may be perfectly appropriate to the history of black culture and religion. Nevertheless, it is a form of Calvinism different from others, and may have different economic and political effects.

Within the several distinctive black cultures to be found within the United States, there seem to be pronounced differences in social profile. Thomas Sowell in *Race and Economics* points out that blacks from the West Indies, U.S. blacks who were early freed from slavery ("freeborn persons of color"), and the descendants of slaves show quite different statistical profiles. An important differential, in his view, is that those whose culture has encouraged a higher degree of self-reliance and independence succeed in higher proportions.

It is precisely at this point that the socialist approach to the needs of American blacks—massive government programs—resembles the paternalism common under slavery. The pattern of dependency is reinforced.

Sowell has also studied the profile of other American ethnic groups. He argues that those groups which historically relied on government jobs and the types of municipal welfare commonly achieved through the nineteenth-century urban "machines" succeeded less well and more slowly than those who enterprisingly sought work in the private sector. Furthermore, those who went into business for themselves, through uncovering needs they could fill in new ways, succeeded best of all.[8]

The Marxist stencil applied to poverty begins by suggesting that the poverty of some is due to the wealth of others. An alternative theory suggests that cultures differ from one another in the mental and emotional disciplines in which they instruct their young, in their economic proclivities, and in other respects significant for economic and political competition. Most analysts of the situation of blacks in the United States consistently neglect the cultural materials which Sowell and others have shown to be so significant.

Many also neglect other significant variables, like age, region of the country, and family status. A population with a median age of twenty-four should, other things being equal, have lower average income than a population whose median age is thirty, since younger workers tend to make less money. Populations disproportionately concentrated in lower-income regions of the nation, like rural areas or the South, will show a lower average income than populations concentrated in higher-income regions (thus Irish-Americans, in the Northern states, have higher average incomes than Irish-Americans in the South). Finally, populations with larger average numbers of children, or with a higher proportion of female-headed households, will have lower average incomes than those whose family status includes fewer children, and those in which husband and wife are together, both of whom may be working. It is a matter of statistical honesty to compare like with like, and to hold significant variables constant. Finally, both I.Q. and level of education correlate with income, and for all ethnic groups these change over time.

Leaving variables to one side, the Census Bureau reports the income for the 6,894,000 black families in the United States in 1978 as follows. The lowest quintile earned up to $4,879. The second, third, and fourth quintiles earned, respectively, up to

$9,081, up to $14,665, and up to $22,195. The fifth quintile includes all who earned more than this. The top 5 percent of black families earned an average of $35,416.[9]

The median age in 1978 for whites was just over thirty, but for blacks just over twenty-four.[10] About one in five black families relied on aid to dependent children, compared to only 3 percent of white families.[11] Nationally, over half of black children by the age of eighteen had no father in the home. In education, the proportion of eighteen- and nineteen-year-old blacks who attended school in 1978 was higher than among whites, but on average, blacks twenty-five years old and over had less schooling than whites.[12]

In 1977, half of all blacks were earning $9,485 or more, and half of all whites $16,782, the figure for blacks being 57 percent of that for whites.[13] This difference is almost wholly accounted for by the disproportionate numbers of female-headed households among blacks as compared to those among whites. Black households with two earners have a median income of more than three-fourths that of white households with two earners,[14] although the wife in two-parent black families is more likely to be working (60 percent) than the white wife (49 percent).[15] Black households with two parents under age thirty-five, *living in the North,* do better than equivalent white households.[16]

If one were boasting of the accomplishments of blacks, one might note that after generations of slavery, years of segregation and discrimination, and the serious disabilities attendant on welfare dependency, 2.1 million black families were earning more than $15,000 per year in 1978 and 820,000 black families were earning more than $25,000 per year.[17]

In 1900, 90 percent of blacks lived in the South under conditions of segregation and in an agrarian economy in the poorest region of the nation.[18] By 1965, half of all blacks in the United States lived outside the South. Meanwhile, the South itself had begun to prosper. By 1970 a large majority of blacks now lived in urban centers (66 percent), with only 21 percent remaining in the rural economy (compared to 27 percent of whites).[19] The poverty of central cities receives predominant attention today, but the poverty of rural areas is probably more acute.

More blacks belong to unions—9.2 million[20]—than belong to any other organizations except the Baptist church and the Democratic Party. The 17 million blacks over the age of sixteen constitute about 11 percent of all U.S. citizens that age, and hold 9 percent of all jobs. Black workers, however, represent 18 percent of the unskilled work force.[21]

A glaring spotlight is often cast upon black teenagers, who in 1978 numbered 2.3 million. Most of these teenagers are in school. A disproportionate number serve in the U.S. military. Of the rest, about 669,000 are employed and, in any given month, some 381,000 (1978 annual average) were seeking work without success.[22] The newspapers often report this as "40 percent black youth unemployment," and such it is. But the actual number needing employment—381,000—seems far less ominous. At the minimum wage of approximately $130 per week, or about $6,500 per year, the full cost of employing all such youths would amount to about $2.6 billion.

Welfare dependency appears to have measurable effects upon the marital behavior of black males. Whereas in 1960 only 22 percent of black children were born out of wedlock, by 1978 the percentage had climbed to 53.2 percent. In cities like Chicago, the total had reached 67 percent. This illegitimacy rate is notwithstanding the fact that of the 1.3 million abortions performed in 1977, 444,000 were for black women. The rise in out-of-wedlock births and male abandonment of families shows some correlation with welfare policies, particularly in Northern cities.[23]

There is widespread debate about whether it is more fruitful to approach the question of poverty among the lowest third of black families as a question of race or of class. The advantage of the language of class is that it tends to unite the poor of all races in common necessities and common strategies. On the other hand, the element of race involves an undeniable psychological factor. It is probably difficult for non-blacks to appreciate the sense of inferiority, barely conscious, which those with black skin often feel thrust upon them. These feelings often have an irrational character, making them exquisitely difficult to face truly and exactly.

Reasonable persons of all races try to build bridges of trust where earlier hurts destroyed them. Yet for many of even the most successful blacks, real blows to self-esteem can fall with startling suddenness. For others of lesser talent or opportunity, there may be a terrible vulnerability to a sense of unfairness and defeat. Such vulnerability cannot be touched merely by job programs or training in skills. In some ways, healing must come less through the political system or the economic system than through the moral-cultural system. Yet in order to make a kind of systematic progress, reaching greater numbers, it is clear that economic opportunity and political potency offer the surest and most satisfactory social strategies. If strategies which engender dependency do not work, the urgent task is to invent strategies which lead to independence.

For it is in the real interests of democratic capitalism—economic, political, and moral interests—to see improvement in the lot of all the poor, including the black poor. The critical point is to break the pattern of dependency. This means that the private sector must be the point of concentration, since about 90 percent of all new jobs are created by small businesses and relatively modest corporations. To the extent that government helps, it should do so indirectly and in the role of facilitator, rather than as a paternalistic agent. Black communities must be regarded as locations for small businesses of many kinds.

Yet serious economic difficulties arise immediately. Insurance rates in black communities are higher than elsewhere. Managerial talents are in lower supply, good managers are harder to retain, and good workers demand higher pay for conditions of relative hardship. Breakage and pilfering are serious problems. Physical intimidation is frequent.[24] Here an indirect role for government makes practical sense. Government policies designed to lower the costs of doing business in black communities may—but, of course, may not—encourage the flow of capital and protect its safety. Such policies might take the form of underwriting the costs of insurance, providing minimal tax rates, guaranteeing mortgages and capital investments, and employing other devices which businessmen and economists might think of more practically than theologians. The key is to overcome the disincentives business presently faces in black communities.[25]

That is one key. Another will require a change of ethos in an isolated portion of the black community. Many employers have tried to hire black youths, only to be disappointed by irregularity and self-destructive personal habits. In order for the political and the economic system to work, certain moral-cultural values must be in order. Many persons in good physical health are "unemployable," not because they lack skills (in many jobs skills are not demanding) but because they lack personal discipline. Some resist regular hours. Some dislike the "hassle" of the daily grind. Their sense of worth is fragile, and some resist service jobs whose character reminds them of the jobs open to earlier generations. Some feel intimidated in cultures not familiar to them. In a word, some blacks seem to suffer a cultural crisis of significant proportions, through no fault of their own. There is little or no guidance to help them through it. The temptation to turn to despair and alienation, or at least to give way to restlessness, is very great. There is acute suffering.[26]

Markets have amazing capacities for invention. Keen eyes may discern needs no one else is meeting. Adjustments and experiments with the minimum wage for teenagers may open up new possibilities for those whose economic skills are not high. Within communities where the unemployed live, buildings need repair, businesses need to be built. There is no lack of work to be done. Workers to do it are available. But to match laborers to labor so that income results is a task for intelligence and wit. Under current conditions, it cannot be said that such communities lack capital. Many beginning with less capital have made much more from it. Some catalyst is necessary. The spirit of democratic socialism, with its litany of statist solutions, seems designed to prevent such a catalyst from ever emerging.

As in domestic affairs, so also in international affairs do ideals of independence and self-reliance give rise to great passions. Most of the disputes concern the role of transnational corporations. Democratic capitalism could exist without such corporations but has, in fact, been the seedbed of their invention. How do they fit the ideals we have been exploring?

XIII
The Transnational Corporation

Socialism accepts the brotherhood of man. It has humanitarianism built into it. It accepts that the resources of a country belong to the people as a whole and therefore must be exploited in the interest of the people as a whole. It rejects exploitation.

I think those are also the principles of Christianity—the common denominator of brotherhood running right through. As for the godless character of dialectical materialism, well, everyone knows there is always the right to accept that or reject it, depending on whether they are atheistic or Christian in orientation.

—Robert Mugabe[1]

Although some socialists focus much hostility upon the transnational corporation, it was a curious fact of early 1980 that the leaders of two new "Christian socialist regimes"—those of Nicaragua and Zimbabwe—spent considerable energy trying to attract transnational corporations to their lands. Robert Mugabe, for example, visited the United States in August 1980 and pledged before bankers and security analysts in New York that the investments of transnationals would be welcomed in Zimbabwe and would be safe, and that profits from them could be expatriated—as long as some profits were reinvested in Zimbabwe. "Union Carbide," he pointed out, defending himself against criticism that talking to capitalists is unorthodox for a Marxist, "has done much good for Zimbabwe. Why can't other companies as well?" His people want material things, a better life, food, clothing, schools, jobs; and it is the business of good government, he said, to provide such things.[2]

It is an anomaly of intellectual life in our era that Mugabe should be obliged to use the idiom of socialism to express the natural workings of his mind. For it is clear that some of what he has in mind is not only consistent with democratic capitalism but integral to it. Socialism is not alone in accepting the brotherhood of man, in having "humanitarianism built into it," in being opposed to exploitation, and in recognizing that "the resources of a land belong to the people as a whole and therefore must be exploited in the interests of the people as a whole." The fallacy of socialism is to imagine that brotherhood demands collectivism. The genius of democratic capitalism is to serve brotherhood by recognizing that the most precious of all common goods is the individuality of each person, and that the best way to increase the common good is to empower people through differentiated systems.

Consider the institutions of capitalism: the corporation, the labor union, banking, the stock exchange. Each of these is communal. None would make sense in a world of isolated individuals. Each depends on bonds of trust which go beyond coercive force, beyond written contracts, and beyond the letter of the law. (An effective way of halting any enterprise is to slow it down by "going by the book.") Most interchanges within a democratic capitalist economy depend upon the good faith implicit behind the spoken word; they depend upon a bond of spirit.

Ironically, a society supposedly based upon competitive individualism and possessiveness seems to favor in its citizens forms of generosity, trust, extroversion, outgoingness, and reliance upon the good faith of others. Meanwhile, existing socialist societies seem to narrow the circles of trust, as groups competing for the same allocations run afoul of each other's interests. Collectivism pits man against man. A system which encourages each to seek first his own interests yields liberty and receives in return loyalty and love.

Liberty, basic trust, and communal purpose underlie the theory of the corporation. As the name suggests, the business corporation is a collective enterprise, voluntarily entered into by individuals. Normally, it is created by those with capital to invest and an idea around which to build an enterprise, although sometimes someone first has the idea but no capital. Before things can begin to be produced and before workers can be hired, someone has to put up the money for the materials and the instruments of production. If the product fails to sell (like the Edsel or the large cars that glutted dealers' lots in 1980), much of the initial investment may be lost. Two circumstances make the business corporation a unique instrument of the common good. First, social cooperation is encouraged, as are social invention, social investment in instruments of production, and real interests in widespread distribution. A nation without such things is poor and underdeveloped. A nation with them is rich. Secondly, although the common good of all is served by the success of such corporations, the state's resources are not directly at stake. "Presently we do not have the capital," President Mugabe said in the United States, appealing to President Carter for aid to Zimbabwe. Future risks, then, will not all be made with Zimbabwe's money. Yet the common good of Zimbabwe is served if *someone* takes the risk. If those who invest are successful, Zimbabwe will gain, too.

President Mugabe invites transnational corporations for several reasons. Through their efforts, Zimbabwe stands to gain: (1) industrial plants that otherwise would not be there; (2) the products those plants produce (which otherwise would have to be imported); (3) the salaries paid to employees; (4) related investments in infrastructure (roads, electricity, sewage); (5) the teaching of skills to the work force; (6) an industrial tax base for the locale; and (7) the amenities foreign corporations usually import with them (clinics, schools, services).

Foreign corporations—for good or ill—will also bring with them a foreign culture. There follows an intense conflict between the foreign ethos and that of the population, a clash of contrasting disciplines, powers, and assumptions. A transnational corporation brings with it not simply an economic system, but at least in some measure a set of political and moral-cultural assumptions as well. Its functioning cannot be understood merely in economic terms.

Nonetheless, business firms are easier for nations around the world to import than are political parties, churches, or religions. Corporations have a certain impersonality that makes them compatible with the Japanese as well as the British, the Taiwanese as well as the Brazilians, the South Koreans as well as the Dutch. Politics, morals, and culture may differ, but fundamental aspects of saving, investment, and organization of means, production, and sales are adaptable in virtually all cultures. Some cultures, it is true, may not wish to adapt. In India, for example, many religious taboos seriously impede the path of commercial development. The incredible inefficiencies of India's dual facilities for ninety million untouchables (beside which *apartheid* in South Africa shrinks in perspective) indicate that some cultures prefer the costs of nonadaptation. In Iran, the Ayatollah Khomeini preferred his own inner vision to modern business practices. These caveats in place, it remains true that the economic system of democratic capitalism is more universal than its political or moral-cultural system. Its curious impersonality (so detested by moralists) makes an economic system oddly adaptable, where the culture it represents might be less so.

When Robert Mugabe imposes a rule on corporations that a "substantial portion" of their earnings "must be plowed back, so there is expansion," he is looking out for his own self-interests. Yet any foreign investment in Zimbabwe necessarily: (a) is largely immovable insofar as it goes into buildings, infrastructure, and salaries; and (b) owes its origins to profits earned somewhere else. Today's investments at place P are yesterday's profits at place Q. Mugabe, however, wishes to eat his cake and have it, too. He wants profits earned elsewhere to be invested in Zimbabwe. But he does not allow profits earned in Zimbabwe to be liberated for investment in yet another place.

Richard J. Barnet, of the Institute for Policy Studies, has made U.S. international enterprises the focal point of criticism. First in *Global Reach* and then in *The Lean Years,* Barnet has cataloged the prevailing socialist wisdom.[3] Three main theses preoccupy him. These are: (1) that the global corporations intend to manage the world; (2) that they exploit the poor nations; and (3) that they are "Latinamericanizing" the United States, i.e., spreading Latin America's weaknesses North.

Against these theses, one may observe that for private business to be able to operate within all nations and to concentrate upon economic matters is not the same as to wish to "manage the world." "Manage the world" is the aim of socialism, not the aim of market systems. The same polemical technique is obvious in Barnet's phrase "exploit the poor." Poor nations seem to prefer the presence of global corporations to their absence. Like Mugabe, they are capable of "exploiting the corporation." Economic transactions are free and consensual. They bring advantages to both parties or else they are abruptly broken off. Finally, the ill effects of large global corporations upon life in the United States, according to Barnet, must be set alongside the advantages which these same corporations bring to the people of the United States. Suppose that all U.S. corporations were forbidden tomorrow to have any branches overseas at all. It is altogether unlikely that the poor and the workers, within or outside the United States, would reap benefits. Absent global corporations, the likelihood that the world would be more prosperous, freer, more peaceful, and more healthful is slim.

One also needs to calculate the cost of alternative instruments. The record of the socialist international economic system in the developing countries must also be evaluated. So must the record of the Catholic church and other international agencies. If aid to developing nations is *not* to come through investment and productivity on the part of transnational corporations, to what sort of agencies shall we turn, and what will *their* deficiencies be? On the surface, Barnet's thesis seems to be that the transnationals need to be reformed. Nearly all the reforms he suggests involve the subordination of economic activities to political authorities. These are statist ideals, and they also have costs. No one argues that transnational companies are without fault, only that they are the best of available instruments and that, on balance, the good they do outweighs their deficiencies.

The UN commission which has studied international corporations (it has not yet studied international socialism) prefers to call them "transnationals" rather than "multinationals."[4] This name better reflects the fact that such corporations—Volkswagen, Royal Dutch, British Petroleum, Toyota, Renault, and many others—have their origin and headquarters in one nation, but have productive operations in other nations. They do not merely *sell* in other nations; they have productive operations there. Usually, these operations are in manufacturing or processing; in the case of banks and insurance companies, they provide financial services.

Within the United States, there are now some two hundred corporations which have significant operations overseas.[5] The first U.S. corporation to establish a branch overseas was Tiffany's in 1868, which opened a Paris branch to show that it could compete with the best. The second was Singer Sewing Machine.[6] Such operations spring from the international vision of Adam Smith, a vision which rivals that of "the socialist international"—a vision of the wealth of *all* nations, an intention to liberate all humans by bettering the material lot of all.

For some generations, as John Kenneth Galbraith has pointed out, three types of overseas enterprise led the way: banking operations; resource industries, mining in particular, followed in the twentieth century by oil; and the trading companies which introduced an international exchange of goods. Each of these has been historically subject to ill repute. The international banker was accused of a lack of national patriotism because of his cosmopolitan interests. When all other accusations failed, anti-semitism could be invoked. Resource industries were accused of being robber barons and exploiters of local labor, and of bending weak governments to their purposes. The trading companies in India, Indonesia, and Indochina were linked to colonialism and in China to foreign penetration and domination. "Thus, like so many children, the multinational industrial corporation was unwise in the choice of its parents and is visited with their sins."[7]

But Galbraith notes a decisive difference recently. The older multinationals almost always traded between rich and poor countries, exchanging needed capital for cheap labor, and exchanging needed manufactured products for needed raw materials and agricultural products. Today, by contrast, nearly all multinational activities take place among the industrial nations. Only a small fraction occurs between them and the poorer nations. Moreover, "the greatest supplier of wheat, feed grains, coal, wood and wood pulp, and cotton fiber are the two North American countries—the United States and Canada." These are the two major hewers of wood and suppliers of food and natural products to the world. Among the old types of multinational organizations, banks now operate almost wholly between industrial countries, the trading corporations have receded in relative importance, and the resource companies have been dramatically limited by expropriation.

The modern transnational corporation, according to Galbraith, is a "nearly inescapable accommodation" to the worldwide need for consumer goods.[8] The world wants goods for the immediate use of its households and its peoples. Following Singer Sewing Machines have been General Electric, General Foods, Nabisco, General Motors, Ford, Control Data, IBM, and scores of other exporters of technology and manufactured products. The economic infrastructures of the world's nations demand heavy industry, and here, too, major manufacturing firms like Dravo have become involved.

By contrast with transnational exchanges of the past, the new exchanges demand intimate contact between maker and purchaser. In the old days, producers of foodstuffs, cloth, coal, and steel never saw or needed to see their purchasers. Indeed, ships often went to sea destination unknown, waiting for word about which markets offered better prices. Today, manufacturers produce products that must be marketed, products which require education in their use and service throughout their useful life. The new corporations spend as much energy on instruction, repair, service, and marketing and sales as upon production—maybe more. They have intimate contact with individuals at every point of sale and service. The relationship is far less distant and less impersonal, far more human, cultural, and political.

Thus the full nature of the system of democratic capitalism—and of its natural child, the large mass-market manufacturing firm—has become visible to the world. Transnational companies are not economic systems only (even if they are primarily that). They require intimate contact with the political system and with the moral-cultural system of host nations. Governments themselves are among their most important customers, purchasing transport systems, power generators, electric grids, office equipment, building materials, and many other necessities. Governments make the basic decisions about national infrastructure (airports, highways, electrical grids, energy systems, television channels, telephone systems). Governments also regulate, prohibit, or restrict conditions of sale and operation.

In some respects, transnationals are utterly dependent upon governments; in some respects their relations are symbiotic and in others their power may suborn those of governments. Transnationals are clearly involved as political agents functioning within political systems. When collaboration between corporations and governments is unstable, unprofitable, or simply too filled with headaches, transnationals must necessarily go elsewhere. This may explain their decisively marked preference for dealing with established industrial societies. There is nothing wrong with this need for harmony between the economic system and the political system; it is wholly natural. Socialist societies solve it by subordinating economics to politics. The preferred democratic capitalist solution is coordination. Each system, political and economic, has something the other wants and needs. Each has power and vulnerabilities. Each loses if the bargain between them is not fair, stable, and long-term. The corporation faces heavy initial investments and a long production period before products are available and markets prepared for their introduction. The local political system has its own needs. When either side cannot deliver, exchange is ruptured. Expulsion, expropriation, and withdrawal mark the twentieth-century history of the transnationals and governments.[9]

Thus the long-term interests of transnationals and local political systems work toward accommodation, even if in the short term new nations are jealous of their sovereignty and pride, and even if transnationals make grevious errors of political or moral-cultural judgment. Both are engaged in a process new to world history. Were a team of U.S. humanists and social scientists sent abroad into cultures not fully known to them, one would not be totally surprised if some of their members made egregious moral-cultural and political errors. The personnel of business enterprises are likely to commit similar offenses against common sense, discretion, and cultural understanding. The room for error is enormous. There is always room for improvement and reform.

Transnational corporations are being forced—in large measure by criticism, defeat, and failure—to face up to their own complex structure. They are political and moral-cultural enterprises, as well as economic enterprises. They must respect local needs along all three dimensions of their life.

Two of the most stunning achievements of the new transnational order, in Galbraith's view, are the lessening of tariff wars and the diminishment of economic conflict. Transnationals have real interests in avoiding tariff wars and in diminishing tensions between the governments with which they cooperate. IBM has absolutely no interest—exactly the reverse—in fomenting troubles between France and Germany, or Brazil and Argentina. "We would wish," Galbraith writes, "that there were more multinational operations between the Soviet Union and the United States."[10] The companies desire less economic conflict, but nations may not.

Again, the transnational corporation "brings into existence the world's first truly effective international civil service—men and women who have a nominal loyalty to their country of origin, a rhetorical commitment to the country in which they serve and a primary loyalty to the company that employs them." In Galbraith's eyes, the transnationals have thus taken "a civilized step from narrow militant nationalism," of which the twentieth century and earlier centuries have suffered quite enough.

Management by its nature must always be partly local. Successful companies stress this development and expend great efforts in realizing it. "Extensive managerial authority must be granted to national entities as a matter of simple necessity. . . . It matters less and less and eventually not at all who ultimately owns the corporation, or where it is owned, for the owners are without power."[11] Indeed, as Ronald Müller states in an article strongly critical of transnationals, most investment is as soon as possible derived from local sources.[12] Transnationals have a real interest in the self-protection afforded by stimulating local ownership. They have urgent capital needs elsewhere.

Whereas Barnet develops the protectionist accusation that transnationals export jobs, capital, and technology, Galbraith makes the classic case for free international trade. In a free world economy, technology is spread more rapidly; the international division of labor follows more realistic and intelligent lines; productivity increases; prices fall (as efficiencies earned in one place displace older inefficiencies); and a greater aggregate of employment around the world is achieved.[13]

Galbraith's views appear to be becoming widely shared. While many from smaller nations resent having to turn to outside assistance, the advantages of doing so appear for most nations to outweigh disadvantages. Dealing with private corporations is a full step short of dealing directly with governments. Thus even when nations are at odds with one another, private corporations are often able to continue operations (as is the case with Gulf and others in Angola). Moreover, to break with a private corporation is a step short of breaking with its nation of origin. The dependence upon the Soviet Union into which Cuba has fallen, by contrast, is far more difficult to break. It is said that, for this reason, Castro in 1980 warned the Nicaraguans against breaking economic relations with the West.

A socialist cannot consistently object to the size of large corporations in the free world. Were all corporations nationalized, the resulting entities would be still larger. Relations with such corporations, furthermore, would constitute political relations with a state government and thus bring into play far vaster concentrations of power. Reinhold Niebuhr wrote in 1956 some words which events have partially overtaken. Since then, the wealth of Western Europe, Japan, and many other nations at that time still relatively prostrate from the Second World War has been greatly increased through market systems and corporate activities. His words are worth recalling:

> Our nation enjoys living standards that are roughly two to three times as high as those of the European nations, and five to ten times as high as those of Asian nations. This wealth is a tremendous hazard to our moral prestige throughout the world. It not only tempts others to envy but it gives a certain plausibility to the Communist charge of "capitalistic exploitation." This charge is not well-founded because our wealth does not even depend upon a great percentage of foreign trade. We have a more nearly self-sufficient continental economy than any other nation. Our wealth is due primarily to the high degree of efficiency of our technics and of our whole industrial enterprise. Other nations may approach our efficiency, but our continental economy, permitting mass production and lowered costs, gives us an advantage over even the most efficient of other nations. Thus our good fortune, gained with a minimum of injustice to others, makes us appear as Dives in a poverty-stricken world.[14]

Since 1956, other nations have much advanced. Many have equalled, some have surpassed, U.S. standards of living. To a remarkable extent, and quite quickly, in twenty-five short years, economic benefits have been broadly spread. Global corporations deserve some credit. What other agency has done as much?

If it is objected that global corporations are international, one must recall that socialism is as well. If it is objected that they are large, one must recall that so are the tasks awaiting the world's 4.4 billion population. If it is objected that they represent "great concentrations of power," it must be noted that socializing them would concentrate power still more tightly. If it is objected that they are "outside the law" or "unaccountable to political institutions," it must be recalled, first, that freedom from law and regulation will come as news to corporate management and, second, that some degree of lack of subordination to political systems is the secret of their liberty, vitality, efficiency, and humanity. There is no evidence that political management of industry better serves the people in whose name it is imposed, and no evidence whatever that state-managed economies more successfully produce the goods that people want. If it is objected, finally, that there have been abuses, that reforms are in order, and that the needs of political systems and moral-cultural systems must be more carefully and thoroughly respected, one can only concur that the ideals of democratic capitalism demand as much.[15]

A final word must be reserved for small corporations which are not transnationals. Large corporations must of necessity commit long-term investment to proven technologies. The main force for innovation belongs with small new pioneers, which many large corporations of today once were. Often enough, engineers and artisans who begin with large corporations break away to start their own firms. In due course, if their inventions prove themselves, their small firms either become large ones or are sold to larger ones with the capital to mass-produce and to market their products. Chances are, the goods which transnationals of twenty years from now will be selling to the peoples of the world (and manufacturing overseas) are being developed today in small firms formed around a powerful new idea. As matters stand, the large firms contract out many of their component processes. By the principle of subsidiarity and by the nature of the human mind, new ideas are born in the minds of single individuals or small teams at work upon specific technical problems, far out of sight of the boardrooms of the top managers of the giants.

It is sometimes said that today's corporations are so large that they are no longer characterized by entrepreneurship and risk. Yet one reads every day of major corporations whose strategic planning involves them in costly, even devastating, mistakes. Others by a few bold decisions achieve stunning success. In every industry, there are advancing companies and declining ones. It seems premature to think that risk-taking and high-stake decision-making are at an end.

On the other hand, executives and workers in very large corporations necessarily encounter problems of morale, spirit, and efficiency quite unlike those present in small pioneering firms. Bureaucratic thinking may afflict them. Private industry has means for removing deadwood and measuring productivity lacking to governmental bureaucracies. It may fire people, close down inefficient operations, open new projects. There is greater systemic vitality in the private sector than in the public sector, independently of personal motivation. Still, the success of corporations in routinizing their problems generates in its own way a crisis in the ethos of democratic capitalism. The spirit of those who work in large enterprises may rigidify or grow lax over time. Thus those who care about the life of the spirit within the corporate sector of democratic capitalism need constantly to stimulate the sense of participation and creativity. According to the principle of subsidiarity, vital decision-making and innovation at each level of work are necessary if the whole is to remain vital.

The collective strength of the human race is rooted in the creative intelligence of individual men and women. A theologian is obliged to observe, by analogy, that Christianity is better represented in its individual witnesses than in its collective apparatus, and may be forgiven, then, for preferring, on balance, small corporations to large, due recognition being paid to the human necessity of large institutions. If our corporations atrophy, or are made into adjuncts of state bureaucracies, we shall all be the losers.[16]

In the real world, the socialist critique of transnationals seems to be losing its ideological simplicity under the pressures of urgent practical need. Having considered the underlying moral structures of democratic capitalism in Part I, and having considered the transformation of socialism in Part II, we must turn more directly to the churches and the theologians. The groundwork has been laid. The work of creative criticism must begin.

Three

A Theology of Economics

Since 1891, the authoritative voices of the Christian churches, Catholic and Protestant, have more and more spoken out on social and economic matters. This effort is entirely in keeping with the Jewish and Christian concept of religious vocation—a vocation not to seek escape from this world but to change the world. On the other hand, there exists no serious disciplined body of theological reflection on the history and foundations of economics. In few areas has Christian theology, in particular, been so little advanced. Yet laypersons in the world, not least in democratic capitalist lands, have need of disciplined inquiry— and an obligation to contribute to it. Corporate executives and workers, white-collar workers and teachers, doctors and lawyers—all have need of spiritual guidance. How can this be given until we have a theology as realistic as the work they do?

XIV

The Catholic Anti-Capitalist Tradition

The popes have no need to study modern economics.
—*The Twentieth Century Encyclopedia of Catholicism*[1]

1
A Theology of Economics

Most theologians recognize that our field requires a new discipline. Precedents exist in the work of the distinguished German thinker Heinrich Pesch (1854–1926) and of John A. Ryan of the United States (1869–1945).[2] Yet a huge systematic task awaits the theologians of the coming generation, as they apply sustained theological reflection to economic realities.

Three separate specializations would seem to be needed. First, theologians must consider economic realities present in every economic system in every age. They need clear and critical concepts about such realities as scarcity, work, money, capital accumulation, production, distribution, inequality, technology, division of labor, and the like. What do such realities mean for religion, and what does religion mean for them? This inquiry might be called a *general* theology of economics.

On a quite different level, theologians must fairly understand and evaluate *systems* of political economy. There have not been many such in human history. Until the twentieth century, systems of slavery appeared on every continent. The human race has experienced systems based on hunting and systems, like feudalism, based on grants of land to nobility. Among other major systems have been state-controlled mercantilist systems, democratic capitalism, socialism in several forms, and communism. Each of these systems needs to be described accurately both in its theory and in its practice.

There is in our day an extended literature on the theology of socialism[3] as old as early religious socialism in nineteenth-century Britain[4] and as new as liberation theology in Latin America.[5] There is virtually nothing on the theology of democratic capitalism.[6] There is no single book even describing the latter accurately. No book compares the inner ideals of democratic capitalism (which have not been adequately stated) with the inner ideals of socialism (which have been profusely stated). No book compares the practice of democratic capitalism with the practice of socialism. The practice of actual socialist regimes is little studied by socialists, who argue less from cases than from visions of what has never been. Nations like Nicaragua, Iran, Angola, Vietnam, and many others are today, through well-armed elites, making choices of political economy, often enough based upon religious claims. Are such claims valid?

Thirdly, theologians must assess institutions, practices, and special ethical dilemmas that occur *within* particular systems. For example, the business corporations so distinctive of democratic capitalism need to be studied in empirical detail and measured by religious standards. So do state bureaucracies. So do the decentralized decision-making bodies imagined by more recent democratic socialists. Political activists face even more serious ethical dilemmas than do economic activists, since they have at their disposal the coercive power of the state. But the ethical dilemmas within economic systems need attention, too.

These three kinds of discourse—general economic theory, specific systems, particulars—need to be distinguished. For often enough, arguments which appear to be about one reality are actually about another. Many but not all objections against transnational corporations, for instance, are really against a free economy. Many but not all objections lodged against particular practices actually have as their intention the establishment of a different system. Such an intention is legitimate. But to state exact disagreements exactly is to state them at the appropriate level of discourse. Someone who thinks that a world of scarcity strengthens the case of socialism may need to look again at the general meaning of scarcity under any economic system, whether that of democratic capitalism or that of socialism or any other. The true locus of disagreement is likely to appear on the first rather than on the second level of discourse.

Even if the new theology of economics did nothing more than to promote critical clarification and to debunk ideological uses of religious language, it would serve a high purpose. In fact, though, carried to its fulfillment, a critical theology ought also to be able to articulate more exactly the worldly import of religious ideals and the religious import of worldly innovations. Discernment is a high spiritual art. It mounts upward on the scaffolding of exact concepts and clear thinking. To move from the myth of Exodus to Marxist theories of exploitation and liberation, on the one hand, or from the parable of the hidden talents to a Spencerian theory of competition, on the other hand, is mere fundamentalism. More exact thinking is needed. For neither Judaism nor Christianity is reducible to Karl Marx or Herbert Spencer, nor is every word of wisdom about economics and politics contained in Keynes or Friedman. To think theologically about economics is, first of all, to learn some economics. It is, at the very least, to distinguish the three levels of discourse.

For the most part, the argument of the present book lies on the second level: the study of systems. I have not been presenting a general theory of economics. Neither have I dealt with all the particulars that fall within each classic system of political economy. These are important tasks, and from time to time clarity has demanded that I ascend briefly to the first level of discourse or descend briefly to the third. But my main intention has been to put into words the actual moral and theological presuppositions of democratic capitalism as it now exists. In a sense, this task is merely descriptive. I have been trying to describe the present system accurately, and to elicit from its actual practice the dynamic intentions and ideals already present within it. Thus I did not begin with an ideal type, nor did I confine myself to the world of conceptual logic. I have tried to reflect upon common experiences within democratic capitalism in order to show how its implicit ideals actually work. I have tried to make its inarticulate wisdom articulate.

In the pages which remain, I wish to consider some of the more prominent objections raised by religious authorities and scholars against democratic capitalism and in favor of socialism. It is not necessary for all Christians or Jews to agree about questions of political economy. Those questions are inherently complex and difficult. Competition between many points of view—even within the same religious body—is appropriate. Furthermore, Judaism and Christianity are religions for all times and all places. Their historical and religious roots run deeper than any one historical system, and their aims and purposes transcend any and all systems of political economy.

Over the years, I have slowly become convinced that the actual practice of democratic capitalism is more consistent with the high aims of Judaism and Christianity than the practice of any other system. Democratic capitalism respects the imperative of self-reform and self-transcendence. It has already changed much and is capable of indefinite future transformation. Yet for various reasons, the Christian churches have failed to comprehend its inner spirit. The laity will probably have to lead the way. They will encounter opposition.

2

The Bias Against Democratic Capitalism

"Any serious Christian," Paul Tillich once said, "must be a socialist."[7] In the history of the last two hundred years, the favored ecclesiastical word for democratic capitalism has been "liberalism." This word is almost always used pejoratively in the papal documents—not only in "The Syllabus of Errors" of Pope Pius IX in 1864, but also in the encyclicals of subsequent popes. In 1980, the superior general of the Jesuits, Father Pedro Arrupe, S.J., wrote: ". . . the type of social analysis used in the liberal world today implies an individualistic and materialistic vision of life that is destructive of Christian values and attitudes."[8]

The traditional accusations against democratic capitalism fall into two categories: those against democracy and those against capitalism. Over the years, the former have fallen away. The churches have learned to cherish democracy and religious liberty, but resistance to capitalism remains. The generic and fundamental accusations against capitalism are that it is individualistic, materialist, and anarchic. At times, it is also suggested that capitalism fosters inequality (although comparisons are seldom undertaken with respect to inequality under other historical systems).

There are some excellent summaries of church teachings in this area.[9] Instead of repeating them, it may be more useful to exhibit the sort of mental horizon, the complex of images and sensibility, which a devout Christian is likely to encounter in the church teachings on economics. There are many misunderstandings.

The first known use of the word "individualism" occurs in an essay by the French writer Joseph de Maistre in 1820.[10] De Maistre used the word in an expression of disdain "for this deep and frightening division of minds, this infinite fragmentation of all doctrines, *political protestantism* carried to the most absolute individualism."[11] In 1829, the prominent French Catholic writer Lamennais assaulted "individualism" as a doctrine which nourishes "power without obedience" and "law without duty." He added: "The same doctrine which produces anarchy among minds produces in addition an irremediable political anarchy, and overturns the basis of human society." Both de Maistre and Lamennais influenced the course of nineteenth-century Catholic liberalism. Both were French, surely among the most individualist of peoples. And both respected social traditions and inarticulate social connections as did British Whigs like Edmund Burke. They were disturbed by the anti-clerical, anti-religious revolutionary secularism of France.

From the nineteenth-century Vatican, democratic capitalism

seemed far away and heretical. In the nineteenth century, the social structure of Catholic Italy, Spain, and Austro-Hungary was still feudal, monarchical, and mercantilist. In 1864, the at first liberal pope, Pius IX (whose reign lasted 32 years, 1846–78), embittered by his experiences with Italian anti-clerical republicans, condemned nearly every thesis of a liberal society root and branch in his famous "Syllabus of Errors."[12] In 1891, Leo XIII at last addressed the large social questions racking the first modern societies in a letter addressed to the entire world, "On the Condition of Labor." He was the first architect of what came to be thought of as the Catholic "middle way."[13] He roundly condemned socialism, even in its milder forms. He upheld the notion of the limited state and the critical role of private property as the protector of liberty.[14] But he was soundly critical not only of certain practices of capitalism but of some of its philosophical bases, especially its individualism and its radical dependence on the free market.

The Catholic bishops of the United States played an important role in persuading Leo XIII to defend the rights of labor.[15] In 1891, Catholics in the U.S. numbered about 9 million in a population of 65 million. Many laymen, priests, and bishops were active in the labor movement. In a sense, the strong social traditions of Catholics and Jews led both communities in the United States to early and strong support for labor. American Protestants, with their strong traditions of individualism, long found it more natural to oppose unionization. Even the "Social Gospel" movement among American Protestants had to struggle mightily to bring authoritative religious support to the cause of the unions.[16]

Forty years after *Rerum Novarum,* in 1931, Pius XI (pope 1922–39) advanced the thought of Leo XIII in a new letter, "On the Reconstruction of the Social Order." Pius XI, not quite as hostile to liberalism as Pius IX had been, nonetheless described individualism and collectivism as "twin evils." Because of the Catholic tradition favoring limited government and private property, his treatment of the twin evils was not symmetrical. He described "Christian socialism" as a contradiction in terms, and held, "No one can be at the same time a sincere Catholic and a true socialist." He did not symmetrically condemn capitalism. But he did blast the "tottering tenets of liberalism" and "the evil of individualism."[17]

Just as the unity of human society cannot be built upon "class" conflict, so the proper ordering of economic affairs cannot be left to the free play of rugged competition. From this source, as from a polluted spring, have proceeded all the errors of the "individualistic" school. This school, forgetful or ignorant of the social and moral aspects of economic activities, regarded these as completely free and immune from any intervention by public authority, for they would have in the market place and in unregulated competition a principle of self-direction more suitable for guiding them than any created intellect which might intervene. Free competition, however, though justified and quite useful within certain limits, cannot be an adequate controlling principle in economic affairs. This has been abundantly proved by the consequences that have followed from the free rein given to these dangerous individualistic ideals.[18]

The pope observed fairly that the horrible "pauperism" of the days of Leo XIII is "less prevalent today. The condition of the workingmen has indeed been improved and rendered more equitable in many respects, particularly in the larger and more developed States, where the laboring class can no longer be said to be universally in misery and want."[19] But how did this happen? The pope showed no inclination to inquire.

Next, Pius XI made a grave charge against "capital":

Capital, however, was long able to appropriate to itself excessive advantages. It claimed all the products and profits and left to the laborer the barest minimum necessary to repair his strength and to ensure the continuation of his class. For by an inexorable economic law, it was held, all accumulation of riches must fall to the share of the wealthy, while the workingman must remain perpetually in indigence or reduced to the minimum needed for existence.[20]

It is not at all clear who "claimed" this. No serious thinker in the democratic capitalist tradition is directly confronted.

Closer to our own time, Pope Paul VI wrote in *Octogesima Adveniens* in 1971:

The liberal ideology . . . asserts itself in the name of

economic efficiency, for the defense of the individual against the increasingly overwhelming hold of organizations, and as a reaction against the totalitarian tendencies of political powers. Certainly personal initiative must be maintained and developed. But do not Christians who take this path tend to idealize liberalism . . . while easily forgetting that at the very root of philosophical liberalism is an erroneous affirmation of the autonomy of the individual in his activity, his motivation and the exercise of his liberty.[21]

Pope John Paul II, in his encyclical *Laborem Exercens* (1981) for the ninetieth anniversary of *Rerum Novarum,* went beyond these early texts in four ways. He clearly distinguished "early nineteenth-century capitalism" from recent capitalism ("rigid capitalism" from modern). He drew from broad experience the lesson that the socialist collectivization of property takes from one class to give power to a new class. He identified as "labor" many sources of creativity—the work of inventors, intellectual workers, management experts and the like—which go far beyond blue-collar workers. Under "labor," he included all those who contribute to production, even entrepreneurs and managers, discoverers of new processes and inventors of new techniques. Finally, he emphasized the creativity of modern work by drawing on the theological symbols of the Creator and his creation. These are giant steps toward the tradition of John Locke, Adam Smith, and later democratic capitalism. In his capsule history of early-nineteenth-century capitalism, however, Pope John Paul II may have intended only to provide an illustration. As illustration, his material works; as history, it appears to be as deficient as the views of his predecessors have been.[22]

All the popes, it is true, have respected some of the fundamental principles of democratic capitalism. All have favored the limited state (in keeping with the liberal tradition) and the indispensable role of private property. They have resisted, however, both "individualism" and the "so-called liberalism of the Manchester School," in part confusing these with the anti-clerical, anti-religious republicanism of Italy, France, and Mexico, and in part simply by misunderstanding Anglo-Saxon cultures. Their resistance to democratic capitalism has not been due to illusions about socialism. On the contrary, they were from the beginning alert not only to the latter's materialism and atheism but to its utopianism and its potential for state tyranny.

In a sense, by standing outside the historical stream of democratic capitalism, the popes were able to make some legitimate criticisms of abuses and errors within it, and to support many proposals for humane reforms eventually adopted by it. Yet, simultaneously, the remnants both of the medieval world and state mercantilism were crumbling all around them. Resisting socialism and standing outside democratic capitalism, Catholic social teaching laid claim to a certain neutrality— but gradually came to seem suspended in air. Catholic thought began to deal with every sort of regime, traditional and modern, even while its talk of a Catholic "middle way" seemed empty, since there are, in fact, no existing examples of that middle way. Catholic social teaching has, therefore, occupied a sort of utopian ground—literally, no-place. It came to seem uncharacteristically abstract, otherworldly, deracinated. Popes and scholars might make astute and valuable comments from time to time, but the platform on which they stood no longer seemed connected to real experience.

For this reason, perhaps, the programs of the 1940s and the 1950s in which Catholic thinkers had invested so much hope for "the reconstruction of the social order"—Catholic Action, the Young Christian Workers, the Christian Democratic parties— achieved some notable successes but lacked the force of an alternative ideal. To be anti-communist and anti-socialist, and only halfheartedly committed to democratic capitalism, is to represent not a "middle way" but a halfway house. Such movements collapsed of their own lack of a serious ideal.

After the Second Vatican Council, first under "good Pope John" (Pope John XXIII) and then under Pope Paul VI, this vacuum in Catholic social thought began to be filled from two directions. First, in Western Europe, chiefly in Germany, the new "political theology" began to move in a socialist direction.[23] Socialism cherishes images of community, unitary authority, and integrated life which are closer to those of traditional feudal society than to those of democratic capitalism. The new political theology practiced by Johannes Metz and others has turned away from the Enlightenment and embraced the philosophy of praxis (understood in the tradition of Marxism rather than in that of the American pragmatists).[24] It has shown contempt for bourgeois society, favored a "Christian-Marxist" dialogue, and taken an almost medieval delight in the supposed rediscovery of an "age of limits." This new political theology provides a novel form of socialism in Europe (to be considered in Chapter XV). More recently, in Latin America and in the formerly French, Belgian, and Portuguese colonies of Africa and Asia, another form of socialism has arisen under the title "liberation theology" (Chapters XVI–XVIII).

Following Vatican II, a special Vatican Commission on Peace and Justice was established, and peace and justice commissions were opened in many dioceses around the world. These commissions freed many priests and sisters from traditional pastoral duties so that they might engage in social action. It was natural for them, in many situations, to ally themselves with an adversarial spirit. Increasingly, these groups appear to have taken on an anti-capitalist and, at times, anti-democratic ideology. Employing the language of "standing with the poor and the oppressed," they easily fall into the language of class struggle. Beginning as reformers, they often find the language of their socialist peers captivating. If they become concerned about world hunger, they seldom blame shortages of foodstuffs on the failures of socialist agriculture; they are more likely to blame "multinational conglomerates." Many such activists deny that they are Marxists or even socialists, but one seldom hears them employing the ideas or the methods of democratic capitalism. Instead, they frequently denounce democratic capitalist societies as selfish, sick, greedy, materialist, individualist, etc. They seem to assume the correctness of their views; the quality of their intellectual arguments suffers from lack of self-criticism.

Perhaps their fatal flaw lies in the omission of the symbol "liberty." Peace and justice there may be even under authoritarian societies. The innermost secret of democratic capitalism is liberty. A Vatican Commission on Peace, Liberty, and Justice would sound a universal clarion.

But more than symbols are at stake. The intellectual model for peace and justice offered by Catholic social teaching is at present closer to a mild form of socialism than to democratic capitalism. It has little to say about markets and incentives, the ethics of production, and the habits, disciplines, and organization necessary for the creation of wealth. It seems to take the production of wealth for granted (as if wealth were as limited and static as in medieval times) and preoccupies itself with appeals for redistribution. The discoveries of modern economics seem to have affected it hardly at all. There are virtually no signs in it of sustained theological reflection upon democratic capitalism. There are many signs in it of conformity to the conventional thinking of socialists in Europe and the Third World. Some interpreters argue that socialism is the emerging wave of the future in Catholic social teaching.[25] A new confluence between secular and ecclesiastical authoritarianism under socialism may seem to some attractive.

One of the themes emergent in this new social teaching is that "development is the new name for peace." Empirically, however, it does not seem to be true that a developing country necessarily commits itself to peace; some are armed to the teeth. Among the nations, socialist models of development—of which since World War II there have been scores—seem woefully gray, economically dependent, and politically oppressive. The social teachings of the Catholic church at present do not seem to be rooted in sound empirical and theoretical reflection upon such outcomes, although Pope John Paul II has begun to make a difference. His reflections on creativity also show promise. Any economic system whatever, if it is not to stagnate, must produce more than it invests. It must yield capital accumulation. Profit is, therefore, a condition of development; without it, there are only losses or stagnation. The church seems poised, at last, to think about the creative causes of wealth.

One would think that Catholic theologians, in particular, would be more modest in speaking of development. The record of wholly Catholic countries in the history of economic and social development is not entirely laudable. (The same is true, alas, of their record in establishing democracies.) Is it possible that there are some intellectual *lacunae* in Catholic teachings on political economy? Are there some insights missing?

Such reflections as these have led me, over the years, to believe that just as the Catholic tradition has something to teach America, so also American democratic capitalism has some new things to add to the Catholic tradition. The Catholic church has heretofore learned from the intellect of Greece and Rome, Germany and France. Why not also from America?

As Reinhold Niebuhr himself experienced (cf. Chapter XIX below), a theology of economics must first proceed by a *via negativa*. It is sometimes necessary to study first what does not work, so as to discover the better by examination of the worse. For the sake of brevity, we will select for study the most prominent representative of Christian socialism in Europe, Juergen Moltmann.

XV
Christian Socialism in Europe

Arthur McGovern, S. J., summarizes the era of Catholic thought between Leo XIII and the present under the title "From Anathemas to Christian Marxists."[1] Those who are in favor of Christian Marxism have noble intentions. They are moved by the "sin" of poverty and oppression to seek "change." Most of them are determined that the socialist society they wish to bring about will be democratic, open, and pluralistic. Yet they have several intellectual blind spots, which will almost certainly occasion the defeat of their good purposes.

1
Historical Development

In his famous *Pacem in Terris* (1963), Pope John XXIII gave the distinction between "historical movements" and the "philosophical teachings" canonical weight, and Paul VI reinforced this distinction by repeating it in more detail in *Octogesima Adveniens* (1971). Christian socialists have exploited this distinction with great vigor.[2] For it offers them a way of escaping the official ideology of Marxism while still finding some way to call themselves socialist.

There are several difficulties in Marxist thought which, as Christians, they wish to avoid. They are not atheist. They are not materialist. They favor neither complete collectivization under the state nor one-party rule. They do not hold that divisive class struggle is the key to history. And they cannot be totally opposed to private property—a decisive limitation on the power of the state—for they generally favor land reform, rural cooperatives, and the ownership of one's own home and personal goods.

After their rejection of atheism, materialism, state collectivization, party rule, class struggle, and the abolition of private property, it is hard to see what is left of the Marxism of Christian Marxists. As a result, many of them drop the claim to being Marxists and insist upon being called non-Marxist socialists or democratic socialists.

Oddly, then, the Christian who would be a Marxist experiences two contrary movements of thought. First, he denies that cooperating with the "historical movement" of Marxism necessarily commits him to its basic "philosophical teachings." The second movement of thought, however, follows the reverse pattern; in order to cooperate with the movement, he re-defines the teachings. In the annual "Christian-Marxist dialogues" which took place in Germany and Czechoslovakia from 1964 through 1967, and in the United States in later years, scholars rejected the actual "historical movements" of Soviet Marxism and Catholic teaching. They wished to redefine the originating "philosophical teachings" of both. Marxist thinkers Ernst Bloch and Roger Garaudy tried to show that Marx never intended the individual to be "sacrificed" to the totalitarian state. On the other side, Catholic theologians like Johannes Metz tried to show that the primary impetus of Christianity is "eschatological," that Jesus should be seen as "a revolutionary," and that the church should consider itself an institution for the collective criticism of society.[3]

The first movement of thought tried to rescue socialism as a humanistic historical *movement*. The second tried to rescue Marxism as a humanistic philosophical *idea*.

As early as 1909, the distinguished American Catholic social thinker Monsignor John A. Ryan had foreshadowed this effort, in an essay titled "May a Catholic be a Socialist?"[4] He distinguished between socialism as a social *movement* hostile to religion, as a social *philosophy* committed to materialism, and as an economic *technique* of limited public ownership. He thought that this last, which he called "essential economic socialism," respectful of home ownership and the private ownership of personal goods, might or might not work in practice. But it is, he taught, consistent with Catholic moral teaching. In a later book, *The Church and Socialism* (1919), Ryan tried to develop a Catholic alternative to state socialism, emphasizing cooperatives and the broad distribution of ownership.[5] His work was influential upon a joint statement by the Catholic bishops of the United States in 1919, the "Bishops' Program for Social Reconstruction," many of the proposals of which were later realized under Roosevelt's New Deal and in subsequent social programs.[6] These proposals were not only consistent with democratic capitalism, they have become part of its substance. The moral-cultural system (the bishops joining with others, like the "Social Gospel" movement among Protestants) helped to move the political system to check, modify, and improve the economic system.

In recent years, the social teaching of the U.S. Catholic bishops has turned toward "essential economic socialism" in a more decisive way. The bishops waste little breath on the long-term needs of the economic system, even in those areas in which the moral dimension is salient, like productivity, savings, investment, and growth, and have shown surprisingly little interest in moral guidance for the worker, investor, manager, and executive in productive industries. Instead, the bishops seem to focus on the state as the fulcrum of their hopes. Their intentions are to help the poor. Their method is usually statist, although cautiously so.

Quite secular socialists in the United States have followed an analogous movement. Not only have they rejected Stalinism and most of Marx, many have also become at least cautiously critical of the welfare state. They have begun to worry about the tyranny of the administrative apparatus, about the ways in which it may be captured by elites, and about its corruptions and its inefficiencies. Some, like Michael Walzer, therefore, call for a "second revolution," this time against the welfare state and in the name of participatory democracy.[7]

What, then, is Christian socialism? When Christian socialists defend private property and personal ownership, a pluralistic political system, an open and tolerant moral-cultural system, and even economic techniques like the market and personal incentives, it is difficult to distinguish their fundamental ideals from those of democratic capitalism.

One clear differentiating feature is hostility to capitalism, corporations, business. This point is made conveniently clear by the new Catholic left in Great Britain, both in *Slant* and in *New Blackfriars*.[8] According to the *Slant* Manifesto of 1966, to be a Christian is to be committed to building community in the world and thus, logically, to oppose capitalism. In the *Slant* view, capitalism is thoroughly destructive of community, systematically creates class antagonisms, encourages egoistic competitiveness, and teaches possessiveness. While opposing rigid Stalinist socialism, the new Catholic left plans to build community through true, democratic, participatory socialism.[9]

We have already observed how democratic socialism seems to nourish an eighteenth-century ideal of community. Even so, the *Slant* group gives utopian socialism the benefit of every doubt, while giving democratic capitalism no credit whatever for its actual character. Although democratic capitalism is not without its injustices, contradictions, and internal evils, still, on crucial points the history of the last ninety years suggests that the "philosophical teachings" and the "historical movement" of democratic capitalism have been vindicated, whereas both the "philosophical teachings" and the "historical movement" of socialism have had to be substantially amended. This is true concerning atheism, materialism, determinism, class struggle, the collectivist state, rule by one party, the supposed resistance of socialism to imperialism, and the utility of the basic economic techniques of democratic capitalism: private property, markets, and incentives.

Socialism has been dying the death of a thousand qualifications. Yet theologians who want the church to give some guidance to the men and women of the late twentieth century have adopted for their use virtually no idiom other than vulgar Marxism. The latter, as Raymond Aron notes, has become the *lingua franca* of the educated classes of the West.[10] So when theologians begin to speak of the world of our time, they sound rather like Willy Brandt. Perhaps a sustained treatment of one major and influential writer, the distinguished Protestant theologian Juergen Moltmann, will illustrate how vague the symbols of Christian socialism have become. Lay readers may be unaccustomed to plowing through theological discussions. Still, they need to see how theological and political-economic matters come to be linked in the minds of scholars who have great influence upon the churches.

2
Christian Socialism in Europe

Moltmann, a professor of systematic theology at Tübingen, West Germany, is one of the two or three most influential theologians in this generation. The underlying movement of his thought owes far more to Hegel than to Aquinas:

> The impulse of the Christian spirit in the history of the West links up again and again with the spirit of the modern age and produces progressively better views of the world and of life. . . . The progress of the human spirit can be interpreted as the self-movement of absolute Spirit.[11]

Moltmann's work is at the center of what is usually known as "the theology of hope" and, more generally, "political theology." The originality of this school lies in two contributions.

First, political theology has focused the attention of Christians upon the future (rather than on the past), stressing the eschatological aspects of Christian hope. The foundations of this emphasis lie both in recent Scripture studies and in reading "the signs of the times." In the early stages of this movement of thought, the new possibilities of John F. Kennedy's "New Frontiers" and of Pope John XXIII's "opening" of the Catholic church were commonly acknowledged.[12]

Second, it breaks away from centuries of Christian emphasis upon the struggle of the individual soul. While it clings to the teaching "What shall it profit a man if he gain the whole world and suffer the loss of his soul?" (Mk. 8:36), it emphasizes the social nature of the Christian vocation—indeed, its *political* nature. In a sense, this new political theology is an attempt to break out of the cultural stream of the Enlightenment, with its emphasis upon the individual and rational consciousness, in order to think of theology (and philosophy) as *practical* activities engaged in the full range of worldly problems.[13]

This last motive was already being explored by earlier twentieth-century thinkers like Maurice Blondel, whose philosophy of action was influential upon William James and, through him, John Dewey and other American philosophers.[14] These Americans also thought that they were healing the classic break between speculative and practical reason, between thought and action, between theory and praxis.[15] European theology is frequently undertaken, however, without reference to American thinkers or the American experience.

Moltmann's most influential books have been *The Theology of Hope* (1967), *The Crucified God* (1974), and a collection of essays on social and political subjects, *The Experiment Hope*.[16] His intention seems to be to articulate a new "Protestant ethic" that would bring Christianity to the support of socialism.

Under the influence of Max Weber, Protestantism is conventionally thought to be the moral force which fills the sails of capitalism. At the other extreme, inheriting a strong emphasis upon individual conscience and upon faith rather than works, many ordinary Protestants tend to define salvation in private terms, apart from questions of social, political, and economic structures. On both these counts, Juergen Moltmann has tried to change the Protestant understanding of God and human history. In his earlier phase (*Theology of Hope*), he seemed to identify God as "a God with 'Future as his essential nature,' " a power exerted upon human life not from the past but from somewhere up ahead and above.[17] As his critics have pointed out, this tendency seemed to involve him in determinism and cosmic optimism.[18] In a later book, *The Crucified God,* Moltmann has seemed to his critics to become "more patient, more realistic, more gradualist."[19] If earlier he wanted to identify Christianity with progressive forces in the world, later he qualifies his optimism. He now tries to steer between the "great refusal" to deal with political and economic responsibilities at all and the "accommodation" of Christianity to established institutions.[20]

In both phases, Moltmann is critical of the existing systems embodied in Stalinist Marxism and in capitalism. He does not, however, stand outside the intellectual mainstream. "In the end, his political ethics boil down to a rather routine endorsement of democracy and socialism."[21] One of Moltmann's favorite terms, nonetheless, is "radical criticism." He thinks of himself as standing outside of all existing systems in order to practice discernment into worldly good and evil. Through his eschatological method, he wishes to show that Christian faith has relevance for human history, without being wholly identified with any one of its historical embodiments. He writes: "The path of a theology of the cross that is critical of society" avoids the Scylla of a Christian identity that is irrelevant, and the Charybdis of a social relevance without Christian identity.[22] He makes this task easier for himself by exaggerating the extremes. He places the Byzantine ideology of Stalinism on the one side and the Constantinian church linked with ruling powers on the other. He then posits two parties of the middle ground, whose dialogue gives most promise for the future: (1) "humanistic Marxism aligned with the downtrodden and the humiliated" and (2) humanistic Christianity which is chiliastic, future-oriented, and concerned for the poor.[23] The latter is, of course, his own position.

For Moltmann, the two chief theological starting points are the resurrection of Jesus, which for him grounds a theology of hope; and the crucifixion of Jesus, which for him reveals the ambiguity of history and identifies Christianity with the poor and the oppressed. In a central passage in one of his later writings, he notes that Jesus "proclaimed the Kingdom of God to the poor." The background Moltmann selects is the trial of Jesus, in which the death of Jesus is decreed because of his ministry and his claims. Since human justice fails Jesus, Moltmann finds a parallel between the history of suffering which God assumed in Jesus and the history of human suffering.[24]

This much is conventional and is found represented in the murals and paintings of Christianity from the beginning. But Moltmann's exegesis takes on new notes almost immediately.

> Only the poor know the oppression of exclusion from riches. Only the humiliated know the pain of humiliation. Only the hated know the wretchedness of hatred. Conversely, the rich, the oppressors, and the haters are unknowing and blind, even if they are of good will. They unconsciously live in terms of an objective communal delusion (Marx) and despite their own effort and critical history, they manage to remain blind to the way things really are. The

oppressed hold in their hand the key for the liberation of mankind from oppression.[25]

These sentences, explicitly derived from Marx, overlook the present situation of millions who live along the broad continuum between being poor and being rich. They neglect the fact that many now rich knew "exclusion from riches" only a short time ago, under conditions of war, the Depression, and ancestral family poverty. Nearly all persons, rich and poor, have known the pain of humiliation. Nearly all have been hated. Sometimes the poor hate. Sometimes the rich (and many who are not rich) exhibit ordinary and heroic moral virtues. Sometimes the poor oppress members of other classes, races, religions, and ethnic groups. Sometimes the rich are intelligent about the lot of the poor and struggle manfully to assist them. Sometimes the poor experience "subjective" communal delusion, being passive under centuries of tyranny. Finally, Moltmann suggests that Marx reveals "the way things really are" and holds "the key for the liberation of mankind from oppression." St. Augustine offers different wisdom in his commentary on Psalm 72, v. 34: "It is not a matter of income but of desires. . . . Look at the rich man standing beside you: perhaps he has a lot of money on him, but no avarice in him; while you, who have no money, have a lot of avarice."

Moltmann next describes the church as "a twofold brotherhood," composed of the visible brotherhood of believers and the hidden brotherhood of the poor, the former "those who are waiting" and the latter "those who are sent," the former belonging "to the resurrection, the latter to the cross."[26] But this, too, flies in the face of ordinary experience. Most of the world's Christians are poor, and they too share in the resurrection of Jesus. The cross is meant also for the rich.

Moltmann, while borrowing heavily from Marx, immediately adds: "This ecclesiology does not mean that the oppressed should become the oppressor. For the gospel reconciles all sinners." But are the poor also sinners? Usually Moltmann treats the poor as objects, victims, and finally as a messianic class, sent to save the rich. "Insofar as the gospel praises the poor as blessed and promises them the kingdom of God, it saves the rich also by revealing their real poverty." But this is true only in the sense that the gospel seems to treat riches and poverty as irrelevant. The gospel does not say that salvation comes through the poor. It does say, though, that it is harder for the rich man than for the poor man to be saved, "but with God all things are possible" (Mt. 19:23–26). The gospel seems neither to insist that poverty is evil nor that it will be removed from human history. Moltmann, however, adds a new dimension: "Unless the 'subversive' character of the Bible as the 'Bible of the poor' pervades eschatology, then the promise of a new and reconciled mankind receives no authentic witness."[27] Does Moltmann mean that poverty must be eliminated? And that a "new and reconciled humanity" will then appear? Does sin occur only because of poverty? Does "the Bible of the poor" define poverty in terms of monetary income?

The suffering and the persecuted, Moltmann warns, "are not made into instruments of God's vengeance but are empowered to save from dehumanizing oppression both the oppressor and the oppressed."[28] Moltmann's thought is colored by images of a class struggle based on wealth. He pays less attention to tyranny based upon total political power.

Given his own circumstances, the Marxist overlay in Moltmann's thought is perhaps inevitable. Some of his general points are orthodox enough. For example; orthodox Christianity does want "to change the world rather than explain it, to transform existence rather than elucidate it." Such orthodoxy generated the special power Max Weber discerned in Judaism and Christianity, the power which enabled modern progress to occur first in Christian Europe. Moltmann observes: "Today the possibilities of consciously controlling the evolution of nature and the progress of history are proliferating immeasurably for the first time."[29] But this is true only in free societies.

Moltmann is correct to chastise those who interpret Christianity as if it were concerned solely with the private salvation of the individual soul. The Christian vocation, particularly the vocation of the layman, is to take up worldly responsibilities, to increase the wealth available to mankind, and to turn the use of such wealth to noble and Christian purposes. No one may deny the importance of personal prayer in secret and apart from public gaze. But the vocation of Christians and Jews extends beyond private prayer to social, political, and economic responsibilities. Moltmann is here on firm ground. "We no longer view the structures of society as given by nature or by God, but know that because they are made by man, they can also be changed by man."[30] For centuries, poverty and hunger were for most persons inescapable. Given the discovery of how wealth may be created, they are now the responsibility of humans.

3
Moltmann's Economics

> That capitalism in which every man preys like a wolf on every other man is utterly un-Calvinistic.
> —Juergen Moltmann, *The Experiment Hope*[31]

The most extended treatment Moltmann gives to economic matters occupies only eight pages of his published work, although of course asides about economics run like a thread through his other writings. In addition, he was written a sharp rejoinder to Max Weber.

Moltmann describes economic history: "Down to modern times, economics was dealt with in the framework of moral theology and moral philosophy." It was only "at the end of the eighteenth century that the autonomy of the economic sciences grew up, an autonomy which is expressed in the concept of 'pure economics.' " Relationships of monetary exchange "cannot be called 'human' relationships. For through them the person only enters into communication as *homo oeconomicus,* as labor and as purchaser."[32]

Yet, if economics must again be subordinated, as it was before the end of the eighteenth century, to politics, and if both the political system and the economic system must again be subordinated to "moral theology" and to "moral philosophy," theologians like Moltmann end up in command of the entire social order. Thus *homo theologicus* will again exert dominion over *homo politicus* and *homo oeconomicus.*

Moltmann's capsule history of capitalism is motivated by the desire to rebut Max Weber. He is eager to claim some credit for Calvinism: "It is a fact that the modern mastery of the world through science and industry was accomplished more quickly among peoples and groups with a Protestant, and to be more exact a Reformed tradition, than it was in other places."[33] Although this "fact" is what pricked Weber's interest in the first place, Moltmann the socialist is extremely uncomfortable with Weber's "famous thesis." He regards as "defamatory slogans" the notion that Calvinism is the "religion of capitalism" or that it mixes *"Geist und Geld* (spirit and money)." He does not regard it as a defamation to call Calvinism the religion of socialism.

Moltmann is especially offended that Max Weber cites only Benjamin Franklin (whom Moltmann paraphrases quite erroneously) and "late Puritan texts" such as those by Richard Baxter (1673) and Richard Steele (1684), from which he accuses Weber of quoting "only half the truth. He suppressed such themes as responsibility for the community, care for the weak, and education for the common good which are expressed in their pastoral writings and belonged to the reality of Puritan life."[34] As we have seen, Weber was not in fact ignorant of such themes, for his own mother, a devout member of the Reformed tradition, tried often to engage him in discussion of such topics, kept a young Reformed theologian in the household since Max would not oblige, and distinguished herself for her practical concern for the poor and the needy.[35] On the other hand, Weber perhaps justly thought that such evidences of Christian practice have been common in every era of Christian life, and that while they are *true* of the capitalist ethos they are not uniquely distinctive of it. Under democratic capitalism in Great Britain, the United States, and elsewhere, the history of community service, universal education, social work, philanthropy, and concern for the needy owes much to religious traditions. It rivals in quantity, quality, organization, and dedication any other era of church history,

Moltmann eagerly exempts Calvin from any "recognizable connection between faith in election and zeal for business." He points out with pride that "the predominance of Calvinism actually hindered rather than promoted capitalism in Geneva itself," and that "in 1568 and again in 1580 the pastors successfully prevented the establishment of a bank." Calvin was still involved in a medieval attitude toward economics, Moltmann believes, and the Reformation in Geneva "included the whole life of the church, society, and politics," and was in this sense more worldly than monasticism. Moltmann asserts that a typical capitalist idea is that "good works" should consist of "ceaseless work at one's job and the egoistic accumulation of capital." He holds that "only the prosaic morality of a businessman in the Victorian period could speak in this way. An inner connection between Calvinist-Puritan faith in election and the spirit of capitalism cannot be demonstrated.[36]

Moltmann is eager to show that "the Fuggers, Welsers, Paumgartners and other merchants belonging to the Catholic confession" were capitalists. He even lists, without any sense of irony, the Catholic Sun King Louis XIV of France (1643–1715) as "capitalistic," ignoring the fact that Louis XIV was one of those "mercantilist absolute princes" against whom Adam Smith's revolution was chiefly directed. Moltmann does admit that "Reformed Christianity has been alive in the great cities"; that "it was spread in France by merchants" and "was carried into other countries by emigrants"; and that it "thus formed a certain alliance with the freedom struggles of the middle class against the medieval structures of feudalism and ecclesiastical domination." He does not note that these "freedom struggles" largely consisted in the struggle for *economic* liberty. Moltmann is outraged that "people have often denounced Calvinist morality as zeal for work, capitalism, and greediness."[37]

Moltmann portrays capitalism as though it were outside the law, destructive of true community, reducing all relations to impersonal monetary relations, inspiring wolflike animosity between man and man, mad and irrational in its pursuit of growth for the sake of growth and work for the sake of work. Consider his indictment point by point:

(1) Today, "economic categories are more comprehensive than political ones, and political institutions are less and less able to regulate the large scale economic organizations."[38] Yet economic unity, as in the Common Market, seems easier to attain than political unity, since in some ways economic activities are more rational and community-building than politics. Moreover, Moltmann seems to be in error about the power and extent of government regulation. In the United States alone, the *Federal Register* of regulations over commerce and industry now fills 36,000 pages.[39]

(2) "World markets have grown up which escape the control of governments and intergovernmental institutions."[40] The *point* of free trade is to be free of political control, so that German autos and other products can be sold outside Germany. Free trade makes

the world economically interdependent. Yet world markets are exceedingly vulnerable to embargoes, tariffs, expropriations, and harassments. Free and open world markets are rare; politically restricted ones dominate.

(3) "Practically speaking, the only 'universal' in the contemporary world is money." The symbols of the Olympic sports appear to be universal, as do ideas of liberty, symbols such as Marxism and nationalism, and governmental controls. Religions, though not as various as currencies, are universal, as is science. Moltmann wishes to show that money is "something like a symbolized possibility," "a speculative reality."[41] He does not see that money symbolizes the health, stability and dynamism of a political community, in such a way that money flees some communities and gravitates towards others, since its value depends on long-term social realities. He finds monetary relationships less than "human" because they are impersonal, without noting that this very impersonality makes them nondiscriminatory, effective without regard to birth, status, race, creed, or ethnic belonging. Monetary relationships are open and indeterminant. They may be as personal as persons desire.

(4) "The economy belongs within the context of a social ethic, and lives from it," he asserts. "The economy has to consider its ethical and political context critically."[42] But this is just the point of democratic capitalism. Invariably, Moltmann subordinates the economic system to the other two. This is a premodern residue in his thought.

(5) "What values have governed modern economics? If we compare modern economics with the economics of premodern societies we find that the most important distinction is the difference between growth, expansion, and universality on the one hand, and equilibrium in limits on the other." Yet economics is always about scarcity and limits. The crucial difference between modern and premodern economics is liberty. Sustained economic development comes slowly, at a very low annual rate, and must be sustained through time by "small savings and gains." Premodern economics left the poor in wretchedness; "equilibrium" is far too rosy a word for premodern wretchedness. "The modern world," Moltmann believes, "is fundamentally out for growth, expansion and conquest, without inward moderation and without external scruple."[43]

Moltmann here confuses two strains of thought: enlightened

progress and unrestrained *hubris*. The world's population has nearly tripled since 1900. Growth in the world's wealth is a compelling moral imperative if all are to be fed, clothed, housed, and given opportunity for self-realization. True enough, given liberty, some persons do want—in Moltmann's phrase—to "live it up" as though there were no limits. By contrast, business leaders usually adopt conservative, moderating voices and point out costs. They tend to stress the need for savings, the obligations of investment for the future, problems of depreciation and reindustrialization, and other limiting realities. Moltmann cites Max Scheler, who describes the modern European's desire for self-improvement negatively: "the eternal 'Faust,' the *bestia cupidissima rerum novarum,* never content with the reality encompassing him, always hungry to break through the limits of his existence-as-it-is-now, always striving to transcend the reality that surrounds him."[44] Yet even the theology of hope depends upon the hunger for a better future. The idea of progress is not identical with the Faustian quest for limitlessness. Economics and commerce are excellent teachers of realism and limits, and often more so than religion and philosophy. This was the point of Montesquieu, Hume and Smith.

(6) For capitalism, "Life is power and the will to power."[45] Actually, the will to power is embodied in every culture. Under democratic capitalism, it is directed in competing, mutually restraining systems. Under socialism, the will to power is channeled into politics.

(7) Capitalism "led to a reinterpretation of the biblical teaching that man was made in the image of God."[46] Since Francis Bacon and René Descartes, Moltmann asserts, it is man's expanding rule over nature that makes him the image of God. This, he says, is a perversion of the Christian picture of man. But the democratic capitalist ideal of stewardship is not based on Bacon and Descartes, both of whom are pre-capitalist figures. Nor did the Anglo-Scottish Enlightenment follow the Continental Enlightenment in this regard. Smith, Madison, Jefferson, and de Tocqueville give evidence of no such views. Their vision is far more conservative, rooted both in a sense of human sinfulness and in the constraints of economic laws, commercial realities, customs, and morals.

(8) "Everywhere processes of growth have come into being which escape our control: growth of populations, growth of the need for raw materials and energy, growth of man's dependence on a flood of outward stimuli, and his inward instability."[47] These

are factual and empirical observations, subject to sharp dispute. There is some danger that international economic growth may end. The world has had long experience of *that* alternative.

(9) "However the 'limits of growth' are described today, it is obvious that unlimited growth is impossible with limited resources, and that unrestricted demands cannot be fulfilled with limited potentialities." But this is a truism. Economics is, precisely, the science of dealing with scarcity. Moltmann denounces "the idols of growth, expansion and exploitation." Yet, all things considered, intelligent persons may prefer realistic growth and sustained material progress to stagnation and decline. "The essential point is to end the race between demand and satisfaction,"[48] Moltmann asserts. This is also the point of "supply-side economics," a renewed emphasis upon discipline and savings, sober attention to capital formation, and sustained innovation in heretofore unexplored directions. Moltmann is intelligent enough to see that new directions are needed; but so are other free economic agents. In this respect, a free system is self-correcting. Everyone's real interests are engaged in the task of ever rethinking the ethos of democratic capitalism and human progress.

(10) "What line ought Christianity to take in economics, and what trend ought it to pursue with the means at its disposal?" Moltmann answers his own questions: "Economics cannot be excluded from the liberating Lordship of Christ. . . . Christian theology is economic theology as well. . . . The change of life's direction towards the Kingdom of God, through which people become Christians, is a comprehensive one."[49] A world in which theology is the lord of economics may be rather more clerical than Moltmann imagines.

(11) "The most important element for the development of a society that deserves the name 'human' is *social justice,* not economic growth . . . the will towards private or group-oriented self-realization must give way to the will to build a just society and a contented existence." No doubt this it true. But whose model of a "just society" and a "contented" existence shall rule? Moltmann does not rank pluralism high on his scale of values. He blames "modern European imperialism" for nourishing merely material desires and thinks that "among other peoples and other cultures, and among many young people in the industrial societies, solidarity is higher up the list of values than the material enrichment of life through production and consumption."[50] Yet

nothing in the West prevents Christians, or other peoples or cultures, or young people, from using their liberties to seek whatever values they choose. Democratic capitalism is pluralist. But no one can have everything. Solidarity, too, has its social costs. So does a no-growth economy.

(12) "This ethic of solidarity and a corresponding new economic orientation . . . includes renunciation of further economic expansion in the wealthy countries for the sake of economic development which is necessary in the hungry ones." This assertion implies that stagnation in the relatively few "wealthy" nations (a majority of whose citizens are far from wealthy) will be a boon to the hungry nations. It implies a direct connection between the wealth, say, of Hong Kong, Taiwan, Singapore, and Japan and the poverty of Vietnam, Cambodia, Thailand, Burma, and other less developed countries. Moltmann concludes: "The line which Christianity in the world ought to follow comes down to 'socialism' in the relationship of people with one another and 'socialism' in the relationship of humanity to nature."[51] The quotation marks which Moltmann places around "socialism" suggest that he does not mean *real* socialism, the socialism of Poland, the USSR, China, Cuba, Tanzania, and Libya; he seems to exclude even West Germany and Sweden (which are "wealthy countries"). What, then, does he mean by socialism?

4
Moltmann's "Socialism"

Moltmann's fullest elaboration of his concept of socialism occurs in Chapter 8 of *The Crucified God,* where he writes: "In socialism the political religions tend toward pantheistic materialism. Capitalism in turn displays primitive forms of fetishism, involving gold and possessions."[52] This formulation fails to identify exactly the fundamental idolatry of socialism, its reverence for the naked will-to-power, its fetishism of political control.[53] It also fails to express the stunning fact that under democratic capitalism, investors do not have the same ethic as the misers of previous eras. They do not treat money as a fetish; they put it to work. Democratic capitalism is not grasping and stagnant, but dynamic, open, inventive, exploring. But let us grant that neither capitalism nor socialism is identical with Christianity. The question is why Moltmann thinks that Christianity should lend its support to socialism.

Moltmann defines his "socialism" in response to five "vicious circles" which he observes in the world today. His picture of the world is quite melancholy.

(1) "In the economic dimension of life there is the *vicious circle of poverty,*" which "consists of hunger, illness, and early mortality, and is provoked by exploitation and class domination." Millions of immigrant workers in North Europe, he says, are caught in this trap; "Most Negroes in the USA are caught in a similar trap: poverty, police, courts and prisons all being linked together." "From a global perspective, the economic systems of the world work in a spiral which makes the rich nations richer and the poor nations poorer." This is an odd reading of the picture of material progress during the last two hundred years. Moreover, in Moltmann's view, the *cause* of poverty is "exploitation and class domination." This theory of causation deserves cold assessment. On its basis, Moltmann proposes "a redistribution of economic power," "economic codetermination and control of economic power by the producers" (apparently he means labor), and "social welfare for those who are weak and so-called development aid for the so-called underdeveloped nations." He concludes: "*If and in so far as* socialism in this sense means the satisfaction of material need and social justice in a material democracy, *socialism is the symbol for the liberation of men from the vicious circle of poverty.*"[54] But democratic capitalism from Adam Smith to the present also aims to break the grip of poverty. Indeed, it has achieved a historically unprecedented success in this respect. This point is not decisive for socialism.

(2) "In the political dimension, the vicious circle of force is produced in various societies by the domination of dictatorships, upper classes or those with privileges." To remedy these defects, Moltmann appeals to democracy as "the recognition of human rights and the basic rights of the citizen in a state," and asserts that "*democracy is the symbol of the liberation of men from the vicious circle of force.*"[55] Democracy is equally crucial to democratic capitalism.

(3) In the cultural dimension of life, many are trapped in "*the vicious circle of racial and cultural alienation,*" through being "shaped in the image of their rulers" or through becoming "apathetic cogs in a technocratic mega-machine."[56] Moltmann here links two different sorts of alienation: under dictatorship and under industrialization. The cure for the first is liberty: political, economic, and moral. The cure for the other is no more to be found in the industrial plants of Poznan, Leningrad, or Hanoi than in Frankfurt, Cleveland, or Kyoto. The "technocratic mega-machine" has its discontents; but it also makes possible liberties never known before. Inherent in these liberties, as we have earlier seen, is an unavoidable and healthy "alienation."

Moltmann then describes "the 'human emancipation of man' (Marx), in which men gain self-respect, self-confidence in the recognition of others, and fellowhip with them." Yet one needn't be a socialist to enjoy communities in which "different kinds of people encounter each other without anxiety, superiority or repressed feelings of guilt and regard their differences as fruitful, working together productively."[57]

In a crowd of strangers, any sensitive person will at times feel "alienated." Such feelings are natural and unavoidable. In a free and mobile society, within which various forms of expert knowledge are unequally distributed (even among experts), everyone will sometimes feel inferior to others (less knowledgeable, less self-confident). In a pluralistic society, no one is equally at home in every one of its many communities. Even if the institutions of a society are perfectly free, just, open, and equitable, such alienation will remain. It does so even in the monastery, in the family, and in the church. It is bound to do so in political and economic life. If there were not such otherness, pluralism would not be necessary, freedom would lead to homogeneity, and all might shout slogans in unison.

(4) "*The vicious circle of the industrial pollution of nature,*" through which "mindless faith in progress has irreparably destroyed the balance of nature," promises "ecological death." Moltmann again cites the Club of Rome. He despises hopes which rest "with messianic fervor on work, the machine, profit and progress" and which demonstrate an "orientation on death."[58] Moltmann's pessimism may reflect an occupational bias, since theologians often employ Doomsday scenarios to frighten their listeners. His images of brimstone overlook the lengthening life-

span of human beings; the fact that many rivers, like the Thames, are now cleaner than in Shakespeare's time; and other such improvements.[59] Humankind seldom does everything right at once. Self-correcting mechanisms are functioning—more so, and better, in democratic capitalist than in socialist societies.

To forestall Doomsday, Moltmann urges "new models of cooperation with nature," in which man will treat nature not as "an object" but as his own "environment," with its own "rights and equilibria." Thus, he says, *"Peace with nature is the symbol of the liberation of man from this vicious circle."*[60] Moltmann here suggests that humans are the aggressors and that nature is peaceful. He makes too little of the ferocity of nature against entire species of living things. In volcanoes, earthquakes, erosions, poisonous waters and gases, floods, windstorms, hurricanes, tornadoes, and weather patterns that pitilessly wipe out entire harvests, the face of nature has often been hostile toward human beings. In paradise, both nature and humans may be at peace. In history, nature as well as humankind has needed to be "tamed." A political and economic program based upon extreme hopes—"socialism with nature"—may have some validity as an ideal for which to strive. Yet impure drinking water, disease, lack of sanitation, and ignorance continue, in nature's way, to kill millions of humans every month.

(5) Worse still, according to Moltmann is *"the vicious circle of senselessness and godforsakenness,"* in which "today we are making the world hell," and "men are transfixed with future shock and become apathetic." Do such descriptions capture the awakening vitalities of the world's populations today? Moltmann believes that "perplexity, resignation and despair are widespread." Are they? He adds: "An inner poisoning of life extends not only through poor societies but through rich societies as well," a poisoning deeper than "economic need, political oppression, cultural alienation and ecological crisis . . . this wound remains open even in the best of all conceivable societies." Moltmann proposes as a remedy the hidden presence of God in "the godforsaken Christ on the cross." For theological reasons, he commends hope and "the courage to do what is necessary, resolutely and patiently, in the vicious circles mentioned above."[61] This quite orthodox conclusion is not particularly socialist. It is not only compatible with democratic capitalism but historically deeply embedded in it. The Reverend Thomas Malthus was preaching Doomsday while

Adam Smith was preparing late editions of *The Wealth of Nations*. European royalty seemed to be sinking in decadence when Madison, Rush, Hamilton, Franklin, and Jefferson were imagining the first "commercial republic." Realists all, they commended the courage to act creatively.

Moltmann asserts that "socialism is impossible without democracy and democracy is impossible without socialism in the sense mentioned above." He ends by describing his vision as "social democracy or democratic socialism." He admits that he uses all such words as symbols, in order to "invite further thought," and without defining "events in process" in such a way as to bring "the process to a standstill." "Thus the cause of liberation is not established, but is consistently in process and is only comprehended by participatory, dialectical thought."[62]

The transformation through which Marx thought to turn Hegel on his head has now ended with Hegel standing Marx upon his head. It was Marx who made the dialectic materialist. Moltmann makes it idealistic. He lifts socialism from the world of events in order to locate it in the world of symbols.

Even those inclined to assume the viewpoint of "social democracy or democratic socialism" must be astonished that socialism no longer seems to rest its case on concrete programs but has become a symbol for large and grand ideals. True, Moltmann exhibits high confidence in governmental control over life. He commends the distribution of wealth and a no-growth economy. But he offers no reasons why government officials should be trusted with economic decisions. He offers no reasons why we should believe that the distribution of wealth, under conditions of stagnation, will actually render the world more humane, healthful, and peaceful. He respects political liberties and moral-cultural liberties, but not economic liberties. He wishes political and moral-cultural growth to occur, but not economic growth. His "theology of economics" gives very little place to economics. It subordinates economics to a system of political allocation and moral-theological dominance. To some this will sound like a return to premodern conceptions.

In Latin America, however, Christian socialism is rather more aggressive, rather less democratic, and rather more clerical. It is, of course, in flux and is composed of several strains. In some ways, it is more practical and immediate, since some of the governments against which it works themselves abuse the law, due process, and the inalienable rights of individuals. Since fundamental problems of economic development are also under debate, our discussion must be somewhat more lengthy and must at least raise some of the empirical, pragmatic questions on which realism turns.

XVI
Guilt for Third World Poverty

The principal guilt for the economic dependence of our countries rests with powers *inspired* by uncontrolled desire for gain, which leads to economic dictatorship and "the international imperialism of money". . . .
—Conference of Latin American Bishops, Medellín, 1968[1]

On few continents of the planet is the socialist myth more vigorous than in Latin America, where it seems well suited to the political culture, if badly suited to the moral culture, of traditional societies. The vision of socialism legitimates an authoritarian (even a totalitarian) order. It ensures order and stability. In Cuba and Nicaragua, it permits the abrogation of elections and the suppression of dissent. It legitimates the wholesale indoctrination of populations in a millenarian vision. It unites the political system, the economic system, and the moral-cultural system under one set of authorities. It now inspires the most heavily armed states on the continent.

Yet one attraction of socialism may also be that it provides an excuse. Confronting the relatively inferior economic performance of their continent, the Catholic bishops of Latin America do not now blame themselves for the teachings about political economy which Latin American Catholicism has nourished for four hundred years. Conveniently, socialist theory allows them to blame the United States and other successful economic powers. No passion better fits the fundamental Marxist stencil, which offers a universally applicable paradigm: *If I am poor, my poverty is due to malevolent and powerful others.*

The use of this stencil illustrates a transformation in socialist theory. Whereas Marx based the promise of socialism upon the predicted failures of democratic capitalism, the new socialists attack its successes, to which they attribute their own failures. Democratic capitalism, they say, is responsible for the poverty of the Third World. It typically creates a "center" which oppresses "the periphery," offers reform and development which either don't work or take too long, imposes unfavorable terms of trade on Third World nations, and acts through multinational corporations which are outside the law. Nearly all these accusations are alluded to in the statement of the Latin American episcopate meeting at Medellín in 1968:

> Another feature of this economic situation is our subjection to capital interests in foreign lands. In many cases, these foreign interests exercise unchecked control, their power continues to grow, and they have no permanent interest in the countries of Latin America. Moreover, Latin American trade is jeopardized by its heavy dependence on the developed countries. They buy raw materials from Latin America at a cheap price, and then sell manufactured products to Latin America at ever higher prices; and these manufactured goods are necessary for Latin America's continuing development.[2]

We ought to weigh these accusations.

1
Do Developed Nations Cause Poverty?

It is odd, on the face of it, to blame the poverty of the rest of the world on democratic capitalism. Such poverty, after all, is hundreds of years older than its purported cause. Two hundred years ago, Latin America was poorer than it is today; but so was North

America. At that time, Adam Smith drew attention to the two contrasting experiments taking place in "the New World," one on the southern continent and one on the northern, one based on the political economy of southern Europe, the other launching a new idea.

In those early days, Latin America seemed to have greater physical resources than North America. Much of its gold, silver, and lead ended up in the ornate churches and chapels of the Catholic church in Spain and Portugal. Columbus himself, seeking gold and other precious resources, sailed under a Spanish flag. By contrast, the first settlers in New England discovered a relatively harsh agricultural environment. Such riches as they won from North America consisted of tobacco, furs, corn, and later cotton, which they traded to Europe for manufactured goods.

In 1800, there were about 4 million European settlers in the United States, about 900,000 blacks, and an estimated 1 million "Indians." The population of South America was then three times larger, numbering 19 million, of which the original population of Indians, estimated at between 25 and 50 million in 1500, had been dramatically reduced. By 1940, the populations of the United States and Latin America were about equal, some 130 million each. By 1977, the population of the United States had reached a relatively stable 220 million but that of Latin America had shot up to 342 million.[3]

In computing average per capita income, population is important in three ways. First, every newborn child lowers the average per capita income. Second, as the cohorts of those under age eighteen increase in proportion, the relative number of productive workers decreases. Third, rapidly increasing populations indicate that many parents have decided in favor of larger families, through whatever combination of motives. This is an admirable preference. But it has, in some but not all respects, economic costs. Those who make that choice cannot properly blame others for its consequences. Since 1940, the population of the United States has grown by 90 million, that of Latin America by 210 million.

In the nineteenth century, on both continents, independence was relatively new. Both had recently been colonies of the then greatest powers in Europe. All through the nineteenth century, trade between Latin America and North America was negligible. Nearly all trade between either continent was transatlantic trade with Europe. In North America, the vast majority of persons became owners of their homes and lands; not so in Latin America. The moral-cultural system of North America placed great emphasis on building and working for tomorrow. The moral-cultural system of Latin America favored other values. Either choice has its own costs and its own rewards.

Consider what might have been. Suppose that Latin America had developed industries and manufacturing before the United States did. Clearly, the resources were available. Latin America is rich in oil, tin, bauxite, and many other important minerals. Its farmlands and tropical gardens are luxuriant. Why, then, didn't Latin America become the richer of the two continents of the New World? The answer appears to lie in the quite different nature of the Latin America political system, economic system, and moral-cultural system. The last is probably decisive. Latin America might have been economically active, progressive, and independent. Indeed, Latin America had the advantage of remaining outside World Wars I and II. It might long ago have placed the United States in its economic shadow. It might yet do so, if it were to organize itself to use its own great wealth in an appropriate way. Yet its Catholic bishops do not blame the Catholic church, the systems of political economy they long supported, or the past values and choices of its peoples. They blame the United States.

Specific emphasis is placed upon practices of trade. During the nineteenth century, trade between Latin America and the United States was minimal. Between 1900 and 1950, trade did begin to grow, but by 1950 the total historical investment of U.S. companies in Latin America totaled only $4.6 billion. During World War II, Western Europe lay in rubble, its economies broken, and Japan lay economically prostrate. After the war, trade between the United States and Latin America grew. Still, by 1965, the total value of all U.S. investments in Latin America was $11 billion.[4] By 1965, investments by Western European nations and Japan, just beginning to revive after World War II, were not of great significance. It seems preposterous to believe that such small sums are responsible for the poverty or the dependence of Latin America. They are neither a high proportion of the wealth of the investing nations nor a high proportion of Latin America's internally generated wealth. The total U.S. investment of $11 billion averages out to $44 per capita for the 250 million Latin Americans of 1965. Moreover, U.S. investments in Western Europe and Japan during that same period were many times higher, without producing similar "dependence." Is it supposed that such investments in Latin America should have been forbidden altogether?

Traditional Catholic ignorance about modern economics may, in fact, have more to do with the poverty of Latin America than any other single factor. Consider the economic history of traditional Latin cultures.

2
Latin Catholic Economics

Max Weber observed that capitalism seemed to succeed first and most steadily in Protestant lands. He traced the origins of the modern capitalist ethos to Calvinism. Unfortunately, scholars also observed that capitalism was retarded for ideological reasons in certain Calvinist lands, too—Calvin's Geneva, for one. The empirical picture is a bit more complicated than Weber thought.

Hugh R. Trevor-Roper, for example, discovered that many of the great entrepreneurs of the sixteenth and seventeenth centuries are to be distinguished less by the fact that many were Calvinists than by the fact that nearly all were immigrants. Among them were some Calvinists, but also others who were Jewish or Catholic. Thus, Trevor-Roper asks, what made these entrepreneurs migrate? Why did they find some cities and some regimes hospitable and others (including Calvinist ones) inhospitable? The details of Trevor-Roper's argument, which I here summarize, are rich and the scholarship he cites broad. The basic picture he draws indicts Catholic Counter Reformation economies, particularly that of the Castilian monarchy of Spain, then at the zenith of its imperial power.

Trevor-Roper uncovers many surprising patterns of fact. He discovers the remote origins of capitalism, both as a system of production and as a technique of financing, in Catholic cities like Antwerp, Liège, Lisbon, Augsburg, Milan, Lucca. "These were the centers of European capitalism in 1500," Trevor-Roper writes. Yet between 1550 and 1620 these centers were "convulsed, and the secret techniques of capitalism were carried away to other cities, to be applied in new lands."[5] Why?

For Trevor-Roper, the decisive factor was a new alliance of church and state, more intolerable with each passing year, which drove the new class of Catholic businessmen in some cases out of their church but in many more cases out of their native cities and homelands. They sought out cities no longer under the control of princes and bishops; they sought self-governing cities of a republican character.

A sharp contrast arose between such cities and the religio-economic shortsightedness of the Spanish Empire. Made rich by silver from South America, the Spaniards, who represented the dominant Catholic state, misperceived the basis of their new economic strength. Officials of church and state grew ever more numerous. They produced little, being parasitic upon the producers, whom they gouged and regulated until the latter emigrated. With relative suddenness, then, the strongholds of the Counter Reformation economically declined and northern European centers of commerce gained the ascendancy. Trevor-Roper concludes: "The Calvinist and for that matter the Jewish entrepreneurs of northern Europe were not a new native growth: they were an old growth transplanted. Weber, in seeing the 'spirit of Capitalism' as something new, whose origins must be sought in the sixteenth century, inverted the problem. The novelty lay not in the entrepreneurs themselves, but in the circumstances which drove them to emigrate."[6]

The Counter Reformation state impugned the religious value of commerce. It banned or restricted enterprise in the private sector. It licensed certain entrepreneurs to develop state monopolies; it favored state mercantilism over private mercantilism. "It was a change," Trevor-Roper reports, "which occurred predominantly in countries of the Spanish clientele":

It is one of the great accidents, perhaps misfortunes, of history that it was the Castilian monarchy, that archiac "feudal" society accidentally raised to world power by American silver, which stood out, in the sixteenth century, as the champion of the Catholic church, and thus fastened something of its own character upon both Church and State wherever their combined patronage prevailed. The Roman Catholic religion, as medieval history had shown, was perfectly compatible with capitalist expansion. The growth of

princely States in the advanced capitalist societies undoubtedly, in itself, marked an economic regression, whether those
States were patronized by Spain or not. Rome, with its swollen
clerical bureaucracy, would have been an unmercantile city
at any time. But the Spanish patronage, by its own character
and by the necessities of State, imposed the pattern in a yet
more extreme form. Moreover, it was fatally successful. The
wealth and military support of Spain enabled the princely
States under its protection to work: to seem economically
viable even if they were not; and this illusion lasted long
enough for the new system to become permanent. In 1610
the patronage of Spain was the natural sustenance of every
princely Court which felt itself no longer secure: even a
Protestant Court, like that of James I, was its pensionary.
Conversely, every mercantile society, even if it were Catholic, like Venice, regarded Spain as its enemy. By 1640 Spanish patronage could be of little help to anyone, but by then
the societies of Counter-Reformation Europe had been fixed:
fixed in economic decline.[7]

At the time of America's founding—Latin America and North
America alike—Spain and Portugal were the world's dominant
and most active powers. But the philosophers and theologians of
Spain and Portugal failed to grasp the inner secret that had made
them so and, careless of it, lost it. For their colonies in the New
World as well as for their nations of birth, this failure of Catholic
intelligence was a calamity. It is sad to see it being taken up again
by a new generation of bishops and theologians, eager once again
to prefer state control to liberty, seeking to ally the church with
state authority as once their predecessors allied it with the *ancien
regime*.

The classical interpretation of Catholic history holds, with Pius
XI, that the tragedy of the nineteenth century was the loss of the
working class. Trevor-Roper's essay suggests a more radical thesis: the tragedy of the seventeenth century, setting in motion the
tragedy of the nineteenth, was the failure of Catholic thinking to
grasp the creative potential of democratic capitalism. One result
was that many early republicans and liberals, opposed to premodern ways of thought, were confirmed in the practical necessity of
being anti-clerical and anti-Catholic. The revulsion against religion on the part of liberals and republicans was most pronounced
in Latin lands, which to this day still suffer under the legacy of

"laicism," as did Pius IX in Italy before he issued his "Syllabus of Errors," and as Mexico has since its anti-clerical revolution. The conflict was not one-sided. Latin Catholic theology bears its due proportion of the blame.

Such theology remains in its premodern phase, as is evident—not only in Latin lands—by such statements as the following, by the Catholic bishops of Peru in 1969:

> Like other nations in the Third World, we are the victims of systems that exploit our natural resources, control our political decisions, and impose on us the cultural domination of their values and consumer civilization. . . . The more we try to change, the stronger the forces of domination become. Foreign interests increase their repressive measures by means of economic sanctions in the international markets and by control of loans and other types of aid. News agencies and the communications media, which are controlled by the powerful, do not express the rights of the weak; they distort reality by filtering information in accord with their vested interests.[8]

"We are the victims," the bishops say. They accept no responsibility for three centuries of hostility to trade, commerce, and industry. They seem to imagine that loans and aid should be tendered them independently of economic laws, and that international markets should operate without economic sanctions. After having opposed modern economics for centuries, they claim to be aggrieved because others, once equally poor, have succeeded as they have not.

Are the bishops really expert in technical matters of international trade? Before pronouncing moral condemnation, do they understand the laws which affect international currencies? Do they wish to enjoy the wealth of other systems without having first learned how wealth may be produced and without changing their economic teachings? The Peruvian aristocracy and military were for three centuries under their tutelage. Did the Peruvian bishops for three centuries teach them that the vocation of the layman lay in producing wealth, economic self-reliance, industry, and commerce, and in being creative stewards thereof?

Yet this intellectual failure appears, as well, among North American bishops. In an unsigned pamphlet, "Development-Dependency: the Role of Multinational Corporations" (1974), the

Catholic bishops of the United States say of themselves and their people, "We are a people so deeply committed in theory, if not in practice, to the philosophy or the ideology of free enterprise in the old-fashioned sense of the word . . ." This statement, in form an empirical statement, is not true of the bishops themselves. It is not true of most American economists. In his introduction, Bishop John J. Dougherty cites the following text from Pope Paul VI:

> A system has been constructed which considers profit as the *key* motive for economic progress, competition as the *supreme* law of economics and private ownership of the means of production as an *absolute* right that has no limits and carries no corresponding social obligations. This unchecked liberalism leads to dictatorship rightly denounced by Pius XI as producing "the international imperialism of money." One cannot condemn such abuses too strongly, solemnly recalling once again that the economy is at the service of man.[9]

Is it a fact that the United States practices the "unchecked liberalism" described with such hostility by Pius XI and Paul VI? Is it a fact that democratic capitalism has led to dictatorship in Great Britain and the United States? If investment in foreign lands is in and of itself "imperialism," where are Vatican funds invested? There was a quite real imperialism building up in the 1930s in Italy and Germany, and it took every resource of the rest of the world to defeat it. Again, under democratic capitalism, private ownership is not, in fact, regarded as "an absolute right." Within a liberal system, moreover, the political system and the moral-cultural system are crucial checks upon the economic system and, within the economic system itself, there are many contrary interests, countervailing forces, and complexities. Thus these papal words seem marvelously remote. If they are intended by Bishop Dougherty to represent the beliefs of the American people, he speaks falsely. If he intends them as a description of the actual system of democratic capitalism, he errs.

The text and footnotes of the bishops' statement which follows Bishop Dougherty's introduction are filled with misinformation and innuendo. The author writes in the name of the bishops:

> In the period between 1950 and 1965, U.S. private cor-

porations invested $3.8 billion in Latin America. Part of the profits were retained in Latin America to increase the total investment of the companies concerned; part of the profits were remitted to the United States. From this investment of $3.8 billion, no less than $11.3 billion in profits were remitted home to the United States, while the profits retained locally increased the investment of $3.8 billion to $10.3 billion.[10]

There are several confusions in this passage, even if we accept its highly problematic figures. First, the total investment made by U.S. corporations between 1950 and 1965, as given, averages out to $253 million per year. This does not seem like sufficient money to make all of Latin America "dependent." Second, the bishops ignore investments made before 1950. As we have seen, these totaled $4.6 billion. This figure must be added to the $3.8 billion invested during 1950–65 in establishing the base on which a return is made. Third, the bishops point out that many profits were reinvested during 1950–65. Presumably the same occurred prior to 1950. The bishops say that with reinvested profits, total investment during 1950–65 reached $10.3 billion. They do not give the cumulative total for the pre-1950 period. Finally, the bishops say that $11.3 billion in profits was remitted to the United States during the fifteen years. There is no way of telling, from their figures, on what base of cumulative investment these returns should be calculated. But perhaps a simple illustration will do. Invested at 8 percent interest, money will double in about ten years. In fifteen years, at that rate of return, an investment of $10 billion should have *more than* doubled, simply if left in a bank. If the bishops intended to shock their readers concerning returns on Latin American investment during 1950–65, they did not make the case.

There is a further illuminating point. The bishops note that "more than half of American profits went to but 16 firms."[11] This suggests that the problem of multinationals is fairly small and quite manageable, since relatively few firms seem to be involved. The total sum of investments is not large, and is to be divided at least sixteen ways (not counting the firms which have smaller investments). If so few firms are heavily involved, it appears that overseas investment brings headaches of its own, which most firms would sooner do without. Finally, in discussing the sixteen firms referred to, the bishops point with innuendo "to the concentration of power in the hands of a few corporations (which in turn are controlled by a few people)."[12] Are the bishops suggesting that it would be better to concentrate the "power" of these sixteen firms, and all others besides, in the hands of the state? What is the meaning of this innuendo? The boards of directors of the sixteen firms and the chief executive officers they hire are, indeed, composed of "a few people"; but for their short terms in office they have fiduciary responsibility for thousands of owners of their stock. It seems as proper for the economy to be separated from the state as for the church to be separated from the state.

The bishops, of course, are not remotely socialist. But they could not have accepted so sloppy a document if economics were not a traditional weak point of Catholic theology.

These two documents from the bishops of Peru and the United States illustrate how great the gap still is between Catholic theological intellect and a grasp of relevant economic reality. Their goal, they say, is to create new wealth for poor nations. What means are likely to result in that end? In recent centuries, the record of Catholic bishops in promoting an economic doctrine that would produce such wealth, particularly in Latin America, has not been brilliant. The fault does not seem to lie in Catholicism but in certain intellectual traditions within it. Surely Catholic bishops in the twentieth century can do better than to blame others for widespread poverty in their own domain.

3
The Center and the Periphery

Inherent in socialist theory are inexorable tendencies toward centralization and dependency. Socialist regimes invariably develop strong centers of planning and authority, which attempt to make the periphery utterly dependent upon the center. Socialist states do this in accord with theory and ideology. So the Soviet Union has rendered Cuba almost wholly dependent upon its own subventions, exacting in return not so much economic repayment as military service in Africa for fifty thousand Cubans. So the Soviet Union controls the economies, politics, and military forces of its Eastern European satellites. Power in socialist societies is neither differentiated nor fragmented; it necessarily accumulates in the capital cities where central authorities are gathered. Outside these central authorities, there are no sources of appeal. Economic development systematically occurs from the center.

Yet, ironically, Marxist thought today uses the theory of center and periphery as an accusation against democratic capitalism. For example, the Canadian theologian Gregory Baum, in celebrating "the remarkable shift to the left found in the Catholic Church's social teaching since the end of the 1960s," rejoices in the discovery of "social sin," a recognition of "sinful structures which exploit and dehumanize people despite the possible good will on the part of those in charge." He believes that this notion offers a "systemic critique" of the evils both of "the existing socialism in the Soviet bloc and the system of corporate capitalism with its center in the industrialized parts of the West." Baum believes that the Church's social teaching "has accepted the neo-Marxist theory of dependency which argues that corporate capitalism enriches the center of the system at the expense of the periphery."[13]

This "neo-Marxist theory" effectively disguises the extreme centralizing tendencies of socialism. With regard to democratic capitalism, however, it expresses only a truism. Wherever there is intense and heightened economic activism, a "center" comes into being and, under democratic capitalism, these centers frequently increase in number, rival one another in influence, and rise and decline. What, for example, is the "center" of democratic capitalism today? Is it in New York, Zurich, Frankfurt, Tokyo, London, Riyadh? The multiplication of centers is a natural effect of the stimulation of local activism. The more such centers, the better.

Is there a "center" within the United States today? Is it New York City, and is that city being enriched at the expense of Atlanta, Miami, Dallas, and Los Angeles? No region of the United States is poorer than it was in 1900. Even those who write about poverty in rural Appalachia must write of its "pockets" of poverty, for its cities are thriving and the renewed importance of coal is sending pulses of vitality through its valleys. Perhaps Dr. Baum believes the "center" is located in industrial cities like Pittsburgh,

Cleveland, and Detroit; or in centers of new technology like Houston, Tulsa, San Jose, and Seattle; or in newly thriving cities like Atlanta, Columbus, and Indianapolis. Many manufacturers have, in fact, begun to locate their operations in the small towns of the rural countryside. Furthermore, the most dynamic part of the American economy appears to be the service industries, which have grown from 11 percent of the work force in 1900 to 28 percent in 1978.[14] Naturally enough, service industries grow fastest where there are concentrations of people to serve.

Thus, under democratic capitalism, regions formerly poorer and at the periphery have rapidly become among the wealthiest and the most powerful. Within these "centers," furthermore, it is not always the central city that has become richer; often it is the "periphery," the suburbs, that have grown wealthier and more powerful. The urban heart of industrial capitalism, the great Northern manufacturing centers of the preceding era, have diminished in wealth, power, population, and dynamism. The center of creativity has swung elsewhere.

No doubt, to build a factory in one place is to create a "center" as opposed to places—largely agricultural, mountainous, etc.—where there are not factories. Economic activism thrives by interaction. Thus democratic capitalism, which grew up with cities and their liberties, rejoices in the cosmopolitanism, rapid exchange of ideas, inventions, and liberties of urban life. It likes "centers." There are signs in the United States and elsewhere that urbanization is losing its attractiveness, however, and that revolutions in communications and transport make urban centers less essential and suburban and rural living more attractive. Furthermore, the world's food supply is less than its demand, so that agricultural regions are entering an era of prosperity and social importance. Here too, systems of privately owned production have demonstrated far greater productivity than collectivized systems. Democratic capitalism—complete with subsidies, parity, and other forms of joint private and public action—seems to be as well designed for rural activism as for urban activism. Indeed, schemes of "land reform" in Latin America and other nations imitate, in effect, the homesteading traditions of democratic capitalism and the small privately owned farms which, in Western Europe, resulted from the earlier breakup of feudal estates. Rural cooperatives are, in effect, the agricultural equivalent of urban corporations.

What, then, does "the center" mean? It appears to mean any place where there is a great deal of economic activity, even if on a large rocklike island (like Hong Kong) far from its markets. "Center" is not a geographic term but an index of economic activity. Where there is a vortex of economic activity, there is a center. Wherever there is a low level of economic activity, there is the periphery.

The theory of the "center" and the "periphery" is merely a clever restatement of the proposition that the poverty of the poor is explained by the wealth of the wealthy. For this there is not a shred of evidence. What causes wealth is intelligent economic activity. Societies can become wealthy through the blessings of nature, which the Creator distributed unequally. Yet richly endowed nations, like the Middle Eastern oil sheikdoms, can remain in poverty for millennia without awareness of the wealth awaiting their awakening. Societies may lack resources and, nevertheless, become wealthy, like Hong Kong and Japan. Societies may be colonies or former colonies, like the United States. Others, like some in Latin America, blessed with climates that make subsistence relatively easy, can languish without significant development for generations. Theories of wealth which try to ignore cultural factors miss the central point. Theories which overlook the importance of a system of liberty miss a crucial lesson of economic history.

Dr. Baum writes of "sinful structures" which have their evil effects independently of the personal intentions of those who work within them. On the other hand, systems may also produce good independently of the personal intentions of those who work in them. This was Adam Smith's point about "the natural system of liberty." The intentions of individual workers may, or may not, be noble; yet the cumulative effect of their actions, if the system is well designed, may be to produce the wealth of nations.

Baum is correct about the need to criticize systems and to design them so as to produce the maximal good which human beings may expect in history. But he is only one in a long historical line of Catholic theologians drawn to authoritarian and unitary systems, of which socialism is the favored contemporary form. In drawing a distinction between systems and personal activities, why does he long for a system able to coerce the latter? In traditional Catholic thinking, all human systems are "sinful." This would seem to include socialism.

What are the credentials of popes, bishops, and clergymen for designing a workable political economy? Do the bishops of Canada, under Dr. Baum's advice, propose the Catholic church as a model of a sinless structure? Would they have Canada organized as Cuba is organized, or as Nicaragua is organized under the Sandinistas? When bishops propose a novel form of political economy (even in documents drafted by experts, of whose content they themselves may not fully approve), they place on trial their own economic realism and political wisdom. They acquire responsibility for the trade-offs certain to result from the implementation of their proposals. Since such proposals will affect the fate of all, all have the right and duty to submit the political economy designed by the bishops to critical review.

Perhaps clergymen resent being on the "periphery" of economic activism. Perhaps they imagine that socialism will place them more at the "center" of things. Father Miguel D'Escoto of Nicaragua, formerly the editor of *Maryknoll* magazine, became the foreign minister of Nicaragua. Father D'Escoto dispatched emissaries to the Soviet Union, Eastern Europe, and North Korea to sign pacts of accord and fraternity. His emissaries gave speeches pledging war on "the imperialists" until they are destroyed. His party postponed elections, suppressed dissent, murdered a key opposition leader, took control of all the media of communication, launched a massive indoctrination campaign throughout the countryside, raised the largest standing army (next to Cuba's) in Latin America, and established a block system of domestic political control. Father Ernesto Cardenal, the minister of culture, had offices in the palace abandoned by the former dictator, Somoza. Father Cardenal, we might say, moved from the "periphery" into the "center." He did so in the name of "liberation theology" and the gospels. To that transformation we now must turn.

XVII
Liberation Theology

We have not come, as Christians, to forge a Christian socialism. That would amount to absolutizing socialism and relativizing Christianity, just as we have absolutized . . . "Western civilization," "democracy," "humanism," and "religion" itself.

I believe that there is one system which, thanks to the grace of God, we have not dared to label "Christian" explicitly and directly—even when Christian ideology had reached its most abject levels. I refer to Capitalism. Today it seems that we are all agreed that it must be rejected. . . .

—Archbishop Mendez of Cuernavaca[1]

One of the most interesting transformations of socialism is occurring in Latin America, under the leadership of Catholic and Protestant theologians. Beginning in 1968 at a meeting in Medellín, the Catholic bishops of Latin America began to criticize the path of economic and political development being followed under "the Alliance for Progress." The Medellín statement and others subsequent to it have increasingly adopted a Marxist perspective, analysis, and future. Some theologians celebrate this development. It is called, generically, "liberation theology."

Recent Catholic theology has deemphasized philosophy and systematic theology in preference to Scripture studies. Reading Scripture as a story of liberation—as Exodus was a liberation—theologians began applying it to problems of poverty and development. They applied the teachings of Scripture not so much to individuals, however, as to social structures and economic systems. In this they were abetted by a new interest among theologians in the social sciences, and by a new interest of social scientists (in Latin America) in religion.

The theme of liberation, one might have thought, would lead theologians away from socialism and toward "the natural system of liberty" described so often in the Anglo-Saxon Whig tradition. It did not. The Anglo-Saxon tradition is perhaps the least known among Catholic theologians trained (as most liberation theologians have been) in Europe.

Thus in Latin America, liberal and republican thinkers have often been rigorously anti-clerical. *Liberalismo* has not been treated kindly by Latin theologians. Moreover, ordinary preaching in Latin America has never favored the commercial virtues or the virtues of republican life; the emphasis has been rather more mystical and otherworldly. The church has played a strong institutional role in Latin America, quite unlike the role played by Protestant and Catholic churches in North America. Its services to the sick and the infirm, the insane and the orphaned, those in need of education and counseling, and other forms of human assistance have been the traditional backbone of Latin America's social services. The vocations of commerce and industry, entrepreneurship and economic activism were treated, however, with the distancing traditional to Catholicism in aristocratic societies. Economic activism was suspect as "materialistic." Latin America has not lacked men of economic talent, but they had little spiritual support from the church or Latin culture. The pedagogy of Benjamin Franklin and the myth of Horatio Alger are relatively absent. Worse than that, they are thought to be spiritually inferior, almost contemptible.

The result is that businessmen in Latin America tend to lack an indigenous intellectual theory and a code of practical behavior. They receive even less theological guidance than their counterparts in North America. This vacuum in Latin theology generates a self-fulfilling prophecy. Economic activism is not given high spiritual value. It follows that even many who engage in it do not hold themselves to spiritual standards which are not, in any case, widely embodied in Latin American literary culture. Business in Latin America, therefore, seldom carries with it the tacit sanctions so powerful in British or North American culture. One feels instantly the difference between business in Latin America and in

North America. It is not just, as some say, that some Latin American nations have never experienced the equivalent of the New Deal. It is, rather, that business operates not only in a political but in a cultural and religious vacuum. The great Catholic thinker of nineteenth-century Spain, Donoso Cortés, for example, whose work is cherished by conservatives in Latin America, is profoundly opposed to Anglo-Saxon *liberalismo*.[2]

The widespread Latin American antipathy toward commerce—antipathy rooted both in an aristocratic culture and in traditional Latin Catholicism—is married in Latin America to a widespread desire for an integral, holistic, unitary system. Such a unity is not afforded by the pluralism of democratic capitalism. The latter seems too anarchic, too individualistic, too materialistic to win much loyalty from the clergy, from the aristocracy, and from the rural peasantry. Its communitarian aspects are not grasped. The absence of a compelling indigenous theory on the part of those in favor of a free private business sector and democracy creates a vacuum, into which liberation theology rushes.

Socialism feeds the strong traditional social sense of Latin American life. It meets the need for a unitary order. In addition, it sharply focuses feelings of resentment and economic inferiority. It provides a simple scheme of good and evil. Among theologians, at least, the debate between capitalism and socialism is one-sided. Not even the conservatives defend democratic capitalism. They focus their worries upon communism and national security. They may oppose the left, but their vision is chiefly negative. They have little to offer that is positive. For these reasons and others, many Latin Americans who have formed Christian Democratic parties—trying to establish a "middle way" between the authoritarian societies of Latin American tradition and the totalitarian tendencies of socialism—have little theoretical or cultural support. They have been especially weak in developing the *economic* component of Christian Democratic theory. Repelled by the absence of an intellectual theory for business enterprise, they have often been in the position of seeming to say "me too" to socialist programs. In such circumstances, the center has little intellectual ground on which to hold off right and left.

In a succinct overview of liberation theology, Michael Dodson points to the inarticulate wisdom of the North American tradition:

North Americans, not feeling any need for self-criticism

and orientation, have largely eschewed political theories and philosophies. . . . [North] Americans subdued an environment and built their civilization on liberal principles, which were simply taken for granted. Since liberal assumptions worked so well, there was no need for critical reflection; indeed [North] Americans were endowed with a pragmatic "genius," which made critical reflection or political theorizing unnecessary.[3]

By contrast, Dodson claims the current rise of liberation theology is highly theoretical. He calls it "prophetic politics." Latin American theologians like Juan Luis Segundo are explicit about their preference for the utopian vision.[4] Such utopianism better fits the aristocratic, otherworldly Latin tradition. Further, Dodson may confuse theory with utopian theory. North Americans, too, live by ideas. Few cultures have produced a classic of political economy as vivid and detailed in theory as *The Federalist*. But it is the opposite of utopian.

Many commentators ascribe to liberation theology not only a superior interest in theory (and "prophecy") but also a superior emphasis on praxis.[5] They understand this concept in the Marxist sense, not in the Anglo-American sense of *practice,* the experimental method, pragmatism, and self-reform.[6] Two elements in the Marxist meaning appeal to liberation theologians. It claims to take shape out of the "revolutionary consciousness" of the oppressed, and to be in touch with the people. It also claims to be in touch with the "real" reality of daily revolutionary struggle. Not everyone may see this reality. Some may live in "false consciousness." But careful *concientización* may bring their unspoken concerns to consciousness. In this sense, Marxism is a form of illuminism familiar enough in mystical and religious writings. Instead of being applied to the other world, it is now applied to this world. Indeed, liberation theologians sometimes identify religious liberation with the this-worldly struggle for revolution against tyranny and poverty.

About 10 percent of the clergy in Latin America, Dodson estimates, have embraced liberation theology. The proportion among theologians appears to be closer to 50 percent. At least, it is chiefly the socialists among them whose work is translated into foreign languages.[7] Many of the liberation theologians were educated at strongholds of socialist theology in France, Belgium, and

Germany. About half of all the clergy in Latin America are foreign missionaries, mainly from Western Europe and the United States. Many of these have experienced culture shock. About half are native Latinos, chiefly of the bourgeois class.

Latin America has long been one of the more capable and yet oddly backward continents of the globe. It inherits Western culture through Spain and Portugal. The poverty of its rural regions is often stark, while the *favelas* that have grown up around the glittering centers of its largest commercial cities offer heartrending glimpses of human suffering and disorganization. The traditional Catholic piety of the continent largely consisted of private devotion with a strong supernaturalist flavor. It did not much reinforce the natural or civic virtues, the practical virtues, or the social "worldly" virtues.

As the liberation theologians themselves picture it, they were too long sheltered in divinity schools and too long content with tepid reformism and scholarship as usual. Dodson reports how in the 1960s many bishops in Argentina, Chile, and Uruguay sent parish priests (often foreigners) to factories and workshops in order to regain contact with the new urban populations, and into various projects of land reform, the forming of cooperatives, and rural development in the hinterland. "For most worker-priests," Dodson reports, "direct involvement was a profoundly unsettling experience. They began to see both religion and the social order through a Marxian lens."[8]

Instead of learning from the gospel "and then applying their insights to the actual world," Dodson observes, the liberation theologians "try to learn from the world and then 'locate' their experience in the gospel."[9] But this world from which they try to learn they already carry with them. They see what they are prepared to see.

Predominantly, the poor of Latin America are peasants in rural areas and now an urban proletariat. Predominantly, the wealthy of Latin America are landholders rather than industrialists. Nonetheless, as in China, Marxist categories can be adapted to local conditions. The liberation theologians speak of "the pedagogy of the oppressed."[10] They are moved by the need to give "voice to the voiceless." They wish to identify with the "authentic" cultures of the poor. Some recognize obstacles to their vision in the culture of Latin American elites and in Latin American folk cultures. Revolution will require some changes in both, yet on the whole liberation theologians wish to maintain Latin American culture intact.[11] They despise the inroads of cultural values from North America and Western Europe. They claim to "learn" about oppression from the oppressed, yet they also take pains to teach literacy simultaneously with instruction about class struggle. In this way, the radical clergy and the communities they make their base speak the same language.

In visiting among the people, liberation theologians at first saw their own lands almost as foreigners might. They experienced *conscientización* and attributed it to lessons learned from the experience of ordinary people. This claim is suspect, since it turns out that "the people," although they formerly did not know it, now report on the world in socialist categories. Under prodding, the people become aware of being "oppressed" and gradually form the resolve of rising up against their oppressors.

Liberation theologians begin from a rejection of "development" theory and "reform" of the North American type, sometimes spoken of contemptuously as *desarrollismo*. Their argument, based upon empirical studies for the years before 1965, which are subject to considerable dispute both on their merits and in the light of later figures, is that development helps the rich to get richer, makes the lot of the poor worse both absolutely and relatively, and takes too long.[12] Worse than that, development through outside help from democratic capitalist lands victimizes Latin America.

The weight of ideology in these charges exceeds the evidence adduced in their favor. For one thing, the dependence of Cuba (and other socialist lands) upon the internationalist socialist system is treated in an altogether different manner. It is simply ignored. For another, the extent of outside investment in Latin America is not by any means large enough to justify the claim of "dependence." Furthermore, as we shall see in the next chapter, the record of internally generated success in Latin America since World War II, and especially since 1965, is no cause for a sense of inferiority or failure. Development takes time—as has socialism under such diverse regimes as those of Cuba, Grenada, Guyana, Nicaragua, and Jamaica (under Manley).

It is alleged that unfair terms of trade imposed by outside financial powers make international capitalism the oppressor in Latin America. It is alleged that the multinational corporations are oppressors in specific ways—by seeking their own interests instead of those of local populations; by strengthening existing (and oppressive) regimes; by buying off political leaders and ignoring the need for popular revolution; by paying wages that are too low; by producing goods that are less needed than other goods, and goods which go only to the rich rather than to the rapidly growing and impoverished masses; by taking more capital (in profits) out of Latin America than they put in, etc. Latin American liberation theologians seem to be ambivalent with respect to multinational corporations. Even if in theory they loathe them, in practice they often seem to think they may be useful. Fidel Castro is said to have advised Nicaragua in 1980 to keep lines open to an internal private sector and to Western financial markets, in order to avoid excessive dependence upon the Soviet Union.[13]

In its hostility to the ideals and institutions of democratic capitalism, liberation theology is clearly socialist in inspiration, in vocabulary, and in its methods of analysis. It is especially socialist in what it is *against*. Positively, liberation theology is vague and dreamy. One reads it in vain for a critical assessment of the socialist experiments in Europe, from which it claims to distinguish itself. The liberation theologians claim originality of thought; but they do not show it. In virtually every respect, their ideas are derivative of European socialist ideas. In an open letter, the leading Protestant theologian and socialist Juergen Moltmann complained that the Latin Americans poorly enlighten scholars from the homelands of Marx and Engels.[14] From the Latin American theologians one learns little about the actual political and economic realities of the diverse societies of Latin America. One finds in them minimal concrete description of persons, events, and institutions. Their tone is inspirational and hortatory, marshaling the "awakening" masses in rebellion against "oppressors." Liberation theology is remarkably abstract.

Further, one finds in liberation theology little reflection on the new institutions which, after the revolution, will replace the old. Such theologians seem to have given little thought to how the church will retain institutional independence under socialism. Will it have full liberty to publish its own papers, magazines, and books, and access to the media? How will public institutions be designed to ensure dissent, free speech, the right to organize, and other human rights? Liberation theologians say much about theology but little about the institutions of liberty that will survive the revolution. They have much to say about poverty—for which, invariably, they blame malevolent others—but little to say about the causes of wealth. In protesting against unfair trade practices, they say little about what would constitute fair practices or how these might be institutionalized. While attacking "private property," they sometimes support giving peasants rights to own their own land and to work for their own profit. They have little to say about instruction in modern methods of agriculture; about mechanization, road-building, and rural electrification; or about the infrastructures required to support modern commerce and industry. There is an oddly conservative, rural cast to liberation theology. One might form the impression from some of it that it wishes to preserve rural life intact, against modernization.

In another way, liberation theology reflects a double standard. Although it is not blind to totalitarianism under existing forms of socialism, its passion seems to be exhausted in attacking democratic capitalism. There has not yet been much thought given to how the "revolution" it calls for will be accomplished. Yet a revolution is not solely a matter of ideas. Guerrilla armies and terrorists need arms, training, communications equipment, stores, salaries, explosives, and many other forms of assistance. Such instruments are readily available through the Cubans, the Palestinians, and others, under funding from the Soviet Union. An armed revolution is not fought with pitchforks.

Many governments in Latin America have never enjoyed legitimacy as it is known under democratic capitalism. Some have had not only a change of government but a change of constitutions many times since 1900. Those elites at any one time in power stay in power less through the consent of the governed than by maintaining sufficient force to cow or to divide their rivals. In such cultures, it is relatively easy to provoke a Hobbesian "state of nature" in which no order is legitimate. In the "war of all against all," rival factions, uncontrolled by any central authority, offer natural cover to large guerrilla armies well armed and well directed.

This picture is not pretty. One would wish that Catholic theologians might support a "middle way." Alas, liberation theologians seem hardly to consider democratic capitalism a "middle way." In addressing the "theological crux" of our time, which he defines as capitalism versus socialism, Juan Luis Segundo simply chooses socialism. Similarly, the cardinal-archbishop of Santiago asserted in November 1970: "In socialism there are more evangelical values than in capitalism."[15] One sympathetic commentator remarks of such choices: "Thereby they risk identifying their church with a particular faction which is not less capable of using religion to its own ends than were capitalists and imperialists of earlier ages. This is a risk which Christians for Socialism in Chile and elsewhere are quite willing to run."[16]

Dodson summarizes the belief of liberation theologians: "Capitalism fosters individualism, competition, materialism, and greed. Socialism offers an alternative set of values, which stress the virtues of participation, community, equality and sacrifice."[17] José Miguez-Bonino draws the contrast between the two theories of liberation in typical fashion: "Humanization is for capitalism an unintended by-product, while it is for socialism an expected goal. Solidarity is for capitalism accidental; for socialism it is essential. In terms of their basic ethos, Christianity must criticize capitalism radically, in its fundamental intention, while it must criticize socialism functionally, in its failure to fulfill its purpose."[18]

In *Christians and Socialism,* the English Catholic John Eagleson defends the unwillingness of liberation theologians to be more concrete: "The construction of socialism is a creative process, and that has nothing to do with dogmatic schemes or an uncritical stance." He applauds the liberation theologians for avoiding "a definitive *a priori* statement of what socialism must entail."[19] The best-selling author of liberation theology Gustavo Gutiérrez summarizes the dream in glowing words: Liberation "means seeing the history of mankind as a process of the emancipation of man all through history, a process which aims at a society in which man will be free from all forms of servitude and in which he will determine his own destiny."[20] These words seem to express the ideal of individuals independent of the state, but Gutiérrez believes emphatically in the immorality of private property and disdains democratic capitalist limitations upon the state. He believes in "emancipation" under a powerful central state.[21]

The strongest argument the liberation theologians make is that socialist nations, even though their economies may stagnate, claim to supply basic necessities to all the poor. They "frequently point to Cuba as evidence that, given the necessary determination, even a poor country can accomplish this goal."[22] In Cuba, they believe, every family at least has basic food, clothing, and medical care. There may be little or no liberty from surveillance and police control. There may be relatively little room for individual imagination and initiative. There may be little hope that tomorrow will be better than today. There may be extreme financial dependence on the USSR. Many liberation theologians seem willing to surrender liberty for bread, both because they prefer the socialist ideal and because the most desperate, they believe, will receive necessities.

But the example of Cuba brings to light the existence of two models of development. In the Caribbean, a beautiful and naturally favored region of nearly 32 million persons distributed over thirty-two independent states, two rival schemes have been followed, one in Cuba, the other in Puerto Rico. In Jamaica, the conflict between these two futures has been especially acute.

The choice between socialism and democratic capitalism in the election of 1980 fell to Edward Seaga, leader of the democratic opposition of Jamaica, who thus describes the appeal of Cuba: "The development strategy of the Cuban model is based on a centrally planned economy in which the allocation of resources is done by the bureaucracy and/or the political directorate." Since the free market does not exist, distribution cannot be affected by the decisions of suppliers or purchasers. "Regimentation rather than personal incentive governs production and compatible with this is the over-rule of one-party government from which all regimentation springs. Naturally, personal and civil rights and freedoms are greatly restricted in this model of development."[23]

Seaga notes that the Cuban model is attractive to an increasing number of governments in the Caribbean. Its rival, the Puerto Rican model, emphasizes the expansion of the economy with continuously improving standards of living. The drawback of the Puerto Rican model, Seaga observes, "is an insufficiency of social programs capable of distributing mass benefits." This deficiency makes the Cuban strategy "more attractive to some, because of the Cuban emphasis on mass social programs and planned distribution." Yet the Cuban strategy "in the longer term results in contraction of the economy and continuous reduction of standards of living leading to shortages and stagnation." Still, elites prefer the Cuban model. Why? Cuba's foreign subsidies temporarily permit distribution of benefits; that is one reason. Seaga adds another: "But it is also true to say that part of the interest shown in the Cuban model is due to the preference of power-hungry politicians who prefer and want the permanent power that this model offers them by way of escape from the electoral system."[24]

Thus liberation theologians, like other socialists, face a dilemma. In developing nations which are only partially democratic (if at all) and only partially capitalist (since the middle class is small, local industries weak, and state control overpowering), direct attention to the poorest seems to be a low priority. On the other hand, socialist economies like those of Cuba claim to provide direct assistance to the very poor, at the cost of economic stagnation and the deprivation of liberties. Liberation theologians seem to desire more liberation than Cuba delivers. Michael Dodson concedes: "No socialist experiment has yet achieved such liberation anywhere in the world."[25] The prognosis for socialism is not good. We must now examine a little more closely the record of economic development in Latin America.

XVIII

A Theology of Development: Latin America

Every year nations like Nicaragua, El Salvador, and Jamaica make momentous choices about their political economy. Ignorance about economics can lead to untold sufferings in decades to come. Here lurks a special danger for nations of Latin Catholic tradition.

Professor Léo Moulin of the College of Europe, who has studied the sociology of economic development, makes an overwhelming case that one cannot ignore cultural factors. He shows how Protestant cultures differ dramatically from Latin Catholic cultures. The four Latin cultures—Spain and Portugal, Italy and France—appear to have occupied a quite different spiritual world from that of the six Anglo-Saxon, five Scandinavian, and six German nations that share with them a European inheritance.[1]

In landmass, Europe is much larger than Central America. Europe bears only a small fraction of the planet's population; its natural resources, while many, are not spectacular. Its economic strength lies in its culture. Even when Latin Catholic lands imitate some of the institutional forms of Protestant lands—constitutional government, industrial development—such institutions work out differently. Patterns of "self-control" are quite different. Emotional constraints and cultural ideals are different. Patterns of authority and liberty are different. There is a tendency for Latin cultures to oscillate between "anarchy and hierarchy," with less moderation and order than is typical of Northern European cultures. Wryly, Professor Moulin notes that Northern cultures produce little by way of a distinguished cuisine, are relatively inferior in the development of many of the arts, and are less relaxed in cultivating sensuality and sensual appreciation.[2] Yet there are also, he notes, economic losses involved in a lack of punctuality, in reluctance to compromise, in the failure to see worldly life as a spiritual vocation, and in other fascinating aspects of the Latin Catholic cultural ethos.

The case of Japan (and other countries) shows that democratic capitalism is not limited by necessity to cultures rooted in Judaism and Christianity. The case of Latin Christianity shows that such roots alone are not sufficient. Furthermore, even the major alternative to democratic capitalism—socialism—has, Moulin points out, Jewish-Christian roots.[3] A theology rooted in realism and in practicality must deal with such cultural facts.

1
Dependency?

Consider the assertion of Archbishop Dom Helder Camara of Brazil before the World Council of Churches in 1970: "It is a sad fact that 80 percent of the world's resources are at the disposal of 20 percent of the world's inhabitants."[4] This assertion is not exactly true. Most of the world's oil, for example, appears to be in the hands of nations like Venezuela, Mexico, Nigeria, Saudi Arabia, Kuwait, Libya, and Iran. Such curious expressions as "the Third World" and "the South" mask many contradictions. It cannot factually be said that all Third World nations are poor. Furthermore, most of the poor in the world—in India and other parts of Asia, for example, including China—are to be found north of the equator. In fact, the word "resources," as used by the archbishop, must also be stripped of ideology. What he describes as "a sad fact" is sad only if looked at from one ideological perspective. It is only a fact, and only a partially true one. Quite diverse cultural histories lie behind it.

The combustion engine was invented under democratic capitalism barely a century ago. The first oil well was dug in Titusville, Pennsylvania, in 1859, and the first oil well in the Middle East was dug only in 1909. If oil is today to be considered a "resource," one must recall how short a time ago the entire human race lay in ignorance of its potential. Most of the materials we today call resources were not known to be such before the invention of a democratic capitalist political economy; many were not known to be such even one hundred years ago. (Presumably, there are others which we do not yet appreciate.) Dumb material remains inert until its secrets are discovered and a technology for bending it to human purposes is invented. The word "resources," therefore, includes within its meaning the factor of culture, of which discovery and invention are expressions. Protestant European culture, in particular, has been exceedingly fertile in the discovery of such resources and in the invention of such technologies. Among Nobel Prize winners in science, Protestants have been conspicuously prominent.

Thus Archbishop Camara might have observed in fairness: "It is a marvelous fact that 80 percent—maybe even 90 percent—of the world's resources have been discovered and put to use during the past century by one of the smaller cultures on the planet. The benefits of such discoveries have been carried to every continent, but more must now be done in this direction." Dom Helder Camara, of course, was trying to make a moral rather than a scientific point. Furthermore, he was trying to make an ideological point. He was trying to suggest that there is something "sad" in the preeminence of a minority culture in the discovery of resources and in the invention of technologies for using them. Some cultures have organized their political economy precisely for this purpose. Others have not.

Nothing prevented Brazilians from inventing the combustion engine, the radio, the airplane, penicillin, and other technologies which give resources their utility. Although Brazil is apparently one of the most richly endowed of all nations in material resources, neither Brazil nor other Latin American nations have so far provided a system favorable to invention and discovery. So, in a sense, the archbishop's observation is merely a truism: Those cultures which value the intelligent and inventive use of God's creation are far better off than those which do not. He cannot mean to imply that intelligence and invention on the part of some

obstruct intelligence and invention on the part of others, for that
would be absurd. Latin America is responsible for its own condition. It had beginnings very like those of North America. The
system established there has not, on the record, been as successful
as many would now like it to become.

As late as 1850, the difference between the per capita income
of Latin America and that of North America was not great. Most
of the new technologies the world now knows had not then been
invented. Sailing vessels were still of creaking wood and billow-
ing sail. Although steam-powered locomotives were in use, they
were still primitive and few. Most agricultural labor was by hand,
and such machinery as had been invented—like the reaper and
the combine—were pulled by animals. Highways were designed
for horseback, carriage, and cart. Wars were fought with muskets
and cannon.

In population, Latin America in 1850 numbered 33 million, the
United States 23 million (and all North America 26 million).[5]
Manufacturing was more highly developed in a few states in North
America than anywhere in Latin America, but both continents
were largely agricultural. The mining industries of Latin America
were far more important than those of North America. The economy of Western Europe was stronger than that of either continent
of the New World, and both continents depended upon Europe for
most of their manufactures. But in some respects, certain regions
of both continents enjoyed a higher standard of living than
southern Italy, parts of Spain and Portugal, and other sectors of
Western and Eastern Europe, and both, therefore, attracted
immigrants.

In 1850, Great Britain was just completing seventy straight
years during which, with a dynamism never before matched in
history, its gross national product grew every year by an average
of nearly 2 percent a year. This seemingly miraculous achievement introduced into the world the reality of economic development. It also gave material substance to the notion of "progress"
which had long fascinated the imagination of the West. The law
of patents had greatly stimulated invention, as had the Royal
Society. In every decade and in almost every year, new technologies excited the populace.

Why after 1850, then, did the journeys of North America and
Latin America dramatically diverge? Why for the next one hundred years did one remain almost static, while the other steadily

but ever more rapidly developed? During that century, North America hardly needed Latin America. Latin America hardly needed North America. The volume of trade between them was highest in 1892, when the United States exported goods worth $96 million in Latin America and imported $290 million.[6] Things did not much improve prior to 1950. By the end of 1929, total U.S. investment in Latin America was valued at $3.5 billion, and by the end of 1950 $4.6 billion.[7]

Latin Americans do not value the same moral qualities North Americans do. The two cultures see the world quite differently. Latin Americans seem to feel inferior to North Americans in practical matters, but superior in spiritual ones. In Latin American experience, powerful personages control almost everything. From this experience, it is easy to imagine that the whole world must work this way, and to project such expectations upon North America. It must be said, then, that relations between North and South America are emotional as well as economic. The "Catholic" aristocratic ethic of Latin America places more emphasis on luck, heroism, status, and *figura* than the relatively "Protestant" ethic of North America, which values diligent work, steadfast regularity, and the responsible seizure of opportunity. Between two such different ways of looking at the world, intense love-hate relations are bound to develop.[8] Looking at North America, Latins are likely to attribute its more advanced status to luck—and also to a kind of aristocratic power. In their experience, wealth is relatively static and what is given to one is taken from another.

By contrast, looking at Latin America, a North American is likely to attribute its backwardness to an ethos better suited to aristocrats, monks, and peasants, who lack respect for commerce and industrial life and the moral virtues on which these depend. As Latin Americans do not admire Northern virtues, North Americans do not entirely approve of Latin virtues. Thus most North Americans are likely to feel not a shred of guilt for the relative economic position of the two continents.

However, some North Americans *are* susceptible to the guilt feelings which flow from the reverse side of the "Protestant" ethic: the demand for perfect charity. Some feel unworthy of their own success. Some take many accusations to heart. They are inclined to believe Gustavo Gutiérrez's accusation in his best-selling *A Theology of Liberation:*

The underdevelopment of poor nations, as a global social fact, is then unmasked as the historical sub-product of the development of other countries. In fact, the dynamic of the capitalist system leads to establishment of a center and a periphery, simultaneously generating progress and riches for the few, and social disequilibrium, political tensions and poverty for the majority.[9]

Gutiérrez believes that the decisive liberation for Latin America will be socialism: liberation from private property. This is not a theological interpretation of development, but an economic one. Moreover, his thesis of dependency is only one economic theory among many. It cannot be said to have biblical authority. It does not square with many of the facts. It has many internal problems of its own.

Official reports of the UN Economic Commission on Latin America give the most accurate account of the available facts. A brilliant young scholar who works for that commission, Joseph Ramos, an economist for the UN's International Labor Organization and a professor at the Catholic Latin American Institute on Doctrine and Social Studies (ILADES) in Santiago, prepared background papers on economics for the Catholic bishops' meeting at Puebla in 1979, and has elsewhere replied to Gutiérrez courteously and eloquently. In what follows, I draw upon the outline of his assessment of the economics of liberation theology, upon the UN statistical record, and upon U.S. Department of Commerce reports. In particular, I follow his review of Gutiérrez's book.[10]

First, in embracing the dependency theory and the center-periphery theory, Gutiérrez inherits all the factual and theoretical weaknesses of those theories. In an interdependent world, every nation is in some ways dependent upon every other. The most highly developed nations are quite dependent upon the oil-producing nations, for example. If one regards the oil nations as part of the periphery, they are, clearly, able to exploit nations in the center. If they are now to be located in the center—having until recently been on the periphery—then the original theory of center-periphery is a truism: a "center" is any self-reliant, economically active locale.

Moreover, interdependence is seldom symmetrical. The economy of the United States is six times larger than that of Latin America. A recession in the United States may seriously affect Latin America; the reverse may not be true. The dependence of the United States on Latin America is real but different in kind from that of Latin America on the United States.

Secondly, Gutiérrez seems to think that progress and riches in one place *must* subtract from what is available in another place. In fact, the world economy, since the industrial revolution, has become expansive and dynamic. There is today far more wealth than there was two hundred years ago. Absolutely, the wealth of virtually every nation and region is greater than it was. Average life expectancy is higher. Hygiene and health are better. Some modernization is in place. Yet, relatively, individual nations rise and fall as events, needs, and exertions favor first one, then another. The rise of Japan has been as spectacular as the decline of Great Britain.

Moreover, the mere existence of dependency does not mean that the underdevelopment of Latin America is due to the development of the United States, or vice versa. A battery of facts must be accounted for: (1) Only 5 percent of total U.S. investment is made abroad, and only 7 percent of its production is exported. The United States depends relatively little on foreign trade.[11] (2) About 70 percent of U.S. foreign investments and exports go to developed countries. Fewer than 20 percent of U.S. foreign investments go to Latin America.[12] U.S. investment in Latin America represents less than 1 percent of the U.S. gross national product. (3) The average rate of return on U.S. investments in Latin America has not been particularly high, either before 1950 or during the years 1950 to 1977. This return has been higher than in Canada but lower than in Europe, Australia, Asia, and Africa. The after-tax return on U.S. capital in Latin America is approximately 10 percent.[13] (4) The often-repeated statement that U.S. investors in the Third World take out more in profit than they invest is, for all sound investments, a truism. To invest $1,000 in a savings account for ten years is to hope to withdraw significantly more than the original $1,000. These new funds are then available for new investment elsewhere. Without such growth, economies stagnate and investment is futile. One might as well be a miser. (5) To argue that U.S. corporate profits depend to a high degree on investments in the Third World is to err. Only about two hundred U.S. firms account for most of U.S. investments overseas. Of these, virtually all make most of their investments in the United States and in the developed world. As a proportion, their investments in Latin America are small. About twenty firms account for half of all U.S. overseas profits. For such U.S. transnationals—General Motors and General Electric, for example—investments and sales within the United States are, year by year, far more significant than those in the Third World. In some years, profits made in some operations make up for costs incurred for new investments elsewhere. One must examine investments over time. (6) The United States has for many years suffered a balance-of-payments deficit; the total value of its imports exceeds that of its exports. The net effect is a weakening of the dollar in relation to other currencies.

These six facts oblige Professor Ramos to reject the center-periphery theory of dependence. Belief in such a dubious theory hinges, of course, on other assumptions. Professor Ramos also deals with these. Suppose, he says, exploitation does exist. The exploitation of one people by another has existed since the beginning of history. "However, until the Industrial Revolution, no people, no matter how exploitative or imperialist they were, could reach a generalized, sustained level of economic development."[14] A few nations first reached this level through science, technology, and economic organization. The "wealth" of the center is due far more to such factors than to its colonies. The contrast between Great Britain and Spain since 1500 permits no other conclusion.

Secondly, Gutiérrez may find it "attractive to place the fundamental blame for our problems on dependency (and by so doing blame others)," Ramos writes, but "might not this dependence rather be a reflection of the internal obstacles which are concentrated within our countries?" Ramos notes that each presently developed country also began in dependency. "The United States broke out of its dependency on what was then the world's greatest power, while Latin America, colonized at the same time, still fails to do so." Since Spain and Portugal are among the most underdeveloped countries of Europe, Ramos suggests that "internal structures common to Latin American and Iberian countries are the fundamental obstacles to overcoming development."[15]

In the same vein, Gutiérrez believes (oddly) that underdevelopment in Latin America is due to "private property." But Ramos calls attention to a special characteristic of Latin American property rights: "the initial extreme concentration of economic and political power (since Colonial times) in the hands of a few, and the consequent limitation of opportunities."[16] In the United States, by contrast, property, power, and opportunities were distributed much more equally from the beginning. For Ramos, a narrow concentration of wealth has negative effects quite visible in regional variations both in the United States and in Latin America. In the U.S. South, where power and wealth were concentrated in the landholding system, vigorous development was delayed until after World War II. By contrast, the Midwest and Far West, even though they were also agricultural regions, experienced more rapid development through a system of family property and relative equality. In Latin America, the regions of least economic and political concentration are most developed. Thus private property is not always narrowly concentrated. Development seems to depend on its diffusion.

Thirdly, when Gutiérrez rejects sentimental appeals to brotherhood, which disguise class conflict, Ramos appreciates his desire to abolish the causes of class conflict. But he finds Gutiérrez "ideological and ahistorical" in overlooking "the most significant economic fact of modern times, namely that wealth can be created." All economies prior to the Industrial Revolution were (relatively) static. Under static conditions, the economic improvement of some is necessarily obtained at the cost of others. For this reason, "the central concern of static economies, like the medieval one, has been the fixing of just prices and wages." In the early medieval economy, capital did not produce new wealth. Thus the taking of interest was judged to involve the terrible sin of usury, since through it one took advantage of those in need. But once capital became creative and its utility in economic progress became clear, moral interpretation was obliged to shift its ground. Thus Ramos urges Gutiérrez to shift ground too, by recognizing that relations of mutual advantage and cooperation are essential to dynamic economies, even though relations of conflict never disappear.[17] To emphasize class conflict but not mutual advantage is to ignore real interests.

Ramos does not accept the Marxian theory that classes are rooted in the relation to property. For him the relation to power is more significant, and assumes different forms in different times and places. Relative scarcity yields one common form of economic power. Such scarcity may involve land, water, transport, capital, technology, knowledge, oil, arms, etc. "It does not suffice to have property in order to dominate; domination requires possession of the critical form of power in each historical moment."[18] At different times in history, the military caste, the clergy, the landlords, the industrialists, the bankers, the politicians, the technocrats have been preeminent. There is not one class struggle but many; and their root is not property but power. As a result, class struggle will not disappear with the abolition of private property. Struggle over the political allocation of power and goods is historically one of the most bitter forms of struggle. Nationalization of ownership always generates class struggle, to the extent that the participation of citizens is only a formality, while decision-making lies in the hands of the party, the bureaucracy, and the police. Private property is a device to limit the power of the state. It undergirds the principle of subsidiarity, by giving citizens rights to make decisions about what each knows best.

Finally, Ramos deplores "the exaggerated tendency of Catholic theology to interpret social relations as though they were interpersonal relations." The error of socialists is to trust the ideals of socialism while disregarding their structural results. Gutiérrez ends his book with a plea for "a definitive stand, and without reservations, on the side of the oppressed classes and dominated peoples."[19] His good motives are clear. But the unintended consequences of his economic theories are not likely to constitute the liberation he desires.

In matters of political economy, much stands or falls on fact. The liberation theologians widely assert that development and reform in Latin America are not working. "Not working" *compared to what?* It is worth pausing to reflect on the facts, first of success, then of failure.

2
The Success of Latin America

In 1945, the population of Latin America was 140 million. Between 1945 and 1960, the gross national product of Latin America averaged an annual growth rate of 4.9 percent. From 1960 to 1965, the rate was 5.3 percent; from 1965 to 1970, 5.7 percent; and from 1970 to 1974, 6.7 percent. The world recession slowed growth in Latin America in 1975 (2.7 percent); in 1976 the rate was back up to 5 percent.[20]

Thus, for the thirty years from 1945 to 1975, Latin America averaged an annual growth of 5.2 percent. Few regions of the world exhibit such a sustained success. In this century, the wealth of Latin America has doubled, and then doubled again, more than once. Since World War II, manufacturing has grown at a rate of 6.5 percent each year. In addition, agricultural output per worker grew by more than 2 percent a year, and total agricultural output by 3.5 percent each year. Since population growth averaged 2.7 percent a year, agricultural yield has grown faster. This compares favorably with agricultural output in the United States from the end of the Civil War until World War I, when agricultural output grew at 2.1 percent a year and average output per worker at 2.5 percent.[21]

In real terms, wages and salaries in Latin America have grown since World War II at an annual average of 2 percent a year. This is better than the United States experienced from 1865–1914.[22] Wages and salaries have not grown as fast, however, as returns on capital. In part, this is because large agricultural sectors, with expanding populations, share slowly in the development of commerce and industry which occurs in cities. Rising returns on capital tend to attract new capital. While dynamic growth in some sectors does not automatically flow to other sectors, it does provide new wealth which sound political systems may invest in rural electrification and other institutions.

The rates of growth in real wages, in manufacturing, and in agricultural income and output per worker are all the more remarkable when one recognizes that during the same thirty-year period, 1945 to 1975, Latin America's population grew from 140 million to 324 million. It is a happy thing on every other index to have a living, healthy child; the one index which each new child lowers, however, is per capita income. Yet despite Latin America's immense growth in population, its per capita income has grown *at rates* seldom equaled on so sustained a basis anywhere in the world. Per capita income in Latin America stood in 1976 at $1,000.[23]

In thirty years, infant mortality was reduced significantly. Life expectancy advanced from approximately forty-two years to sixty-two years. Despite immense population growth, illiteracy has been reduced from 50 percent to 25 percent (absolute numbers, though, remain large: about 80 million persons). In 1945, only 55 percent of primary-school-age children attended school; the figure in 1975 was 90 percent. In high school, the jump was from 10 percent to 35 percent. The percentage of those from twenty to twenty-four years old attending universities has gone from 2 percent to 9 percent.[24]

Obviously, these figures cry out for improvement. Still, what accounts for the sudden explosion of growth in 1945, after centuries of relative stagnation? Foreign aid and foreign investment cannot account for it, since together these make up less than 4 percent of Latin America's annual internal investment.[25] Favorable terms of foreign trade do not account for it, for these terms have been lower than in the nineteenth century. Structural reforms cannot account for it, for these have been relatively few; there have been few major land reforms, tax reforms, or dramatic institutional reforms.

In the opinion of Ramos, the most satisfactory explanation is that the advantages of being a "late starter" have finally been seized. Latin Americans are closing the technological, organizational and management gaps which once separated them from the developed world. The power of ideals and intelligence, learning and application, is much in evidence. Religion itself is becoming more dynamic. There has been a breakthrough beyond the ranks of the narrow elite at the top. It has not yet reached millions at the bottom, but revolutions in "human capital" have set a great dynamism in motion. Whereas, for example, U.S. AID officers once struck Latin Americans as better prepared than their local counterparts, today Latin American economists and experienced officials possess training and skills superior to those of the average foreign adviser. Finally, late-starting nations may take advantage of already developed technologies and thus deploy relatively less capital in research and development.

3
The Failure of Latin America

Impressive growth in GNP, in per capita income, in literacy, in education, in health, and in longevity represent human goods of great value to Latin America. But such figures also mask inequalities, uneven distributions, and massive suffering.

In a paper produced for DOCLA (Documentación Social Católica Latinoamericana) in 1978, Sergio Molina and Sebastian Piñera calculated that in 1970 about 40 percent of all Latin Americans (some 115 million persons) received an income below the poverty line of approximately $200 per year. Still lower on the scale of poverty, at the destitution level, about 19 percent (some 56 million persons) received less than the $100 per year required to purchase foodstuffs providing a minimum level of calories and protein for subsistence.[26] It is clear that the fruits of spectacular economic growth are not reaching all parts of the population. The 56 million destitute need urgent care. The total 115 million poor need rapid improvement of their condition. Between 1960 and 1970, the percentage of the poor fell from 51 percent to 40 percent and of the destitute from 26 percent to 19 percent.[27] But because of population growth, absolute figures were virtually unchanged (down only about 2 million in each category).

What would it take to raise all Latin Americans above the *destitution* line? Molina, Piñera, and Ramos calculate $100 per year for 56 million persons, or over $5 billion annually. To raise all the destitute and the poor above the *poverty* line would require another $11 billion per year. Compared to the GNP of Latin America, this $16 billion represents (depending upon its exact calculation) about 5 percent. As a percentage of government spending in 1970 it would have represented 22 percent. As a percentage of the continent's total disposable income in 1970, it represented about 6 percent.[28]

These figures show that Latin America already has at its disposal sufficient annual income and gross national product to raise the level of its 56 million destitute persons almost immediately. The economic capacity is present. The political will and the economic techniques may not yet be present. Techniques which do not discourage greater production are indispensable. On the other hand, the diffusion of purchasing power to the poorest 25 percent of the population is in the interest of domestic manufacturers, farmers, and traders. An additional healthy 56 million persons would provide markets for goods and promote new forms of economic activism. In a dynamic economy, the economic activities and skills of each person offer mutual advantage to all others.

Molina and Piñera observe that income differentials among employees explain only about half the difference in per capita income between poor and non-poor households. The rest is explained because the non-poor tend to have a higher number of employed adults per household and a lower number of dependent minors. The vast majority of heads of households are employed. A high percentage complains of underemployment (less than thirty-nine hours a week) and desires more. Simultaneously, many large social tasks remain unaccomplished. The economic infrastructure to support future growth will require investment and labor to build roads and bridges, sewage and sanitation, generators and power lines, communications facilities and urban water supplies, rural irrigation and facilities for transport.

The case of Brazil is often cited. Ramos points out that prior to 1964 the nonmilitary governments in Brazil sustained an average annual growth rate of 5.5 percent a year. After the military coup in 1966, the growth rate jumped to 9 precent a year. By 1970, every decile of the population had benefited in real terms. Relatively, however, the poorest deciles were receiving a lesser proportion of national income, the upper deciles a larger proportion. Between 1970 and 1976, the relative position as well as the absolute position of the poorest deciles improved.[29] Still, the contrast between the richest and the poorest is stark. Behind the cold statistics there are families whose children lack sufficient calories and protein for normal activities and normal growth.

Ramos proposes that $5 billion be invested every year for ten years (a total of $50 billion), from funds already internally generated in Latin America, to improve the lot of the destitute. The exact schemes he proposes for this ten-year crash program need not detain us, for they are matters best decided by those closest to them.[30] The central point Ramos makes is that of scale. The problem of reaching the destitute and the poor is not insuperable. Resources are available. The ideals of democratic capitalism command that the task be accomplished.

4
The Crux

When they write of institutions, the liberation theologians seem to be in favor of socialism. When they write of individual persons, they seem to be in favor of economic independence, self-reliance, personal creativity, and self-determination. They write of land distribution and of land ownership on the part of peasants. Is it conceivable that by "socialism" many liberation theologians actually intend an ideal compatible with, and more accurately described as, democratic capitalism? They are in favor of self-reliance, the communitarian individual, a sense of providence and serendipity compatible with equal opportunity and self-improvement. They seem to favor an open, mobile, pluralist society. They seem to want private property, independence from the state, institutions of human rights, and full liberties for the moral and cultural system.

On the other hand, they give little encouragement to economic activism, much to political activism. While they do not seem intent upon banning the activities of foreign corporations from Latin America entirely, they do not seem to grasp the role business corporations—especially domestic ones—might play in building up the structures of middle-class democracy. Their rage against the existing order and against foreign multinationals prevents them from thinking *institutionally* about how to devise checks and balances against corporate power, while using it creatively to check clerical and military power. They have not thought *theologically* about the vocation of laymen and laywomen in the world, particularly in commerce and industry. They have not discerned the spiritual hunger of the commercial and industrial classes (including white-collar and blue-collar workers) for a theological vision of daily work. They have not seen how the three strongest institutions in Latin America—the clergy, the military, and the traditional landholding class—may be checked by the growth of a new middle class based in commerce and industry. They have not grasped the importance of economic growth to the sense of legitimacy on which democracy depends.

There are many in Latin America who perceive that tyranny necessarily follows from the unitary system of socialism. Many also see that an alliance of the clergy and socialist leaders will result in the same sort of arrangement which has plagued traditional Latin American societies. Many are alarmed at the bleakness and grayness of life in Cuba, at Cuba's total financial dependency on the Soviet Union (funds which may be cut off at any time), and at its subservience to Soviet military and police power. Many are dismayed at Nicaragua's growing army and network of domestic surveillance, its failure to hold elections, its assassinations of dissidents, its economic stagnation, and its international alliances. In Jamaica, large enough popular forces were disgusted by the economic shambles to which the socialists had reduced the nation to vote them out on October 30, 1980. Thus support for a democratic capitalist alternative to socialism still exists.

Yet at present there is no intellectual vision of the liberation yet to come through democratic capitalism. There are neither books nor parties, neither leaders nor dedicated followers. This intellectual vacuum is dangerous. But the *institutional* vacuum is also dangerous. Democratic capitalism depends upon the vigor of many rival institutions. It needs strong, disciplined, intellectually alert unions. It needs churches committed to pluralism, democracy, and the lay vocation. It needs a business community with a vision larger than that of free enterprise alone—a vision of the pluralist system of democratic capitalism—and with a real concern for bringing the entire population into the market system as self-determining agents. It needs a military respectful of legitimacy, the consent of the governed, and constitutional succession in political office. It needs political leaders who can act upon a vision that breaks the traditional oscillation of Latin political cultures between hierarchy and anarchy.

In this respect, liberation theologians have yet to show intellectual mastery of the institutional requirements of a free political economy. Choosing the utopian road, they seem to imitate the Grand Inquisitor, who out of pity for the people promised bread, not liberty.

The continent of Latin America is richly favored in natural resources and immense human vitalities. Its biblical heritage gives it a spiritual basis for that realism which alone leads to political and economic liberation. During this century, its peoples have already experienced a great awakening. Their economic and social achievements are many and more are yet to come.

Yet Latin America does face a crux. Shall the church in Latin America encourage its people along the road of unitary socialism—or along the road of pluralistic democratic capitalism? More than good intentions and high motives are needed. Decisions about the shape of the system *qua* system, about the political economy *qua* economy, will have consequences far beyond those willed by individuals. The people desire bread. They also desire liberty. Not only is it possible to have both, the second is a key to the first.

In thinking about political economy, some theologians, myself included, praise the liberation theologians for sustained work that raises important questions. Still, we worry that their path to liberation is ill-defended against state tyranny, is vulnerable to a new union of church and state (this time on the left), and is likely to lead to economic decline. Such results would not be looked upon kindly by future generations.

Furthermore, the temptation to believe that democratic capitalism is too lowly a path, and that socialism offers a more noble way, has also been known in North America. Reinhold Niebuhr— the greatest of all American theologians—knew that bent of spirit well, experimented, and learned from experience. He placed theology on the lowly track of realism. To have learned from him is to have had a wise man for a teacher—and to find in his reflections on politics a model for reflection on economics. Work in such a complex field always requires learning much from others, so it seems useful to walk in Niebuhr's shoes before attempting to press beyond.

XIX

From Marxism to Democratic Capitalism

Reinhold Niebuhr leaned toward Marx early in his intellectual life, but soon he became critical of Marxism and, later, of democratic socialism. Although in the early 1930s he predicted the imminent collapse of capitalism and energetically spread the conviction that capitalism *ought* to collapse, he later discovered virtues in it he had not seen before. For many years, Niebuhr was a leading figure in American religious socialism, running once for Congress in New York City on the Socialist Party ticket. For more than a decade, he was closely and publicly allied with Norman Thomas. Yet as John C. Cort, the editor of *Religious Socialism,* fairly concludes: "The problem with Niebuhr as a spokesman for either Christian or non-Marxist socialism is the fact that, for all practical purposes, he gave up on it."[1]

Niebuhr's career, in this sense, prefigured that of the "neoconservatives" three decades later.[2] Like theirs, his life story moved from disillusionment with liberal rationalism to Marx, to socialism, to democratic socialism. He finally became disillusioned with democratic socialism too and attempted to understand democracy and capitalism more exactly.

Niebuhr's intellectual odyssey has been followed by many others since. But it is important to read this story, not as that of one who eventually "saw the light," but rather as that of a man committed to realism and practical results. Niebuhr was not an ideologue. He cherished practical wisdom.

1
The Early Years

In 1931, Niebuhr was predicting in *The Christian Century* that "the growth of socialistic political philosophy will be the most significant development in our political life in the next decades." In his eyes, "the chief root of economic and social inequality" at that time appeared to be "the unqualified right of private property." He proposed a continued abridgement, qualification, and destruction of absolute property rights, and adequate unemployment and other social insurance financed through "heavier and heavier taxation," including "steeply graduated income and inheritance taxes." Conservatives, he wrote, are quite right to see that such a program points in the direction of socialism. "Every extension of the claims of the general community upon the property of individuals is a development in the direction of socialism." The more idealistic element in the Christian church does not "find any difficulty with the aim of socialism," and "recognizes the identity between its ideal and that of socialism."[3]

Niebuhr in those days insisted upon being a hardnosed, and not merely an idealistic, socialist. Idealistic Christians are "afraid of class consciousness and class conflict." But the class struggle, he replied, is not "an invention of socialism. It is a fact of history."[4]

Nonetheless, by the next year Niebuhr was insisting upon "closer recognition of the conflict, whatever the affinities, between Christianity and socialism." This is "not necessarily an irresolvable conflict, but it is a real one." He felt that the whole Christian socialist movement in Britain never came to grips with this conflict, at least not as vigorously as German socialists had.[5] Soon, though, he also became disillusioned with German socialists, although all ninety-six of them voted against the grant of dictatorial powers to Hitler.[6] Indeed, the specter of Hitler dominated his thinking for several years. He thought that the decline of capitalism would lead industrialists to seek the protection of other fascist leaders like Hitler, and that charismatic fascists like Hitler would galvanize the working classes. "Both in Germany and in England," he wrote in *Harper's Magazine* in 1932, "there are indications that any final effort to socialize modern industrial society will result in fascist ventures." He foresaw that it would be "practically impossible to secure social change in America without the use of very considerable violence."[7]

In 1932, Niebuhr supported Norman Thomas and disparaged both the Republican and the Democratic parties, both of which "represent the financial and the commercial classes" and succeed in holding farmers and workers only because of "the political ignorance of these classes." Roosevelt's policies "modify the Hooverian ones so slightly that the net difference in results will probably be very inconsequential."[8]

In March 1933, Niebuhr wrote "on the assumption that capitalism is dying and with the conviction that it ought to die." Its death was deserved "because it is unable to make the wealth created by modern technology available to all." He confidently asserted that "capitalism will not reform itself from within." He ridiculed Roosevelt's "pretension to liberalizing the Democratic Party," and called "the efforts of liberals who stand to the left of Mr. Roosevelt" equally futile, offering "pills of diluted socialism coated with liberalism."[9]

Niebuhr saw an "inevitable line of moral decadence" leading from "the austere morality of John Calvin to the highly prudential business ethic of a Benjamin Franklin." He recognized that Protestantism "gave the businessman a sense of religious sanctification for his activities," and honored "the virtues of the lower middle classes. . . . It championed diligence as against leisure; thrift against extravagance; and continence and temperance against the vices which flourished in luxury." In this way, it "increased honesty in business and thereby laid the foundations for the intricate credit structure" of modern capitalism, a system of trust and cooperation. But all these high virtues eventually became too functional, too utilitarian, too merely economic. Worse, they made the middle-class person—businessman and worker alike—far less class-conscious than the aristocracy had been, or than the proletariat was becoming.[10]

The first half of 1933 may perhaps have marked the high-water mark of Niebuhr's Marxism. By August, he was beginning to apply a pragmatic capitalist critique to Marxian dogma about private property. "The big centers of finance and industry must be socialized if modern society is to live. But what shall be done with private property where property is not power but merely a chance to perform a social function in terms of relative security: the property of the small trader and the farmer for instance?"[11] Niebuhr was outraged at the blind dogmatism and immense cruelty of the slaughter of millions of peasants under enforced collectivization in the Soviet Union. Yet at that time he worried more, incredibly, about socialism's *liberal* illusions, and did not fully trust parliamentary democracy.

Niebuhr did not regard the historical materialism of orthodox Marxism as basic to a socialist politics. He began slowly but surely to distinguish Christian socialism from Marxism. Christian socialists, he wrote in June 1934, believe in establishing "a basic justice in society," while recognizing that "the imperfections of human nature" will make such justice "relative."[12] He was pleased in the same year by a survey of 20,000 Protestant ministers in 1934, which showed that "about one-half are in favor of a drastically reformed capitalism. Almost 6,000 favor socialism. Many others choose other political systems which represent left-wing thought. It is rather remarkable that 123 are ready to vote for Communism. This number is actually larger than the number who voted for fascism."[13] He had flirted with revolution and violent struggle and even with high admiration for the Soviet model, but something always held him back from the worst extremes.[14]

2
The Lessons of Experience

Before examining Niebuhr's middle years—1935 to 1945—two features of socialist thought deserve comment. Socialism has been from the beginning a protest against radical individualism and a search for lost community. As James H. Billington suggests in *Fire in the Minds of Men*, socialism was in part a rebellion of Catholics and Jews (mostly from German, Slavic, and Latin lands) against Protestant individualism.[15] When it attracted Protestants, its revolutionary strains were modified by respect for the individual, an empirical temper, and esteem for parliamentary methods. Secondly, socialism was from the beginning a mythic force. Socialists adopted the red flag as a dramatic simplifying device, deliberately contrasting their single color (at first black, then red) with the conventional tricolor of existing democratic revolutions. They wished to represent a simple universal idea transcending any one nation. The color red glowed ominously by torchlight, Victor Hugo observed, signifying fire, danger, struggle, and a universality of shared blood.[16] It had a kind of Pentecostal echo, important to many whose attachment to socialism was based upon evangelical religion. In a certain sense, socialism is a kind of secular fundamentalism. So, in any case, Reinhold Niebuhr slowly came to treat it.

Niebuhr's German roots made him more aware than most American Protestants of events on the Continent; they also gave him a profound sense of linguistic and cultural community, rooted in family life but extending through networks of parishes and schools all across America. His father's church was the German Evangelical Synod, which in 1915 numbered 1,074 German-speaking pastors and 1,381 U.S. churches. The family migrated often, from close community to close community, from Missouri to Illinois. Young Reinhold went to school in Missouri, where the faculty and students elected him *Abschiedsredner* (valedictorian) in 1913.[17] Niebuhr inherited from his family an implicit rebuke to the classic American rational individualism of the frontier. He belonged to real communities, and these in turn linked him to Germany.

Thus the accession of Hitler to power through democratic methods deeply disturbed him. He recognized that democracy and capitalism had grown up together, and that democracy transcended class interests. Yet he thought that "the development of fascism proves conclusively that capitalists will seek to destroy democracy before capitalism is destroyed by it." In 1935, in *The American Socialist Quarterly* he wrote: "Now, the Russian revolution remains a beacon light to workers in the whole world." Yet he warned that the Russians, knowing nothing of American institutional history, falsely believed that "American constitutional rights are nothing but a facade for capitalism." A worker's movement in the United States would need "a tremendous mechanism of social cohesion." Practical socialists must therefore make compromises and proceed by degrees, and not expect enthusiasm for "pure socialism."[18]

In 1935, Niebuhr helped to launch *Radical Religion* as a quarterly for the Fellowship of Socialist Christians. The reversal of the usual term "Christian Socialists" was deliberate, for Niebuhr and his friends conceived "our primary loyalty to be to Christianity and our primary task to help divorce the Christian religion from its too intimate embrace with bourgeois society and its capitalistic culture." On the other hand, they wanted to avoid socialist sectarianism. They were not a new type of socialist, Niebuhr wrote, only socialists who shared three basic Marxian views: that capitalistic society was destroying itself and must be destroyed; that the social ownership of the means of production was the only basis of health and justice in a technical age; and that such a society could be achieved only through social struggle. "In these things we support socialism wholeheartedly."[19]

In the same issue, Niebuhr pointed out that radical religion must "turn against the spiritual pretensions of a proletarian culture" as well as against bourgeois culture, recognizing that "history relativizes all ideals." It must sharply criticize "the strategy of radicalism."[20] Subtly, then, Niebuhr was extricating himself from full commitment to socialism. His point of view aimed to transcend that of socialism. He wished to submit socialism, too, to empirical tests.

In 1938, he stood firmly against "the intolerable injustices of capitalism," although recognizing that "Russia is not the holy land." Capitalism was dynamic and "at present its dynamic is self-destructive." The church could not be neutral; an attempt to be so would put it "on the side of reaction." It must fight "for a socialist commonwealth against a dying capitalist society."[21] He added later that "Roosevelt is still better than most of his reactionary critics. But no final good can come of this kind of whirligig reform."[22] He begged Roosevelt to choose: "If that man could only make up his mind to cross the Rubicon!"[23] He was afraid Roosevelt, like Lot's wife, might look backward.

But he took hope from the growing sophistication of Christian socialists (whose number, he fondly hoped, "is growing"). Such Christians are socialists "because they believe it is the duty of a Christian to affirm the highest possible justice in every society." But they "do not believe that a socialist society would eliminate the sinfulness of men as simply as socialists expect." While they still regard the "social ownership of the means of production" as "the minimal requirement of social health in a technical age," they had learned by now that "the problem of power . . . always will remain the crucial issue in any scheme of social justice. They mean to equalize economic power but not at the price of creating political tyranny in a socialist society. They do not trust any irresponsible power in the long run, whether it is wielded by priests, monks, capitalists, or commissars." A Christian can give only "qualified loyalty" toward any political program. A Christian can never regard "one particular class as Messianic, though he may assign a very high historic mission to the industrial workers of the world."[24]

Niebuhr was now focusing more and more on the distance between the "City of God" and any historical "City of Man" (he had been reading much Augustine). And he appealed more and more to "political wisdom." Like the founders of the American idea, he was concentrating on the problem of tyranny. He was slowly becoming a realist rather than a utopian revolutionary.

In the campaign of 1940, Niebuhr was banished from the Socialist Party because he supported U.S. intervention in Europe. He wrote, "Nothing is more obvious than that socialism must come in America through some other instrument than the Socialist Party."[25] Contemplating Wendell Willkie, he recognized him as "the most intelligent and liberal aspirant for the Republican nomination," but faulted him for not recognizing that "economic power is essentially irresponsible power." The problem is to "preserve and increase its responsibility through checks, not to destroy it."[26] Then, after the election, Niebuhr felt Roosevelt's election was a "heartening revelation of the ability of democracy to arrive at a right decision in a crisis."

A special word might be said about the "wisdom" of a democracy in making such a choice. No election in our history has validated the principle of universal suffrage more than this one. The "good" people and the "wise" people, the intellectually respectable, the "leaders" voted generally for Willkie. He had a majority on most college campuses, though it is only fair to say that the faculties were usually less conservative than the students.

It was the common people who reached the right decision. This merely proves that the counsels of democracy are not complete if the "disinterested" intelligence of college presidents, "cultured" businessmen, Christian journalists and prima donna preachers is not balanced by the wisdom which resides in hungry stomachs and anxious hearts. "Blessed are the poor" for many reasons, including this reason— that there is a wisdom in their direct experience with the insecurities of life which is withheld from the wise and prudent.[27]

Thus, Niebuhr had a new experience to contemplate. Democracy, which failed in Weimar Germany, worked in the United States. Besides, there was an inarticulate wisdom which proved itself superior to the wisdom of the articulate. He saw in this a new empirically founded source of hope.

Niebuhr was to appeal increasingly to the lessons of experience in the late 1940s and 1950s. He began to look to Roosevelt, whom he had long ridiculed, as wiser than he. On Roosevelt's death in 1945, he penned a restrained but lovely tribute:

The idea that economic power is self-regulating belongs to the childhood of an industrial era and is refuted by all of its maturer experience. Roosevelt was no systematic political thinker; but he saw the main issue clearly and acted upon his convictions with as much consistency as the confused state of American public opinion would allow. Even his lack of consistency and his infinite capacity for improvisation had its virtuous side; for it is a question whether a more consistent or doctrinaire exponent of his policy could have achieved as much national unity around his central purpose as he achieved. While it is much too early to assess his place in American history adequately, one may hazard the guess that future historians will regard his administration as a new level of maturity in domestic policy.[28]

In the same vein, Niebuhr reflected on the joint condemnations of capitalism and communism produced by the World Council of Churches meeting in Amsterdam in 1948. He thought the "equilateral indictment unfair at one point." The capitalist belief that justice will be achieved automatically through freedom "is a mistaken belief which has resulted in much injustice in modern society. But it could hardly be said that it generates the demonic fury which characterizes modern Communism." To be absolutely fair, "one would have to point out that the mistaken ideology of capitalism is not wholly incompatible with the preservation of a free society, while the Communist dogma results inevitably in the destruction of freedom." Of course, only a decade earlier Niebuhr had shared views like those victorious in Amsterdam. Perhaps for this reason, he felt obliged to be far kinder to the church on the left than to the church on the right. He indulges the judgments of Amsterdam as merely a "mood."[29]

That same year, the Fellowship of Socialist Christians changed its name to "Frontier Fellowship: Christians for Social Reconstruction." The name of its journal had already been changed from *Radical Religion* to *Christianity and Society*. He offered three reasons for such important changes. The term "socialist" in the United States is "subject to too many misinterpretations." The official Socialist Party was pacifist, Niebuhr and friends were not. Finally, he no longer shared the orthodox Marxist belief that the institution of property is the primary root of evil in human society and that the abolition of property will usher in the millennium.[30]

By 1952, Niebuhr was still clearer about the lessons of history concerning "Marxist dogma," even elements which had once attracted him. "Its theory of revolution is incompatible with democratic responsibility; its theory of class conflict does not fit the multiple-class structure of modern industrial societies and is incompatible with the principle of 'class collaboration' upon which democratic politics depends; above all, its utopianism interferes with an interest in proximate, rather than ultimate goals, and that is the point which distinguishes a sane political movement from one that is corrupted by false religious visions." Even in a democratic framework, socialism constantly disappoints utopian hopes. The Labour Party in Great Britain had had to learn that the socialization of property does not overcome collective poverty, and that the same problems of authority plagued workers with the "coal board" and the "steel board" as had formerly plagued them with private owners. "A high degree of empiricism is a basic requirement for democratic health. All sweeping generalizations and assumptions must be eschewed and the questions must constantly be asked. . . ." He now believed that a healthy democracy "never gives all the power to the proponents of any one dogma; it holds all claims to truth under critical review; it balances all social forces, not in an automatic, but in a contrived harmony of power. In this way it distills a modicum of truth from a conflict of error."

When Marxism is applied in a democratic setting, "its sweeping generalizations are refuted by daily experience."[31]

Daily experience, diffusion of power, balances of group interests, contrivances of checks and coalitions—Niebuhr was one by one rediscovering the lessons of *The Federalist*. He was rethinking the structural pluralism of democratic capitalist societies, as corrected by the experiences of the generations.

By 1961, Niebuhr was writing of a trinity of goods necessary to a healthy society: freedom, community, and justice. Every community first of all needs social peace and order, even at the price of some freedom. Yet no one social class must pay too high a price, so justice is also needed. "Since in the long history of Western democracy, no one has offered accurate criteria by which each man's due is measured, we must come to the conclusion that open societies have solved the problem by allowing a free competition of social forces, which enables every force in society to make its claims upon society and to acquire enough social and political power and prestige to enforce its claims." Niebuhr then noted that liberty and equality are the twin principles of justice. But abstract libertarianism and abstract egalitarianism demand more than history can give. A society is not under a suicide pact, and therefore makes claims against liberty in the name of security, order, and social justice. Similarly, a society cannot function on one identical plane, and therefore makes claims against equality in the name of a hierarchy of social function and the integration of its daily life and work. "That is why history has refuted the Jacobin libertarianism and the Marxist egalitarianism."[32]

3
"Capitalistic-Democratic Culture"

Scholars are agreed that Niebuhr broke decisively with Marx and later with the Socialist Party. There is room for some disagreement about how far he broke from socialism and how highly he came to regard the virtues of a reformed capitalism. To the end, he continued to insist upon a balance between political powers, economic powers, and moral-cultural powers. He relativized the absolute claims of private property. He believed that human sinfulness made private property indispensable for defensive purposes; i.e., for the defense of individual liberty. He came to recognize that revolutions could be achieved pragmatically, incrementally, experimentally, for in his lifetime and in the history of the West he had seen that happen with his own eyes. He came to see that there were spiritual resources and vitalities inarticulate in the conception of the "commercial republic," present *both* in a democratic polity *and* in capitalistic institutions, which produced from cultures which sustained them moral victories which ideologues had been too blind to expect.

Finally, Niebuhr came to see that "political encounters in a free society involved not only contests of interest and power, but the rational engagement and enlargement of a native sympathy, a sense of injustice, a residual moral integrity, and a sense of the common good in all classes of society." Human communities are reservoirs of virtue as well as of conflict; moral-cultural systems undergird and enliven institutions. Moral realities have their own hidden power, different from those pointed to both by the bourgeois rationalists, who expect too much reason, and by the antibourgeois cynics, who expect too little from the human heart. He regretted speaking too simply in an earlier book of "moral man" and "immoral society."[33] Life had taught him that both in individuality and in collective life, the human being is more complex than simple ideologies recognize.

Central to Niebuhr's vulnerability to Marxism was his vision of the American tradition into which he had been born. For many years, he understood this tradition in a quite shallow way. He saw it as no more than a too simple religious individualism, wed to a merely political realism. Thus he believed that Alexander Hamilton was a realist when he recognized the importance of self-interest and wished to make it "profitable for the wealthy classes to support the new American Constitution," by promising to harness self-interest to the common good of the civic community rather than to suppress it. The impact of Spengler and Darwin on this tradition almost a century later, Niebuhr felt, was devastating. If biological life is a fateful competition among individuals in which the fittest survive and through which alone progress is wrested from nature, then the "confluence of social Darwinism and moribund Calvinism''[34] works to blunt the social conscience which plainly confronts the growing disparity between rich and poor. Moreover, the invention of the machine transferred power from the skills and simple tools of craftsmen to the possessors of capital and the builders of factories. Before such power, religious individualism and democratic realism are rendered naive.

Jeffersonian idealism boasted that ''a government of reason is better than one of force.''[35] But reason and force, Niebuhr notes, are not the only factors at play. Idealists praise reason; realists (like Hamilton) recognize interests. Yet neither noted the ''collective or class character'' both of reason and of interests. Of course, Jefferson and Hamilton were not the sole architects of the American tradition. Only in his later years, however, did Niebuhr absorb the significant additions made by James Madison.

After the passages we have been citing, from Niebuhr's last (and wisest) book, Niebuhr in the end paid his highest homage to Madison. Madison, he wrote, ''was the only one of the founding fathers who made a realistic analysis of both power and interest from a political and democratic perspective.'' Madison was governed by a basic insight of political realism: into the ''intimate relation'' between reason and self-love. (Niebuhr does not note that Adam Smith wrote with the same insight.) Unlike the idealists, Madison ''knew the need for strong government.'' Unlike Thomas Hobbes and the Marxists, ''he feared the dangers of strong government'' and insisted upon the separation of powers to prevent tyranny. Madison ''gave us the best pre-Marxist analysis of the basis of collective and class interests in the varying 'talents' and consequent economic interests of various classes.''[36] This is high praise indeed from one who had to learn from Marx what Madison had already seen.

Thus Niebuhr came to see that ''the whole historical process by which Western democracies righted the injustices of early industrialism . . . is an eloquent testimony more to the virtues of a free society than to the virtues of any agents in the process.'' But this too, as we have seen, was the reason for Adam Smith's insistence upon attention to unintended consequences rather than to virtuous motivations. ''This triumph of free institutions involved the refutation of bourgeois ideologies,'' Niebuhr went on, ''which might have proved Western democracy to be as captive to middle-class interests as the Marxists contended.'' It refuted the bourgeois idealists who placed too much confidence in pure and disinterested reason and who naively believed that political struggles involve individuals but not classes. It refuted the bourgeois realists who "pretended that competition in the market would ensure justice and that bargaining in the labor market would defend the worker's interest, despite the disparity of power between worker and employer."[37]

There is not much evidence that Niebuhr ever read Adam Smith with the same care or energy he invested in Karl Marx. He continued to use Smith as a foil for Marx.[38] He saw "elements of truth" in classical economics:

> It was the great achievement of classical economic liberalism to gain recognition of the doctrine that the vast system of mutual services which constitute the life of economic society could best be maintained by relying on the "self-interest" of men rather than on their "benevolence" or on moral suasion, and by freeing economic activities from irrelevant and often unduly restrictive political controls. It released the "initiative" of men to exploit every possible opportunity for gain and thus to increase the resources of the whole of society, at first through the exploitation of commercial opportunities and subsequently through the endless development of technical and industrial power.[39]

He believed such insights to be "a permanent treasure of a free society," since some forms of a "free market" are essential to democracy. The alternative, he says, "is the regulation of economic process through bureaucratic-political decisions. Such regulation, too consistently applied, involves the final peril of combining political and economic power."[40]

More and more, Niebuhr saw the moral advantages of capitalist techniques of liberty. But he never lost his critical watchfulness for balances of power. He argued consistently that the free market alone is not a sufficient instrument of justice and that rights of private property must be approached not as absolutes but pragmatically. He tried manfully to distinguish between "defensive" and "offensive" forms of property: "No sharp line can be drawn between its two functions. It is defensive only so long as the individual possesses so little of it that he will not be tempted to use it for domination over others."[41]

Niebuhr rejoiced in two other aspects of capitalism: its realism about self-interest and that sense of sympathy, benevolence, and fairness that meant so much to Adam Smith (and to Niebuhr in his last works).

In the perspective of the Christian understanding of human nature, it becomes apparent not only why self-interest must be harnessed and not merely suppressed, but also why the self-interest has a different dimension than was assumed in the theories of classical economics and in the whole of modern naturalistic thought. Self-interest must be harnessed for two reasons. It is too powerful and persistent to be simply suppressed or transmuted. Even if individual life could rise to pure disinterestedness so that no human mind would give the self in which it is incarnate an undue advantage, still it would not be possible for collective men to rise to such a height. . . .

But self-interest must be allowed a certain free play for that additional reason that there is no one society good or wise enough finally to determine how the individual's capacities had best be used for the common good, or how his labor is to be rewarded, or how the possibilities of useful toil, to which he may be prompted by his own initiative, might be anticipated.[42]

He grasped clearly that the economic system is checked both by a political system and a moral system while possessing its own integrity: "Thus even now, when we know that all economic life must submit to moral discipline and political restraint, we must be careful to preserve whatever self-regulating forces exist in the economic process. If we do not, the task of control becomes too stupendous and the organs of control achieve proportions which endanger our liberty."[43]

At the end, Niebuhr referred to the U.S. system as a whole in the phrase " 'capitalistic-democratic' culture."[44] The quotation marks and the clumsiness of the expression testify to the complexity of the concept.

Earlier we briefly noted that a contemporary of Niebuhr's, the French Catholic philosopher Jacques Maritain, went through a similar change in judgment about capitalism and, like Niebuhr, struggled for a phrase to describe it. From an article in *This Week* (March 4, 1951), Maritain seized on a quote which captured his own observations. The nineteenth-century system had given place to a new one:

How shall we describe this system—imperfect, but always improving, and always capable of further improvement—where men move forward together, working together, building together, producing always more and more, and sharing together the rewards of their increased production?[45]

The author requested suggestions and received over fifteen thousand replies. Never, said the editor, "have I touched so raw a nerve." Among the suggestions: "the new capitalism," "democratic capitalism," "economic democracy," "industrial democracy," "distributism," "mutualism," and "productivism." Maritain himself favored "economic humanism."[46] Maritain saw "a new social and economic regime" developing in the United States "in actual fact," which had come about "by virtue of the freedom and spirit of man," by virtue of "the American mind and conscience, and of the American collective effort of imagination and creation." He saw in this "a decisive fact in modern history," "a considerable success of the experimental approach dear to the American mind."[47]

Thus Reinhold Niebuhr, like Jacques Maritain, was obliged by experience to unlearn the ideology through which he had long looked at America, especially at its economic system. Neither thinker dwelt much upon the capitalist component of democratic capitalism. Both were far more concerned with its political and cultural components. Both had the courage to trust their own experience.

4
The Failures of Democratic Socialism

Niebuhr never took back his criticism of dangerous concentrations of economic power if the free market is left entirely to itself; nor did he ever withdraw his critique of individualism in the light of man's social nature. As he mentioned, both Catholics and Jews have in these matters a different starting place from Protestants, particularly from those Calvinists whose theories of individualism are extreme. On the other hand, the attachment of Protestants to traditions of dissent and, therefore, to a kind of empiricism, practicality, and respect for democratic compromise seems to have made Protestantism a soil more resistant to the utopian illusions of socialism.[48] Capitalist democracy, Niebuhr knew, established no perfect justice. In 1959, however, he looked back on his own socialist critique:

> But it is now perfectly clear that the "capitalist" culture which was also a democratic one had more moral and political resources to avoid catastrophe than either the Marxists or their Christian fellow travelers believed. The religious and moral sense of catastrophe as judgment upon injustice was invalidated by a complicated array of historical, economic and political factors. . . .
> We Christian "prophetic" sympathizers with Marxism were as much in error in understanding the positive program of socialism as we were in sharing its catastrophism. For the positive program was utopian, despite the explicit anti-utopianism of the Marxist. It sought to establish the kingdom of perfect brotherhood or of perfect justice on earth. It completely failed to appreciate the possibility of corruption through self-interest in any structure of society.[49]

Niebuhr noted that no one with any real influence in the Christian church had espoused the communist cause. "We were, almost without exception, democratic socialists." Still, he did not doubt that communism is a legitimate form of orthodox Marxism. He did not try to "revise" Marx so as to make communism seem an aberration. He judged, further, that democratic socialism "really represented a domestication and revision of orthodox Marxism to fit into the framework of a free society." Moreover, until after the Second World War, "almost all democratic socialists believed in the nationalization of all basic industries." But they did not accurately count the costs of bureaucratization and inflexibility. They did not sufficiently fear that "even when the bureaucratic power was under democratic control the policy of nationalization would lead to too great centralization of power."[50]

Further transformation in socialism followed. "Increasingly, the socialist parties have modified their goals and have sought for

more equal justice by social security measures, by taxation policies, in which political society intervened in economic society
where centralization of power led to inordinate privilege." Socialists used political power to equalize economic privilege.
In short, they "have accomplished the same ends as our own
capitalist nation has achieved in its welfare measures. Thus, the
nineteenth-century conception of a class struggle, which even
democratic socialists accepted, has been invalidated by the complex
realities and social forces of a modern society."[51]

Niebuhr further concluded that democratic socialism was "until
recently, weighed down with ideological baggage which prevented
it from becoming a truly creative third force." Failing to understand the complexities of modern social classes, democratic socialists trusted too naively in "socializing property." They gave
the abolition of property a false "halo of redemption" it did not
deserve. Believing in the dignity and freedom of the individual,
democratic socialists "furnished no spiritual foundation for this
belief" consistent with their own premises. They were parasitic
on a liberal culture they affected to despise. Finally, democratic
socialism never deepened its theory of human nature beyond "the
Marxist belief that human egoism is caused by a social institution
and would therefore be eliminated by getting rid of that institution."[52] Thus, socialism is a "spent force in current history." A
free society, with its competing political forces, is able to "come
to terms with historical contingencies," and to absorb socialism
while moving onwards.[53]

Niebuhr saw clearly that "a religious passion for justice must
be balanced by a pragmatic consideration of all the factors in a
historical situation."[54] He did not allow such pragmatism to blind
him to claims coming from Asia, Latin America, and Africa,
which he was one of the first American Christians to hear. He saw
disguised moral esteem in the accusatory appeals directed at the
United States by underdeveloped nations.

In a paper for UNESCO in 1956, Niebuhr observed that the
people of the United States then enjoyed living standards that
were roughly two to three times as high as those of European
nations, and five to ten times as high as those of Asian nations.
This wealth, he wrote, "is a tremendous hazard to our moral
prestige through the world. It not only tempts others to envy but
it gives a certain plausibility to the Communist charge of 'capitalistic exploitation.' " Niebuhr observed that "this charge is not

well-founded," for the solid reasons we have already quoted from him in Chapter XIII. He worried then about "the inability of the world to sell as much to us as it is forced to buy," and complained of U.S. tariff barriers to foreign trade. By 1980, these circumstances had changed, and U.S. pressures were mounting to *restore* tariff barriers previously lowered (for Japanese and European autos, for example, and for textiles and shoes from many other regions). But Niebuhr's conclusion of 1956 is as valid today as then: "The fact is that the complexities of the problem of our wealth and the world's poverty are so great that all simple moral judgments about the problem, whether expressed by ourselves or by our critics, tend to be irrelevant."[55]

After Vietnam, an experience which deeply shook the intellectual class in the United States, a new tide of democratic socialism and Marxism began to sweep through some circles of intellectual and journalistic life, and especially through the liberal churches. Some argue that if Reinhold Niebuhr were still alive and could see the "economic crises" and "multinational outrages" of the '70s, he "might well have returned to the more radical commitments of his youth and middle age." John C. Cort believes that the "spreading disillusionment of democratic socialists throughout the West with nationalization and their shift toward other forms of socialization such as workers' ownership or control might also have encouraged him to return to those commitments."[56] Cort speaks of needing Niebuhr again.

But perhaps Niebuhr is needed again, rather, to penetrate the utopianism, perfectionism, and moralistic passions sweeping through our highly educated and religious classes as they did when Niebuhr first wrote.[57] Niebuhr is needed because so many uncritically accept the oppressed of the Third World as a messianic force, attribute Third World poverty to U.S. exploitation, discount the military threat posed for the West by an armed force greater than Hitler's, and resume again the attacks of the 1930s on "concentrations of economic power" in the multinational corporations.

Niebuhr showed us a way to be faithful to the ideals America helped invent.

XX

A Theology of Democratic Capitalism

The industrial regime inherited from Europe has now become unrecognizable in this country. It has been superseded by new economic structures which are still in the making, and in a state of fluidity, but which render both capitalism and socialism things of the past. Free enterprise and private ownership function now in a social context and a general mood entirely different from those of the nineteenth century.
—Jacques Maritain, *Reflections on America*[1]

1
The Importance of Ideals

The ideals a system is designed to serve, especially if they are transcendent ideals, stimulate each new generation to advance the work of its forebears. Building a humane social order is not a task for one generation merely. It is a journey of a thousand years. For democratic capitalism, barely two hundred have been traversed. To know its ideals is to be restless under the status quo and to wish to do better in the future.

It is important to grasp the ideals of a system clearly for another reason. There are many on the democratic left in the United States who interpret their own experience, judge the system in which they live, and try to direct its development, according to the ideals of socialism. Democratic capitalism, which is exceedingly flexible and experimental, has learned much from their efforts. Yet in the end, it is surely better for them and for the American system to be clear about each other. Insofar as socialism is a unitary system, dominated in all its parts by a state apparatus, socialism is not an improvement upon democratic capitalism but a relapse into the tyrannical unities from which the latter has emerged. A unitary, dominant, central state authority has been tried before. The enforcement of high moral ideals by coercion of law has been tried before.

Insofar as democratic socialism has given up the classic positions of Marxism and the collectivized state, it may now be no more than a left-wing variant of democratic capitalism. Insofar as it separates the moral-cultural system from the state, and also separates the economy (in some degree) from the state, it preserves the pluralist structure of democratic capitalism intact. In practice, of course, the political, economic, and moral-cultural programs of democratic socialists do not run helter-skelter. Running through them is a consistent thread of statism. In general, the left wishes to strengthen the political system at the expense of the economic system and the moral-cultural system.

It is the role of socialists on the Democratic left, as Michael Harrington and Irving Howe, the editor of *Dissent*, instruct their readers, to become the "conscience" of the Democratic Party.[2] But this conscience is *not* the conscience of democratic capitalism. It is the conscience of the socialist system they wish America yet to become.

My reasons for not wishing to march into the cold with them have already been given. Here I would like merely to summarize some of the important doctrines of Christianity (of which there are analogues in Judaism and other major religions) which helped to supply the ideas through which democratic capitalism has emerged in history.

It is no accident that democratic capitalism arose first in Jewish-Christian lands (or that it is imitable only in analogous cultures). Apart from certain specific views of human life and human hope, neither a democratic polity nor a market economy makes sense. If those who live under democratic capitalism lose sight of the moral foundations of the system, a loss of morale is likely to occur. Moral ignorance will bring moral paralysis. Necessary reforms and advances cannot be attempted when individuals within the system have lost sight of its proper ideals.

Some theologians may be dismayed that I do not more often cite Scripture in what follows. A host of texts is at my disposal. The economy of biblical nations in the Near Eastern basin was, after all, an economy of caravans and traders, a desert crossroads of active commercial life.[3] Nonetheless, writers of the biblical era did not envisage questions of political economy such as those we face today. The revelation of God which Christians and Jews (and Muslims) hold to have been given through these writings was intended for all human beings universally, in all conceivable systems, even in systems of slavery (which have dominated world history) as well as in societies of hunters, in agricultural societies, in urban societies, in primitive societies, in modern societies, in future societies. For all such contexts, Scripture has words of universal power. It is a mistake, I believe, to try to bind the cogency of Scripture to one system merely. The Word of God is transcendent. It judges each and every system, and finds each gravely wanting. Liberation theologians in the Third World today err in binding Scripture to a socialist political economy, and I do not wish to indulge in a parallel mistake.

For candor's sake, I must add that the emphasis upon Scripture studies during the past generation does not seem to have effected, as its sponsors hoped, the revitalization of Christian life and practice. There is a great gap between the Word of God and systems of economic, political, social, and cultural thought in modern societies. The human mind requires a powerful set of philosophical and theological concepts in order to relate the pure and simple Word of Scripture to the complex body of modern thought. By trying to take a shortcut around systematic philosophical and theological reflection, and by ignoring intellectual and social history, too many contemporary clergymen, theologians, and devout laypersons have ensnared themselves in pious simplicities which falsify reality. Quoting Scripture, they do not manage to relate the Word of God *incarnationally* to every fiber of modern civilization. They fail to understand that Scripture applied to the real world without exact intellectual analysis echoes emptily. Those who would apply Scripture to public policy cannot take shortcuts.

On this terrain, there can scarcely be certainty. Perhaps they are right who believe that "Christianity is the religion of which socialism is the practice." I do not think they are right, and I have tried to set forth reasons for this judgment. For my part, I do not claim that democratic capitalism is the practice of which Christianity and Judaism are the religions. That is not my view. Both Christianity and Judaism have flourished, or at least survived, in every sort of social system known to humankind. If democratic capitalism were to perish during the next fifty years, as well it may, Christianity and Judaism could still survive; according to God's promise, they will survive to the end of time. It is essential, then, not to confuse the transcendence of Christianity and Judaism with the survival of democratic capitalism. If democratic capitalism were to perish from the earth, humankind would decline into relative darkness and Jews and Christians would suffer under regimes far more hostile to their liberties and their capacities. Yet Judaism and Christianity do not *require* democratic capitalism. It is only that without it they would be poorer and less free. Among political economies, there may be something better than self-correcting democratic capitalism. If so, it is not yet in sight.

It is, therefore, a sad commentary on the sociology of knowledge in the Christian churches that so few theologians or religious leaders understand economics, industry, manufacturing, trade, and finance. Many seem trapped in pre-capitalist modes of thought. Few understand the laws of development, growth, and production. Many swiftly reduce all morality to the morality of distribution. They demand jobs without comprehending how jobs are created. They demand the distribution of the world's goods without insight into how the store of the world's goods may be expanded. They desire ends without critical knowledge about means. They claim to be leaders without having mastered the techniques of human progress. Their ignorance deprives them of authority. Their good intentions would be more easily honored if supported by evidence of diligent intelligence in economics.

Yet it is not economics that is our proper subject here. Our task is to cite, if all too briefly, religious doctrines which have been powerful in leading humanity, slowly and fitfully, to those formulations of institutional practices which have made economic development, political liberty, and a moral-cultural commitment to progress on earth emerge in history as a realistic force. I judge six such doctrines most important, and will address them in their Christian form.

2
Six Theological Doctrines

1. *The Trinity.* The first of these is the symbol of the Trinity. No one has seen God. What we know of God can only be inferred from our experience and from what God has chosen to reveal of Himself. These are the two sources of our knowledge: what we learn from the works of the Creator and the Lord of History, and what we learn from His self-revelation. Characteristically, therefore, humans develop a language about God, inadequate as they recognize it to be, based upon what they most value in their own experience. They seek signs of the godly in everything. "Grace," George Bernanos tells us, "is everywhere."[4]

The one God of Christians is also plural; appropriately, then, the mind becomes accustomed to seeing pluralism-in-unity throughout creation, even in social systems.

Some Protestants fear that any knowledge of God which arises from human experience is bound to be flawed and distorted—to be, in the final measure, idolatrous compared to God as He knows Himself. Yet in this matter experience and Scripture are at one: Community is essential to our notion of God. Jesus described Himself as the Son, one with the Father, and one as well with the Holy Spirit of love whom the Father would send. These are dark words. But they do suggest that even God is not best thought of as the Aristotelian *Nous,* a lonely individual in solitariness. A plural God, yet one?

No one sees God or comprehends what can be intended in speaking of God as Three-in-one. Yet it is at least clear that God is more to be conceived as a kind of community than as a solitary individual. From human experience, human beings have learned to place highest value upon communities of love, however humble and flawed. The image of the solitary loner, however noble and heroic, however brave in facing the darkness alone, somehow rings false as a representation of the highest of human experiences. What is most valued among humans is that community within which individuality is not lost. To build such community is to share God's life. (It is through this strong sense of community that Judaism supplies an analogous way to God.)

I do not think it wrong to hold that this lesson of experience is consistent with the teaching of Scripture. Experience and Scripture alike suggest that what is most real in human life, of highest value, most godlike, is a community of persons. Thus the creation images the Creator, and the creature is made to be in God's image, through community. When Jesus says, "Forsake all and follow me" (Matthew 16:24), he is giving his life for the entire human community. So must we all.

It is true that socialism aims at community. It is less clear that its institutional arrangements effect, or can effect, the survival of individuality. This deficiency makes the community socialism builds suspect. In practice, it exhibits itself more as collective than as community.

The problem posed for political economy by the doctrine of the Trinity is how to build human community without damage to human individuality. How can there be one and yet many? How can all humans be united as one, yet retain personal liberty in insight and choice? This is the systemic problem which democratic capitalism has set out to solve. Its solution is remote from being perfect. Democratic capitalism is by no means the Kingdom of God. It remains in partial bondage to the world, the flesh, and the devil. Yet St. Patrick saw a metaphor for the Trinity in a shamrock. St. Augustine saw a metaphor for God in the procession of an insight (the Word) from an active intelligence (the Father), and in the procession of the choice of love (the Spirit) from both. These metaphors do not represent God adequately. They are merely arrows shot, as it were, in God's direction and fated from the beginning to fall short. Yet they do direct our attention in the direction of awe, silence, and wonder. Metaphors taken from silent nature and from the inner life of the human person are dangerous. Those taken from political economy may be even more so. Yet analogy is the air the Catholic mind breathes.

In everything I have been taught to seek God's presence. Thus also in political economy. I find attractive—and resonant with dark illumination—a political economy differentiated and yet one. Each of its component systems has a certain autonomy from the others; each system is interdependent with the others. Each has its distinctive operations, methods, rules. Each tames and corrects and enhances the others.

Moreover, this systemic differentiation is designed to permit many other sorts of communities to flourish. To be sure, the *forms* of each of these communities—families, neighborhoods, local agencies, interest groups, voluntary associations, churches, unions, corporations, guilds, societies, schools—are transformed under democratic capitalism into modalities unfamiliar in previous history. Less and less are they rooted in kith and kin, blood and status, propinquity and immobility. They have become more voluntary, fluid, mobile. They are nonetheless communities for that. Further, for too long the philosophers of democratic capitalism have neglected them, being hypnotized by the two dominant historical emergences, the *individual* and the *state*. Yet in fact, even if insufficiently studied in theory, these "mediating communities" make the life of individuals and the life of states possible. In Poland, for example, the clumsy state apparatus is the despair of millions, who derive their real sustenance from their families, neighbors, friends, churches, and other social institutions. Strong individuals need strong mediating structures both in order to become what they are and in order to act effectively in the world. States need strong mediating structures in order to accomplish more cheaply and efficiently and with greater love what the state either cannot do at all or can do only at prohibitive expense and badly. When mediating communities suffer and are broken, both individuals and states are crippled.

Under democratic capitalism, the individual is freer than under any other political economy ever experienced by the human race, and this fact has led some scholars to speak of anomie, alienation, fragmentation. Such abstractions move us when we imagine others as strange, discrete objects separate from ourselves. Yet the scholars who write of such things do not appear to be particularly anomic, alienated, or fragmented; nor do their readers; nor our own families, loved ones, and mediating communities. In all societies, one meets lost souls, but there is no evidence that their number increases under conditions of modernity. It is obviously true that *old* forms of community die and that *all* forms of community become subtly different. It is also obvious that new forms bring their own pains, doubts, and uncertainties. But under democratic capitalism mediating communities multiply and thrive, become subject to choice, and afford enormous variety and possibility.

Under democratic capitalism, each individual participates in many vital communities. The social life of each is not exhausted by the state or controlled by the state. The federal government alone presently has at its disposal an annual budget reaching $452 billion, excluding intergovernmental transfer payments. State and local governments spend another $381 billion. This communal spending averages out for a population of 225 million to about $3,072 for every man, woman, and child.[5] It does not include the communal spending of private associations, churches, guilds, unions, art leagues, schools, sporting activities, and other social institutions. In terms of money alone, the social vitalities of democratic capitalism are significant.

It may seem blasphemous to some to go from the Trinity to communal patterns of monetary expenditures. Yet in the patterns of its communal and individual life, a society does reveal its highest ideals, if darkly. Ideals of community oblige it constantly to do better.

2. *The Incarnation.* The second great Christian symbol is the Incarnation. According to this doctrine, God stooped low to enter human history as a man in one underdeveloped country in one particular location in the world's geography. Thus, God did not overpower history but respected its constraints. He accepted for Himself the human condition, including the worst it might offer, death at the hands of the state under conditions of ridicule and hatred. (Analogous to this conception is that of the chosen people—the transcendent again revealed through the particular.)

The implications of this doctrine are many and profound: for the meaning of history and human narrative, of time and evolution, of progress and decline, of respect for the laws of the human body, of reconciliation to the world's sinfulness and its capacity for cruelty, of hope and acceptance, of mercy and justice, of love and humility. Many millions have contemplated these meanings in silence, picturing before their hearts the events which gave rise to them.

One of the most poignant lessons of the Incarnation is the difficult teaching that one must learn to be humble, think concretely, face facts, train oneself to realism. There are some who always imagine hope in utopian terms. Their hope depends upon the world changing: either back into the Paradise of time's beginnings or ahead into the Nowhere of the future. The Incarnation is a doctrine of hope but not of utopia. If God so willed his beloved Son to suffer, why would He spare us? If God did not send legions of angels to change the world for Him, why should we idly dream of sudden change for us? Christian hope is realistic, braced for darkness and cruelty, alert to the forces of unreason and of sin. In an analogous way, the diaspora of the Jewish people and the horror of the twentieth-century death camps have given Jews a profound instinct of realism, a readiness for the worst. Illusionlessness is a high form of Christian and Jewish consciousness.

Actually, both communities are also prone to escapism. In Christianity, this usually takes the form of perfectionism. Its less political form is piety kept pure from the ambiguities of political economy, a quest for personal salvation in the private recesses of the heart. Its more political form includes hostility toward merely realistic ideals, coupled with the utopian expectation of a coming time of justice and peace under socialism. In Judaism, this otherworldly strain sometimes takes the form of the separate community, as among the Hasidim. Among the more political, it sometimes takes the same form as among political Christians: the content of expectation is deliverance into socialism. Socialism has become the name for deliverance from temptation and evil, "the dream that will never die." It is a powerful mythic force.

I do not mean to employ theological reflection as an argument for or against any form of political economy. My aim is more modest. The point of Incarnation is to respect the world as it is, to acknowledge its limits, to recognize its weaknesses, irrationalities, and evil forces, and to disbelieve any promises that the world is now or ever will be transformed into the City of God. If Jesus could not effect that, how shall we? If the tears of six million victims pleading for their loved ones could not effect that, how shall we? The world is not going to become—*ever*—a kingdom of justice and love. This is not a counsel against hope. It is a moderate and realistic response to the questions of Kant: "Who are we? What ought we to do? What may we hope?"

We may hope that God does not abandon us (though He did abandon Jesus); and that, even in His abandonment, His will shall be done. We may hope that great deeds may be done through us, even though we in person never live to see their fruits. We may hope that time is God's narrative and that through its fullness yet more of His justice and mercy will be revealed. We may hope His kingdom will unfold in our midst partially and gradually, as yeast unfolds in dough or as seeds do in the ground. We may hope in modest progress but not in final victory over irrationality and sin. We may hope in revolutions if they are rooted in realism, but not in utopia. We may hope in the capacities of human decency, but not without vigilance. We may hope in common sense and in practical wisdom, in plain love and heroic virtue, but we must be ready for betrayals. There are, alas, many vices humans are prey to.

These hopes are modest hopes. Such hopes would have been necessary had we lived with Christ and seen Him die, or struggled to retain humanity in the pitiless desolation of Buchenwald. They are illusionless hopes. They are conservative by comparison with every form of utopia. They are progressive by comparison with every form of cynicism.

A political economy patterned upon the doctrine of the Incarnation or upon the bittersweet history of the Jews—those two symbols so powerful in the minds of Thomas Jefferson and others of his generation—must necessarily seem to the perfectionist mind and to the angelic temperament too limited, even reactionary, too stubbornly mired in the stuff of present perplexities. Some speak of an "eschatological break" with the past, a "new beginning" for the human race. Such utopianism was not absent among those who thought to establish in America a "New World" apart from the tangled sins and distortions of the "Old World." In the name of such utopianism, righteous intolerance and feigned innocence have not been unknown. In the coercive power of Christian love, the world has had reason to learn that there is no hate like Christian hate. (Except that every human being may fall prey to hate.) The pure fury of reformers can kill. Those who claim enlightened virtue often carry unexamined viciousness in their hearts.

Although the Founding Fathers, too, were tempted by perfectionism, they strove manfully to design institutions proportionate not to angels or to saints but to sinners. They did not try to construct utopia. They tried to check and limit vice, tyranny most of all, even tyranny in the name of morality and religion. They chose as their model citizen, for whom the system was designed, neither the saint nor the preacher, neither the hero of war nor the aristocrat, neither the poet nor the philosopher, neither the king nor the peasant, but the free man of property and commerce. They did that precisely because they thought such a man was more common, more visibly human both in virtues and in vices, thus cut to the size of sinfulness and plain expectation. (Not incidentally, Jesus the carpenter was such a man, and even Jesus the preacher stressed plain wisdom.) There would be room enough within the system they designed for every form of heroism and high virtue, noble thought and brilliant deed. But the system *as a system* was cut to common cloth. It is easily enough subjected to ridicule and scorn. Their aim was to have it commended not for its exhilaration but for its simplicity and practicality.

They called theirs a "revolution," but in the history of the world's revolutions it was more nearly than any other designed upon common and practical lines, hardly at all pretentious, and by no means free from sin. They did not design it to be a vessel of grace and salvation, but simply as a *removens prohibens* within which human beings might work out such destiny as they judged themselves to be called to. They went about it not as poets build up visions but as carpenters lay a hull and set in place its beams. They designed it, like Noah, against whatever floods and hazards history might have in store for it. What dreams it sailed toward they left to each generation's crews and captains. They understood their role to be, not that of priests or philosophers charting stars the ship should follow, but that of builders whose rule was that the system as a whole be seaworthy. Paradise and salvation, peace and justice, they did not promise. The task of political economy is not to guide the ship but to make a voyage possible.

Not every dream of political economy is equally credible. Among the limited possibilities, one must choose. Before abandoning ship, moreover, one would wish to observe the other ships a little.

The single greatest temptation for Christians is to imagine that the salvation won by Jesus has altered the human condition. Many attempt to judge the present world by the standards of the gospels, as though the world were ready to live according to them. Sin is not so easily overcome. A political economy for sinners, even Christian sinners (however well intentioned), is consistent with the story of Jesus. A political economy based on love and justice is to be found beyond, never to be wholly incarnated within, human history. The Incarnation obliges us to reduce our noblest expectations, so to love the world as to fit a political economy to it, nourishing all that is best in it.

3. *Competition.* The great Catholic spiritual writer Tanquerey once observed that on the whole, candidates attracted to the priesthood and religious life tend to be drawn disproportionately from those of passive, sweet, and noncompetitive temperaments. This was, he thought, a fair enough distribution of temperaments, given their role and function in the Mystical Body. Wide experience of life teaches one the astuteness of this observation. Religious professionals are expected, in the main, to be conciliators and reconcilers. They counsel those in grief and in perplexity. They tend the sick and dying. They teach the unruly and the stubborn. Men and women of peace, they are not expected to display a flagrant will-to-power, self-assertion, a bold pride of person. Many exceptions test the generalization but do not invalidate it.

But the danger this tilt in temperament presents to religious communities, as communities intended for all personalities of every type, is plain enough. Given the work they have to do, chaplains and ministers, church workers and nuns, teachers and nurses, professors and canon lawyers are lucky if they have temperaments to match their duties. To try to impose upon the Christian people at large, however, the style that works for them is bound to make other kinds of Christians ill at ease. A political economy needs bold political leaders who thrive in contests of power and willful dreamers and builders who delight in overcoming economic difficulties in order to produce. The will-to-power must be made creative, not destroyed.

In this respect, Judaism and Christianity are religions of narrative and liberty. In every story in the Bible, attention is focused upon the moment of decision. In any given story, dramatic interest is aroused because the outcome remains in doubt until the closing lines. King David might, or might not, betray his closest friend. In some episodes, David is virtuous; in others, vicious. The same human being, in his liberty, may say yes to grace, or like the rich young man turn sadly away in declination. Judaism and Christianity, in other words, envisage human life as a contest. The ultimate competition resides in the depths of one's own heart. Much is to be gained, much lost. "What does it profit a man if he gain the whole world and suffer the loss of his soul?" (Mk. 8:36). The stakes are real; there are winners and losers. "Many are called, few are chosen" (Mt. 20:16).

The Jewish and Christian view shows that God is not committed to equality of results. One steward differs from another in his performance; some virgins are foolish, some wise. The faithful son receives no celebration comparable to the one given by his father for the prodigal. Workers who arrive at the eleventh hour receive the same wage as those who bore the whole day's heat. St. Paul bids all to compete, to measure themselves as he measures himself, and to outdo him if one can: God will be the judge. Religious compassion does not entail levelling.

It is altogether natural within a Jewish and Christian civilization for autobiography to enter the world as a literary form, and to accept as its natural dynamic the image of "pilgrim's progress," a journey, a race, a combat, a struggle against the self and the world and the devil. Implicit in such a life form is not only the possibility of failure but standards of *more* and *less*. Life is under judgment. All are not equal. Some who receive many talents do little with them, squander them, or bury them; some produce from them more even than they were given. Human dignity, as Jews and Christians understand it, depends upon the power of such inequalities. Otherwise, human responsibility is empty. Granted that even those who are "elected" are so through God's grace, not through any initiative or power of their own, still, each is free to say yes or no. Success may be due to God alone; but failure is due to self. For God made this world a world of liberty, gave each the capacity freely to choose, and nourishes each in a multiplicity of ways, so that even the power to say yes is given as a gift.

To jump from the laws of the life of the spirit to the laws of political economy is a big and inappropriate jump. Success in this world is often entirely the opposite of success in the life of grace. "Many who are now last will be first, and many who are now first will be last" (Mt. 20:16). God regards not the worldly success of man but his response to God's Word in his heart and deeds. There is, therefore, much reason to be skeptical of Max Weber's view that the Calvinist world view of election through grace led to the worldly pursuit of success as a confirmation of such grace. God did not give Job such a confirmation; he took everything away. The Bible is replete with warnings that worldly success is not only not the same as salvation, and surely no sign of it, but even a common obstacle to grace. "It is as difficult for a rich man to enter the Kingdom of Heaven as for a camel to pass through the eye of a needle" (Mt. 19:24). There is reason to believe that Calvinist preachers in Great Britain were as likely as any other preachers to inveigh often and sulphurously against worldly success.

One might imagine, though, that those virtues which arose from the worldly asceticism of the plain Christian life turned out, under specific conditions in the urban markets of eighteenth-century Great Britain and North America, to result in hard work, thrift, savings, prudent investments, and, in short, worldly success. It may even have seemed obvious that lewdness, profligacy, laziness, gluttony, intemperance, pride, envy, and other habitual sins were costly, not only in expenses paid but also in investments lost. I have heard corporate leaders even today say that those with factories among present-day Mormons—perhaps our nearest equivalent to the sound people Weber described—have one of the most faithful, honest, hardworking, and self-reliant work forces in the country.

It would be odd if the virtues recommended by the Creator were *entirely* out of keeping with the laws of creation. One recalls that the Rule of St. Benedict instructed monks to rationalize their hours, to work as if to work were to pray, and to attain not only communal self-reliance but a surplus to share in open hospitality. Still later, the great Cistercian abbeys were very factories of productivity—transnationals, at that—in the heart of early-medieval Europe. Virtue can hardly help bearing material fruit, when conditions are right. The relation of Creator to creation would otherwise seem odd.

Still, one must insist that Christian grace is never measured either by virtue or by worldly success. Indeed, Christians sometimes bear down on this point so hard—I remember many such sermons in my youth—that success typically makes a Christian feel *guilty.* Indeed, Weber's theory would be much more plausible if he were trying to explain why Western Christians are so uniquely susceptible to guilt feelings. One could not make Attila the Hun feel guilty for sacking cities. Christian teaching runs in so many ways counter to worldly success that its appearance—in Protestant nations, at least; the wealthy of Latin America do not seem so easily moved to feelings of guilt—is almost certain to generate moral anxiety.

Nonetheless, onward Christian soldiers are called, bound to daily combat with the self, inspired to noble competition by the example of the saints who have gone before, hearts burning in emulation of Abraham, Sarah, the good David, Jesus, Paul, Stephen, and the others. The competition is relentless. Judgment is constant. Critics sometimes suggest that competitiveness is foreign to a religion of love, meekness, and peace. They have no idea how hard it is to be meeker than one's neighbor. There are abuses of the competitive spirit, of course, as there are of love, meekness, and peace. But to compete—*com + petere,* "to seek together although against each other"—is not a vice. It is, in a sense, the form of every virtue and an indispensable element in natural and spiritual growth. Competition is the natural play of the free person. All striving is based upon measurement of oneself by some ideal and under some judgment. When that judgment is omniscient and omnipotent, such measurement is keener than any scalpel. Human sports, lotteries, and contests of every sort—in oratory, song, drama, horsemanship, the arrangement of flowers, the winning of tenure—would make no sense if the competitive spirit were foreign to human nature and learning. Most humans rejoice in it.

Furthermore, it is unlikely that individuals could ever discover their own potential unless they were blessed with good friends and rivals, whose exploits teach them how to push themselves harder than they yet have. To live in a slack age of low standards is a curse upon self-realization. To live among bright, alert, striving rivals is a great gift to one's own development. De Tocqueville much admired the distinctive and widespread spirit of competition that he found in Americans of every station. It made the nation seem alive. Ralph Lerner summarizes John Adams's views as follows:

> Whereas in other lands, he thought, "ambition and all its hopes are extinct," in America, where competition was free, where every office—even the highest—seemed within one's grasp, the ardor for distinction was stimulated and became general. In America, "the lowest can aspire as freely as the highest." The farmer and tradesman pursued their dream of happiness as intensely as any man. Most revealing, however, were the objects of those dreams. "The post of clerk, sergeant, corporal, and even drummer and fifer, is coveted as

earnestly as the best gift of major-general.'' No man was so humble but a passion for distinction was aroused; no object so small but it excited somebody's emulation.[6]

It does not seem to be inconsistent with the gospels for each human being to struggle, under the spur of competition with his fellows, to become all he can become.

It is absurd to believe, as some sentimentalists will have it, that the world knew no competition before the advent of democratic capitalism. Earlier, it is true, hopes of bettering one's own condition were vain; immobile status was inherited at birth. Yet competition was vital among the Greeks, as it is among all awake and advancing peoples. Otherwise discoveries by genius would not be studied and imitated by others, and progress would stop. The soul of the spirit of progress is the desire to do better. A noncompetitive world is a world reconciled to the *status quo*. It is further absurd to suppose that the competitive spirit dies in a socialist society. Among zero-sum games, the struggle for power is the most deadly. This is why there are so many disappearances, exiles, and jail sentences in socialist experience.

Among the things for which humans compete, money is neutral and may be used in wise stewardship or foolish. Since it is impersonal and instrumental, its possessors may accept it with an infinite range of human attitudes and use it for a vast range of choices. More to the point, those who have money are obliged by it to become careful stewards, under pain of losing it or cutting foolishly into their capital. Their natural interest lies in investing it soundly and well. This interest leads them to produce more of it than there was in the first place. Thus a money economy is inherently dynamic. What one wins in the competition is not, as in the zero-sum game of political allocation, taken from others, for the original sum is invested so as to be added to, and its investment opens new opportunities for others. In such an economy, it is in the real interest of those with money to see others prosper along with themselves. Those who earn power or honor cannot make their rewards multiply as can those who earn money. Power and honor, widely shared, are diminished. Not so with money.

Money has value only within a system. The soundness of the system is its only protection. Thus de Tocqueville observes that in "the doctrine of self-interest properly understood," private interest and public interest are fused in such a way that "a sort of selfishness" obliges the individual to "care for the state."[7] Only the soundness and dynamism of the society as a whole permits investments to retain their value; otherwise money becomes as worthless as "a Confederate dollar" or a German mark before and after World War II. Money *seems* to be a material thing. But it is actually only a symbol, whose value is entirely upheld by social health. In a healthy society, its certificates are as broadly distributed as possible to bind the loyalty of all to a common enterprise. Few societies have invented an incentive so innocent in itself, so self-multiplying, so socially binding, and so utterly dependent upon the common social health.

For all these reasons, it seems wrong to imagine that the spirit of competition is foreign to the gospels, and that, in particular, competition for money is humankind's most mortal spiritual danger. Under God, a wealthy nation faces an especially harsh judgment, but that judgment will not be aimed so much at the existence of wealth as at the character of the uses made of it. On Judgment Day, the rich may find it especially hard to get through the eye of the needle, but this will not be because they had money but because their use of it will be subjected to an accounting on different ledgers from those scrutinized by the Internal Revenue Service. The rich have reason to tremble. If their wealth has been productive for others, though, the world has reason to be merciful to them even if God's standards are higher.

4. *Original sin.* The fourth doctrine is original sin, which we have already explored under a more general heading in Part One. The force of the word "original" may, however, need exposition. Its effect is to deflate human pretensions of unambiguous virtue.

Some among the Greeks, some rationalists of the Enlightenment, and some socialists and other utopians seem ready to imagine healthy, normal, moral, reasonable human beings coming into existence somewhere or someday under stipulated favorable conditions. This is either because they think that the evils and inconstancies of the human heart are superable, or because they think that individuals are evil only through living within evil structures. In the latter case, they try to imagine a new society which will enable men to stand taller, achieve a nobility never before achieved, give spontaneous expression to altruistic and creative impulses, and, for good measure, have only pure and reasonable thoughts.[8]

The force of the doctrine of original sin is to steel the gullible mind against such illusions. Human liberty is subject to evil expression as well as to good. Human intelligence is not only limited but often biased and distorted. The human passions are subject to common disorders. Those who believe in original sin believe that it is cruel, in such circumstances, to expect too much of other human beings. They believe, furthermore, that the root of evil does not lie in our systems but in ourselves.

Every form of political economy necessarily begins (even if unconsciously) with a theory of sin. For every system is designed *against* something, as well as in *favor* of something. Every system nourishes, every system inhibits. That is why some types of persons do particularly well within one system, others within another. The system of democratic capitalism, believing itself to be the natural system of liberty and the system which, so far in history, is best designed to meet the premises of original sin, is designed against tyranny. Its chief aim is to fragment and to check power, but not to repress sin. Within it every human vice flourishes. Entrepreneurs from around the world, it appears, flock to it and teach it new cultural specialties, of vice as well as of virtue, of indelicacy as well as of delicacy. *Nil humanum mihi alienum,* such a system might well say: "Nothing from the world's cultures is alien to me." Outsiders like Solzhenitsyn are often shocked by such a nation's public immoralities: massage parlors, pornography shops, pickpockets, winos, prostitutes, pushers, punk rock, chambers for group sex—you name it, democratic capitalism tolerates it and someone makes a living from it.

One can imagine a form of democratic capitalist society which would put an end to public vice. The United States used to be stricter than it now is. Halfhearted measures in this direction are still sometimes made. But the heart of most citizens is clearly not in the wholesale legal repression of all sinful behavior. Socialist societies repress sin much more effectively. They begin by repressing economic activities.

If there is to be reform concerning the public exhibition of vice in the modern United States, such reform will probably have to emanate from the moral-cultural system rather than from the political system. But the present ethos is still in an anti-bourgeois phase, in which some forms of decadence are not only not ridiculed, but are admired as "liberation." The wheel may turn again, more than once. The denizens of *Playboy* eventually inspire a "moral majority," whose own errors and decline are inevitable. Sin is where the majority is. Its fashions change from time to time.

A free society can tolerate the public display of vice because it has confidence in the basic decency of human beings, even under the burden of sin. The concept of original sin does not entail that each person is in all ways depraved, only that each person sometimes sins. Belief in original sin is consistent with guarded trust in the better side of human nature. Under an appropriate set of checks and balances, the vast majority of human beings will respond to daily challenges with decency, generosity, common sense, and even, on occasion, moral heroism.

5. *The separation of realms.* The classic text is: "Give to Caesar the things that are Caesar's, and to God the things that are God's" (Mt. 22:21). In earlier chapters, we have already explored the importance of structural pluralism to democratic capitalism. This pluralism renders the mission of Christianity uniquely difficult. Some traditional societies imposed Christianity upon their citizens. Some socialist societies could conceivably do so. Under pluralism, no democratic capitalist society has a right to do so.

This means that the political system of democratic capitalism cannot, in principle, be a Christian system. Clearly, it cannot be a confessional system. But it cannot even be presumed to be, in an *obligatory* way, suffused with Christian values and purposes. Individual Christians and their organized bodies may legitimately work through democratic means to shape the will of the majority; but they must also observe the rights of others and, more than that, heed practical wisdom by respecting the consciences of others even more than law alone might demand. On the question of abortion, for example, no one is likely ever to be satisfied with the law, but all might be well advised not to demand in law all that their own conscience commands.

Dietrich Bonhoeffer has written about the impossibility of a Christian economy.[9] For one thing, a market system must be open to all regardless of their religious faith. Economic liberty means that all must be permitted to establish their own values and priorities. The churches and other moral-cultural institutions may seek to persuade persons to avoid some actions and to take others. Public authority properly forbids some practices, regulates others, commands others. Nonetheless, a wide range of economic liberties remains. This liberty is valued as the atmosphere most favorable to invention, creativity, and economic activism. To repress it is to invite stagnation.

For another thing, Christian values in their purity command a high level of charity that is not of this world. Christians are urged to moral behavior that seems counter-natural: to love enemies; to do good to those that hate them; when struck, to turn the other cheek. Such counsels are high standards by which to fault even our best daily practice. They are not rules cut to the expected behavior of most persons most of the time. Again, it is said: "Love your neighbor as yourself" (Lev. 19:18). It is not easy to love oneself. Escape from too much self often affords sorely needed relief. Often it is easier to love the poor and the oppressed than to love one's nextdoor neighbor. Part of the attraction of Christianity derives from the moral heroism to which such counsels call. Christianity in this sense is like a mountain peak. There is danger in such mountains. Christians who are not alpinists easily deceive themselves about their virtue.

No intelligent human order—not even within a church bureaucracy—can be run according to the counsels of Christianity. Not even saints in company assembled can bear such a regimen. Monasteries are designed for sinners, beginners, and backsliders. In the world at large, moreover, the consciences of all Christians are not identical. An economy based upon the consciences of some would offend the consciences of others. A free economy cannot—for all these reasons—be a Christian economy. To try to run an economy by the highest Christian principles is certain to destroy both the economy and the reputation of Christianity. Each Christian can and should follow his or her conscience, and cooperate in coalitions where consensus may be reached.

Liberty is a critical good in the economic sphere as well as in the sphere of conscience. Yet the guardians of the moral-cultural system are typically less concerned about liberty in the economic system than about their own liberty. Intellectuals insist upon a free market for their own work, but easily endorse infringements upon the liberty of economic activists. Journalists are quick to resist encroachments upon the laws which protect their own liberties; they are slow to protest—if they do not themselves encourage—infringements upon the liberties of industry and commerce. So it is and always was.

These different interests and different concerns illustrate the systematic distortions in human perception to which the doctrine of original sin draws attention. The perception of each of us is regularly more self-centered than our ideal selves can plausibly commend. We are not often as objective as we would like to be. That is why the separation of systems is appropriate to our weakness. At the heart of Judaism and Christianity is the recognition of sin, as at the heart of democratic capitalism is a differentiation of systems designed to squeeze some good from sinful tendencies.

6. *Caritas.* The highest of all theological symbols for Judaism and Christianity is the one closest to the personality of God: compassion, sacrificial love, *caritas. Caritas* is the proper name of the Creator.[10] Thus this symbol is the highest, but also the most difficult to penetrate. Consider such passages as these: "Love your neighbor as yourself" (Mt. 22:39). "Love your enemies" (Mt. 5:44). "Love is the highest law" (Rom. 13:10). "The greatest of these is love" (I Cor. 13:13). Such passages make clear that something considerably more profound than feelings is involved. A certain conquering of feelings—a disciplining and tutoring of the feelings—is required. Indeed, something larger, more powerful, more profound than the love of one's own heart, mind, and soul is involved: the very love of God flowing through human lives and shaping the world of history—"the Love," Dante saw, "which moves the sun and all the stars."

The distinguishing feature of Jewish and Christian conceptions of love is that love is realistic. It is the very energy of reality itself. For centuries, it was expressed in the philosophical language of "being" and "the existent." It is love that makes things "to be," to "stand out" from nothingness (*ex + sistere*).

Moreover, even in human relations, true love is distinguished from its counterfeits by its realism. "To love," Aquinas wrote, "is to will the good of the other as other."[11] This means that the lover must not be possessive, reducing the loved one to an adjunct of the self. The loved one is other—an autonomous person. Furthermore, the lover must will *the good* of the other, not simply illusions about that good. In a word, such love, like God's love, is realistic.

The ideal of "willing the good of the other as other" represents a profound and complex insight. It suggests to the lover that he (or she) must be wary both of the illusions of the self and of the illusions of the other. It means that the lover must not be led solely by desire, pleasure, or the wish to please, but must attempt to activate a more difficult capacity for realism and judgment. The question a true lover faces is not What do I want? and not What does my beloved want? but What is the good of my beloved? In this way, true friends give each other correction, lead each other beyond their own infantile fantasies, and grow together in wisdom and friendship.

There are, then, many counterfeits of love. True love is experienced like a clearing of the eyes. It teaches one to see what one did not at first see, and what one usually cannot see without struggle and trial and error. "Hell," Jean-Paul Sartre once wrote, "is other people." For Aquinas, love is exactly the reverse: to learn to see the good of another, precisely as other, and to cherish and pursue that good together with the other. In this sense, love is a teacher and leads two friends beyond one level of development after another. Ultimately, the good of each of us is to become all each can become. For someone to love that good latent within us is to call us to grow as we might otherwise not. Friends give each other the most precious gift humans can, not so much the comfort of sympathy as the call to self-realization. They do this, often enough, through painful candor, puncturing our cramped self-images, freeing us from those petty tyrannies to which self-love blinds us.

Love, then, is a great teacher of realism about ourselves. Marital love, in particular, the most intimate and noble of all human friendships, is ruthless in destroying the illusions of each about each.

In this sense, too, love is the inner form of all the virtues.[12] In teaching the self a certain realism, it teaches wise judgment about human frailties and hidden possibilities. Love clarifies the intelligence and the heart, disciplines the merely self-loving emotions, corrects the aberrations of personality, brings one down to earth, teaches one respect for the other as other. Love listens. Yet love can hardly afford to be sentimental; so many vices lurk where good judgment is left at the door. Love is demanding, a disciplinarian, although it brings such sweetness as poetry sings of (in its disciplined meters).

In English, the word "love" is used in so many vulgar ways, to express so many self-centered sentiments, that one instinctively feels a better word is needed. For this reason, I have headed the present section with the Latin word *caritas*. For Thomas Aquinas, whom I here follow, *amor* refers to physical attraction, even of the sort involved in the "desire" of a stone for earth, the motions of the sun and all the stars, the movement of a kitten toward a saucer of milk, the flutter of the heart at the striking presence of another of the other sex. *Dilectio,* as in our English "predilection," suggests a further and more complex activity, the exercise of choice or election. In a sense, one loves one's parents instinctively, but one *chooses* friends. (It is a happy event when one begins to choose one's parents as one's friends, passing with them from *amor* to *dilectio.*) Next comes *amicitia,* or friendship, the form of *dilectio* that is reciprocated, the circuit which is complete when two independent persons each begin to love the other as other. Courtships begin in *amor,* proceed to *dilectio,* only gradually develop—many quarrels shared, many illusions shattered—into *amicitia.*[13] Finally, *caritas* appears in the recognition that the good which one loves in one's friend, and the good one's friend loves in oneself, is God. Then the recognition arises that, of all things known to human experience, the love of friends for one another is not only the most *like* God, but in fact the way by which humans *participate* in the life of God. "Ah! The fire that breaks from thee, then . . . !"[14]

To look upon human history as love-infused by a Creator who values others as others, who sees in those originating sources of insight and choice which we have come to know as "persons" the purpose of his creation; and who in loving each as an individual creates of the contrarious many an unseen, hidden, but powerful community, is to glimpse a world in which the political economy of democratic capitalism makes sense.

In order to create wealth, individuals must be free to be other. They are not to be understood as fragments of a collective, members of a kinship group or ethnic enclave, but as individual others; originating sources of insight and choice. Such persons are not isolated and alien from one another. Sympathy, cooperation, and association are to them as natural, and as necessary, as breathing air. Yet when they form communities, they *choose* them, *elect* them, *contract* for them. The natural state of political community for persons is arrived at not by primordial belonging but by constitutional compact. Before the human race chose its communities, it had only a form of *pietas,* a type of *amor,* love of country.

It had not yet glimpsed the possibility of *dilectio*. Even primordial love of country is good. But choice, compact, election, is better. In this scheme, the individual is not atomic. Although the individual is an originating source of insight and choice, the fulfillment of the individual lies in a beloved community. Yet any community worthy of such love values the singularity and inviolability of each person. Without true individualism, there is no true community.

In the economic sphere, creation is to be fulfilled through human imitation of the Creator. Creation is no morality play. Nor is it a Panglossian perfect harmony. Many species perished in its evolutionary emergence, and within each species countless individuals have been untimely stricken. Winds have eroded fertile lands. Ice has covered the earth. Rushing waters have eaten away entire territories. Earthquakes, tornadoes, and volcanic ash have wreaked their havoc. The earth bears many scars that antedate the emergence of humankind. The beasts of the jungle are hardly kind to one another. Yet in the caves one is right to imagine that human beings loved one another as well as slew one another. Not so high as the angels, not so low as the beasts, the creation of humans is the most wondrous act of the Creator. Respecting liberty, the Creator allowed sin.

The problem for a system of economy is how to unleash human creativity and productivity while coping realistically with human sinfulness. To love humans as they are is to accept them in their sinfulness, while seeking a way to transform such sinfulness into creative action for the commonweal. Some argue that the best way to do this is to appeal to social solidarity and high moral ideals. They erect economic systems accordingly. Others hold that the common good is better served through allowing each individual to work as each judges best and to keep the rewards of such labor. For them, the profit motive is designed to inspire a higher level of common benefit by respecting the individual judgment of economic agents. The more the latter risk and invest, the greater return they may gather in. Most will not be selfish with this return; most will share it liberally. If they bury their talent, or squander it, that is their choice; they will hardly be thought to be good stewards. The idea is that greater incentives will stimulate greater economic activism. The more economically active most citizens are, the greater should be the common prosperity.

According to socialist theory, the rich get richer and the poor get poorer. The implication is that the poverty of the poor is caused by the wealth of the wealthy. The theory of democratic capitalism is quite different. It holds that economic activism creates wealth, and that the broader the stimulation of economic activism the greater the wealth created. It does not hold that economic activists are equal in talent, judgment, exertion, or luck, nor does it expect equal outcomes. Yet it does hold that economic activism, whether on the part of a few or on the part of many, benefits not only its agents but the entire community.

A system of political economy imitates the demands of *caritas* by reaching out, creating, inventing, producing, and distributing, raising the material base of the common good. It is based on realism. It respects individuals as individuals. It makes communal life more active, intense, voluntary, and multiple. An economic system which makes individuals dependent is no more an example of *caritas* than is a lover whose love encourages dependency. A collectivist system which does not respect individuals as originating sources of insight and choice is no more an example of *caritas* than is a beehive or a herd of cattle.

The highest goal of the political economy of democratic capitalism is to be suffused by *caritas*. Within such a system, each person is regarded as an originating source of insight, choice, action, and love. Yet each is also a part of all the others. The goal of the republic is to inspire in each and every citizen the desire to become all that each can become, as the motto of New York State—"Excelsior!"—succinctly expresses. A cognate goal is to inspire the disciplines of realistic judgment: "Confirm thy soul in self-control!" as the hymn puts it. The vision is that of a republic of independent, self-reliant, fraternal, and cooperative citizens, each of whose interests includes the interests of all in brotherhood "from sea to shining sea."

Under external assault and adversity, citizens forget petty contentions and are naturally drawn together. It is less easy for a pacific republic to maintain its unity. Under conditions of prosperity, the same diverse interests that defend all against the tyranny of the few tend to block the full unity of the many. Hence a democratic capitalist republic, in its pluralism, is nearly always in disequilibrium. Neither its political system nor its economic system nor its moral-cultural system can function as they are intended to function without the leadership which draws on the ideals of fraternity and community and inspires all to self-sacrifice for the common good.

Caritas is at one and the same time an ideal of individual autonomy—respecting the good of the other as other—and an ideal of community. It is the spiritual ideal which attracts from afar the only approximating drives of a democratic polity, a capitalist economy, and a liberal pluralist moral-cultural system. It is the spiritual ideal whose betrayal most injures the system in its every part. It is not an easy ideal to realize. That is why the institutions which try to approximate it in practice are best guided by the motto "In God we trust," for no lesser source suffices for its full self-realization. Renewal, reform, and self-transformation are, in the light of that transcendent ideal always called for.

3
Under God

All things considered, democratic capitalism will carry a heavy burden to Judgment Day. Its fundamental structure has proved to be productive, its liberties are broad; consequently, its responsibilities are many. Had the experiment failed, had the United States remained a primitive country, badly governed, surly and anarchic, the world might love it more. If the United States were unable to govern itself, the world could scarcely look to it for leadership. If the United States were still poor, no others could blame it for their own poverty. A former colony like other former colonies, it might be eligible for help from the World Bank.

But the United States is not stricken weak with poverty. Its system has been productive beyond compare. Its experiment has (so far) worked. Its people are free. Its burden of responsibility is, therefore, higher.

In this book, I have not been concerned to pass judgment on the practice of capitalism. I have been concerned to grasp the

ideals latent in its practice. This procedure seems to me legitimate. There are hundreds of books about the ideals of socialism,
many of them written before there was even a single instance of
socialist practice, many others written by ignoring socialist practice. If it is legitimate for socialists to dream and to state their
ideals, it is also legitimate for democratic capitalists to dream and
to state our ideals. One must compare ideals with ideals, practice
with practice.

Some will retort that the real world of democratic capitalism is
harsher and more evil than I describe. The question is, By which
standards should we *judge* harshness and evil? In order to judge
the practice of democratic capitalism severely but fairly, the first
step is to judge it in the light of its own ideals. These must first be
stated. They are latent in its own practice; they do not have to be
pulled out of the sky.

To say that democratic capitalism does not meet the ideals of
socialism is plainly inadequate. It does not even attempt to do so.
It has its own ideals. Whether in *practice* it achieves, as well, the
ideals of socialism—and does so better than any extant socialist
state—is an empirical question. Someone should assemble the
evidence to answer it.

Nor does it suffice to say that democratic capitalism does not
measure up to the full standards of Jewish and Christian visions
of the Kingdom of God. It does not pretend to do so. No political
economy dares to pretend that it measures up to that Kingdom.
Yet democratic capitalism does welcome judgment under that
Kingdom's clear light. For it is a system designed to be constantly
reformed and transformed, and it alone of all known systems has
within it resources for transformation through peaceful means.

In the light of its own ideals, criticism of democratic capitalism
is both possible and necessary. Undoubtedly, the system has failed
its own ideals, in large ways and in small. It is designed to
be a free system within which individuals, interest groups, and
moral minorities may try to direct it according to their lights.
"Many things," Shakespeare writes in *Henry V,* "may work
contrariously."

Almighty God did not make creation coercive, but designed it
as an arena of liberty. Within that arena, God has called for
individuals and peoples to live according to His law and inspiration. Democratic capitalism has been designed to permit them,

sinners all, to follow this free pattern. It creates a noncoercive society as an arena of liberty, within which individuals and peoples are called to realize, through democratic methods, the vocations to which they believe they are called.

Under God, they may expect to meet exact and just judgment.

NOTES

INTRODUCTION

[1]Karl Marx and Frederick Engels, *The Communist Manifesto* (New York: International Publishers, 1948), pp. 13–14.

[2]See Max Weber, *The City,* trans. D. Martindale and G. Neuwirth (New York: The Free Press, 1958), p. 94.

[3]In conceptual logic, *socialism* and *democracy* are mutually compatible. The problem of realizing both at the same time arises from the conditions of actual history. In the real world, a socialism which is rationally planned and coercively imposed by a state bureaucracy is not likely to arise from popular interests, unless one supposes an incredibly passive, docile, and homogeneous populace. Another type of socialism, decentralized and participatory, must deal with the refractoriness of individual agents and groups. If it reconciles diverse interests, it is unlikely to be "rational." If it is "rational," it is unlikely to express diverse interests. Thus democratic socialism, while possible in the world of logic, appears to be incoherent in actual history.

By contrast, *democracy* and *markets* do not mutually entail each other in the world of conceptual logic. One may imagine democracy without markets, and a market system without democracy. But in the real world of actual experience, a polity which recognizes individual rights is bound to be drawn to an economic system which empowers individual agency. Similarly, an economic system based upon markets and individual incentives is, over time, bound to be drawn to a political system recognizing individual rights and liberties.

I call such entailments "dialectical," to suggest the tendencies and preconditions which are operative in the real world of history, as distinct from the merely conceptual necessities of the world of logic.

[4]Robert Lekachman writes: "Political democracy seems to be consistent only with some versions of capitalism. Capitalism, embarrassingly, flourishes in places like Chile, Brazil, South Korea, Taiwan, the Philippines, Indonesia, and other bastions of repression. In the past, it has been comfortable in fascist Italy, Spain, Portugal, Greece and elsewhere. In short, capitalism has certainly existed without political democracy and without free play for intermediate organizations. In fairness, of course, one must say that it is difficult to find examples of democratic socialism without some significant degree of capitalism." "The Promise of Democratic Socialism," in *Democracy and Mediating Structures,* ed. Michael Novak (Washington: American Enterprise Institute, 1980), p. 35.

The nations Professor Lekachman points to are not fully formed examples of democratic capitalism. Their economic systems may be more

free than their political systems, although even the latter, as he generously suggests, provide a wider range of liberties than those available in
neighboring socialist societies (North Korea, Cuba, etc.). Their political
authoritarianism, however, diminishes liberty, social mobility, and the
circulation of elites. Their typical patterns of corruption, favoritism,
nepotism, and other vices violate economic and moral ideals. Thus, to
liberate the economy from the state is a necessary but not a sufficient
step toward the attainment of fully formed democratic capitalism.

It is true that in Germany, for example, a certain form of capitalism
has survived for more than a hundred years under regimes as various
as those of Bismarck, the Kaiser, the Weimar Republic, National
Socialism, and the Federal Republic of Germany. Still, the economic
liberties presupposed in a genuinely broad diffusion of capitalism are
best served by the political liberties and individual rights guaranteed
under democracy.

In Great Britain, the historical situation seems to have been in some
ways the reverse: First there was democracy and, only gradually, capitalism. Still, the political liberties which were so long the rights of
Englishmen had as their natural expression the broadening of such rights
in the economic sphere. Economic rights and liberties could not forever
be beholden to charters and privileges meted out solely by the Crown.
There are many interpretations as to how and why capitalism first arose
in Great Britain. Yet rights in the political sphere seem also to have
encouraged limits upon the state in the economic sphere.

My intention is not to simplify the many underlying schemes of causation, but only to call attention to the underlying consonance of political
and economic liberties, and to note, further, their common source in
liberties of conscience, morals, and culture.

[5]Henry Hazlitt, *The Conquest of Poverty* (New Rochelle, N.Y.: Arlington
House, 1973), pp. 13–18.

[6]See Paul Johnson, "Has Capitalism a Future?" in *Will Capitalism Survive?* ed. Ernest W. Lefever (Washington, D.C.: Ethics and Public Policy
Center, 1979), p. 5.

[7]Oscar Handlin, "The Development of the Corporation," in *The Corporation: A Theological Inquiry,* eds. Michael Novak and John W.
Cooper (Washington, D.C.: American Enterprise Institute, 1981), p. 2.

[8]Johnson, "Has Capitalism a Future?"

[9]"One of the merits of the factory system was that it offered, and
required, regularity of employment and hence greater stability of consumption. During the period 1790–1830 factory production increased
rapidly. A greater proportion of the people came to benefit from it both
as producers and as consumers. The fall in the price of textiles reduced
the price of clothing. . . . Boots began to take the place of clogs, and
hats replaced shawls, at least for wear on Sundays. Miscellaneous commodities, ranging from clocks to pocket handkerchiefs, began to enter
into the scheme of expenditure, and after 1820 such things as tea and
coffee and sugar fell in price substantially. . . . In 1837 or 1838 Thomas
Holmes, an old man of eighty-seven born in 1760 [*sic*], gave . . . his
impressions of the changes that had taken place since his youth . . .

'There has been a very great increase in the consumption of meat, wheaten bread, poultry, tea and sugar. But it has not reached the poorest, except tea, sugar and wheaten bread. The poorest are not so well fed. But they are better clothed, lodged and provided with furniture, better taken care of in sickness and misfortune. So they are gainers.' " T. S. Ashton, "The Standard of Life of the Workers in England, 1780–1830," in *Capitalism and the Historians,* ed. F. A. Hayek (Chicago: University of Chicago Press, 1954), pp. 152–54, n. 26.

[10]In March 1925, receiving Monsignor Joseph Cardijn of Belgium. See John Tracy Ellis, *American Catholicism* (Chicago: University of Chicago Press 1956), p. 106.

[11]"J. B. Bury, in his *Idea of Progress,* also denied the existence of the idea of progress in Greek and Roman thought (and in Christian thought as well) on the grounds, first, that their philosophers lacked awareness of a long historical past within which progress could be discerned; second, that they were victims of their own belief in a theory of historical degeneration (with the story of mankind perceived as one long decline from an original golden age); and third, that Greek and Roman philosophers were generally committed to an envisagement of human history as endlessly and recurrently cyclical, thus making any thought of linear advancement through the ages quite impossible. . . . Weighty testimony indeed. But the truth, I believe, lies in the opposite corner." Robert Nisbet, *History of the Idea of Progress* (New York: Basic Books, 1980), pp. 10–11.

[12]Jacques Maritain, *Reflections on America* (New York: Charles Scribner's Sons, 1958), p. 118.

[13]Irving Kristol, *Two Cheers for Capitalism* (New York: Basic Books, 1978), pp. 262, 270.

[14]See Jacques Maritain, *Integral Humanism,* trans. Joseph W. Evans (New York: Charles Scribner's Sons, 1968); *Christianity and Democracy,* trans. Doris C. Anson (New York: Charles Scribner's Sons, 1944); *The Person and the Common Good,* trans. John J. Fitzgerald (New York: Charles Scribner's Sons, 1947); and *Man and the State* (Chicago: University of Chicago Press, 1951).

In 1958, Maritain wrote: "I would like to refer to one of my books, *Humanisme Intégral,* which was published twenty years ago. When I wrote this book, trying to outline a concrete historical ideal suitable to a new Christian civilization, my perspective was definitely European. I was in no way thinking in American terms, I was thinking especially of France, and of Europe, and of their historical problems, and of the kind of concrete prospective image that might inspire the activity, in the temporal field, of the Catholic youth of my country.

"The curious thing in this connection is that, fond as I may have been of America as soon as I saw her, and probably because of the particular perspective in which *Humanisme Intégral* was written, it took a rather long time for me to become aware of the kind of congeniality which existed between what is going on in this country and a number of views I had expressed in my book.

"Of course the book is concerned with a concrete historical ideal which is far distant from any present reality. Yet, what matters to me is the *direction* of certain essential trends characteristic of American civilization. And from this point of view I may say that *Humanisme Intégral* appears to me now as a book which had, so to speak, an affinity with the American climate by anticipation." Maritain, *Reflections on America,* pp. 174–75 (italics his).

[15] See John Courtney Murray, S.J., *We Hold These Truths* (New York: Sheed & Ward, 1960); and Walter Lippmann, *The Public Philosophy* (New York: New American Library, 1955). Reinhold Niebuhr wrote: "If the experiences of America as a world power, its responsibilities and concomitant guilt, its frustration and its discovery of the limits of power, constitute an ironic refutation of some of the most cherished illusions of a liberal age, its experiences in domestic politics represent an ironic form of success. Our success in establishing justice and insuring domestic tranquility has exceeded the characteristic insights of a bourgeois culture. Frequently our success is due to social and political policies which violate and defy the social creed which characterizes a commercial society." *The Irony of American History* (New York: Charles Scribner's Sons, 1952), p. 89.

European writers have also tried to capture the unique American spirit. See Jean-Francois Revel, *Without Marx or Jesus,* trans. J. F. Bernard (New York: Doubleday, 1971), chaps. 1, 14, 16; Raymond L. Bruckberger, *Image of America* (New York: Viking Press, 1959); and J.-J. Servan-Schreiber, *The American Challenge,* trans. Ronald Steel (New York: Avon, 1969).

[16] Joseph Gremillion, *The Gospel of Peace and Justice* (Maryknoll, New York: Orbis Books, 1976), p. 35.

[17] See Arthur McGovern, S.J., *Marxism: An American Christian Perspective* (Maryknoll, New York: Orbis Books, 1980). Official Protestant documents on political economy from the World Council of Churches and National Council of Churches include "Report on Church, Community and State in Relation to the Economic Order," in *The Churches Survey Their Task,* ed. J. H. Oldham (London: Allen & Unwin, 1937), pp. 87–129; "The Church and the Disorder of Society," in *First Assembly of the World Council of Churches: Amsterdam, Holland, August 22nd–September 4th, 1948* (Geneva, Switzerland: World Council of Churches, 1948), pp. 39–47; "Economic Development in a World Perspective," in *World Conference on Church and Society: Geneva, July 12–26, 1966* (Geneva, Switzerland: World Council of Churches, 1967), pp. 51–93; National Council of Churches, "Christian Concern and Responsibility for Economic Life in a Rapidly Changing Technological Society," New York, February 24, 1966 (mimeographed); and National Council of Churches, "World Poverty and the Demands of Justice," New York, February 20, 1968 (mimeographed). Recent critiques of the official Protestant agencies include Ernest W. Lefever, *Amsterdam to Nairobi: The World Council of Churches and the Third World* (Washington, D.C.: Ethics and Public Policy Center, 1979); Edward Norman, *Christianity and the World Order* (New York: Oxford Univ. Press, 1979).

[18] See, by contrast, the essays by Joseph Ramos et al. in Michael Novak,

ed., *Liberation South, Liberation North* (Washington, D.C.: American Enterprise Institute, 1981).

[19]Michael Novak, *The Guns of Lattimer* (New York: Basic Books, 1978).

[20]Michael Novak, *A Time to Build* (New York: Macmillan, 1967); and *The Open Church* (New York: Macmillan, 1964).

[21]See, for example, Richard M. Griffiths, *The Reactionary Revolution: The Catholic Revival in French Literature* (New York: Frederick Ungar, 1965).

[22]Reinhold Niebuhr, *Man's Nature and His Communities* (New York: Charles Scribner's Sons, 1965), p. 19.

[23]McGovern, *Marxism: An American Christian Perspective,* p. 135.

[24]Walter Lippmann notes, for example: "It was no accident that the century which followed the intensified application of the principle of the division of labor was the great century of human emancipation. In that period chattel slavery and serfdom, the subjection of women, the patriarchal domination of children, caste and legalized class privileges, the exploitation of backward peoples, autocracy in government, the disfranchisement of the masses and their compulsory illiteracy, official intolerance and legalized bigotry, were outlawed in the human conscience, and in a very substantial degree they were abolished in fact." *An Inquiry into the Principles of the Good Society* (Boston: Little, Brown and Co., 1937), pp. 192–93. Other volumes important to a revised history are: F. A. Hayek, ed., *Capitalism and the Historians* (Chicago: University of Chicago Press, 1954); Ludwig von Mises, *The Anti-Capitalistic Mentality* (South Holland, Ill.: Libertarian Press, 1972): Earnest van den Haag, ed., *Capitalism: Sources of Hostility* (New Rochelle, N.Y.: Epoch Books, 1979); Michael Novak, ed., *The Denigration of Capitalism: Six Points of View,* especially the chapter by Edward R. Norman, "Denigration of Capitalism: Current Education and the Moral Subversion of Capitalist Society," pp. 7–23; and George J. Stigler, "The Intellectual and the Market Place," *New Industrialist Review* 2 (Autumn 1962): 3–9.

[25]"I readily agree the contemplation of his works gives us occasion to admire, revere, and glorify their Author: and, if rightly directed, may be of greater benefit to mankind than the monuments of exemplary charity that have at so great charge been raised by the founders of hospitals and almshouses. He that first invented printing, discovered the use of the compass, or made public the virtue and right use of *kin kina* [quinine], did more for the propagation of knowledge, for the supply and increase of useful commodities, and saved more from the grave, than those who built colleges, workhouses, and hospitals." John Locke, *An Essay Concerning Human Understanding,* 2 vols. (New York: Dover, 1959), II: 352. For a discussion of Locke's views of resources and economic development, see Robert A. Goldwin, "Locke and the Law of the Sea," *Commentary,* June 1981, pp. 46–50.

CHAPTER I: WHAT IS DEMOCRATIC CAPITALISM?

[1]Bogdan Denitch, untitled essay, in Robert L. Heilbroner et al., "What Is Socialism?" *Dissent* 25 (Summer 1978): 353.

[2]Michael Harrington, in Heilbroner et al., "What Is Socialism?" p. 357.

[3]J. H. Oldham, ed., *The Churches Survey Their Task* (London: Allen & Unwin, 1937), pp. 104–05.

[4]See R. H. Tawney, *Religion and the Rise of Capitalism* (New York: Harcourt, Brace & Co., 1926); and Max Weber, *The Protestant Ethic and the Spirit of Capitalism*, trans. Talcott Parsons (New York: Charles Scribner's Sons, 1958), p. 181.

[5]"Religious socialism calls the capitalistic system demonic, on the one hand, because of the union of creative and destructive powers present in it; on the other, because of the inevitability of the class struggle independent of subjective morality and piety. The effect of the capitalist system upon society and upon every individual in it takes the typical form of 'possession,' that is, of being 'possessed'; its character is demonic." Paul Tillich, *Political Expectation*, ed. J. L. Adams (New York: Harper & Row, 1971), p. 50.

[6]I am indebted to Arthur Mitzman's *The Iron Cage: An Historical Interpretation of Max Weber* (New York: Knopf, 1970) for most of the biographical details that follow.

[7]Useful samplings of such bibliography may be conveniently found in S. N. Eisenstadt, ed., *The Protestant Ethic and Modernization* (New York: Basic Books, 1968), pp. 385–400; David Little, *Religion, Order, and Law* (New York: Harper & Row, 1969), pp. 226–237. See also the introductions to various editions of Weber's work, especially R. H. Tawney, "Foreword," *The Protestant Ethic and the Spirit of Capitalism* (New York: Charles Scribner's Sons, 1958); and Anthony Giddens, "Introduction," *The Protestant Ethic and the Spirit of Capitalism* (New York: Charles Scribner's Sons, 1976). Among the strongest critics of Weber's thesis are Kurt Samuelson, *Religion and Economic Action*, trans. E. G. French (New York: Harper & Row, 1964); and Jacob Viner, *Religious Thought and Economic Society* (Durham, N.C.: Duke University Press, 1978). The best single essay on the subject, in my view, is H. R. Trevor-Roper, "Religion, the Reformation and Social Change" in *The European Witch-Craze of the Sixteenth and Seventeenth Centuries and Other Essays* (New York: Harper & Row, 1969), pp. 1–45.

[8]In a somewhat different context, Locke observes: "He who appropriates land to himself by his labor does not lessen but increase the common stock of mankind. For the provisions serving to the support of human life produced by one acre of enclosed and cultivated land are (to speak much within compass) ten times more than those which are yielded by an acre of land of an equal richness lying waste in common. And therefore he that encloses land, and has a greater plenty of the conveniences of life from ten acres than he could have from a hundred left to nature, *may truly be said to give ninety acres to mankind.*" John Locke, *Second Treatise of Civil Government* (New York: Macmillan, 1947), p. 20 (italics his). In reality, Locke observes, the ratio is closer to one hundred to one.

[9]Montesquieu, *Esprit des Lois*, Book XX, chap. 7; quoted in Weber, *Protestant Ethic*, p. 45. On the differences between the Continental and

the Anglo-Scot Enlightenment toward religion, and the difference it made, see Irving Kristol, in *Capitalism and Socialism: A Theological Inquiry,* ed. Michael Novak (Washington, D.C.: American Enterprise Institute, 1979), pp. 17–19.

[10]Benjamin Franklin, *The Autobiography of Benjamin Franklin* (New York: Washington Square Press, 1955), p. 102.

[11]"We have no intention whatever of maintaining such a foolish and doctrinaire thesis as that the spirit of capitalism . . . could only have arisen as the result of certain effects of the Reformation, or even that capitalism as an economic system is a creation of the Reformation. . . . We only wish to ascertain whether and to what extent religious forces have taken part in the qualitative formation and quantitative expansion of that spirit over the world." Weber, *The Protestant Ethic,* p. 91.

[12]Ibid., p. 17 (italics his). Weber notes that the drive to "better one's condition" is not always ardent. "Since the interest of the employer in a speeding-up of harvesting increases with the increase of the results and the intensity of the work, the attempt has again and again been made, by increasing the piece-rates of the workmen, thereby giving them an opportunity to earn what is for them a very high wage, to interest them in increasing their own efficiency. But a peculiar difficulty has been met with surprising frequency: raising the piece-rates has often had the result that not more but less has been accomplished in the same time, because the worker reacted to the increase not by increasing but by decreasing the amount of his work." Ibid., pp. 59–60.

[13]The references that follow are to Weber, *The Protestant Ethic,* pp. 17–27.

[14]How many nations at the present time might be classified as democratic capitalist? A useful survey of the approximately 160 independent nations in the world is provided each year by Freedom House. Each year, the Freedom House survey classifies these nations by type of political economy. It then ranks the degree of civil liberties and political liberties achieved within each of them on a scale from one to seven. Based upon the Freedom House definitions, descriptions, and typologies, the following nations are truest to the ideal type of a democratic capitalist society: Australia, Belgium, Canada, Cyprus, West Germany, Lebanon (before its dismantling), Switzerland, and the United States. The other multi-party democracies, somewhat more centralized, are: Bahamas, Barbados, Colombia, Costa Rica, Djibouti, Dominican Republic, France, Greece, Grenada, Iceland, Ireland, Italy, Japan, Luxembourg, Mauritius, New Zealand, Spain, Surinam, Trinidad and Tobago, and Upper Volta. Among "capitalist-socialist" nations which somewhat grudgingly recognize capitalism as legitimate, Freedom House lists Austria, Denmark, Finland, Israel, the Netherlands, Norway, Portugal, Sweden and the United Kingdom. Nearly all such civil liberties and political liberties as exist on this planet are to be found in the nations on these short lists. See the longer discussion in Raymond D. Gastil, ed., *Freedom in the World: Political Rights and Civil Liberties* (New York: Freedom House, 1980), pp. 40–41.

[15]Robert Heilbroner is brutally frank about the loss of liberties to be

expected even under democratic socialism: "Capitalism alone exposes its constituents to the anxiety of life without the succor of a collective morality. One can argue that the repair of these damages is worth far more than the curtailment of economic freedom or the diminution of personal liberty that socialism will require. . . . A generation accustomed to the supporting discipline of socialism will not miss [the liberties] of bourgeois individualism. . . . Nor can we wriggle off this hook by asserting that, among its moral commitments, socialism will choose to include the rights of individuals to their Millian liberties. For that celebration of individualism is directly opposed to the basic socialist commitment to a deliberately embraced collective moral goal. . . . Because socialist society aspires to be a good society, all its decisions and opinions are inescapably invested with moral import. Every disagreement with them, every argument for alternative policies, every nay-saying voice therefore raises into question the moral validity of the existing government. . . . Dissents and disagreements thereby smack of heresy in a manner lacking from societies in which expediency and not morality rules the roost." Robert L. Heilbroner, "What Is Socialism?" *Dissent* 25 (Summer 1978): 346–48.

CHAPTER II: PLURALISM

[1]The precise characteristics of this *spirit* of capitalism were the subject of an extended dialogue between Max Weber and Werner Sombart. See Sombart, *Der moderne Kapitalismus* (1905); and *Der Bourgeois* (1913), which appears in English as *The Quintessence of Capitalism,* trans. M. Epstein (New York: Howard Fertig, 1967); see esp. chap. 19. Also, see Weber, *The Protestant Ethic and the Spirit of Capitalism,* trans. Talcott Parsons (New York: Charles Scribner's Sons, 1958), pp. 63–65; Weber gives detailed replies to Sombart in four lengthy footnotes on pp. 193–204. There is a discussion of the dialogue between Weber and Sombart in Arthur Mitzman, *The Iron Cage: An Historical Interpretation of Max Weber* (New York: Alfred A. Knopf, 1970), pp. 258–61.

[2]Erik Peterson, *Der Monotheismus als politisches Problem* (Leipzig: Jakob Hegmer, 1935). Peterson argues that a political theology of imperialism was eventually undercut by a trinitarian doctrine of God and an eschatological hope which relativized all existing empires. See the discussion of these issues in Jüergen Moltmann, *The Experiment Hope,* trans. M. Douglas Meeks (Philadelphia: Fortress Press, 1975), pp. 106–08.

[3]Aleksandr Solzhenitsyn, *A World Split Apart* (New York: Harper & Row, 1978), pp. 51, 49.

[4]Pius XI, for example, describes as deplorable the "liberalistic tenets of the so-called Manchester School," which he further describes: "This school, forgetful or ignorant of the social and moral aspects of economic activities, regarded these as completely free and immune from any intervention by public authority, for they would have in the market place and in unregulated competition a principle of self-direction more suitable for guiding them than any created intellect which might intervene." *Quad-*

ragesimo Anno, paragraphs 54, 88; see *Seven Great Encyclicals* (Glen Rock, New York.: Paulist Press, 1963), pp. 140, 149–50.

[5]Solzhenitsyn, *A World Split Apart,* p. 51.

[6]So taught St. John of the Cross, whose teaching on the subject I have tried to relate to the cultural context of democratic capitalism in *The Experience of Nothingness* (New York: Harper & Row, 1970).

[7]Peter Berger develops this metaphor in *The Sacred Canopy: Elements of a Sociological Theory of Religion* (Garden City, New York.: Doubleday, 1967). "Every society is engaged in the never completed enterprise of building a humanly meaningful world. . . . Viewed historically, most of man's worlds have been sacred worlds" (p. 27). "If the nomos of a society is to be transmitted from one generation to another, so that the new generation will also come to 'inhabit' the same social world, there will have to be legitimating formulas to answer the questions that, inevitably, will arise in the minds of the new generation. Children want to know 'why.' Their teachers must supply convincing answers. Furthermore, as we have seen, socialization is never completed. Not only children but adults as well 'forget' the legitimating answers. They must ever again be 'reminded' " (pp. 30–31).

[8]Irving Kristol, untitled essay in "The Francis Boyer Lectures on Public Policy," *AEI Public Policy Papers* (Washington, D.C.: American Enterprise Institute, 1981), p. 219. See also C. P. Snow, *The Two Cultures and the Scientific Revolution,* (New York: Cambridge University Press, 1959).

[9]"It is of great importance in a republic not only to guard the society against the oppression of its rulers, but to guard one part of the society against the injustice of the other part. . . . If a majority be united by a common interest, the rights of the minority will be insecure." Alexander Hamilton, John Jay, and James Madison, *The Federalist* (New York: Modern Library, 1941), No. 51, p. 339.

[10]See Jacques Maritain, *The Range of Reason* (New York: Charles Scribner's Sons, 1952), p. 140. In my own writings, see *A Time to Build* (New York: Macmillan, 1967), chap. 17, "The Traditional Pragmatism"; *The Experience of Nothingness,* chap. 3; and *A Theology of Radical Politics* (New York: Herder & Herder, 1969), chaps. 1–3.

[11]Theodore Lowi, *The End of Liberalism* (New York: W. W. Norton, 1969), p. 97.

[12]See John Rawls, *A Theory of Justice* (Cambridge, Mass.: Harvard University Press, 1971), esp. pp. 251–57.

[13]See, for example, the argument for grounding liberalism in conscience in John H. Hallowell, *Moral Foundation of Democracy* (Chicago: University of Chicago Press, 1973), esp. pp. 73ff.

[14]Berlin's text deserves full citation: "One belief, more than any other, is responsible for the slaughter of individuals on the altars of the great historical ideals—justice or progress or the happiness of future generations, or the sacred mission or emancipation of a nation or race or class, or even liberty itself, which demands the sacrifice of individuals for the freedom of society. This is the belief that somewhere, in the past or in the future, in divine revelation or in the mind of an individual thinker, in

the pronouncements of history of science, or in the simple heart of an uncorrupted good man, there is a final solution. This ancient faith rests on the conviction that all the positive values in which men have believed must in the end, be compatible, and perhaps even entail one another." Isaiah Berlin, *Four Essays on Liberty* (New York: Oxford University Press, 1968), p. 167.

[15]Early Christian thinkers faced a difficulty in distinguishing intellectually between what in Jesus Christ was human, what was divine, and what remained constant. Orthodox believers wished to affirm that Jesus is both God and man. To make this clear to themselves, they hit upon this formula: Jesus is one *person* sharing simultaneously in two *natures,* that of other humans and that of God. One can say of him that he is a human *individual* who, like all others, is also a distinctive *person.* "Person" became the preferred term for speaking of the single human being. This is because, in inner life, one person differs from another far more than in bodily presence. We may know an individual for a long time and familiarly without being certain that we have ever plumbed the person. Moreover, with the birth of new insights and new choices, each person may radically alter the direction and meaning of his life. *Person* points to the bottomless capacity of humans to inquire and to choose. In their exercise of these capacities more than any other, humans differ one from another. See Bernard Lonergan, *Divinarum Personarum* (Rome: Gregorianum, 1957); *De constitutione Christi* (Rome: Gregorianum, 1956); and *Verbum: Word and Idea in Aquinas* (Notre Dame, Ind.: University of Notre Dame Press, 1967).

[16]See Albert C. Outler, ed., *John Wesley* (New York: Oxford University Press, 1964), p. 498.

[17]"What is, then, the object of the *secular faith* that we are discussing? This object is a merely practical one, not a theoretical or dogmatic one. The secular faith in question deals with *practical* tenets which the human mind can try to justify—more or less successfully, that's another affair—from quite different philosophical outlooks." Jacques Maritain, *Man and the State* (Chicago: University of Chicago Press, 1951), p. 111.

[18]Ibid (emphasis his).

[19]"But the important thing for the political life of the world and for the solution of the crisis of civilization is by no means to pretend that Christianity is linked to democracy and that Christian faith compels every believer to be a democrat; it is to affirm that democracy is linked to Christianity and that the democratic impulse has arisen in human history as a temporal manifestation of the inspiration of the Gospel. The question does not deal here with Christianity as a religious creed and road to eternal life, but rather with Christianity as leaven in the social and political life of nations and as bearer of the temporal hope of mankind; it does not deal with Christianity as a treasure of divine truth sustained and propagated by the Church, but with Christianity as historical energy at work in the world." Jacques Maritain, *Christianity and Democracy,* trans. Doris C. Anson (New York: Charles Scribner's Sons, 1950), p. 37.

[20]"We may well designate the moral cynics, who know no law beyond

their will and interest, with a scriptural designation of 'children of this world' or 'children of darkness.' Those who believe that self-interest should be brought under the discipline of a higher law could then be termed 'the children of light.' . . . The children of light are virtuous because they have some conception of a higher law than their own will. They are usually foolish because they do not know the power of self-will. They underestimate the peril of anarchy in both the national and the international community. Modern democratic civilization is, in short, sentimental rather than cynical. . . . It does not know that the same man who is ostensibly devoted to the 'common good' may have desires and ambitions, hopes and fears, which set him at variance with his neighbor." Reinhold Niebuhr, *The Children of Light and the Children of Darkness* (New York: Charles Scribner's Sons, 1944), pp. 9–11.

CHAPTER III: EMERGENT PROBABILITY

[1]Thomas Aquinas, *Summa Contra Gentiles,* III: 74: 3, trans. Vernon J. Bourke (Garden City, N.Y.: Doubleday, 1956), Book Three, part I, p. 274.

[2]Bernard J. F. Lonergan, *Insight: A Study of Human Understanding,* rev. ed. (New York: Philosophical Library, 1958); see esp. pp. 121–28. I have also benefited from Michael Polanyi's emphasis upon insight in *Personal Knowledge* (Chicago: University of Chicago Press, 1958) and other books.

[3]Ibid., pp. 596–98.

[4]Ironically, since about 1955, many students of development have forgotten Adam Smith. One British critic describes the situation quite harshly: "The field of development economics, at least as written about by the major stars of the economics profession concerned with it and as taught by their followers in most universities, has been until recently the scientifically weakest and most intellectually dishonest branch of economic studies, dominated by a socialist mythology of poverty applied to the less developed countries by Western intellectuals. . . . The success of capitalism in winning the Second World War and producing unprecedented prosperity and economic growth left these people emotionally unemployed. They easily found new employment by turning to the less developed countries and the problems of development as fodder for the expression of their criticisms of capitalism." Harry G. Johnson, "The Achievement of P. T. Bauer," *Encounter* 39 (November 1972): 64.

[5]See Chapter XVI for a fuller treatment of this point.

[6]"Though the development of economic rationalism is partly dependent on rational technique and law, it is at the same time determined by the ability and disposition of men to adopt certain types of practical rational conduct. . . . We approach the side of the problem which is generally most difficult to grasp: the influence of certain religious ideas on the development of an economic spirit, or the *ethos* of an economic system. In this case we are dealing with the connection of the spirit of modern economic life with the rational ethics of ascetic Protestantism." Max Weber, *The Protestant Ethic and the Spirit of Capitalism,* trans. Talcott

Parsons (New York: Charles Scribner's Sons, 1958), pp. 26–27. Cf. David Little's criticism: "Weber's own conclusion about the association between Puritanism and rational capitalism as stated in *The Protestant Ethic* is, finally, oversimple. . . . Calvinist Puritanism has its own inner dynamics; just as it does not lead automatically to a 'free Church,' neither does it lead automatically to a 'free economy.' . . . We can agree with Weber's conclusions in *The Protestant Ethic* up to a point: when Puritanism appears, there will be special pressure toward voluntary, self-initiated economic behavior." *Religion, Order, and Law* (New York: Harper & Row, 1969), pp. 222–23.

CHAPTER IV: SIN

[1]Thomas Hobbes vividly described the difficulties of establishing social order in his description of the life of man in a mythical state of nature: ". . . no Arts; no Letters; no Society; and which is worst of all, continuall feare, and danger of violent death; and the life of man, solitary, poore, nasty, brutish, and short." *Hobbes's Leviathan,* ed. W. G. Pogson Smith (London: Oxford University Press, 1929; reprint of 1651 ed.), p. 96.

[2]R. H. Tawney, *Equality,* 4th ed. (London: Allen & Unwin, 1952; originally published in 1931), p. 222. Tawney complained that the working class is lacking in moral indignation over the conditions of capitalist society: "As it is, though they resent poverty and unemployment, and the physical miseries of a proletariat, they do not always resent, as they should, the moral humiliation which gross contrasts of wealth and economic power necessarily produce" (p. 29).

[3]Michael Walzer criticizes the meritocratic aspect of democratic capitalism in his *Radical Principles: Reflections of an Unreconstructed Democrat* (New York: Basic Books, 1980); see esp. pp. 250–51. See my review in *Commentary* 71 (February 1981): 78–80.

[4]Charles Péguy once placed these words on the door of his room. Another famous line of his runs: "Socialism is a new life not just a policy" (Letter to Camille Bidault, February 27, 1887). Three useful biographies are Daniel Halévy, *Péguy and the Cahiers de la Quinzaine,* trans. Ruth Bethell (London: Denis Dobson, 1946; translation of the 1919 ed.); Marjorie Villiers, *Charles Péguy: A Study in Integrity* (New York: Harper & Row, 1965); and Hans A. Schmitt, *Charles Péguy: The Decline of an Idealist* (Baton Rouge, La.: Louisiana State University Press, 1967).

[5]For a comparison of the two paths, see Michael Novak, ed., *Liberation South, Liberation North* (Washington, D.C.: American Enterprise Institute, 1981).

[6]Juan Luis Segundo, "Capitalism—Socialism: A Theological Crux," in *The Mystical and Political Dimensions of the Christian Faith,* eds. Claude Geffré and Gustavo Gutiérrez (New York: Herder & Herder, 1974), pp. 105–23. This essay is reprinted in the text cited in the preceding note.

[7]Robert Heilbroner's interpretation of Adam Smith is typical: "As regularly and as inevitably as a series of interlocked mathematical proposi-

tions, society is started on an upward march. . . . In a sense the whole wonderful world of Adam Smith is a testimony to the eighteenth-century belief in the inevitable triumph of rationality and order over arbitrariness and chaos.'' The truth is that Smith's conceptions of rationality and order are simply different from Heilbroner's, and far less utopian. *The Worldly Philosophers*, 5th ed. (New York: Simon & Schuster, 1980), pp. 64, 68.

⁸Late in his career, reconsidering the title of his early classic, *Moral Man and Immoral Society* (New York: Charles Scribner's Sons, 1932), Reinhold Niebuhr wrote: "A young friend of mine recently observed that, in the light of all the facts and my more consistent 'realism' in regard to both individual and collective behavior, a better title might have been *The Not So Moral Moral Man in His Less Moral Communities*." *Man's Nature and His Communities* (New York: Charles Scribner's Sons, 1965), p. 22.

⁹Eric Voegelin, *Order and History*, 4 vols. (Baton Rouge, La.: Louisiana State University Press, 1956–1975); see esp. vol. 1, preface and introduction.

¹⁰See Friedrich A. Hayek, *The Constitution of Liberty* (Chicago: Henry Regnery, 1960), pp. 397–411.

¹¹See Paul Johnson, "Is There a Moral Basis for Capitalism?" in *Democracy and Mediating Structures: A Theological Inquiry,* ed. Michael Novak (Washington, D.C.: American Enterprise Institute, 1980), p. 56.

¹²See Alexis de Tocqueville, *Democracy in America,* ed. J. P. Mayer (Garden City, N.Y.: Doubleday, 1969), pp. 544–46.

¹³See Kathleen Nott, *The Good Want Power: An Essay in the Psychological Possibilities of Liberalism* (New York: Basic Books, 1977).

¹⁴Milton and Rose Friedman, *Free to Choose* (New York: Harcourt Brace Jovanovich, 1980), p. 27.

¹⁵Adam Smith, *The Theory of Moral Sentiments* (Indianapolis: Liberty Classics, 1969), pp. 204, 71.

CHAPTER V: PROVIDENCE AND PRACTICAL WISDOM

¹See Thomas Aquinas, *Summa Contra Gentiles,* III, esp. chap. 64; trans. Vernon J. Bourke (Garden City, N.Y.: Doubleday, 1956), Book 3, part 1, pp. 209–14.

²Benjamin Franklin, *The Autobiography of Benjamin Franklin* (New York: Washington Square Press, 1955), p. 103.

³See Raymond Williams, *Keywords: A Vocabulary of Culture and Society* (New York: Oxford University Press, 1976), pp. 42–44.

⁴See John T. Noonan, Jr., *The Scholastic Analysis of Usury* (Cambridge, Mass.: Harvard University Press, 1957).

⁵See Léo Moulin, *L'Aventure Européenne* (Brussels: De Tempel, 1972), chaps. 4–7. Also: Jacob Viner, *The Role of Providence in the Social Order* (Philadelphia: American Philosophical Society, 1972), chaps. 2 and 3.

⁶See George Gilder, "The Moral Sources of Capitalism," *Imprimis* 9 (December 1980): 1–6; and *Wealth and Poverty* (New York: Basic

Books, 1981), chap. 21. My differences with Gilder are well expressed by Ernest Van den Haas in *Fortune* (July 13,1981), pp. 151–52.

[7]Alexis de Tocqueville, *Democracy in America,* ed. J. P. Mayer (Garden City, N.Y.: Doubleday, 1969), p. 453.

[8]Walter Lippmann, *The Good Society* (New York: Grosset & Dunlap, n.d.), pp. 193–94.

[9]Franklin, *The Autobiography of Benjamin Franklin,* pp. 107–08. Bernard Murchland has commented on the close relationship between existentialism—the philosophy of self-making—and capitalism. Both center on freedom and its risks. See his essay "The Socialist Critique of the Corporation," in Michael Novak and John W. Cooper, eds., *The Corporation: A Theological Inquiry* (Washington, D.C.: American Enterprise Institute, 1981), pp. 167–70.

[10]The routinization of work, leisure, and prayer is a recurring theme, for example, in *The Rule of St. Benedict:* "The abbot shall have the responsibility, day and night, of calling the time for the Divine Office. . . . For all things ought be done at the designated hours. . . . Idleness is an enemy of the soul. Therefore, the brothers should be occupied according to schedule in either manual labor or holy reading." *The Rule of St. Benedict,* trans. Anthony C. Meisel and M. L. del Mastro (Garden City, New York: Image Books, 1975), pp. 85–86.

[11]"Since Judaism made Christianity possible and gave it the character of a religion essentially free from magic, it rendered an important service from the point of view of economic history. For the dominance of magic outside the sphere in which Christianity has prevailed is one of the most serious obstructions to the rationalization of economic life. Magic involves stereotyping of technology and economic relations." Max Weber, *General Economic History,* trans. Frank H. Knight (New York: Collier Books, 1961), p. 265.

[12]P. T. Bauer and John O'Sullivan observe that "economic achievement depends principally on people's attitudes, motivations, mores, and government policies. People in LDC's [less developed countries] may place a high value on factors that obstruct material progress. They may be reluctant to take animal life, they may prefer the contemplative life over an active one, they may oppose paid work by women, or they may simply be fatalistic. If on account of such factors, they are uncongenial to material progress, then external doles will not promote development. For if the conditions for development other than capital are present, the capital will either be generated locally or be available commercially from abroad. If the required conditions are not present, aid will be ineffective and wasteful." "Foreign Aid for What?" *Commentary* 66 (December 1978): 42.

[13]"Economy is essentially the transformation of natural forces and natural goods into forces and goods that serve humanity. It is an order created by thinking people, and one that has developed as a result of people's intellectual and spiritual growth. Further, it should be clear that when we regard economy as the creation of thinking human beings, economic wealth becomes nothing more than the transformation of natural wealth. There is no material wealth except that of nature and that created by

humans from nature." Stephen Roman and Eugen Loebl, *The Responsible Society* (New York: Regina Ryan Books/Two Continents, 1977), pp. 22–23. Chiding Europeans, Jean-Jacques Servan-Schreiber points out that the American character, culture, and educational systems are admirably ordered to experimental intellect and technological innovation. He writes: "Modern power is based on the capacity for innovation, which is research, and the capacity to transform inventions into finished products, which is technology. The wealth we seek does not lie in the earth or in numbers of men or in machines, but in the human spirit. And particularly in the ability of men to think and to create." *The American Challenge,* trans. Ronald Steel (New York: Avon, 1969), p. 240. Relevant examples of creative intelligence can be found in John Chamberlain, *The Roots of Capitalism* (Indianapolis, Ind.: Liberty Press, 1976; reprint of 1959 ed.), pp. 25–27.

[14]John J. McDermott develops an aesthetic of the city in his essay "Nature, Nostalgia and the City," in *The Culture of Experience* (New York: New York University Press, 1976). He writes: "We have failed to articulate our distinctively city experience in aesthetic terms. . . . The city is now our home; in the most traditional and profound sense of the word, it is our land" (pp. 197–99).

[15]U. S. Bureau of the Census, *Statistical Abstract of the United States: 1979,* 100th ed. (Washington, D.C., 1979), tables 58, 1101.

[16]Charles E. Lindblom, *Politics and Markets* (New York: Basic Books, 1978), p. 79.

[17]See Charles E. Lindblom, *The Intelligence of Democracy* (New York: Free Press, 1965); and *A Strategy of Decision* (New York: Free Press, 1963).

[18]"Insofar as intellectuals as a social class are motivated by the intellectual process, their positions might be expected to be as diverse as the different readings possible on the complexities of political issues. . . . Actual studies of opinions among academics, however, show 'exceptionally high correlations among opinions across a broad array of issues.' . . . These cohesive beliefs among intellectuals have been politically to the left of the general public for as long as such surveys have been taken." On experts: "The enormous investment of time and effort required to acquire familiarity with intricate regulations and labyrinthine administrative procedures is unlikely to be made by someone unsympathetic to a program, both because the philosophic or cognitive interest would not be sufficient and because such an investment offers large payoffs only to those whom the bureaucracy would employ as consultants or officials—obviously *not* those unsympathetic to its programs. . . . Under this set of incentives and constraints, it may be a truism that 'all the experts' favor this or that program, but that may indicate very little about its value to the larger society." Thomas Sowell, *Knowledge and Decisions* (New York: Basic Books, 1980), pp. 353, 361.

[19]Ibid., pp. 362–63.

[20]See John Kenneth Galbraith, *American Capitalism* (Cambridge, Mass.: Riverside Press, 1952), pp. 13–17.

[21]See William Jovanovich, "Businesses Catering to Popular Culture Are

Suffering Many Unhappy Returns," *New York Times,* December 26, 1980.

[22]Barbara Ward, *Nationalism and Ideology* (New York: W. W. Norton, 1966), p. 81.

[23]See P. T. Bauer, *Equality, the Third World, and Economic Delusion* (Cambridge, Mass.: Harvard University Press, 1981), pp. 67–68.

[24]"The Cuban governmental structure was faced in 1978 with seemingly unending economic problems, as well as its own inadequacy. . . . In a revealing speech on 24 December 1977, Castro said that some Cuban investment projects had to be 'sacrificed' and that the country was going through a 'period of austerity . . . and [economic] adjustment. . . . Until 1985 we cannot talk about [improving] standards of living, only about consolidation of what we have. . . . For the next seven or eight years, our spendings and investments will be guided by economic, not social, criteria. . . . We have to fight against indolence, bourgeois spirit, delinquency. . . . This generation has to make sacrifices' " (*Granma,* January 2, 1978); George Volsky, "Cuba," *Yearbook on International Communist Affairs, 1979,* ed. Richard F. Staar (Stanford: Hoover Institution Press, 1979), p. 336.

[25]See Weber, *General Economic History,* p. 129.

[26]Henry Fairlie, "Mencken's Booboisie," *Washington Post,* July 27, 1980.

[27]I once uncritically accepted these conventions, writing of "the hollowness of so much of American life; the vacant eyes watching television and drinking beer; the tired eyes of the men on the commuter train; the efficient eyes of the professor and the manager, the sincere eyes of the television politician. Americans . . . do not know who they are, only what they are useful for; they are bored and apathetic because they are manipulated; they are violent because they secretly resent the lies they are forced to live. Unable to live with themselves, Americans level the earth, build and destroy, attempt to master matter and space and human history. Americans play god." Michael Novak, *A Theology for Radical Politics* (New York: Herder & Herder, 1969), p. 28. That this was a superficial, unfair, and ideological description of real Americans became clear to me when I looked more closely at my neighbors and companions and less at literary conventions.

[28]See Andy Stark, "The Public Policy: An Even More Dismal Science," *American Spectator* 14 (January 1981): 26–29.

[29]See *The Theory of Moral Sentiments,* IV, i, 10 and *An Inquiry into the Nature and Causes of the Wealth of Nations,* IV, ii, 9. Irving Kristol notes that "this famous phrase appears only once in *The Wealth of Nations,* and then in the hypothetical mood." "Adam Smith and the Spirit of Capitalism," in *The Great Ideas Today: 1976* (Chicago: Encyclopedia Britannica, 1976), p. 294.

[30]Adam Smith, *An Inquiry into the Nature and Causes of the Wealth of*

Nations, ed. Edwin Cannan (New York: Modern Library, 1937), p. 423.

[31]See Irving Kristol, "The Spiritual Roots of Capitalism and Socialism," in *Capitalism and Socialism: A Theological Inquiry,* ed. Michael Novak (Washington, D.C.: American Enterprise Institute, 1979), p. 1.

[32]See Noonan, *The Scholastic Analysis of Usury,* chap. 3.

[33]Ralph Lerner, "Commerce and Character: The Anglo-American as New-Model Man," *William and Mary Quarterly* 36 (January 1979): 3–26; see p. 5. See also Stephen Miller, "Adam Smith and the Commercial Republic," *Public Interest* 61 (Fall 1980): 106–22. In what follows, I have borrowed extensively from Lerner's argument; for several quotations the author and title only are given, along with the page number of the Lerner article where the quotation appears. For convenient reference, the Lerner article also appears in *Liberation South, Liberation North* (Washington, D.C.: American Enterprise Institute, 1981).

[34]Adam Smith, *The Theory of Moral Sentiments* (Indianapolis: Liberty Classics, 1969), pp. 407, 416.

[35]Ibid., p. 416.

[36]In the New World, two contrasting experiments in political economy caught the attention of Adam Smith. Whereas the colonies of Spain and Portugal in South America imitated the existing social orders of southern Europe, he wrote, the frugal, simple, yet decent civil and ecclesiastical establishments in the North American colonies displayed "an ever memorable example at how small an expense three millions of people may not only be governed, but well-governed." By contrast, the oppressive practices of South America plunged all but a very few into unnecessary poverty. Smith disdained the "numerous race of mendicant friars, whose beggary" placed "a most grievous tax upon the poor people." The elaborate ceremonials of the South American rich perpetuated "ruinous taxes of private luxury" already well known in Europe. Smith, *Wealth of Nations,* p. 541.

[37]Ibid., p. 364.

[38]See de Tocqueville, *Democracy in America,* pp. 400–07. Ralph Lerner properly stresses the deliberate lowliness of the commercial republic: "This way of getting rid of a kind of unreason did not presuppose that men at large would use their reason more. Far from seconding the proud aspirations of Reason to grasp the whole of society and to direct its complex workings in detail, the commercial republicans counseled humility. They thought human behavior was adequately accounted for by dwelling upon the wants by which men are driven—wants that are largely, though not exclusively, physical; wants that cannot in most cases be satisfied. Butchers, bakers, prelates and professors—all could be understood in more or less the same way. Once the similitude of our passions was recognized (however much the objects of those passions varied from man to man), our common neediness and vulnerability became apparent." "Commerce and Character," p. 8.

[39]De Tocqueville, *Democracy in America,* quoted by Lerner, p. 10. Another early visitor to America, J. Hector St. John Crèvecoeur, saw a new type of human being shaped by the new civic order: "Urged by a variety of motives, here they came. Everything has tended to regenerate them; new laws, a new mode of living, a new social system; here they are become men: in Europe they were as so many useless plants; wanting vegetative mould, and refreshing showers, they withered, and were mowed down by want, hunger, and war; but now by the power of transplantation, like all other plants they have taken root and flourish! Formerly they were not numbered in any civil lists of their country, except in those of the poor; here they rank as citizens. By what invisible power has this surprising metamorphosis been performed? By that of the laws and that of their industry. The laws, the indulgent laws, protect them as they arrive, stamping on them the symbol of adoption; they receive ample rewards for their labours; these accumulated rewards procure them lands; those lands confer on them the title of freemen, and to that title every benefit is affixed which men can possibly require. This is the great operation daily performed by our laws." *Letters from an American Farmer* (New York: Fox, Duffield & Co., 1904; reprint of 1782 ed.), pp. 52–53.

[40]De Tocqueville, *Democracy in America,* see Lerner, p. 10.

[41]Charles Francis Adams, ed., *The Works of John Adams,* see Lerner, p. 12.

[42]Montesquieu, *Esprit de lois,* see Lerner, p. 14.

[43]Thomas Paine, "Common Sense," see Lerner, p. 14.

[44]Benjamin Rush, "Of the Mode of Education Proper in a Republic," see Lerner, p. 15.

[45]David Hume, *Essays,* see Lerner, p. 15.

[46]Ibid., see Lerner, p. 15.

[47]Smith, *Wealth of Nations,* p. 385.

[48]Smith, *The Theory of Moral Sentiments,* see Lerner, p. 16.

[49]De Tocqueville, *Democracy in America,* see Lerner, pp. 16–17.

[50]Ibid., p. 404.

[51]Montesquieu, *Esprit de lois,* see Lerner, p. 21.

[52]Smith, *Wealth of Nations,* see Lerner, p. 22. Elsewhere Smith criticizes certain landlords with withering contempt: "All for ourselves, and nothing for other people, seems, in every age of the world, to have been the vile maxim of the masters of mankind." *Wealth of Nations,* pp. 388–89.

[53]"Commerce and manufactures can seldom flourish long in any state which does not enjoy a regular administration of justice, in which the people do not feel themselves secure in the possession of their property, in which the faith of contracts is not supported by law, and in which the authority of the state is not supposed to be regularly employed in enforc-

ing the payment of debts from all those who are able to pay." Smith, *Wealth of Nations*, p. 862.

[54]Smith, *Wealth of Nations*, see Lerner, p. 22.

[55]See Joseph A. Schumpeter, *Capitalism, Socialism and Democracy*, 3d ed. (New York: Harper & Row, 1950), esp. the section entitled "The Sociology of the Intellectual," pp. 145–55.

[56]De Tocqueville, *Democracy in America*, p. 705.

[57]See Paul Johnson, "Has Capitalism a Future?" in *Will Capitalism Survive?* ed. Ernest W. Lefever (Washington, D.C.: Ethics and Public Policy Center, 1979), p. 4.

[58]Jack D. Douglas, "The Welfare State as a Zero-Sum Game," *The Freeman*, July 1980, p. 408.

[59]Thomas Wilson, "Sympathy and Self-Interest," in *The Market and the State*, eds. Thomas Wilson and Andrew S. Skinner (London: Oxford University Press, 1976), p. 77.

[60]Milton and Rose Friedman, *Free to Choose* (New York: Harcourt Brace Jovanovich, 1980), p. 13.

[61]Lester C. Thurow, *The Zero-Sum Society: Distribution and the Possibilities for Economic Change* (New York: Basic Books, 1980), p. 24.

[62]See Erik Erikson, *Identity: Youth and Crisis* (New York: Norton, 1968), pp. 91–107; and *Insight and Responsibility* (New York: Norton, 1964), chap. 4.

[63]John Dewey, *The Quest for Certainty* (New York: Putnam, 1929), esp. chaps. 5, 6, 9. Chaps. 4 and 5 represent one of many excellent contributions to the philosophy of community which democratic capitalism has produced.

[64]The table on p. 380 appears in an appendix to Sylvia Ann Newlett, *The Cruel Dilemmas of Development* (New York: Basic Books, 1980); the figures were compiled from Montek S. Ahluwalia, "Inequality, Poverty and Development," *Journal of Development Economics* 34 (1976): 340–41.

CHAPTER VI: COMMUNITY

[1]Pope Paul VI, *Octogesima Adveniens*, para. 35; in *The Gospel of Peace and Justice*, ed. Joseph Gremillion (Maryknoll, N.Y.: Orbis Books, 1976), p. 501.

[2]See Roger Heckel, S.J., *Self-Reliance* (Vatican City: Pontifical Commission on Justice and Peace, 1978).

[3]Even Karl Marx was honest enough to observe that the possibility of socialism depends upon the prior achievements of the democratic capitalist revolution. See Karl Marx and Friedrich Engels, *The Communist Manifesto* (New York: International Publishers, 1948), chap. 1. The argument culminates with the final words of the chapter: "The advance of industry, whose involuntary promoter is the bourgeoisie, replaces the

THE DISTRIBUTION OF INCOME IN A NUMBER OF UNDERDEVELOPED AND
DEVELOPED COUNTRIES

Underdeveloped Countries	Per Capita Group (1970 U.S.$)	Income Shares				
		Bottom 20%	Second Quintile	Third Quintile	Fourth Quintile	Top 20%
Ecuador	313	2.5	3.9	5.6	14.5	73.5
Kenya	153	3.8	6.2	8.5	13.5	68.0
Mexico	697	4.0	6.5	9.5	16.0	64.0
Brazil	457	3.1	6.9	10.8	17.0	62.2
Turkey	322	3.0	6.5	11.1	18.8	60.6
Ivory Coast	328	3.9	6.2	11.8	20.9	57.2
Philippines	224	3.9	7.9	12.5	20.3	55.4
Developed Countries						
West Germany	3,209	5.9	10.4	15.6	22.5	45.6
Japan	1,713	4.6	11.3	16.8	23.4	43.8
Sweden	4,452	5.4	9.9	17.6	24.6	42.5
United Kingdom	2,414	6.0	12.8	18.2	23.8	39.2
United States	5,244	6.7	13.0	17.4	24.1	38.8
Australia	2,632	6.6	13.5	17.8	23.4	38.7

isolation of the laborers, due to competition, by their revolutionary combination, due to association. The development of modern industry, therefore, cuts from under its feet the very foundation on which the bourgeois produces and appropriates products. What the bourgeoisie therefore produces, above all, are its own grave-diggers. Its fall and the victory of the proletariat are equally inevitable" (p. 21).

[4]See Michael Novak and John W. Cooper, eds., *The Corporation: A Theological Inquiry* (Washington, D.C.: American Enterprise Institute, 1981); and Michael Novak, *Toward a Theology of the Corporation* (Washington, D.C.: American Enterprise Institute, 1981).

[5]See Richard B. Madden, "The Large Business Corporation as a Mediating Structure," in *Democracy and Mediating Structures: A Theological Inquiry,* ed. Michael Novak (Washington, D.C.: American Enterprise Institute, 1980), pp. 121–22. See also Heckel, *Self-Reliance,* pp. 21–23.

[6]See Peter Berger's account of these accusations in *Pyramids of Sacrifice: Political Ethics and Social Change* (Garden City, N.Y.: Doubleday, 1976), chap. 2.

[7]Pius XI argued for a higher, more effective guiding principle than economic liberty alone: "Still less can this function be exercised by the economic supremacy which within recent times has taken the place of free competition: for this is a headstrong and vehement power, which, if it is to prove beneficial to mankind, needs to be curbed strongly and ruled with prudence. It cannot, however, be curbed and governed by

itself. More lofty and noble principles must therefore be sought in order to regulate this supremacy firmly and honestly: to wit, social justice and social charity." Pope Pius XI, *Quadragesimo Anno,* para. 88–89; see *Seven Great Encyclicals* (Glen Rock, N. J.: Paulist Press, 1963), p. 150.

[8]John Barron, *MIG Pilot* (New York: Reader's Digest Press, 1980), p. 162.

[9]"Liberalism has to assume the responsibility for making it clear that intelligence is a social asset and is clothed with a function as public as is its origin, in the concrete, in social cooperation." John Dewey, *Liberalism and Social Action* (New York: Capricorn Books, 1963), p. 67.

[10]Jacques Maritain, *Reflections on America* (New York: Charles Scribner's Sons, 1958), pp. 178–79, 101. Maritain also observed: "This industrial civilization, which I had learned to know in Europe, appeared to me, here, both as gigantically developed (like many things transplanted from Europe over here) and as a kind of ritual dedicated to some foreign goddess. Its inner logic, as I knew it—originally grounded as it was on the principle of the fecundity of money and the absolute primacy of individual profit—was, everywhere in the world, inhuman and materialistic" (p. 21).

[11]While visiting America, Maritain noticed "the sense of human fellowship" prominent in the country, and observed that attributes of "human reliability, good will, devotion, [and] helpfulness" are characteristic of Americans. "Hence, that American kindness which is so striking a feature to foreign visitors. Americans are ready to help. They are on equal terms of comradeship with everybody. And why? Simply because everybody is a human being. A fellow man. That's enough for him to be supposed worthy of assistance and sympathy—sometimes of exceedingly thoughtful and generous attention." *Reflections on America,* pp. 72, 67–68. I have written further on Maritain's views in "The Economic System: The Evangelical Basis of a Social Market Economy," *Review of Politics* 43 (July 1981): 355–80.

[12]See Charles E. Brown, *Personal Recollections of Rev. Charles E. Brown, 1813–1893 (and the Family Record, 1767–1907)* (Ottumwa, Iowa: Ottumwa Stamp Works Press, 1907). Brown writes: "Pioneer life on the far western border had its compensations as well as its hardships, privations and trials. The early settlers were proverbially hospitable. Neighbors were sociable, kindly, sympathetic and helpful; and people who lived this life, as a rule loved it and preferred it to any other" (p. 48). "With our neighbors we at once began work on a log school house, a few rods south of our cabin, where without floor, doors or windows, we opened a Sunday School" (p. 32).

"In 1845 the Maquoketa people began to plan for an Academy, and Mr. Goodenow, always public spirited, generous and enterprising, donated a handsome site for the building. In 1849 the work was taken up and vigorously prosecuted.

"Early in the fall of that year at the instance of the trustees, I went to Eastern New York to solicit funds. Many of the early settlers came from that section and had friends and acquaintances there. . . . Business was dull, times hard and money scarce, and very little could be done in the way of obtaining aid for the Maquoketa Academy. But in spite of discouragement the work went on, and the building, handsome and commodious for the time and place, was completed.

"Mechanics and laborers engaged on the work were boarded in the families of enterprising citizens to help along, the pioneer wives and mothers cheerfully contributing time and toil in the good cause. Competent teachers were employed and many of the children of the Maquoketa settlers laid there the substantial foundation for their education" (pp. 52–53).

[13]David Riesman et al., *The Lonely Crowd* (New Haven, Conn.: Yale University Press, 1961).

[14]See Michael Harrington, *Socialism* (New York: Saturday Review Press, 1972), p. 118.

[15]In 1978 Americans contributed $39.6 billion in private philanthropic funds, including $32.8 billion contributed by individuals, and the remainder by foundations, corporations, and bequests; see U.S. Bureau of the Census, *Statistical Abstract of the United States: 1979,* 100th ed. (Washington, D.C.: 1979), table 582.

[16]See John Barron, *KGB* (New York: Reader's Digest Press, 1974), Appendix C, "Recruiting Americans in the U.S.A. and Third Countries."

CHAPTER VII: THE COMMUNITARIAN INDIVIDUAL

[1]John Lukacs, *The Passing of the Modern Age* (New York: Harper & Row, 1970), p. 195.

[2]See Michael Walzer, *Radical Principles: Reflections of an Unreconstructed Democrat* (New York: Basic Books, 1980), pp. 9, 15.

[3]Ibid., p. 10.

[4]This aspect is especially prominent in *The Theory of Moral Sentiments.* For treatments of this subject see especially Thomas Wilson, "Sympathy and Self-Interest," in *The Market and the State,* eds. Thomas Wilson and Andrew S. Skinner (London: Oxford University Press, 1976), pp. 73–112; and Garry Wills, "Benevolent Adam Smith," *New York Review of Books,* February 9, 1978.

[5]See Wilson, "Sympathy and Self-Interest," pp. 75–78; and Jacob Viner, "Adam Smith and Laisser Faire," in *Adam Smith 1776–1926: Lectures to Commemorate the Sesqui-Centennial of the Publication of the Wealth of Nations* (Chicago, 1928).

[6]Adam Smith, *The Theory of Moral Sentiments* (Indianapolis: Liberty Classics, 1969), p. 71.

[7]Ibid., pp. 203–04.

[8]Ibid., pp. 235–36.

[9]The medieval Scotsman Duns Scotus held that each individual being has a characteristic action which reveals the agency of God. He spoke of the "thisness" of each thing, each itself and no other. Gerard Manley Hopkins delighted in this insight. He spoke, then, of the "inscape" of each thing:

Each mortal thing does one thing and the same:
Deals out that being indoors each one dwells. . . .

In this same Scotland, Adam Smith was also to perceive an "inscape" of human agency, the economic activism by which each human agent defines himself. Emphasis on "thisness" is a celebration of the God of particulars and contingencies. For a useful introduction see John Pick, ed., *A Hopkins Reader* (New York: Oxford University Press, 1953), esp. pp. xvi–xvii.

[10] Smith, *The Theory of Moral Sentiments*, p. 161.

[11] Ibid.

[12] Ibid., p. 162.

[13] See Reinhold Niebuhr, *Moral Man and Immoral Society* (New York: Charles Scribner's Sons, 1932).

[14] This clarification is made by Tom Bethell, "The Death of Keynes: Supply-Side Economics," *National Review*, December 31, 1980, p. 1562.

[15] Smith, *The Wealth of Nations*, p. 14.

[16] Ibid., p. 718.

[17] J. Hector St. John Crèvecoeur, *Letters from an American Farmer* (New York: Fox, Duffield & Co., 1904; reprint of 1782 ed.), p. 55.

[18] James Boswell, *Life of Johnson*, ed. R. W. Chapman (London: Oxford University Press, 1970), p. 597.

[19] Johann Baptist Metz, ed., *Christianity and the Bourgeoisie* (New York: Seabury Press, 1979).

[20] See, for example, Iring Fetscher, "The 'Bourgeoisie' (*Bürgertum*, Middle Class): On the Historical and Political Semantics of the Term," in ibid., pp. 9–10.

[21] See Gregory Baum, "Middle Class Religion in America," in ibid., p. 15. Baum notes that this phrase was originally employed by Marx.

[22] Fetscher, "The 'Bourgeoisie,' " p. 8.

[23] Ibid., pp. 13–14.

[24] See Max Weber, *The City*, trans. Don Martindale and Gertrud Neuwirth (New York: The Free Press, 1958), chap. 2.

[25] "In the bourgeois era, new words entered modern languages and new forms of consciousness were expressed in homes, furnishings, painting and other arts: *Self-love, Self-confidence, self-command, self-esteem, self-knowledge, self-pity;* other words such as *disposition, character, ego, egoism, conscience, melancholy, apathy, agitation, embarrassment, sensible, sentimental,* appeared in English or French in their modern sense only two or three hundred years ago. And as their appearance marked the emergence of something new in the minds of peoples, something new appeared, too, in their daily lives. As the self-consciousness of medieval people was spare, the interiors of their houses were bare, including the halls of nobles and of kings. The interior furniture of houses appeared together with the interior furniture of minds." John Lukacs, *The Passing of the Modern Age*, pp. 198–99.

[26] "By a similar process, the idea of freehold property was established. The freehold was unknown to barbarian Europe; indeed, it was only imperfectly developed in imperial Rome and Byzantium. The church needed it for the security of its own properties and wrote it into the law codes it processed—wrote it, indeed, so indelibly that the freehold sur-

vived and defied the superimposed forms of feudalism. The instrument of the land deed or charter, giving absolute possession of land to a private individual or private corporation, is one of the great inventions of human history. Taken in conjunction with the notion of the rule of law, it is economically and politically a very important one. For once an individual can own land absolutely, without social or economic qualification, and once his right in that land is protected—even against the state—by the rule of law, he has true *security of property.* Once security of property is a fact, the propensity to save—which, as Keynes noted, is exceedingly powerful in man—is enormously enhanced. Not only is it enhanced; it is translated into the propensity to invest." Paul Johnson, "Is There a Moral Basis for Capitalism?" in *Democracy and Mediating Structures,* ed. Michael Novak (Washington, D.C.: American Enterprise Institute, 1980), p. 52.

[27]Two important books on the "invisible poor" were Ralph Ellison's *Invisible Man* in the 1950s and Michael Harrington's *The Other America* in the 1960s. See, by contrast, George Gilder, *Visible Man* (New York: Basic Books, 1978), pp. ix–x.

[28]Gilder, *Visible Man,* p. ix.

CHAPTER VIII: THE FAMILY

[1]Joseph Sobran, "What Is This Thing Called Sex?" *National Review,* December 31, 1980, pp. 1604–05.

[2]See Nathan Kefitz, *Applied Mathematical Demography* (New York: John Wiley & Sons, 1977), chap. 1. Rough estimates for total world population from 8000 B.C. to A.D. 2000 are in the neighborhood of 110 billion. Current world population is approximately 4.4 billion. Of the latter, approximately 37 percent live in countries classified as "free," 21 percent "partly free," and 42 percent "not free." Raymond D. Gastil, ed., *Freedom in the World* (New York: Freedom House, 1980), p. 5. A more recent survey estimates that 9 percent of all humans who have ever lived are alive now. See *The New York Times,* October 6, 1981, p. C-1, reporting on the calculation of Dr. Arthur H. Westing published in the July-August issue of *Bio–Science.*

[3]In a recent survey, 96 percent of Americans polled rated "having a good family life" as "very important" (3 percent said "only somewhat important" and only 1 percent said "not very important"). *The Harris Survey,* No. 1 (January 1, 1981), pp. 1–2.

[4]U.S. Bureau of the Census, *Statistical Abstract of The United States: 1979,* 100th ed. (Washington, D.C., 1979), table 48; and U.S. Bureau of the Census, *Marital Status and Living Arrangements:* March 1978 (Washington, D.C., 1979), tables D, H.

[5]See Mary Jo Bane, *Here to Stay: American Families in the Twentieth Century* (New York: Basic Books, 1976), chap. 1. John Lukacs writes: "The idea of the family in the Middle Ages was much weaker than we are accustomed to think. In any event, it was much different from ours. In the Middle Ages the lives of children were separated from those of their parents; this practice endured for a long time, especially among the

aristocracy and among the poor. The idea that children were full-fledged human beings, that they were entitled to a kind of protected equality within the family, this, too, was the result of the bourgeois spirit. By the seventeenth century it ceased to be customary to entrust children to strangers. As Ariès puts it: 'This return of the children to the home was a great event: it gave the seventeenth-century family its principal characteristic, which distinguished it from the medieval family. The child became an indispensable element of everyday life, and his parents worried about his education, his career, his future. He was not yet the pivot of the whole system, but he had become a much more important character.' " *The Passing of the Modern Age* (New York: Harper & Row, 1970), pp. 200–01; the quotation is from Philippe Ariès, *Centuries of Childhood* (London: 1961).

[6]See David Friedman, *The Machinery of Freedom* (New Rochelle, N.Y.: Arlington House, 1973), esp. the introduction.

[7]See Thomas Sowell, *Race and Economics* (New York: David McKay Co., 1975), pp. 128–38; and Thomas Sowell, ed., *Essays and Data on American Ethnic Groups* (Washington, D.C.: Urban Institute, 1978).

[8]See Michael Novak, *Jonestown* (Washington, D.C.: American Enterprise Institute, 1979).

[9]See Matthew Arnold, *Culture and Anarchy,* ed. J. Dover Wilson (London: Cambridge University Press, 1969), chap. 3.

CHAPTER IX: CONTINUOUS REVOLUTION

[1]Daniel Bell, *The Cultural Contradictions of Capitalism* (New York: Basic Books, 1976), p. 10 (italics his).

[2]Where governmental power impinges on the economic sector, "the disincentives to business are of two kinds: (1) those that affect productivity because they increase the cost of a U.S. product and hence make it less competitive for sale in international trade; (2) those that directly affect the movement of goods in international trade to the disadvantage of a U.S. business concern." Thibaut de Saint Phalle, *U.S. Productivity and Competitiveness in International Trade* (Washington, D.C.: Center for Strategic and International Studies, 1980), p. 74.

[3]U.S. Bureau of the Census, *Statistical Abstract of the United States: 1979,* 100th ed. (Washington, D.C., 1979), table 509.

[4]"The *Fortune* Directory of the 500 Largest Industrial Corporations," *Fortune,* May 5, 1980, p. 275.

[5]See Barbara Blumenthal, "Uncle Sam's Army of Invisible Employees," *National Journal,* May 5, 1979, p. 730.

[6]Bell, *The Cultural Contradictions of Capitalism,* pp. 226–27.

[7]Ben Stein, *The View from Sunset Boulevard* (New York: Basic Books, 1979); see chap. 4, "Businessmen on Television." See also Leonard J. Theberge, ed., *Crooks, Conmen and Clowns: Businessmen in TV Entertainment* (Washington, D.C.: The Media Institute, 1981).

[8]John C. Bennett, "The Cuban Revolution and Liberation Theology: Matters of Principle," *Christianity & Crisis* 40 (July 21, 1980): 207.

[9]See Michael Novak, *The Guns of Lattimer* (New York: Basic Books, 1978).

[10]Charles E. Lindblom, *Politics and Markets* (New York: Basic Books, 1977), p. 356. Lindblom writes: "Polyarchal politics and government in market-oriented systems take on a distinctive structure. There exists a basic governmental mechanism, given by inheritance to each generation of citizens. At any time, that existing mechanism provides a system of controls for controlling authority. The system is a combination of market, privileged business controls in government, and polyarchal politics" (pp. 199–200). "Communist systems, everyone knows, largely refuse to their citizens the civil liberties: freedom of thought, speech, religion, assembly, and movement, as well as privacy. In liberal societies these are all highly valued liberties not only for themselves but also because they are specific requirements for polyarchy. . . . Yet Communists are not foolish in holding that their societies provide freedom of another kind . . . [and] that in the polyarchies men are not really free; they only think they are. A communist intellectual asks: 'What are people free from in the Soviet Union? They are free from exploitation, from all moral oppression, and consequently their thinking and deeds are free from age-old shackles created by the economic, political and moral rule of the exploiters.' It is not a ridiculous argument" (pp. 264–65). In my view, it is the Grand Inquisitor's argument. Lindblom should try it on Solzhenitsyn.

[11]"The *Fortune* Directory," pp. 276–77.

[12]U.S. Department of Health, Education, and Welfare, *Employees in Institutions of Higher Education 1976–77* (Washington, D.C., 1977). These figures represent professional and nonprofessional employee totals only; they do not include students.

[13]"Because of cost efficiencies, corporations create savings and jobs that are not possible for smaller, less competitive enterprises. . . . For any nation to achieve its societal goals, productivity must improve. Individual productivity can improve only so far; then machines and large-scale efficiencies must take over. The Chinese have finally realized the inevitability of this shift. Self-sufficient local economics cannot produce the efficiencies of scale of great industrial concentrations and technological advancement. These efficiencies can only be created by companies of great financial strength, and they can only occur with huge modern facilities.

"Efficiencies of scale make it possible for the large corporation to tackle the challenge of the mediating role. Any organization has to guard against diverting resources that are necessary for its own survival, and the smaller the structure, the more critical is each of its parts. Corporations with large resources can afford to devote more attention to subjects unrelated to bare survival than smaller ones can. For only after survival has been assured can attention be given to perfecting the structure and its environment—including a social climate that encourages the development of the individual abilities a large organization needs to continue to be efficient." Richard B. Madden, "The Large Business Corporation as Mediating Structure," in *Democracy and Mediating Structures,* ed. Michael Novak (Washington, D.C.: American Enterprise Institute, 1980), p. 113.

[14]Richard B. Madden has begun to explore the notion of subsidiarity as it relates to the corporation; see ibid., pp. 121–22, and "The Importance of the Individual—A Basic Challenge of the 1980s," speech to the SRI International 20th Anniversary Client Conference, September 19, 1978. For a treatment of the concept in Catholic social teaching, see the following: Roger Heckel, S.J., *Self-Reliance* (Vatican City: Pontifical Commission on Justice and Peace, 1978), pp. 21–23; Oswald von Nell-Breuning, "Subsidiarity," in *Sacramentum Mundi: An Encyclopedia of Theology*, 6 vols. (New York: Herder and Herder, 1970), VI: 114–16; and Jean-Yves Calvez, S.J., and Jacques Perrin, S.J., *The Church and Social Justice* (London: Burns and Oates, 1961), pp. 317–42.

[15]Charles E. Lindblom, untitled essay, in "Capitalism, Socialism, and Democracy: A Symposium," *Commentary*, April 1978, p. 29.

[16]According to Gallup, 69 percent of Americans are currently members of a church or synagogue, and 40 percent attend services in a typical week. *Religion in America 1981* (Princeton, N.J.: Princeton Religion Research Center, 1981), pp. 4–5. The Gallup Organization has also compiled comparative figures on church/synagogue attendance for the world's youth, who typically attend worship services less frequently than adults. In a survey of eleven nations, Gallup found that a considerably higher percentage of young Americans (18–24 years old) attend weekly services (25 percent) than do youth in any other country except the Philippines (49 percent). *Religion in America 1979–80* (Princeton, N.J.: Princeton Religion Research Center, 1980), pp. 50–57. See also *The Connecticut Mutual Life Report on American Values in the '80s: The Impact of Belief* (Hartford, Connecticut: Connecticut Mutual Life Insurance Co., 1981).

[17]P. T. Bauer, *Dissent on Development* (London: Weidenfeld and Nicolson, 1971) and *Equality, the Third World and Economic Delusion* (Cambridge, Mass.: Harvard University Press, 1981).

[18]P. T. Bauer, "Ali Mazrui, a Prophet out of Africa," *Encounter* 54 (June, 1980): 70, 77.

[19]"Unlike any other type of society, capitalism inevitably and by virtue of the very logic of its civilization creates, educates and subsidizes a vested interest in social unrest. . . . Intellectuals are not a social class in the sense in which peasants or industrial laborers constitute social classes; they hail from all the corners of the social world, and a great part of their activities consists in fighting each other and in forming the spearheads of class interests not their own. Yet they develop group attitudes and group interests sufficiently strong to make large numbers of them behave in a way that is usually associated with the concept of social class." Joseph A. Schumpeter, *Capitalism, Socialism and Democracy*, 3rd ed. (New York: Harper & Row, 1950), p. 146.

[20]See B. Bruce-Briggs, ed., *The New Class?* (New Brunswick, N.J.: Transaction Books, 1979). The notion of the new class was first employed by writers on the left: David T. Bazelon, *Power in America* (New York: New American Library, 1967); John Kenneth Galbraith, *The Affluent Society*, 3d rev. ed. (Boston: Houghton Mifflin, 1976; revision of 1958 edition), chap. 14; Michael Harrington, *Toward a Democratic Left*

(New York: Macmillan, 1968), chap. 10. See also my "Needing Niebuhr Again," *Commentary* 54 (September 1972): 52–60.

CHAPTER X: THE TRANSFORMATION OF SOCIALISM

[1] Leszek Kolakowski, *Main Currents of Marxism,* 3 vols., trans. P. S. Falla (Oxford: Clarendon Press, 1978), III: 523, 525, 530.

[2] See Bernard Murchland, *The Dream of Christian Socialism: An Essay on Its European Origins* (Washington, D.C.: American Enterprise Institute, 1981).

[3] See C. Wright Mills, *The Marxists* (New York: Dell, 1962), chap. 6, "Critical Observations."

[4] See Leszek Kolakowski, "How to be a Conservative-Liberal Socialist: A Credo," *Encounter* 51 (October 1978): 46–47.

[5] See Mihajlo Mihajlov, *Underground Notes* (London: Routledge and Kegan Paul, Ltd., 1977), esp. pp. 105–24.

[6] See Zdenek Mlynar, *Nightfrost in Prague: The End of Humane Socialism,* trans. Paul Wilson (New York: KZRZ Publishers, 1980).

[7] Kolakowski, *Main Currents of Marxism,* III: 529.

[8] "Marxism performs the function of a religion, and its efficiency is of a religious character," Kolakowski writes. "Marxism is a doctrine of blind confidence that a paradise of universal satisfaction is awaiting us just round the corner. Almost all the prophecies of Marx and his followers have already proved to be false, but this does not disturb the spiritual certainty of the faithful, any more than it did in the case of chiliastic sects: for it is a certainty not based on any empirical premises or supposed 'historical laws,' but simply on the psychological need for certainty." Ibid., p. 526.

[9] Ibid.

[10] Ibid., p. 527.

[11] Ibid.

[12] Ibid., pp. 527–28.

[13] Ibid., p. 528.

[14] Ibid.

[15] Ibid., p. 529.

[16] Ibid.

[17] Ibid., "Epilogue," *passim.*

[18] Ibid., p. 529.

[19] Ibid., p. 530.

[20] Ibid., p. 529.

CHAPTER XI: SOCIALISM AS HIGH MINDEDNESS

[1] Leszek Kolakowski, "Introduction," in *The Socialist Idea: A Reappraisal,* eds. Leszek Kolakowski and Stuart Hampshire (New York: Basic Books, 1974), pp. 15–16.

[2] For a record of the entire conference, see Kolakowski and Hampshire, eds., *The Socialist Idea.*

[3] Stuart Hampshire, "Epilogue," in *The Socialist Idea,* eds. Kolakowski and Hampshire, p. 249.

[4]See *supra,* Chapter IV, note 4.

[5]Eugene V. Debs in *Eugene Debs Speaks,* ed. Jean V. Tussey (New York: Pathfinder Press, 1970), p. 22.

[6]Stuart Hampshire identifies socialism with: "more equality, more security, more welfare, more justice, more freedom, more participation in economic decision." See "The Myth of Human Self-Identity" in *The Socialist Idea,* eds. Kolakowski and Hampshire, p. 34.

[7]Jacques Maritain, *Reflections on America* (New York: Charles Scribner's Sons, 1958), pp. 21–22.

[8]"The communists, in fact, are as backward about ecology as they are about women and contraception. But, just as Europeans still believe that Americans are puritanical, they still picture Americans as slaves to 'gadgets' and pollution-creating machines. The truth is that there is no country in the world where automobiles, for example, are treated more like ordinary tools—nor where people drive less like maniacs. Moreover, it is in America that the moral revolution, and the ecological revolution that is part of it, has initiated an era of caution, if not of outright mistrust, with respect to machines and 'the techno-electronic society.' " Jean-François Revel, *Without Marx or Jesus* (New York: Doubleday, 1970), p. 214.

[9]"The anomie, alienation and purposelessness of an individualistic way of life extend far and deep under capitalism, robbing existence of the stabilizing certainties that have guided it under all other forms of social organization." Robert L. Heilbroner, "What Is Socialism?" *Dissent* 25 (Summer 1978): 348. See *supra,* Chapter I, note 15.

[10]For three analyses of literary modernism and adversary culture, see Irving Kristol "The Adversary Culture of Intellectuals," *Encounter* 53 (October 1979): 5–15; Daniel Bell, "Beyond Modernism, Beyond Self," in *The Winding Passage* (Cambridge, Mass.: Abt Books, 1980), pp. 275–302; and Lionel Trilling, *Beyond Culture* (New York: Viking, 1968). Trilling writes: "Any historian of the literature of the modern age will take virtually for granted the adversary intention, the actually subversive intention, that characterizes modern writing—he will perceive its clear purpose of detaching the reader from the habits of thought and feeling that the larger culture imposes, of giving him a ground and a vantage point from which to judge and condemn, and perhaps revise, the culture that produced him. . . . It is a belief still pre-eminently honored that a primary function of art and thought is to liberate the individual from the tyranny of his culture in the environmental sense and to permit him to stand beyond it in an autonomy of perception and judgment. . . . Between the end of the first quarter of this century and the present time there has grown up a populous group whose members take for granted the idea of the adversary culture. This group is to be described not only by its increasing size but by its increasing coherence. It is possible to think of it as a class. As such, it of course has its internal conflicts and contradictions, but also its common interests and presuppositions and a considerable efficiency of organization, even of an institutional kind" (pp. xii–xiii).

[11]"Just think of the monumental deception we had lived with for almost

fifty years. . . . When Marxism-Leninism was in question, a mysterious impunity seemed to preserve it. . . . Here, too, we needed Solzhenitsyn the *zek,* Solzhenitsyn the tramp, to set things straight, to be able to proclaim what appears, once the book is closed, to be obvious, so monumentally obvious that it is astonishing we were able to ignore it for so long. The Soviet camps are Marxist, as Marxist as Auschwitz was Nazi. Marxism is not a science, but an ideology like the others, operating like the others to conceal the truth at the same time that it forms it. The horror is not a deviation, a blemish, an abscess in the body of the proletarian State, but one effect among others of the laws of *Capital.*" Bernard-Henri Levy, *Barbarism with a Human Face,* trans. George Holoch (New York: Harper & Row, 1979), pp. 155–56.
¹²F. A. Hayek, *The Intellectuals and Socialism* (Menlo Park, Cal.: Institute for Humane Studies, 1971), p. 5.
¹³Kolakowski, "Introduction," p. 15.
¹⁴See Irving Howe, ed., *Twenty-Five Years of "Dissent": An American Tradition* (New York: Methuen, 1979), esp. the introduction by Howe.
¹⁵Irving Howe, "Introduction," in *Twenty-Five Years of "Dissent,"* ed. Howe, p. xiv.
¹⁶Ibid., p. xix.
¹⁷Ralf Dahrendorf of the London School of Economics observes: "The welfare state takes a large part of people's earnings and tells them what to spend them on while leaving them only pocket money for their disposal. . . . The day may come on which historians note with surprise how governments came to be expected to deal with virtually every aspect of people's lives until the limits of their arrogance of power were discovered." "Woes of Europe's Bloated Welfare States," *Washington Star,* January 11, 1981; from the European edition of *Time,* January 12, 1981, pp. 32–33.

There are other reasons for finding the democratic socialist program unworkable: (1) Some activists with special talents for declamation, organizing, iron-bottom endurance, and managing public assemblies gain disproportionate political power. (2) Mob passions and public censorship frequently limit which voices may be heard and which opinions may be voiced. (3) The real interests of disparate minorities are exceedingly difficult to respect in participatory gatherings governed by majority sentiment. (4) Local communities and factions thereof differ on crucial issues, so that consensus is difficult to reach in small groups, and is increasingly diluted as it reaches outward to ever more inclusive communities. (5) Thus, at broader regional and national levels, participatory politics resembles negotiation more than participation. (This outcome does not surprise partisans of interest-group politics, but it eviscerates the ideal of participatory politics.) (6) The divergent real interests and diverse capacities of local communities make long-range planning from above unworkable, even in principle. (7) Long-range planning necessarily favors some communities at the expense of others. If it is planning, it cannot be democratic; if it is democratic, it is not planning. If it is more than a suggestion, it is coercive; if coercive, it will tend to represent the most highly organized.

[18]Theodore Jacqueney, "I Want 'Rotten Bourgeois Democracy'!" (An Interview with Rumanian Dissident Paul Goma), *Worldview* 22 (October 1979): 20–23.

[19]Michael Walzer writes: "Market relations are probably defensible under the doctrine of right reasons. Here in the world of the petty-bourgeoisie, it seems appropriate that people able to provide goods or services that are novel, timely, or particularly excellent should reap the rewards they presumably had in mind when they went to work. . . . No one would want to feed blintzes to strangers, day after day, merely to win their gratitude. But one might well want to be a corporation executive, day after day, merely to make all those decisions. It is precisely the people who are paid or who pay themselves vast sums of money who reap all sorts of other rewards too . . . rewards, like the pleasure of exercising power, that are intrinsic to certain jobs . . . prestige, status, deference, and so on. . . . We pay political leaders much less than corporation executives, precisely because we understand so well the excitement and appeal of political office. Insofar as we recognize the political character of corporations, then, we can pay their executives less too." Michael Walzer, *Radical Principles* (New York: Basic Books, 1980), pp. 251–52.

[20]U.S. Internal Revenue Service, *Preliminary Report: Statistics of Income—1978 Individual Income Tax Returns* (Washington, D.C.: 1980), table 2.

[21]See ibid., which includes the following data:

Size of adjusted gross income	Number of returns	Total adjusted gross income ($\times$ $1,000)	Total income tax ($\times$ $1,000)
$100,000–$200,000	285,161	37,471,450	12,908,164
$200,000–$500,000	60,075	16,726,346	6,944,938
$500,000–$1,000,000	6,872	4,572,184	2,112,475
$1,000,000 or more	2,092	4,185,621	2,086,121
TOTALS:	354,200	62,955,601	24,051,698

[22]Colin Welch, "Crosland Reconsidered," *Encounter* 52 (January 1979): 95.

[23]Ibid.

[24]"Are not freedom and independent art and thought in all their variety, the future of *Encounter* itself, if you like, are they not certainly in far less danger if they can rely for their protection and patronage on one or more millionaires of varied interests and tastes or, better still, upon the variously cultivated members of a whole wealthy and leisured class rather than just upon the monopolistic and monopsonistic State alone, which is all that Crosland proposes to leave them?" Ibid., p. 89.

CHAPTER XII: INCOME DISTRIBUTION AND RACE

[1]See Gary MacEoin and Lourdes Arguelles, "The Cuban Revolution and Liberation Theology: Matters of Fact," in *Christianity and Crisis* 40

(July 1, 1980): 210; the wage differential of between 1 to 5 and 1 to 8 in the early 1970s is said to have increased in recent years. Cf. George Volsky, "Cuba," in *Yearbook on International Communist Affairs, 1979,* ed., Richard F. Staar (Stanford, Cal.: Hoover Institution, 1979), who reports that a farm worker in Cuba receives about $120 per month, while a top scientist receives $1,200 per month.

[2]U.S. Bureau of the Census, *Money Income and Poverty Status of Families and Persons in the United States: 1979 (Advance Report)* (Washington, D.C.: 1980), p. 1.

[3]U.S. Internal Revenue Service, *Preliminary Report: Statistics of Income—1978, Individual Income Tax Returns* (Washington, D.C.: 1980), table 4; see *supra,* Chapter XI, note 21.

[4]Ibid. Also: Telephone inquiry, The Tax Foundation, June 6, 1980 (For information on top 2 percent of earners); and "Top Half of Earners Pay 90% of Tax Bill," *Monthly Tax Features* 24 (June–July 1980): 3, which gives the following figures for 1978:

Adjusted gross income class	Income level	Percent of tax paid	Average tax
Highest 10 percent	$29,414 or more	49.7	$10,430
Highest 25 percent	19,860 or more	73.8	6,208
Highest 50 percent	10,960 or more	93.5	3,924
Lowest 50 percent	10,959 or less	6.5	272
Lowest 25 percent	5,039 or less	0.4	32
Lowest 10 percent	1,988 or less	<0.1	6

[5]See Paul Johnson, "Sick Man of the West," *Policy Review* 14 (Fall 1980): 128–39, esp. pp. 136, 139.

[6]See Andrew Brimmer, "Economic Perspectives" and "Facts and Figures," *Black Enterprise* 8 (April 1978): 62, 64; Parke D. Gibson, *Seventy Billion in the Black: America's Black Consumers* (New York: Macmillan, 1978); and Joseph M. Katz, "An Introduction to Market Segmentation and Selected Segments of the American Population," in *Burrell's Special Groups Media Directory,* ed. Nancy Herriman (Livingston, N.J.: Burrell's Media Directories, 1980), pp. 1–11.

[7]Thomas Sowell notes that, formidable barriers notwithstanding, blacks in America have persistently sought education. See Thomas Sowell, *Ethnic America: A History* (New York: Basic Books, 1981), pp. 202–05. See also Sowell's earlier work *Race and Economics* (New York: David McKay, 1975), especially chap. 5, "Comparisons of Ethnic Groups" and *passim.* Also: Thomas Sowell, ed., *Essays and Data on American Ethnic Groups* (Washington, D.C.: Urban Institute, 1978).

[8]See George Gilder, *Wealth and Poverty* (New York: Basic Books, 1980), chaps. 10 and 11; and Michael Novak, "The New Plantation," *Public Welfare* 38 (Fall 1980): 31–35.

[9]See Sowell, *Race and Economics,* pp. 87–88; also Milton and Rose Friedman, *Free to Choose* (New York: Harcourt Brace Jovanovich, 1980), pp. 131–34.

[10]U.S. Bureau of the Census, *Money Income of Families and Persons in the United States: 1978* (Washington, D.C.: 1980), table 13.

[11]U.S. Bureau of the Census, *Statistical Abstract of the United States: 1979*, 100th ed. (Washington, D.C., 1979), table 29.

[12]Alfred Malabre, Jr., "Recession Hits Blacks Harder Than Whites," *Wall Street Journal*, August 21, 1980; and Frederick S. Klein, "Black Families Headed by Women Still Rise," *Wall Street Journal*, August 28, 1980.

[13]Bureau of the Census, *Statistical Abstract of the United States: 1979*, table 223; and Malabre, "Recession Hits Blacks Harder Than Whites."

[14]Bureau of the Census, *Statistical Abstract of the United States: 1979*, table 744. The same table shows a decline in the black/white income ratio from 61 percent in 1970 to 57 percent in 1977. Steven Sandell explains, "The main reason for the decline in the aggregate ratio is that black female-headed families grew by 12 percentage points to 40.5% (between 1970 and 1978) compared to an increase of 2 1/2 percentage points by white female-headed families to 11.6%" "Black-White Income Differences in the '70s," unpublished manuscript, (mimeographed) p. 2.

[15]Bureau of the Census, *Statistical Abstract of the United States: 1979*, table 744.

[16]Sandell, "Black-White Income Differences in the '70s," mimeo table 5.

[17]See Katz, "An Introduction to Market Segmentation," p. 10. See also Ben J. Wattenburg and Richard M. Scammon, "Black Progress and Liberal Rhetoric," *Commentary* 54 (April 1973): 36. Analyzing data from the 1970 census, the authors found that for black families in the North and West in which both husband and wife work and the head of the family is under 35 years of age, the median income in 1970 was 104 percent of that of white families similarly situated. Thus "young married blacks outside of the South, with husband and wife both working, earn as much as or a trifle more than comparable whites."

[18]Ibid.

[19]U.S. Bureau of the Census, *The Statistical History of the United States from Colonial Times to the Present* (New York: Basic Books, 1976), tables A172–94.

[20]Ibid., tables A73–81, A82–90.

[21]See "Black Clout in the Unions," *Ebony*, December 1980.

[22]U.S. Bureau of the Census, *Statistical Abstract of the United States: 1979*, tables 29, 645; and Malabre, "Recession Hits Blacks Harder Than Whites."

[23]Calculation of black population aged 16–19 based on Bureau of the Census, *Statistical Abstract of the United States: 1979*, table 29. Overall percentage of blacks in the military in 1978 was 17.3 percent (table 607). Employment status figures for "black and other" aged 16–19 in 1978 are found in table 650.

[24]Nancy Fisher Schulte, "Illegitimacy Soars, Begets Legacy of Health, Social Hardships," *Chicago Reporter* 9 (June 1980): 1; U.S. Bureau of

the Census, *Statistical Abstract of the United States: 1979*, tables 81, 93, 97. See also George Gilder, *Visible Man* (New York: Basic Books, 1978), chap. 15.

[25]See Sowell, *Race and Economics*, pp. 222, 236.

[26]Congressman Jack Kemp's "Urban and Enterprise Zone Act" is one example. See Stuart Butler, "Urban Renewal: A Modest Proposal," *Policy Review* 13 (Summer 1980): 95–107. Entrepreneurial skills and skills in the managing of small business do not seem to be equally distributed through all ethnic cultures. See, e.g., the comments of P. T. Bauer on an international level, in *Equality, The Third World, and Economic Delusion* (Cambridge, Mass.: Harvard University Press, 1981), chap. 1. Such reflections suggest that innovations and new techniques must aim at solving some economic problems through the transfer of skills from one culture to another. No one doubts that the required cultural skills can be *learned*. Not much thought seems to have been given to how to *teach* them.

CHAPTER XIII: THE TRANSNATIONAL CORPORATION

[1]Quoted in Caryle Murphy, "Mugabe: The Making of a Marxist," *Washington Post*, August 27, 1980. Zimbabwe's President Canaan Banana has called for the Christian church in Africa to develop a "socialist outlook." He thinks that "it should discard the individualistic ethic of Western culture and emphasize the collectivism found in African culture." See "Zimbabwe's President Calls for Revolutionary Church in Africa," *Lutheran World Information*, Release No. 13, April 1, 1981, p. 17.

[2]Quoted in Bailey Morris, "Mugabe Set to Talk Aid with Carter," *Washington Star*, August 27, 1980. Mugabe made a plea for "massive financial help"; "we are waiting for . . . real offers to invest. . . . Our people look to the Government for concrete benefits." Bernard D. Nossiter, "Mugabe, in New York, Invites Foreign Investment," *New York Times*, August 27, 1980.

[3]Richard J. Barnet and Ronald E. Müller, *Global Reach: The Power of the Multinational Corporations* (New York: Simon & Schuster, 1974), esp. chap. 9, "The Latinamericanization of the United States"; Richard J. Barnet, *The Lean Years: Politics in the Age of Scarcity* (New York: Simon & Schuster, 1980), esp. chap. 9. See also Richard J. Barnet, *The Crisis of the Corporation* (Washington, D.C.: Institute for Policy Studies, 1975).

[4]United Nations Economic and Social Council, *Transnational Corporations in World Development: A Re-examination* (New York: United Nations, 1978); this document is the product of the Fourth Session of the UN Commission on Transnational Corporations. See also Raymond Vernon, *Sovereignty at Bay: The Multinational Spread of U.S. Enterprises* (New York: Basic Books, 1971); C. Fred Bergsten, Thomas Horst, and Theodore H. Moran, *American Multinationals and American Interests* (Washington, D.C.: The Brookings Institution, 1978); and Ben J. Wattenberg and Richard J. Whalen, *The Wealth Weapon: U.S. Foreign Policy*

and Multinational Corporations (New Brunswick, N.J.: Ⴑⴑ⧸⧸ⴖⴖⴖⴖ Books, 1980).

[5]"Strictly speaking, MNCs [multinational corporations] comprise only a relatively few of the swelling number of firms operating internationally. Investigators have developed meaningful distinctions on the basis of such criteria as size, the importance and geographic spread of foreign operations, and the locus of decisionmaking. In very round numbers, only about 300 firms—of which 200 are American—qualify as bona fide MNCs by the tighter definitions." Sperry Lea and Simon Webley, *Multinational Corporations in Developed Countries: A Review of Recent Research and Policy Thinking* (Washington, D.C.: British-North American Committee, 1973), p. 1. Sidney M. Robbins and Robert B. Stobaugh identify 187 U.S. transnationals from the *Fortune* 500 which controlled manufacturing subsidiaries in six or more foreign countries in 1965 or before; see *Money in the Multinational Enterprise* (New York: Basic Books, 1973), pp. 10–11. See also "The 150 Largest U.S. Multinationals," *Forbes,* June 25, 1979.

In 1967, Jean-Jacques Servan-Schreiber urged Europeans to compete with the American system of innovation. By 1980 the Japanese and Western Europeans seemed to have turned the tide, putting more savings and investment into innovation and productivity than the United States. For a picture of the situation in 1967, see his *The American Challenge* (New York: Avon, 1969), esp. chaps. 5 and 6.

[6]See Oscar Handlin, "The Taxonomy of the Corporation," in *The Corporation: A Theological Inquiry,* eds. Michael Novak and John W. Cooper (Washington, D.C.: American Enterprise Institute, 1981), pp. 22–23.

[7]John Kenneth Galbraith, "The Defense of the Multinational Company," *Harvard Business Review,* 56 (March–April 1978): 83–93; see esp. p. 84.

[8]Ibid., p. 85.

[9]See Paul E. Sigmund, *Multinationals in Latin America: The Politics of Nationalization* (Madison, Wisc.: University of Wisconsin Press, 1980), esp. chap. 8.

[10]Galbraith, "The Defense of the Multinational Company," p. 90.

[11]Ibid.

[12]Ronald E. Müller, "The Multinational Corporation: Asset or Impediment to World Justice?" in *Poverty, Environment, and Power,* Paul Hallock, ed. (New York: International Documentation on the Contemporary Church, May 1973), p. 42.

[13]Galbraith, "The Defense of the Multinational Company," pp. 89–91.

[14]Reinhold Niebuhr, *Our Moral and Spiritual Resources for International Cooperation* (New York: The U.S. National Commission for UNESCO, 1956), p. 34.

[15]Walter Lippmann noted what a great moment it was, in the long history of conquest, rapine and oppression, when David Hume wrote in "Of the Jealousy of Trade" (1742): "I shall therefore venture to acknowledge, that, not only as a man, but as a British subject, I pray for the flourishing commerce of Germany, Spain, Italy, and even France itself. I am at least

certain that Great Britain, and all those nations, would flourish more, did their sovereigns and ministers adopt such enlarged and benevolent sympathies toward each other." David Hume, *Essays Moral, Political, and Literary,* vol. 1, part II, no. VI. Lippmann adds: "It is the unfinished mission of liberalism to discover the guiding principles by which this revolutionary readaptation of mankind can proceed." *An Inquiry into the Principles of the Good Society* (Boston: Little, Brown and Co., 1937), p. 194.

[16]See Gottfried Haberler, "Schumpeter's *Capitalism, Socialism, and Democracy* after Forty Years"; and William Fellner, "March into Socialism, or Viable Postwar Stage of Capitalism?" Both papers are contributions to the forthcoming Schumpeter *Festschrift,* tentatively titled *Capitalism, Socialism and Democracy: A Review of Schumpeter's Predictions,* ed. Arnold Heertje (London: Holt-Saunders, forthcoming).

CHAPTER XIV: THE CATHOLIC ANTI-CAPITALIST TRADITION

[1]Jacques Leclerq, "Christianity and Money," in *The Twentieth Century Encyclopedia of Catholicism,* vol. 59, trans. Eric Earnshaw Smith (New York: Hawthorn Books, 1959), p. 108.

[2]See Heinrich Pesch, *Lehrbuch der Nationaloekonomie,* 5 vols., rev. ed. (Freiburg im Br.: Herder, 1920–26); Robert Mulcahy, S.J., *The Economics of Heinrich Pesch* (New York: Holt, 1952); Franz H. Mueller, *Heinrich Pesch: Sein Leben und seine Lehre* (Cologne: Verlag J. P. Bachem, 1980); and John A. Ryan, *Distributive Justice* (New York: Macmillan, 1916). Other titles in the Ryan corpus are *The Church and Socialism, Alleged Socialism of the Church Fathers, A Living Wage, Industrial Democracy, Social Reconstruction,* and *Social Doctrine in Action.*

[3]See, for example, the following surveys of Christian Marxism: Peter Hebblewaith, *The Christian-Marxist Dialogue* (New York: Paulist Press, 1977); and Arthur F. McGovern, *Marxism: An American Christian Perspective* (Maryknoll, N.Y.: Orbis Books, 1980).

[4]Particularly significant was the Anglican F. D. Maurice, who was the architect of Christian Socialism in mid-nineteenth-century England. Continental thinkers were involved at that time in similar tasks. See Torben Christensen, *Origin and History of Christian Socialism, 1848–54* (Aarhus, Denmark: Universitetsforlaget, 1962); and Bernard Murchland, *The Dream of Christian Socialism: An Essay on Its European Origins* (Washington, D.C.: American Enterprise Institute, 1981).

[5]See Rosino Gibellini, ed., *Frontiers of Theology in Latin America* (Maryknoll, N.Y.: Orbis Books, 1979); also see the following titles from Orbis Books: Gustavo Gutiérrez, *A Theology of Liberation* (1973), Juan Luis Segundo, *The Liberation of Theology* (1976), Enrique Dussel, *History and the Theology of Liberation* (1976), and Joseph Gremillion, ed., *The Gospel of Peace and Justice* (1976). See also *infra.,* Chapter XVII, note 7.

[6]Among the few titles on the subject are Edmund A. Opitz, *Religion and Capitalism: Allies, Not Enemies* (New Rochelle, N.Y.: Arlington House, 1970); and Abraham Kuyper, *Christianity and the Class Struggle,* trans.

D. Jellema (Grand Rapids, Mich.: Piet Hein Pub., 1950; reprint of 1891 ed.).

[7]"Once, following a lecture to students, Paul Tillich was asked whether he still supported socialism. The eminent theologian's answer came quickly: 'That is the ony possible economic system from the Christian point of view.' This exchange took place in 1957." J. Philip Wogaman, *The Great Economic Debate* (Philadelphia: Westminster Press, 1977), p. 133.

[8]Pedro Arrupe, S. J., "Marxist Analysis by Christians," *Origins* 10 (April 16, 1981): 693.

[9]See, for example, Franz H: Mueller, "The Church and the Social Question," in *The Challenge of Mater et Magistra*, eds. Joseph N. Moody and Justus George Lawler (New York: Herder & Herder, 1963), pp. 13–153.

[10]See Steven Lukes, "Types of Individualism," in *Dictionary of the History of Ideas*, 4 vols. (New York: Charles Scribner's Sons, 1973), II: 594–604.

[11]Ibid., p. 594 (emphasis added). Ibid., also, for Lamennais.

[12]See E. E. Y. Hales, *Pio Nono* (Garden City, N.Y.: Doubleday-Image, 1962), pp. 266–73.

[13]See E. E. Y. Hales, *The Catholic Church in the Modern World* (Garden City, N.Y.: Doubleday-Image, 1960), chap. 16.

[14]"We have seen that this great labor question cannot be solved except by assuming as a principle that private ownership must be held sacred and inviolable. The law, therefore, should favor ownership, and its policy should be to induce as many people as possible to become owners." Again: "The *Socialists*, working on the poor man's envy of the rich, endeavor to destroy private property, and maintain that individual possessions should become the common property of all, to be administered by the State or by municipal bodies. . . . But their proposals are so clearly futile for all practical purposes, that if they were carried out the working man himself would be among the first to suffer. Moreover, they are emphatically unjust, because they would rob the lawful possessor, bring the State into a sphere that is not its own, and cause complete confusion in the community." Pope Leo XIII, *Rerum Novarum*, para. 35, 3; see *Seven Great Encyclicals* (Glen Rock, N.J.: Paulist Press, 1965), pp. 22, 2.

[15]See John Tracy Ellis, *American Catholicism* (Chicago: University of Chicago Press, 1956), p. 105–06.

[16]See Reinhold Niebuhr, "Walter Rauschenbusch in Historical Perspective," in *Faith and Politics* (New York: George Braziller, 1968), pp. 33–45 (an essay written in 1957).

[17]Pope Pius XI, *Quadragesimo Anno*, para. 120, 27, 78; see *Encyclicals*, pp. 158, 131, 147.

[18]Ibid., para. 88; see *Encyclicals*, pp. 149–50.

[19]Ibid., para. 59; see *Encyclicals*, p. 142.

[20]Ibid., para. 54; see *Encyclicals*, p. 140.

[21]Pope Paul VI, *Octogesima Adveniens*, para. 35, in *The Gospel of Peace*

and Justice, ed. Joseph Gremillion (Maryknoll, N.Y.: Orbis Books, 1976), p. 501.

[22]See John Paul II, *On Human Work: Encyclical "Laborem Exercens"* (Washington, D.C.: U.S. Catholic Conference, 1981).

[23]See Dorothee Soelle, *Political Theology* (Philadelphia: Fortress Press, 1974). In the *Concilium* series, published in New York by Herder & Herder and Seabury Press, see the following collections of essays, primarily by Europeans: *The Mystical and Political Dimension of the Christian Faith* (1974), *Christianity and Socialism* (1977), *Christianity and the Bourgeoisie* (1979), and *Christian Ethics and Economics: The North–South Conflict* (1980).

[24]Metz uses the Marxist rather than the Anglo-American sense of *praxis,* most notably in *Faith in History and Society: Toward a Practical Fundamental Theology* (New York: Seabury Press, 1980); see esp. chap. 4.

[25]Bishop Dom Helder Camara of Recife, Brazil "has called for a synthesis of Marxism and Christianity like the synthesis St. Thomas Aquinas achieved between Aristotle and Christianity in the Middle Ages." See McGovern, *Marxism: An American Christian Perspective,* p. 2. In a similar regard, Jacques Maritain once wrote, ". . . to do with Hegel what St. Thomas did with Aristotle, would involve . . . making over Hegel from head to toe. Just let them try it, they will break their teeth." *The Peasant of the Garonne* (New York: Macmillan, 1969), p. 169.

CHAPTER XV: CHRISTIAN SOCIALISM IN EUROPE

[1]Arthur F. McGovern, *Marxism: An American Christian Perspective* (Maryknoll, N.Y.: Orbis Books, 1980), chap. 3.

[2]See Pope John XXIII, *Pacem in Terris,* para. 159, in *The Gospel of Peace and Justice,* ed. Joseph Gremillion (Maryknoll, N.Y.: Orbis Books, 1976), pp. 235–36. Pope Paul VI distinguished three meanings: "Distinctions must be made to guide concrete choices between the various levels of expression of socialism: a generous aspiration and a seeking for a more just society, historical movements with a political organization and aim, and an ideology which claims to give a complete and self-sufficient picture of man." *Octogesima Adveniens,* para. 31, in *The Gospel of Peace and Justice,* ed. Gremillion, pp. 499–500. See also McGovern, *Marxism: An American Christian Perspective,* pp. 118–21.

[3]See Johannes Baptist Metz, *Theology of the World* (New York: Seabury Press, 1969); *Faith in History and Society,* trans. D. Smith (New York: Seabury Press, 1980).

[4]John A. Ryan, "May a Catholic be a Socialist?" *The Catholic Fortnightly Review* 16 (February 1909): 70–73.

[5]John A. Ryan, *The Church and Socialism and Other Essays* (Washington, D.C.: Catholic University of America Press, 1919), p. 21.

[6]See McGovern, *Marxism: An American Christian Perspective,* p. 101.

[7]Michael Walzer, *Radical Principles: Reflections of an Unreconstructed Democrat* (New York: Basic Books, 1980), esp. p. 9 and chap. 1.

[8]See Adrian Cunningham et al., *Catholics and the Left: Slant Manifesto* (Springfield, Ill.: Templegate, 1966).

[9]For example, Denys Turner, "Can a Christian Be a Marxist?" *New Blackfriars* 56 (June 1975): 244–53; and the replies in subsequent issues.

[10]See Raymond Aron, *In Defense of Decadent Europe* (South Bend, Ind.: Regnery/Gateway, 1979), chap. 3.

[11]Juergen Moltmann, *Theology of Hope*, trans. J. W. Leitch (New York: Harper & Row, 1967), p. 225–26.

[12]Among works about "new frontiers" by theologians of the early sixties see: O. Basse et al., *Geplante Zukunft? Perspektiven fiis die Welt von morgen* (Gottingen: Vandenhoeck & Ruprecht, 1966).

[13]See Johannes Baptist Metz, *Faith in History and Society*, esp. chap. 4.

[14]A few Catholic writers, in the tradition of Aristotelian realism, have responded sympathetically to the realist elements of American philosophy. See, in particular, John J. McDermott, "To Be Human Is to Humanize: A Radically Empirical Aesthetic," and Robert C. Pollock, "Dream and Nightmare: The Future as Revolution," in *American Philosophy and the Future*, ed. Michael Novak (New York: Charles Scribner's Sons, 1968), pp. 21–59, 60–86.

[15]See John Dewey, *Reconstruction in Philosophy* (New York: New American Library, 1950; reprint of 1920 ed.); Richard J. Bernstein, *Praxis and Action* (Philadelphia: University of Pennsylvania Press, 1971); and Stuart Hampshire, *Thought and Action* (New York: Viking, 1960). More recently, see Alasdair MacIntyre, *After Virtue* (Notre Dame, Ind.: University of Notre Dame, 1981).

[16]See Moltmann's *Theology of Hope; The Crucified God* (New York: Harper & Row, 1974); and *The Experiment Hope*, trans. M. Douglas Meeks (Philadelphia: Fortress Press, 1975).

[17]Moltmann, *Theology of Hope*, p. 16.

[18]See Dale Vree, *On Synthesizing Marxism and Christianity* (New York: Wiley–Interscience, 1976), pp. 90–109; and Nelson R. Chamberlain, "Juergen Moltmann: Apostle of Christian Hope?" *Christianity Today* 18 (June 21, 1974): 6–10.

[19]Vree, *On Synthesizing Marxism and Christianity*, p. 109.

[20]Juergen Moltmann, *Man*, trans. John Sturdy (Philadelphia: Fortress Press, 1974), p. 44.

[21]Vree, *On Synthesizing Marxism and Christianity*, p. 109.

[22]Moltmann, *The Crucified God*, "Introduction."

[23]Juergen Moltmann, "Die Revolution der Freiheit," *Perspectiven der Theologie: Gesammelte Aufsaetze* (Munich: Kaiser, and Mainz: Matthias–Gruenewald, 1968), pp. 193, 198.

[24]Juergen Moltmann, "The Cross and Civil Religion," in Juergen Moltmann et al., *Religion and Political Society* (New York: Harper & Row, 1974), pp. 42–44.

[25]Ibid., p. 43.

[26]Ibid., p. 44.

[27]Ibid.

[28]Ibid., p. 45.

[29]Juergen Moltmann, *Religion, Revolution, and the Future*, trans. M. Douglas Meeks (New York: Charles Scribner's Sons, 1969), pp. 5, 26.

[30]Ibid., p. 35.

[31]Moltmann, *The Experiment Hope*, p. 127.

[32]See Juergen Moltmann, *The Church in the Power of the Holy Spirit,*

trans. Margaret Kohl (London: SCM Press, 1977), pp. 168–76; the subheading reads: "Christianity in the Process of Economic Life: Symbiosis." On Moltmann's critique of Max Weber, see *The Experiment Hope*, pp. 124–27.

[33]Moltmann, *The Experiment Hope*, p. 124.

[34]Ibid., p. 125. By contrast, Max Weber had in mind a creative, progressive force: "Now Calvinism was the faith over which the great political and cultural struggles of the sixteenth and seventeenth centuries were fought in the most highly developed countries, the Netherlands, England, and France." In a footnote, Weber adds: "For the following discussion I may here say definitely that we are not studying the personal view of Calvin, but Calvinism, and that in the form to which it had evolved by the end of the sixteenth and in the seventeenth centuries in the great areas where it had a decisive influence and which were at the same time the home of capitalistic culture. For the present, Germany is neglected entirely, since pure Calvinism never dominated large areas here. Reformed is, of course, by no means identical with Calvinistic." Max Weber, *The Protestant Ethic and the Spirit of Capitalism*, trans. Talcott Parsons (New York: Charles Scribner's Sons, 1958), pp. 98, 220, n.7.

[35]See Arthur Mitzman, *The Iron Cage* (New York: Alfred A. Knopf, 1970), pp. 43–46.

[36]Moltmann, *The Experiment Hope*, pp. 125–26.

[37]Ibid., pp. 123–26.

[38]Moltmann, *The Church in the Power of the Holy Spirit*, p. 169.

[39]See Milton Friedman and Rose Friedman, *Free to Choose* (New York: Harcourt Brace Jovanovich, 1980), pp. 190–91.

[40]Moltmann, *The Church in the Power of the Holy Spirit*, p. 169.

[41]Ibid., p. 170. "U.S. dollar notes are not only a claim to confidence in the nation," he writes unkindly. "They are a claim to religious confidence, as well: with their assertion: 'In God we trust.' " By such expressions, including "under God," Americans seem to have in mind a republic always under divine judgment.

[42]Ibid.

[43]Ibid.

[44]Max Scheler, *Die Stellung des Menschen in Kosmos* (Munich, 1949), p. 56; quotation translated and cited in Moltmann, *The Church in the Power of the Holy Spirit*. p. 171.

[45]Moltmann, *The Church in the Power of the Holy Spirit*, p. 171.

[46]Ibid.

[47]Ibid., p. 172.

[48]Ibid., pp. 172–73.

[49]Ibid.

[50]Ibid., pp. 172–73.

[51]Ibid.

[52]Moltmann, *The Crucified God*, p. 323.

[53]Reinhold Niebuhr, by contrast, analyzed the will to power under socialism: "A second source of Marxist illusion is its belief that the ownership of property is the sole and only source of economic power. . . .

The development of a managerial class in Russia, combining economic with political power, is an historic refutation of the Marxist theory. . . . The Marxist theory fails to anticipate the inevitable rise of an oligarchy in a new society, partly because it has utopian ideas of idyllic relations in such a society, which obviate the necessity of the use of any form of coercive power; and partly because it identifies economic power too absolutely with the power of private ownership." *The Children of Light and the Children of Darkness* (New York: Charles Scribner's Sons, 1944), pp. 111–12.

[54]Moltmann, *The Crucified God,* pp. 330–32 (italics his).

[55]Ibid., p. 333 (italics his).

[56]Ibid., p. 331 (italics his).

[57]Ibid., p. 333.

[58]Ibid., p. 331.

[59]See Seymour Martin Lipset, "Predicting the Future of Post-Industrial Society," in *The Third Century,* ed. Seymour Martin Lipset (Stanford: Hoover Institution Press, 1979), esp. pp. 18–24; and Paul Johnson, *Enemies of Society* (New York: Atheneum, 1977), chap. 7, "Ecological Panic."

[60]Moltmann, *The Crucified God,* p. 334 (italics his).

[61]Ibid., p. 331–35 (italics his).

[62]Ibid., pp. 335–37.

CHAPTER XVI: GUILT FOR THIRD WORLD POVERTY

[1]From the official English translation of the Medellín documents, *The Church in the Present-Day Transformation of Latin America in the Light of the Council* (Washington: U.S. Catholic Conference, 1970); cited in Joseph Gremillion, ed., *The Gospel of Peace and Justice* (Maryknoll, N.Y.: Orbis Books, 1976), p. 457.

[2]Cited in *Development-Dependency: The Role of Multinational Corporations* (Washington: U.S. Catholic Conference, 1974), p. ii.

[3]Population figures for earlier eras are difficult to find and subject to dispute. We have utilized the following sources: U.S. Bureau of the Census, *The Statistical History of the United States* (New York: Basic Books, 1976), table A 91-104; U.S. Bureau of the Census, *Statistical Abstract of the United States: 1979,* 100th ed. (Washington, D.C. 1979), tables 1541, 1545; Robert Burnette and John Koster, *The Road to Wounded Knee* (New York: Bantam, 1974), appendix; Colin Clark, *Population Growth and Land Use,* 2nd ed. (London: Macmillan, 1977), p. 64; Celso Furtado, *Economic Development of Latin America,* 2d ed., trans. Suzette Macedo (Cambridge: Cambridge University Press, 1976), p. 6; W. S. and E. S. Woytinsky, *World Population and Production* (New York: Twentieth Century Fund, 1953), pp. 34–36.

[4]Bureau of the Census, *Statistical History of the United States,* table U 41–46; combined figures for "Latin American Republics" and "Western Hemisphere dependencies."

[5]H. R. Trevor-Roper, "Religion, the Reformation and Social Change," in *The European Witch-Craze of the Sixteenth and Seventeenth Centuries and Other Essays* (New York: Harper & Row, 1969), p. 21.

[6]Ibid., p. 28. "In the United States, the land tenure created by the colonial regime was swept away by the American Revolution, and the Homestead Act of 1862 helped to divide the cropland into sound, medium-size farming units. In Latin America, on the other hand, the system of primogeniture, according to which landed property was inherited by the eldest son or the nearest kinsman, kept the latifundia intact. Thus the wealth of the landowner class was preserved, and at the same time that the vast majority of the population was prevented from acquiring land, there was little if any land available for prospective settlers." Edmund Gaspar, *United States—Latin America: A Special Relationship?* (Washington & Stanford: American Enterprise Institute & Hoover Institution, 1978), pp. 34–35. Adam Smith noted the relative wealth of Latin America: "In the plenty of good land the English colonies of North America, though, no doubt, very abundantly provided, are, however, inferior to those of the Spaniards and Portugueze and not superior to some of those possessed by the French before the late war. But the political institutions of the English colonies have been more favourable to the improvement and cultivation of this land, than those of any of the other three nations." *An Inquiry into the Nature and Causes of the Wealth of Nations,* ed. Edwin Cannan (New York: Modern Library, 1937), pp. 538–39.

[7]Trevor-Roper, "Religion, the Reformation and Social Change," pp. 30, 37–38.

[8]Peruvian Bishops Conference, "La Justicia en el Mundo," 1969; cited in *Development-Dependency,* pp. 7–8, n. 16.

[9]U.S. Catholic Conference, *Development-Dependency,* pp. i, iii (emphasis added).

[10]Ibid., p. 7, n. 9.

[11]Ibid.

[12]Ibid.

[13]See Gregory Baum, R. James Sacouman, Thomas Langan, and Gerald Schmitz, "The Maritime Bishops: Social Criticism," *Ecumenist* 18 (March–April, 1980): 35.

[14]Bureau of the Census, *Statistical History of the United States,* table D 127–41; and *Statistical Abstract: 1979,* table 668.

CHAPTER XVII: LIBERATION THEOLOGY

[1]Address of Bishop Sergio Mendez Arceo to the First Convention of Christians for Socialism, April 1972; cited in *Christians and Socialism,* ed. John Eagleson (Maryknoll, N.Y.: Orbis Books, 1975), p. 153.

[2]See Juan Donoso Cortés, *Essay on Catholicism, Liberalism, and Socialism* (New York: Lippincott, 1862).

[3]Michael Dodson, "Prophetic Politics and Political Theory in Latin America," *Polity* 12 (Spring 1980): 389.

[4]See Juan Luis Segundo, "Capitalism-Socialism: A Theological Crux," trans. J. P. Donnelly, in *The Mystical and Political Dimension of the Christian Faith,* eds. Claude Geffre and Gustavo Gutiérrez (New York: Herder & Herder, 1974), pp. 105–23.

[5]"The theology of liberation is self-consciously political . . . it shares the general Latin American concern with a 'place in history,' and . . . its most distinguishing feature is the link it forges between social conditions (praxis) and basic human values (theory)." Dodson, "Prophetic Politics," p. 391. See also Goulet, *A New Moral Order,* chap. 3, "Orlando Fals-Borda: Subversion as a Moral Category."

[6]Richard J. Bernstein contrasts the views of Marx and Dewey in *Praxis and Action* (Philadelphia: Univ. of Pennsylvania Press, 1971). The subject would reward much further study.

[7]Among the most significant of the socialist or Marxist titles are José Miranda, *Marx and the Bible,* trans. John Eagleson (Maryknoll, N.Y.: Orbis Books, 1974; Leonardo Boff, *Liberating Grace,* trans. John Drury (Maryknoll, N.Y.: Orbis Books, 1979); Ernesto Cardenal, *The Gospel in Solentiname,* trans. Donald D. Walsh (Maryknoll, N.Y.: Orbis Books, 1978); and Dom Helder Camara, *Revolution Through Peace,* trans. Amparo McLean (New York: Harper & Row, 1971). See also *supra,* Chapter XIV, note 5. Among the critical works on liberation theology are Alfonso Lopez Trujillo, *Liberation or Revolution?* (Huntington, Ind.: Our Sunday Visitor, 1977); James V. Schall, S.J., *Liberation Theology* (San Francisco: Ignatius Press, forthcoming); Arthur J. McGovern, S. J., *Marxism: An American Christian Perspective* (Maryknoll, N.Y.: Orbis Books, 1980); Dennis P. McCann, *Christian Realism and Liberation Theology* (Maryknoll, N.Y.: Orbis Books, 1981); Juan Gutiérrez González, M.Sp.S., *The New Libertarian Gospel: Pitfalls of the Theology of Liberation,* trans. Paul Burns (Chicago: Franciscan Herald Press, 1977); and Bonaventure Kloppenburg, O.F.M., *Temptations for the Theology of Liberation* (Chicago: Franciscan Herald Press, 1974).

[8]Dodson, "Prophetic Politics," p. 395.

[9]Ibid., p. 397.

[10]See Paulo Freire, *Pedagogy of the Oppressed* (New York: Herder & Herder, 1970).

[11]Dodson, "Prophetic Politics," pp. 389–91.

[12]For a sympathetic account of this argument see Peter L. Berger, *Pyramids of Sacrifice* (Garden City, N.Y.: Doubleday, 1976), chap. 2. On the subject of reformism, Paolo Freire writes: "In reality, no mere reformism—bourgeois or proletarian—can bring about this radical triumph over the situation of dependency. Bourgeois reformism does not extend any farther than the modernization of a dependent society; moreover, it helps to preserve the subordinate character of that entire society as well as the power of the dominating classes." Foreword to Denis Goulet, *A New Moral Order: Development Ethics and Liberation Theology* (Maryknoll, N.Y.: Orbis Books, 1974), p. xii.

[13]Cuba's debt to the Soviet Union was estimated at $5 billion in 1978 and annual Soviet aid at $2–3 billion, double the 1977 figure. *The Europa Yearbook: 1979,* 2 vols. (London: Europa Publications Ltd., 1979), II: 208–10.

[14]Moltmann argues that liberation theologians from Latin America "only quote a few basic concepts of Marx. And they do this in such a general way that one learns only something about the fruits of the theologians'

reading and scarcely anything about the struggle of the Latin American people. In them one reads more about the sociological theories of others, namely Western Socialists, than about the history or the life and suffering of the Latin American people." "An Open Letter to José Miguez Bonino," in *Mission Trends No. 4: Liberation Theologies,* eds. Gerald H. Anderson and Thomas Stransky (Glen Rock, N.J.: Paulist Press, 1978), p. 77.

[15]The statement by Cardinal Silva Henriquez is cited in an early document of "Christians for Socialism"; see *Christians and Socialism,* ed. John Eagleson (Maryknoll, N.Y.: Orbis Books, 1975), p. 4.

[16]Goulet, *A New Moral Order,* p. 127.

[17]Dodson, "Prophetic Politics," p. 399.

[18]José Miguez-Bonino, *Christians and Marxists* (Grand Rapids, Mich.: Eerdmans, 1976), p. 115; cited in Dodson, "Prophetic Politics," pp. 404–405.

[19]From the Final Document of the First Convention of Christians for Socialism, April 1972; see *Christians and Socialism,* ed. Eagleson, p. 169.

[20]Gustavo Gutiérrez, "The Choice Before the Church in Latin America," mimeograph, p. 6; cited in Dodson, "Prophetic Politics," p. 399.

[21]"The poor countries are becoming even more clearly aware that their underdevelopment is only the by-product of the development of other countries. Attempts to bring about changes within the existing order have proven futile. This analysis of the situation is at the level of scientific rationality. Only a radical break from the status quo, that is, a profound transformation of the private property system, access to power of the exploited class, and a social revolution that would break this dependence would allow for the change to a new society, a socialist society—or at least allow that such a society might be possible." Gustavo Gutiérrez, *A Theology of Liberation,* trans. Sister Caridad Inda and John Eagleson (Maryknoll, N.Y.: Orbis Books, 1973), pp. 26–27.

[22]Dodson, "Prophetic Politics," p. 404.

[23]Edward Seaga, "Address on the Caribbean," lecture at the American Enterprise Institute, May 1980, mimeograph, pp. 3–4. Seaga later won election as prime minister of Jamaica.

[24]Ibid., p. 4.

[25]Dodson, "Prophetic Politics," p. 407.

CHAPTER XVIII: A THEOLOGY OF DEVELOPMENT: LATIN AMERICA

[1]Léo Moulin, *L'Aventure Eurpoéenne* (Brussels: De Tempel, 1972), *passim.*

[2]Ibid. p. 51, and *passim.*

[3]Ibid, pp. 47–49.

[4]"It is a sad fact that 80% of the world's resources are at the disposal of 20% of the world's inhabitants, while one segment of humanity is rich and growing richer, the rest will struggle in varying degrees of poverty and have little certainty of breaking out of their stagnation in the next decades. Our responsibility as Christians makes us tremble. The Northern Hemisphere, the developed area of the world, the 20% who possess

80% of the world's resources are of Christian origin. What impression can our African and Asian brethren and the masses in Latin America have of Christianity if the tree is to be judged by its fruits? Christians are largely responsible for the unjust world in which we live. . . ." Dom Helder Camara, "A Christian Commitment Is Needed for Latin American Development," in *Latin America Calls,* March 1970, p. 4.

[5]U.S. Bureau of the Census, *Statistical History of the United States* (New York: Basic Books, 1978), tables A-6–8. See also W. S. Woytinski and E. S. Woytinski, *World Population and Production* (New York: Twentieth Century Fund, 1953), table 14.

[6]U.S. Bureau of the Census, *Statistical History of the United States,* tables U-318–323.

[7]Ibid., tables U-43–45.

[8]See Carlos Rangel, *The Latin Americans: Their Love-Hate Relationship with the United States,* (New York: Harcourt Brace Jovanovich, 1977).

[9]Gustavo Gutiérrez, *A Theology of Liberation,* trans. Sr. Caridad Inda and John Eagleson (Maryknoll, N.Y.: Orbis Books, 1973), p. 84.

[10]See Joseph Ramos, "Reflections on Gustavo Gutiérrez's Theology of Liberation"; "Dependency and Development: An Attempt to Clarify the Issues"; "On the Prospect of Social Market Democracy (or Democratic Capitalism) in Latin America"; and "Latin America: The End of Democratic Reformism?" in Michael Novak, ed., *Liberation North—Liberation South* (Washington, D.C.: American Enterprise Institute, 1981).

[11]Ramos, "Dependency and Development," p. 61. Since 1975, however, the volume of U.S. exports to and imports from the Third World has risen. The point still holds, since earlier levels of independence could be borne far more easily by the U.S. than by its poorer partners.

[12]Ibid.

[13]Ibid.

[14]Ramos, "Reflections on Gustavo Gutiérrez's Theology of Liberation," p. 55.

[15]Ibid., pp. 55–56.

[16]Ibid., p. 56.

[17]Ibid., n. 2, p. 57.

[18]Ibid., p. 58.

[19]Ibid.

[20]Ramos, "Latin America: The End of Democratic Reformism?," p. 74.

[21]Ibid., p.75.

[22]Ibid.

[23]Ibid.

[24]Ibid., pp. 75–76.

[25]Ibid., p. 76.

[26]Sergio Molina and Sebastian Piñera, "Extreme Poverty in Latin America," in Novak, ed., *Liberation South—Liberation North,* p. 82.

[27]Ibid., p. 83.

[28]Ibid., p. 85.

[29]Ramos, "Latin America: The End of Democratic Reformism?" p. 77. See also Peter Berger, *Pyramids of Sacrifice* (Garden City, N.Y.: Doubleday, 1976), p. 65; and Chapter V, note 64, *supra.*

[30]Ramos, p. 79. Useful background material on Latin America may be found in Willard L. Beaulac, *The Fractured Continent: Latin America in Close-Up* (Stanford, Calif.: Hoover Institution Press, 1980); and Robert B. Williamson, William P. Glade, Jr., and Karl M. Schmitt, eds., *Latin America—U.S. Economic Interactions: Conflict, Accommodation, and Policies for the Future* (Washington, D.C.: American Enterprise Institute, 1974).

CHAPTER XIX: FROM MARXISM to DEMOCRATIC CAPITALISM
—*Author's Acknowledgement:* I owe great thanks to my colleague at Syracuse University D. B. Robertson, who helped me compile a large file on Niebuhr's early writings on capitalism and socialism. —M.N.

[1]John Cort, "Can Socialism Be Distinguished from Marxism?" *Cross Currents* 29 (Winter 1979–80): 428. Niebuhr broke from the Socialist Party in 1940, after which, as Cort writes, "He remained a socialist for perhaps another ten years or more, but his politics became that of the ADA (Americans for Democratic Action), of which he was also a founder" (p. 427).
[2]The history of the term is fuzzy. As best I can determine (I have not exhausted the subject), the term was first used as a derisive label for backsliders and former socialists by guardians of the true faith. Although "neo-liberal" would have been a more fair epithet, the intention of "neo-conservative" was not fairness. It was first applied to Nathan Glazer, Daniel Patrick Moynihan, and Daniel Bell in a discussion of their work by Michael Harrington, "The Welfare State and Its Neoconservative Critics," *Dissent* 20 (Fall 1973): 453–54. This issue contains a symposium of six articles, including Harrington's, entitled "Against the New Conservatism." The next year, Lewis A. Coser and Irving Howe edited a collection of critical essays on *The New Conservatives* (New York: Quadrangle, 1974). Coser untruly wrote of its central subject, the men who had "belonged to the Left camp not so very long ago," that they "have now made it, and having made it they are concerned with the maintenance of an order that has been good to them" (pp. 4–5). In 1976, stories in *Newsweek, Time,* and the *New York Times* brought this school of thought to public notoriety; e.g., Irving Kristol, "What is a 'Neo-Conservative'?" *Newsweek,* January 19, 1976. Subsequently, *Esquire* (February 13, 1979) devoted a cover story to Irving Kristol and "neo-conservatism." Later stories elsewhere often confounded the "neo-conservatives" with the emergence of the "New Right," a quite different movement altogether (by region, ethnicity, and philosophy) which was beginning to be noticed at about the same time.
[3]Reinhold Niebuhr, "Socialism and Christianity," *Christian Century,* August 19, 1931, pp. 1038–40.
[4]Ibid.
[5]Reinhold Niebuhr, Review of G. C. Binyon's *The Christian Socialist Movement in England,* in *Christian Century,* March 16, 1932, p. 355.
[6]Reinhold Niebuhr, "Why German Socialism Crashed," *Christian Century,* April 5, 1933.

[7]Reinhold Niebuhr, "Catastrophe or Social Control?" *Harper's Magazine,* June 1932, pp. 114–18.

[8]Reinhold Niebuhr, letter to the editor, *Christian Century,* November 9, 1932, pp. 1379–81.

[9]Reinhold Niebuhr, "After Capitalism—What?" *The World Tomorrow,* March 1, 1933, pp. 203–05.

[10]Reinhold Niebuhr, "Protestantism, Capitalism, and Communism," in *Religion Today, a Challenging Enigma,* ed. A. L. Swift (New York: McGraw-Hill, 1933), pp. 139–54. In Niebuhr's view, middle-class Christians were under an "illusion of individual independence." Their religion became "devitalized." They did not feel "the tragedy of life either as individuals or as groups." By contrast, the aristocrat stuck with his class and its special higher ethic, and the proletarian, more like a Mohammedan than a Christian, was "not squeamish about the ethical means" he chose toward his goals, nursing "a cynical attitude toward the ideal of love." Communists spoke more successfully than socialists to this cynicism, since "the true Communist does not trust moral forces at all." The proletarian "is a collectivist and not an individual."

[11]Reinhold Niebuhr, "A New Strategy for Socialists," *The World Tomorrow,* August 31, 1933. He concludes that "every legal system must be regarded as a rationalization of a given equilibrium of political and economic power and can therefore hardly be a perfect instrument." A few months later he was still despairing of "the evolutionary hopes of parliamentary Socialists," since "it is now quite apparent that the dominant economic power can abrogate democracy" when its interests are endangered. Labor may "press concessions from the lords of industry and finance" but not "the final concession of a new collectivist society." Reinhold Niebuhr, "Making Radicalism Effective," *The World Tomorrow,* December 21, 1933.

[12]Reinhold Niebuhr, "The Fellowship of Socialist Christians," *The World Tomorrow,* June 14, 1934. He writes: "A Christian Marxian has a more pessimistic view of human nature than liberal Protestantism and a less evolutionary conception of history."

[13]Reinhold Niebuhr, "Ex-Cathedra," *The World Tomorrow,* May 10, 1934. See also Niebuhr's earlier writings on Ford, including. "Henry Ford and Industrial Autocracy," *Christian Century,* November 4, 1926; "How Philanthropic Is Henry Ford?" *Christian Century,* December 9, 1926; "Ford's Five-Day Week Shrinks," *Christian Century,* June 9, 1927.

[14]"My reaction to bourgeois individualism prompted me to the error of using Marxist ideas to emphasize our new collective realities. I can only say in self-defense that, despite these absurd inconsistencies, I did succeed in escaping all the hallucinations of the left, who hailed the Russian Revolution as an emancipation for all mankind without noting that its annulment of freedom made the Stalinist depotism almost inevitable. If I mention the fact that I dimly foresaw the evil roots of this new monopoly of power, it must be because I became so conscious of my many mistakes in my revolt against secular and Christian individualism. I made so many mistakes that I now pathetically seek to claim credit for

avoiding the cardinal mistake of many of the left." Reinhold Niebuhr, *Man's Nature and His Communities* (New York: Charles Scribner's Sons, 1965), pp. 21–22.

[15]James H. Billington, *Fire in the Minds of Men* (New York: Basic Books, 1980), pp. 203–04.

[16]Ibid., pp. 155, 159, 165.

[17]William G. Chrystal, "Introduction," in *Young Reinhold Niebuhr: His Early Writings—1911–1931*, ed. William G. Chrystal (St. Louis: Eden, 1977), pp. 22, 26, 30.

[18]Reinhold Niebuhr, "The Revolutionary Moment," *American Socialist Quarterly*, June 1935.

[19]Reinhold Niebuhr, "Why a New Quarterly?" *Radical Religion*, Autumn 1935.

[20]Reinhold Niebuhr, "Is Religion Counter-Revolutionary?" *Radical Religion* (Autumn 1935). In the following spring, he wrote: "In some respects a socialist society, with its higher cohesiveness, will be more perilous than a capitalist society. . . . Equally pathetic is that the new society will not face the problem of power. . . . The new society will have very strong centers of power, though the state will be predominantly political rather than economic. . . . The whole Christian insight into life and history make these utopian illusions untenable." Such illusions are "the vestigial remnants of bourgeois optimism and romanticism." Reinhold Niebuhr, "The Idea of Progress and Socialism," *Radical Religion*, Spring 1936.

[21]Reinhold Niebuhr, "Socialist Decision and Christian Conscience," *Radical Religion*, Spring 1938.

[22]Reinhold Niebuhr, "Roosevelt's Merry-go-Round," *Radical Religion*, Spring 1938.

[23]Reinhold Niebuhr, "Brief Notes," *Radical Religion*, Spring 1938.

[24]Reinhold Niebuhr, "The Creed of Modern Christian Socialists," *Radical Religion*, Spring 1938. Niebuhr tried to elaborate a radical form of Christian Socialism, but he had profound doubts about the anti-radical tendencies in American thought: "On the American frontier the world seemed no longer to defy 'the law of Christ.' A new society of Christians hoped for the realization of the kingdom of God on earth through a simple cooperation of the church and the world. When the sober realities of capitalism disappointed these dreams, they were only slightly remodeled and postponed. The ideal society would be established when economic life would achieve the same degree of democracy which political life had achieved. The watchword was 'industrial democracy.' In short, Christian socialism of the nineteenth and early twentieth century was really very similar to the ethical and utopian socialism which preceded Marx in Europe, the socialism of Saint-Simon and Fourier."

[25]Reinhold Niebuhr, "The Socialist Campaign," *Christianity and Society*, Summer 1940.

[26]Reinhold Niebuhr, "Editorial Notes," *Christianity and Crisis*, Summer 1940.

[27]Reinhold Niebuhr, "Roosevelt's Election," *Christianity and Society*, Winter 1940.

[28]Reinhold Niebuhr, "The Death of a President," *Christianity and Crisis,* April 30, 1945.

[29]Reinhold Niebuhr, "The World Council of Churches," *Christianity and Society,* Autumn 1948.

[30]"We continue to be socialists in the sense that we believe that the capitalist order of society stands under divine judgment and that there is no justice in modern technical society without a completely pragmatic attitude toward the institution of property. It must be socialized whenever it is of such a character that it makes for injustice through inordinate centralization of power. There is however no redemption in the abolition of a social institution if too much is expected of it. Extravagant religious hopes become then the basis of political errors. In the case of the socialization of property the most dangerous error is the centralization of both economic and political power in the hands of a communist oligarchy." Reinhold Niebuhr, "Frontier Fellowship," *Christianity and Society,* Autumn 1948.

[31]Reinhold Niebuhr, "The Anomaly of European Socialism," *Yale Review,* December 1952.

[32]Reinhold Niebuhr, "Reflections on Democracy as an Alternative to Communism," *Columbia University Forum,* Summer 1961.

[33]See Reinhold Niebuhr, *Man's Nature and His Communities* (New York: Charles Scribner's Sons, 1965), pp. 22, 68.

[34]"The combination of errors was in fact so great in the bourgeois age that it must be regarded as one of the wonders of history that Western democracies did not completely succumb to the Marxist rebellion prompted by the glaring injustices of early industrialism." Reinhold Niebuhr, *Man's Nature and His Communities,* pp. 64–65.

[35]Andrew Libscomb and Ellery Bergh, eds., *Writings of Thomas Jefferson* (Washington, D.C.: Thomas Jefferson Memorial Assn., 1903), XV; 284; quoted in Niebuhr, *Man's Nature and His Communities,* p. 65.

[36]Niebuhr, *Man's Nature and His Communities,* pp. 66–68.

[37]Ibid. Niebuhr concludes that the bourgeois revolution led to further accommodation to proletarian interests: "Perhaps the most important triumph was the final one, when it became apparent that political power was not enough to guarantee economic justice. Then, the pressures of free communities forced the reluctant middle-class employers to allow the workers to organize, bargain collectively, and thus to create a tolerable equilibrium of power between organized industry and organized labor."

[38]"Adam Smith contributed mightily to a free society, but he almost wrecked that society with the unfulfilled promise that justice would flow inevitably from freedom. Karl Marx contributed mightily to a just society by his partial understanding of the realities of power in an industrial age, but he laid the foundations for a new despotism by not understanding those realities well enough. Fortunately, we are living in a day in which healthy nations do not concern themselves too much with the dogmas of either Smith or Marx, but profit by the truths they have winnowed from the errors of both." Reinhold Niebuhr, "Neither Adam Smith Nor Karl Marx," *New Leader,* December 23, 1957, p. 9.

410   THE SPIRIT OF DEMOCRATIC CAPITALISM

39Reinhold Niebuhr, "The Christian Faith and the Economic Life of Liberal Society," in *Goals of Economic Life*, ed. A. Dudley Ward (New York: Harpers, 1953), p. 433; reprinted in Reinhold Niebuhr, *Faith and Politics*, ed. Ronald H. Stone (New York: George Braziller, 1968).

40Niebuhr, *The Irony of American History*, p. 93.

41Reinhold Niebuhr, *The Children of Light and the Children of Darkness* (New York: Charles Scribner's Sons, 1944), pp. 117–18.

42Reinhold Niebuhr, "The Christian Faith and Economic Life of Liberal Society," pp. 441–42, 445–46.

43Niebuhr, *The Children of Light and the Children of Darkness*, p. 76.

44Niebuhr, *Man's Nature and His Communities*, p. 81.

45William I. Nichols, "Wanted: A New Name for Capitalism," *This Week*, March 4, 1951. Cited in Jacques Maritain, *Reflections on America* (New York: Charles Scribner's Sons, 1958), pp. 112–13.

46Ibid., p. 113.

47Ibid., pp. 114–15.

48See Billington, *Fire in the Minds of Men*, pp. 204–05.

49Reinhold Niebuhr, "Biblical Faith and Socialism: A Critical Appraisal," in *Religion and Culture: Essays in Honor of Paul Tillich*, ed. Walter Leibrecht (New York: Harper and Bros., 1959), p. 51.

50Ibid., p. 54.

51Ibid., pp. 54–55.

52Reinhold Niebuhr, "The Spiritual Weakness of the Third Force," *Christianity and Society*, Summer 1949, p. 6.

53Reinhold Niebuhr, "The Fact of European Socialism," *New Leader*, December 23, 1957, p. 8.

54For example, Niebuhr criticized the religious passion which would make of the poor a Messianic class: "The one difficulty is that when the poor are historically 'blessed' they become successful. In that case they cease to be poor and become powerful. They become too powerful in fact. The other difficulty is that the poor are too sharply defined as the industrial poor. They are to have the reins of destiny in their hands. But in the nations in which the Marxist apocalypse seems plausible most of the poor were peasants. They were not propertyless. In fact they loved the property in the soil and were therefore not ripe for the Marxist creed. The industrial poor, having the fanaticism with which the creed endows them, seized the levers of power in the State and used their power to force the poor peasants to conform to the collectivist creed. Many peasants starved and were killed in the resulting 'class struggle.' The religious appreciation of the poor as the Messianic class was too undiscriminating in defining the poor, in appreciating their virtues, in forgetting that resentment against injustice may turn into an evil fanaticism, and in failing to estimate the effects of success and power upon the poor." Reinhold Niebuhr, "Biblical Faith and Socialism," p. 53.

55Reinhold Niebuhr, *Our Moral and Spiritual Resources for International Cooperation* (New York: U.S. National Commission for UNESCO, 1956), pp. 33–35.

56Cort, "Can Socialism Be Distinguished from Marxism?" p. 428.

[57]See Michael Novak, "Needing Niebuhr Again," *Commentary,* September 1972, pp. 52–62.

CHAPTER XX: A THEOLOGY OF DEMOCRATIC CAPITALISM

[1]Jacques Maritain, *Reflections on America* (New York: Charles Scribner's Sons, 1958), p. 101.

[2]See Michael Harrington, *Toward a Democratic Left* (New York: Macmillan, 1968), chap. 10; and Irving Howe, ed., *Twenty-five Years of "Dissent"* (New York: Methuen, 1979), esp. the contributions by Howe and Harrington.

[3]See Jacob Neusner, "Max Weber Revisited: Religion and Society in Ancient Judaism," the Seventh Sacks Lecture, Oxford Centre for Postgraduate Hebrew Studies, May 12, 1981 (mimeographed). In addition, the encyclical of Pope John Paul II, *Laborem Exercens,* lists dozens of Scriptural passages referring to work, wages, creativity, talents and the like. See note 10, *infra.*

[4]See the final lines of the novel by Georges Bernanos, *Diary of a Country Priest,* trans. Pamela Morris (New York: Macmillan, 1962).

[5]U.S. Bureau of the Census, *Governmental Finances in 1978–79* (Washington 1980), tables 2, 3; the figures are for 1979.

[6]Ralph Lerner, "Commerce and Character: The Anglo-American as New-Model Man," *William and Mary Quarterly* 36 (January 1979): 17; Lerner is quoting from *The Works of John Adams,* ed. Charles Francis Adams (Boston, 1850–56).

[7]DeTocqueville, *Democracy in America,* cited in Lerner, "Commerce and Character," p. 13.

[8]Michael Harrington makes his own the "audacious optimism" of Trotsky: "Man will become immeasurably stronger, wiser and subtler; his movements more rhythmic, his voice more musical. The forms of life will become dynamically dramatic. The average human type will rise to the heights of an Aristotle, a Goethe, a Marx. And above this ridge, new peaks will arise." *Socialism* (New York: Saturday Review Press, 1972), p. 370.

[9]"For the sake and purpose of Christ there is and ought to be worldly order in state, family and economy. For the sake of Christ the worldly order is subject to the commandment of God. It is to be noted that there is no question here of a 'Christian state' or a 'Christian economy,' but only of the rightful state and economy as a secular institution for the sake of Christ. There exists, therefore, a Christian responsibility for secular institutions, and within a Christian ethic there exist propositions which relate to this responsibility." Dietrich Bonhoeffer, *Ethics* (New York: Macmillan, 1955), pp. 322–23.

[10]For this reason, I rejoiced in Pope John Paul II's use of the theology of creation in his reflections on economic progress in *Laborem Exercens.* (*Origins, N.C. Documentary Service* 11, September 24, 1981.) I have not dwelt at length on Pope John Paul's teachings on economics, because that teaching was still evolving as I labored on this book, begun before

his election. I sense in him—and not just because we share a Slavic heritage—an unaccustomed kinship of spirit. We share similar convictions about person and community. Our experiences of political economy have been vastly different.

[11] "Since to love is to wish the good of someone, that which is said to be loved has a two-fold consideration: it is considered either as one for whom we wish the good; or as the good which we wish for someone." St. Thomas Aquinas, *On Charity*, trans. Lottie H. Kendzierski (Milwaukee: Marquette University Press, 1960), article VII, pp. 61–62. For a correlative treatment, see St. Thomas Aquinas, *Summa Theologica*, II-II, qq. 23–27, and I-II, qq. 65 and 26–28.

[12] "Charity is the form, the mover, and the root of the virtues." Ibid., article III; see *On Charity*, pp. 35–36.

[13] For the different meanings of love, see St. Thomas Aquinas, *Summa Theologica*, I-II, q. 26.

[14] Gerard Manley Hopkins, "The Windhover," in *A Hopkins Reader*, ed. John Pick (New York: Oxford University Press, 1953).

Acknowledgments

This book was a cooperative effort, undertaken to enlarge "the competition of ideas." Many persons contributed ideas, objections, and bibliographical references to it. William J. Baroody, Sr., before his untimely death, took the first risk in inviting a theologian to consider such problems. His contagious zest pulled me away from the Watson-Ledden chair in Religious Studies at Syracuse University, in order to accept a life without tenure in the extraordinary fraternity of the American Enterprise Institute. A man could not have better daily company. My colleagues have taught me much, but could not keep me from the personal views and errors that remain.

I especially thank John W. Cooper, without whose daily labors over three productive years all the vast quantities of materials we were obliged to consider could not have been assembled, and Terry Hall. The Summer Intern program at AEI also enabled me to secure the assistance of Paul T. Stallsworth from Duke and John R. Madden from Dartmouth during the record-breaking heat of the summer of 1980. They have reason to recognize how greatly their efforts helped me to improve the second draft. The next year, the extraordinary editorial abilities of Neal Kozodoy helped me to sculpt the third draft from the second. His contribution is incalculable.

I owe thanks to Paul Johnson, Jeane Kirkpatrick, Stephen Miller, Herbert Stein, Arthur Burns, Irving Kristol, Norman Podhoretz, Pedro San Juan, Murray Weidenbaum, Michael Kerlin, James Finn, Avery Dulles, Edward R. Littlejohn, Lesley Lenkowsky, Thomas Langan, and Elmer Johnson, among many others, for help along the way. Debbie Eccles took my handwritten copy, transformed it, and did not blanch at the enormous labors of continual retyping.

My editor, Erwin Glikes, guided the finished product.

My wife, Karen Laub-Novak, and our three children, Richard, Tanya, and Jana, while busy enough with their own arts and inquiries, surrounded me with that blend of love and familial counterirritants which turns the lonely and even alienating labor of writing into a family enterprise.

The living reality of democratic capitalism is exemplified in the communities from which this book springs.

Michael Novak
June 1981

INDEX

Gutiérrez, Gustavo *(cont.)*
  Ramos's criticism of, 303–7
  socialism advocated by, 303,
    404
  on underdevelopment of poor
    nations, 302–5, 404

Haeccitas, 146
Hamilton, Alexander, 325, 326
Hampshire, Stuart, 197, 198,
  201, 202, 203, 389
Harrington, Michael, 139–40,
  406, 411
Hayek, Friedrich, 89, 205–6
Heckel, Archbishop Roger, 129
Hegel, Georg Wilhelm Friedrich,
  255, 270, 398
Heilbroner, Robert, 46, 367–68,
  372–73
history, 98
  as cyclical vs. progressive, 38–
    40, 363
  order desired by God in, 18,
    50, 73
  as purposive, 50–51, 72
  two tracks of (Lonergan), 73–
    74
  utilitarian concept of, 61–62
History of the Idea of Progress
  (Nisbet), 18
Hitler, Adolf, 316, 319
Hobbes, Thomas, 326, 372
hope, realistic, 341–42
Hopkins, Gerard Manley, 146,
  382
household, workplace divorced
  from, 44
Howe, Irving, 207–9, 406
Hugo, Victor, 319
Hume, David, 119, 264, 395–96

Ibsen, Henrik, 153
idealism, dangers inherent in, 59,
  62–63
ideas and symbols:
  as new reality, 183
  socialism dependent on, 205–6

supremacy of, 19–20, 172,
  183–84
systems of political economy
  inspired by, 184–85
universal, 263
imperialism, 133, 265, 280
Incarnation doctrine, 340–44
  political economy related to,
    342–44
  realism as lesson of, 340–44
income, 215–24
  of blacks, 218–24, 393
  of corporate executives, 211–
    212
  in developed and underdevel-
    oped countries (table), 380
  distribution of, 215–18
  equality of, as unworkable,
    207, 211, 391
  purchasing power of masses
    and, 218
  statistics on, 211, 216–17,
    220–21, 393
  variables in comparisons of,
    220
income taxes, statistics on, 211,
  217, 391, 392
India, commerce hindered in, 228
individual, 159–60
  caritas and, 355–56, 357, 358
  family and self-transcendence
    of, 165–66
  as insufficient unit of economic
    analysis, 160–61
  person vs., 63–65, 370
  see also communitarian individ-
    ual
individualism, 17, 94, 128
  Americans as lacking in, 138–
    139
  British tradition of, 144, 145,
    147
  Catholic criticisms of, 243,
    244–46
  collective morality vs., 368
  Niebuhr's critique of, 329–30,
    407–8
  origin of word, 243